Learning Legacies

THE NEW PUBLIC SCHOLARSHIP

SERIES EDITORS

Lonnie Bunch, *Director, National Museum of African-American History and Culture*
Julie Ellison, *Professor of American Culture, University of Michigan*
Robert Weisbuch, *President, Drew University*

The New Public Scholarship encourages alliances between scholars and communities by publishing writing that emerges from publicly engaged and intellectually consequential cultural work. The series is designed to attract serious readers who are invested in both creating and thinking about public culture and public life. Under the rubric of "public scholar," we embrace campus-based artists, humanists, cultural critics, and engaged artists working in the public, nonprofit, or private sector. The editors seek useful work growing out of engaged practices in cultural and educational arenas. We are also interested in books that offer new paradigms for doing and theorizing public scholarship itself. Indeed, validating public scholarship through an evolving set of concepts and arguments is central to **The New Public Scholarship.**

The universe of potential contributors and readers is growing rapidly. We are teaching a generation of students for whom civic education and community service learning are quite normative. The civic turn in art and design has affected educational and cultural institutions of many kinds. In light of these developments, we feel that **The New Public Scholarship** offers a timely innovation in serious publishing.

Civic Engagement in the Wake of Katrina, edited by Amy Koritz and
    George J. Sanchez

*Is William Martinez Not Our Brother?: Twenty Years of the Prison Creative Arts
Project*, Buzz Alexander

The Word on the Street: Linking the Academy and the Common Reader, Harvey Teres

For the Civic Good: The Liberal Case for Teaching Religion in the Public Schools,
    Walter Feinberg and Richard A. Layton

Learning Legacies: Archive to Action through Women's Cross-Cultural Teaching,
    Sarah Robbins

DIGITALCULTUREBOOKS is an imprint of the University of Michigan Press and the Scholarly Publishing Office of the University of Michigan Library dedicated to publishing innovative and accessible work exploring new media and their impact on society, culture, and scholarly communication.

Learning Legacies

Archive to Action through
Women's Cross-Cultural Teaching

SARAH RUFFING ROBBINS

UNIVERSITY OF MICHIGAN PRESS

ANN ARBOR

Published in the United States of America by the
University of Michigan Press
Manufactured in the United States of America
⊗ Printed on acid-free paper

2020   2019   2018   2017   4   3   2   1

A CIP catalog record for this book is available from the British Library.

Library of Congress Cataloging-in-Publication data has been applied for.

ISBN 978-0-472-07351-1 (hardcover : alk. paper)
ISBN 978-0-472-05351-3 (paper : alk. paper)
ISBN 978-0-472-12284-4 (e-book)
ISBN: 978-0-472-90070-1 (open access e-book)
DOI: dx.doi.org/mpub.4469010

To teachers, archivists, writers, and other stewards of cross-cultural exchange
who seek social justice through stories of shared learning

Contents

Acknowledgments

Learning Legacies, though designated as a monograph, has many coauthors.

This book's many collaborative writers include inquiry partners who are referenced, in upcoming chapters and the bibliography, as "interviews." But during one memorable lunchtime conversation with Renée Gokey and Dennis Zotigh of the National Museum of the American Indian (NMAI), we three discussed differences between "research on" and "research with." Throughout this book, I have certainly aimed for the "with" approach, and I hope the much-appreciated colleagues who contributed to each chapter will see clear signs of that commitment throughout. In that context, for adding their insightful voices to chapters 4 and 5, besides Renée and Dennis, I send heartfelt thanks to Namorah Byrd, Lisa King, Kimberli Lee, and Malea Powell. Chapter 3 would not have been possible without the energizing contributions of Lisa Lee, Lisa Junkin Lopez, and Heather Radke from the Jane Addams Hull-House Museum in Chicago and from all the authors of *Jane Addams in the Classroom*, particularly Todd DeStigter and David Schaafsma, whose leadership in teacher education has been a benchmark for me across multiple decades. For chapter 2, I send a special shout-out to Deborah Mitchell, Kassandra Ware, and the now much-missed Taronda Spencer of Spelman College.

Additional research partners for *Learning Legacies* include generous readers who provided feedback on various drafts—asking sometimes tough and always generative questions to push my thinking. Chief among that group of early readers and conversation partners were fellow faculty members and graduate students in the English Department at Texas Christian University (TCU). Thanks especially, from that incomparable home base of collaboration, to these "gentle" (to use a favorite nineteenth-century term) readers: Richard Enos, Charlotte Hogg, Carrie Leverenz, Brad Lucas, Anne George, Layne Craig, Stacie McCormick, and Theresa Gaul. While all of you have generously guided my work, I must give special thanks to my visionary friend, Carrie Leverenz, who has been an incomparable shepherd of my thinking on this project through literally countless conversations. Five graduate student colleagues gave helpful time at various stages: Carrie Tippen, Tyler Branson, Natasha Robinson, Adam Nemmers, and Samantha Allen will certainly see signs of their contributions here. Your research was attentive, your copyediting clear, your feedback insightful, and your belief in the work inspiring. Thanks as well to all the energetic students in undergraduate and graduate classes who contributed to my thinking about teaching across cultures.

More broadly, being housed in an English Department where literature and rhetoric speak appreciatively to each other daily, in the classroom and in collegial exchanges, was essential to this book's development. In that regard I thank Linda Hughes, Mona Narain, and Karen Steele and all my other department colleagues for teaching, conversations and collaborations crossing the divide that sometimes separates "British Studies" from "American" and "Writing Studies" from "Literature," but does not at TCU. And I salute Dean Andrew Schoolmaster as well; his support of professional development for faculty in AddRan College has left its imprint here too.

Internal funding sources such as the Discovering Global Citizenship (DGC) Visiting Scholar program at TCU were also important to this volume's content, and the chance to serve with the visionary members of the DGC committee has left its mark throughout this text. In the John V. Roach Honors College, where I was serving as acting dean while completing the manuscript, I also found supportive staff colleagues (including Lauren Nixon, Colby Birdsell, Marie Martinez, Donna Schonerstedt, Jason Dunn, Renda Williams, and Lynn Herrera), who strategized ways to give me occasional time away from "dean duties" to do writing. Special thanks to Darren Middleton, Ron Pitcock, Dan Williams, Juan Carlos Sola-Corbacho, Elisa Foster, and Wendy Williams—and to all faculty then teaching in Honors—for continually confirming to me the importance of linking teaching and scholarship. Thanks as well to the talented "administrative fellows" team members (Amanda Allison, Aaron Chimbel, Will Gibbons, and Marla McGhee) for making "part-time" administrative support a creative approach to freeing up your busy acting dean colleague for *Learning Legacies* and other writing tasks, not to mention survival of a super-busy transition.

While I take full responsibility for any shortfalls in this book's content, I know its stories are the better for having had super-smart guidance from specialist scholars in key fields relevant to *Learning Legacies'* case studies. From beyond TCU, I thank Barbara McCaskill, Joycelyn Moody, and Roxanne Donovan for giving essential feedback on chapter 2. Encouraging written reflections from Beth Steffen and Heather O'Rourke reenergized me at a moment when I was losing steam on chapter 3. Conversations with Philip DeLoria helped me believe I could write thoughtfully and (I hope) usefully about the National Museum of the American Indian. Encouraging words from Jessica Enoch about potential use for the book among rhetoric scholars came at a pivotal time of revision. As always, my colleague historian Ann Pullen has been my most demanding and most supportive reader.

Much of the project-based work revisited in this volume was possible only by virtue of funding from the National Endowment for the Humanities and the National Writing Project (NWP). Participants in programs like Keeping and Creating American Communities and the various NWP Teachers Teaching Teachers institutes and continuity programs that I helped facilitate while directing Kennesaw Mountain Writing Project will undoubtedly see ways that they shaped the stories here.

As indicated in the bibliography, a number of archives, museums, and cultural sites have been vital to this book's development, and staff members at each of those locations have been unfailingly helpful. Archivists and librarians also assisted with the acquisition and permission-for-use process for images appearing here. Thanks to Kassandra Ware of the Spelman College Archives, Mark Thiel and Amy Cary of Marquette University's Baynor Memorial Libraries, Nicole Joniec of the Library Company of Philadelphia, Deborah Richards of Mount Holyoke's Archives and Special Collections, and Kay Peterson of the National Museum of American History (Behring Center, the Smithsonian Center Archives), as well as multiple staff members at the Richard J. Daly Special Collections and Archives at the University of Illinois Chicago. Laura Micham of Duke University and Ammie Harrison of TCU's library helped me think through my use of the archive(s) term. More broadly, the outstanding collections and services of TCU's Mary Couts Burnett Library, under the leadership of Dean June Koelker, were, as always, a gift to my scholarship. I am especially thankful for Dean Koelker's direct support of this book via funds contributing to the publication process.

The editorial team at the University of Michigan Press has been patient through the long time it took to complete the manuscript, while providing speedy support at pivotal moments. In particular, Editorial Director Mary Francis and Editorial Associate Christopher Dreyer always gave timely and encouraging guidance, as did talented production editors Elizabeth Frazier and Mary Hashman. Series editor Julie Ellison, who imagined this book in the first place, never lost faith and knew when to prod. It's a special pleasure to have this project published by the press where I completed my doctorate in the Joint Program in English and English Education. Without that interdisciplinary training—including multiple chances to reconnect with the program by meeting with current students—a book like this would not have been possible to conceive. Thanks to Anne Ruggles Gere, therefore, and also to wonderful scholar-teachers like June Howard in the American Culture Program, where I was frequently welcomed as a student for interdisciplinary course work. To David Scobey, who gave hours and wisdom to many projects referenced here and whose vision for public partnerships has been an inspiration: thank you for leading the way.

At home, John Robbins gave many hours of assistance to the preparation of images included here. His patient listening to status reports on the book's overall progress kept my mental wheels turning, and his belief in its content was crucially encouraging.

Years ago, my daughters Patty and Margaret Robbins guided much of the thinking for my first monograph, *Managing Literacy, Mothering America*, by affirming the connections between home-based teaching and parents' potential impact on the larger culture. Between that book and this one, there have been quite a few others, and each one has held traces of their personal stories, however implicit. These days, watching them skillfully navigate professional careers in dynamic institutional contexts continues to inspire, reminding me that family matters most. With my equally brilliant son-in-law Ethan Davis, they show every day how the next generation is surely the best avenue we all have for leaving meaningful learning legacies.

CHAPTER ONE

Introduction

Counter-narratives and Cultural Stewardship

In the late fall of 2014, an Ebola outbreak crossed the Atlantic from Africa and came to America. In its early stages, the disease had seemed remote—a somewhat exotic subject of world news reports, a "problem," certainly, but one having no direct impact within US borders. But suddenly, Ebola exploded among us. In Texas, no less. And, for the community of Texas Christian University (TCU), where I was teaching in Fort Worth, Ebola became personal, almost tangible, when Nina Pham, one of our own, a nursing program alumna working in a nearby hospital in Dallas, contracted the disease from a patient, Thomas Eric Duncan. Ebola was now *local* news, not something far-removed.

And yet, even as the disease cried out for our attention—generating real fear, even—our responses also provided a powerful learning opportunity. As an acting dean in the Honors College, I hosted a meeting of alumni on campus just as news of Pham's illness hit the airways. TCU alumna Linda Newman, one attendee, shared a vivid anecdote with the group: she had just been to the same emergency room a few days before Duncan's trip to that hospital. As she reenvisioned her near-encounter with contagion, the conversation also led her to a memory of reading: she said that, since the news of Ebola's arrival in the Metroplex via her own neighborhood hospital, she had been mentally revisiting Albert Camus's *The Plague*, which she had first studied as a TCU undergrad. She wondered aloud if rereading it now, and inviting others to join in, might be a way of encouraging all of us to examine some worthwhile questions: How can we cultivate a stronger sense of empathy, perhaps even responsibility, for the pain of others? How would we respond, as individuals and as a community, if the initial outbreak of Ebola in our own homeland couldn't be contained?

As organically as that, through an informal conversation, a modest humanities-oriented community-building project was born. "Contagion, Quarantine, and Social Conscience," we called it.[1] I tapped into a small fund that TCU's teaching and learning center provides to support "global learning" and purchased about twenty paperback copies of Camus's novel to distribute, first-come, first-serve. Working with graduate student assistant Marie Martinez (who had been studying "contagion literature" for her dissertation on Victorian disease narratives) and with undergraduate student leaders, Linda and I planned a roundtable for an evening near the end of the semester. To promote involvement beyond whoever might be able to attend in person, another doctoral candidate, Tyler Branson, a frequent partner in civic engagement projects, set up an online discussion board.

This short-term project was only a small-scale endeavor. And it was far from fully successful. The residence hall's main lobby that we chose for the roundtable was loud and distracting. The main doors slammed repeatedly; most of the heavy student traffic that evening exhibited little interest in our gathering, passing through without even pausing to join in, despite the many paper and digital posters we had distributed ahead of time. Most of the undergraduates in attendance were actually students from the Popular Literature class I was team-teaching with grad student Thomas Jesse, so the effort to attract attendees from the dorm didn't really take off. And, with the weather far chillier than usual for a Texas late-fall evening, we didn't draw a crowd of area alumni either.

Yet, I'd argue, worthwhile learning certainly happened. Both the panelists for the roundtable and the other participants that night were fully engaged, beyond the scheduled time, in topics that reminded all of us how powerful cross-cultural interdisciplinary learning in a public context can be. One speaker, biologist Giri Akkaraju, started out by apologizing for the (supposed) limits of his literary interpretation skills, then insightfully launched into a series of ethical questions that galvanized the room. Brite Divinity School professor Nancy Ramsey extended Giri's themes, which were then further complicated by a postcolonial take on Camus offered up by English professor Rima Abunasser. Katherine Fogelberg, who had recently completed a dissertation on enhancing undergraduate science education, pushed us to contemplate how reading Camus's text in light of current events might encourage a shift in teaching foci in the "hard" sciences to more direct examination of public health issues.

All the panelists, and the thoughtful audience members who responded to their lead, told stories. Many were informed by the gear-up conversations on our virtual discussion board. Ephemeral though this shared moment of learning seemed to be, it nonetheless affirmed the need, as Native/First Nations writer Thomas King has so eloquently pointed out, to tell each other stories when confronting challenging social issues.[2] And this project also, however modestly, reasserted ways in which shared reading and discussion can generate stirrings of empathy—empathy that might, upon reflection, lead to social action.[3]

For my own ongoing scholarship on collaborative learning that blends textual studies with analysis of educational practices, this project resonated with longstanding questions. How can we capitalize on the potential of the humanities—especially when set in dialogue with other fields—to enhance cross-cultural understanding? How can teaching, when conceived as a public enterprise, move learners from engagement with cultural resources to actions supporting social justice aims? And, in terms of guiding and assessing such work, what does narrative inquiry look like and why is it a valuable enterprise? What are the most productive methods for documenting the impact of civic engagement projects—from modest ones like our Ebola-inspired novel study to larger-scale, sustained, and complex ones? This book is part of my ongoing effort—supported by many colleagues—to address such questions.

For the majority of that particular fall 2014 evening's participants, as well as most who had joined the dialogue online, this project ended with the roundtable. For some of us, however, an archive of activity remains as a source for ongoing analysis.[4] When I reread the postings, they prompt me to reimagine ways of teaching in the future. In that vein, Sam, one of the members of that Popular Literature class that so commendably swelled the roundtable audience, wrote later about the project in an end-of-course narrative reflection: a future secondary teacher, he contrasted that collaborative learning experience with the focus on standardized assessments that he had been observing in school visits and tried to envision approaches for promoting open-ended, interdisciplinary teaching in his own classroom.

By leaving at least a partial record of our shared learning experience behind—in this case, through our record of online conversations—participants in the "Contagion, Quarantine, and Social Conscience" project invited others to join in future narrative inquiry. To accept such an invitation, by writing into the archive or carrying out new social practices inspired by it, would affirm that these kinds of collaborations seek communal more than individual agency.

In a sense, within the framework I'll be using for this book, we left a "learning legacy"—a story about an intercultural learning process that used collaborative epistemologies toward potential social agency. The knowledge being made was admittedly tenuous and exploratory, grounded in writing linked to questions we had encountered in our daily lives and examined through the lens of shared study. I like to picture others reading through our postings and imaginatively joining our community—maybe even adding to its textual record, so that our online archive grows a bit, expanding its potential reach to others beyond the original participant community. I realize people seeking out that narrative space (or even stumbling upon it) wouldn't have a full understanding of the transdisciplinary and pragmatic applications that emerged for some of us later. They wouldn't have access to the reflection Sam wrote at the end of the semester about his future teaching; they wouldn't have gotten to read Ben's letter of application to divinity school, where he described future ethical leadership goals by echoing, and also extending, some of his previous online postings. Anytime we study archival records, we catch knowledge in fragments, at a remove from the actual lived experiences that shaped their construction. But any community that self-consciously leaves behind a learning legacy—adaptable accounts of narrative inquiry in process—surely does so as an aspirational act of rhetorical intervention, hoping it will be useful to others in the future. And learning legacies that emerge from efforts at cross-cultural teaching have a particularly crucial role to play today, given the many contact zones of social difference we are all encountering in our classrooms and the larger society.

Fortunately, there are numerous past learning legacies far more extensive and fully realized conceptually than the tiny set of exchanges generated through the brief "Contagion, Quarantine, and Social Conscience" program. Therefore, although I am especially committed to scholar-teachers' intercultural community-building within and beyond the classroom today, I am eager to tap into cultural resources from prior generations to guide such work.

The three particular instances of learning legacies I will explore in this book come from my longstanding study of gendered social interventions at the turn between the nineteenth and twentieth centuries. Specifically, I'll be drawing from archival sources to recover narrative texts responding to three pivotal educational issues in that era: what learning opportunities should be afforded to African-American women in the post-slavery decades; how to acculturate the exploding immigrant population of that time;

and what role white and/versus Native cultural resources and teaching approaches should play in educating Indigenous Americans. Focusing here on a specific body of narratives around each of these ongoing debates—from Spelman College's founding period, from Jane Addams's leadership at Hull-House, and from the negative model of assimilationist Carlisle Indian Industrial School set in dialogue with alternative Native teaching practices—I will mine generative learning legacies from these knowledge-making sites.

As those three points of research attest, this previous era provides an especially fruitful ground for study. For one thing, in a seeming forecast of our twenty-first-century moment, these earlier decades in US history represented a period of intense social transformation (including increasing urbanization, a rapid rise in immigration, and enhanced educational opportunities across previous class divides). Educational sites both in and out of school—anticipating parallel American settings in the early twenty-first century—brought together learners from widely diverse backgrounds, often crossing generations; regional and national identities; and race, gender, and social class affiliations. Also similar to our current national context, the transition between the nineteenth and the twentieth centuries prompted sustained efforts by powerful groups to maintain social hierarchies (such as Jim Crow tactics directed against African Americans; a rise in anti-immigrant campaigns; oppressive containment strategies used to undermine Native peoples' own national and individual rights; and continued reluctance to give US women full political and economic access). The echoes of that era's struggles over educational values and practices resonate quite strikingly today, thereby underscoring how relevant stories of cross-cultural collaborations from the past can be for us now. In particular, I have found transportable models of rhetorical activism in cultural work by the institution-founding women who generated published accounts of Spelman College's early days, by women settlement leaders recording stories of Hull-House's Progressive-Era programs, and by students/teachers creating resistant responses to the boarding school movement aimed at Native American youth. I will link these historically situated examples of archive-making with current applications of those legacies by self-conscious heirs today and with my own analysis of stories from both time frames—the past and today. I will analyze these textual records both in their specific historical moments and across time, so as to demonstrate how humanities-oriented knowledge systems and practices from the past can enable meaningful intercultural work in our own day.

Narrative Pathways to Knowledge

To embody this project's arguments rhetorically, I've constructed three layers of narrative writing in the book's structural content. For each core chapter, I've composed a historical narrative about a specific learning legacy; I've also shared a story about how those cultural resources are being used in social action today; and I've woven in a personal narrative about my own learning process along with that analysis.

I realize that using narrative as my own primary writing mode brings risks. There is a long history of women's knowledge-making being downplayed or even ignored when that work is situated in everyday experience and language—or, said another way, when women writers and others on the margins of power "story" rather than "theorize" knowledge. Accordingly, throughout this book, I will sometimes foreground analysis, even as I also seek to establish the efficacy of individual stories and, more specifically, counter-narratives developed by knowledge-makers whose marginalized positions initially constrained their access to agency.

Despite its challenges, first-person narrative does bring important benefits to this project. As feminist epistemology has emphasized, whenever we construct knowledge, however hard we try to be fair, our personal standpoints shape our processes and conclusions. Identity is a particularly crucial factor to consider in my authorship of this book, in terms of my writing about educational practices carried out "for," along with or managed by, marginalized peoples. As a white woman positioned in a highly privileged role as a university professor, I have a clear responsibility to reflect on how my own standpoint restricts my work.[5] I must try to nurture a sensitive and responsive capacity for interpreting the experiences of the educators I am studying from the past, as well as those whose current work I seek to understand, while recognizing that complete empathy and identification with others are never fully achievable.[6] Said another way, I must acknowledge the epistemic challenges to deep empathy that are associated with *who* and *where* I am.

Given these inherent limits, I have sought a rhetorical strategy for textually marking the standpoint-based constraints on my own learning and my scholarship. I do so by calling on interpretive methods and stylistic features of autoethnography. That is, I align my writing with this self-reflective research approach to make visible to my readers, rather than to mask, my own struggles with claiming a voice for this project. In employing features of autoethnographic writing, I also hope to affirm that knowledge derived from storytelling carries value, that analysis and narrative can work together productively, and that scholarly commitments to reach broad audiences may require us to write in a more personal way than when discipline-centered researchers talk only to each other. Overall, I'm seeking to represent textually the process of reflection that, I believe, is a necessary step between archive-guided learning and social action.[7]

Therefore, while this book is not, strictly speaking, an autoethnography, it does weave into each chapter techniques from that research method and conventions from that narrative genre. Admittedly, this partial approach makes for some stylistic jumps in my writing—shifts between a voice that takes a distanced, analytical perspective when interpreting textual records from the archive and one that speaks more directly to readers in an "I" voice, narrating personal experiences of using cultural resources to guide teaching, learning, and civic activism. To craft this hybrid language, I've drawn on Heewon Chang's *Autoethnography as Method*. He advises that autoethnography "combines cultural analysis and interpretation with narrative details," so that "the stories of autoethnographers" can be "reflected upon, analyzed, and interpreted within their broader context" (46).[8] I've also tried to emulate the best storytelling by the women writer-educators from previous eras who originally inspired this project—authors like Carrie Walls and Sophia Packard in the *Spelman Messenger*, Jane Addams in *Twenty Years at Hull-House*, and Zitkala-Ša in her stories for *Atlantic Monthly* and other periodical venues. And I've drawn upon models of writing by colleagues currently doing similar work in a range of civic engagement and community-building projects.[9]

In calling upon a narrative epistemology, I affiliate with a gendered tradition but also with values and practices central to Native American and First Nations teaching approaches. As Gail Guthrie Valaskakis has explained in *Indian Country: Essays on Contemporary Native Culture*: "stories are not just the cultural glue that holds communities together and transports them over time. Stories express the dynamic cultural ground in which individuals and communities are formed through a continual process of adopting and enacting allied or conflicting representations and the ideological messages they signify" ("Introduction," *Indian Country*, 4). Drawing on the work of Stuart Hall, Valaskakis emphasizes that both individual and group conceptions of identity are "contested and reconstructed in the discursive negotiation of the complex alliances and social relations that constitute community" (4). Further, echoing Thomas King, Valaskakis notes that taking control of the stories told about yourself and your community represents a vital step toward claiming agency (6–7).

Significantly, this vision of agency doesn't assume that all problems will be resolved, that irrefutable answers will emerge from story-made knowledge. Given the contingent versions of our individual selves and the communities where we work, knowledge itself is also contingent and fluid. So narrative, given its open-ended qualities, becomes not just an appealing way to convey our understandings; it's also a mode that acknowledges its own limitations. Like the archive from which many humanities scholars seek to construct meaning,[10] narrative is tentative and exploratory. Similarly, the actions we may be able to take from studying cultural resources need not be definitive to be worthwhile. Particularly when collaborating to create or refine communal stories, part of the value of the enterprise is its ongoing process.

I am well aware that my claims for interactive archival inquiry and associated collaborative enterprises growing out of such study fly in the face of ongoing anxiety about the relevance of the liberal arts. I recognize, of course, that we live in a period when the "practical" hard sciences and technical expertise often hold sway in educational value systems. Just ask our political leaders. The governor of North Carolina, Patrick McCrory, and former Secretary of Education Bill Bennett (in)famously advocated public education's abandonment of fields like philosophy and women's studies; and though he later apologized to offended art historians, even President Obama extoled the superior importance of "job training programs" meeting "employer needs" over such liberal arts fields in today's educational hierarchy.[11]

Meanwhile, quantitative assessment orientations place a premium on "objective" testing over measures such as students' own reflective self-evaluations of learning or their stories of how they use, in daily life, what they have studied in the humanities' cultural records. This emphasis on supposedly objective and finely measurable standards undermines the educational value systems and practices for knowledge-making of minority cultural groups, whose members often "score" in lower "levels" on such measures than the white majority. Thus, Marlene Brant Castellano, Lynne Davis, and Louise Lahache have noted, in the context of tensions between First Nations educational curricula and dominant North American practices: "This aggressive gate-keeping of 'standards' has repeatedly challenged the legitimacy of Aboriginal knowledge and values, imposing an assimilative cultural agenda that is both pervasive and coercive" ("Conclusion," *Aboriginal Education*, 251).

On a more hopeful front, a growing chorus of voices has been calling into question such assumptions about the limits of learning avenues in the liberal arts and, conversely, the supposed universal superiority of "hard" knowledge fields. In the K-12 arena, thoughtful parent groups and activist scholars have begun to resist the loss of meaningful learning time arising from "test prep" (i.e., teaching to/for the test) and the seemingly never-ending increase in testing days themselves.[12] In university settings, enterprises such as Campus Compact, Imagining America, and local civic engagement endeavors (often combining curricular and cocurricular approaches) are reasserting the "soft" communal responsibilities of higher education.[13] Such projects reenvision how scholars working in the arts, education, social sciences, and humanities can create, sustain, and assess public partnerships. Furthermore, since civic engagement work is inherently complex, too multifaceted to be fully encapsulated in charts, graphs, and numbers, some are saying, it's time to reassert more qualitative ways to track what we learn through the liberal arts, fine arts, and everyday teaching and learning experiences linked to them.

Accordingly, a subtext of this project might read as follows: let's quit being defensive about the humanities and affiliated fields of study. It's time to stop limiting our measures of effectiveness to strategies more suited to disciplines where knowledge is more easily quantified. Instead, let's foreground knowledge-making and assessment practices best suited to the epistemological systems, tools, and, yes, the aspirations at the core of the humanities and their sister fields of the arts and education.[14] Stories emerging from community-building collaborations offer one such avenue. Therefore, one goal of this book is to interpret legacies from a number of such cross-cultural enterprises, from the past and today.

Knowledge-Making as Public Work

One social efficacy-seeking approach that "soft"-knowledge, liberal-arts-oriented fields have in common when they operate in the public sphere, and thus one framework for tracing their influence, is their rhetorical underpinning. In that context, whereas a hard-scientific drug trial would set up an intervention treatment and a control group, then measure the impact of the medication in question via comparative quantitative data between the two groups, a social intervention project framed through the humani ties would assert the impossibility of isolating all variables in daily life. Instead, a story-based avenue to knowledge would draw on admittedly messier but more rhetorical means of evaluating impact. How, for instance, did participants respond affectively to a particular project's activities? What elements within the language and social practices of the program seemed to impact that audience's belief systems for day-to-day life choices, and why? What did they do with their learning, in their lived experiences afterward? What aspects of the cultural context shaping the project's conception in the first place, as well as pathways through which it was experienced, have implications for future work? These are the kinds of questions an educator like Jane Addams, affiliating with narrative ways of knowing, would address in her writings about the Hull-House settlement. Curators working more recently at the Chicago museum honoring Addams's legacy have asked similar questions about exhibits they developed or public programs they sponsored, as have Native leaders envisioning programming (both on-site and virtual) for the National Museum of the American Indian, and as have planners and performers in the annual Founders' Day pageant held at Spelman College every spring.

This kind of active questioning around text-making and related social interactions aligns with scholarship in cultural rhetoric.[15] In their introduction to a special issue of *Enculturation* dedicated to articulating cultural rhetoric's evolving work, Phil Bratta and Malea Powell noted, "In practice, cultural rhetorics scholars investigate and understand meaning-making as it is situated in specific cultural communities." Hence, they say, cultural rhetoric is a "situated scholarly practice," one that responds to calls from voices like Steven Mailloux's to "'use rhetoric to practice theory by doing history.'" For my work on *Learning Legacies*, Bratta and Powell's description of cultural rhetoric as "More than anything, . . . a practice, and more specifically an embodied practice" is especially helpful, since it reminds me to be vigilant about my own personal standpoint's impact on my inquiry. Similarly useful, I find, is their assertion that cultural rhetoric examines "issues of power," particularly when doing comparative work, as I aim for here by bringing together several different case studies of archive-building and archive use. For Bratta and Powell, positioning our scholarly work within cultural rhetoric entails addressing power differentials ethically, attending to interpersonal relations as influencing cultural action, noting the interactive connections ("constellations") that shape all knowledge-making, and using story as a central form of communication.[16] My project strives to follow this mandate.

In line with such antihierarchical knowledge-building commitments, *Learning Legacies* affiliates with cultural rhetoric as both a conceptual formulation for scholarly study and a pathway toward political agency. Similar to Steven Mailloux's self-positioning in a dialogue with Keith Gilyard for *Conversations in Cultural Rhetoric and Composition Studies*, I see benefits to linking rhetoric with pragmatism. Mailloux, for example, acknowledges the downside of hanging on to "rhetoric" as a term that can elicit negative responses from members of the general public, who may associate it more with verbal performance for effect than with sustained social action (40). Yet he nonetheless argues that there are potentially productive "associative" links between what he terms "rhetorical pragmatism" and "a commitment to radical democracy." Both, he suggests, "share tropes of conversation and dialogue," as well as "arguments about the primacy of empowerment and the protection of minority rights" and "narratives about the way that you come up with knowledge of truth: through deliberation" (39).[17]

If Mailloux admits to both drawing on and resisting some aspects of his training in American literature in order to affiliate with the field of rhetoric, so will I. If the legacy of New Criticism gave me an intellectually appealing tool kit, it has sometimes seemed divorced from one-half of the mandate promoted by the nineteenth-century American women writers whose work has driven much of my prior scholarship: writing both *to delight* and *to improve*—that is, to use language in inherently artistic ways, but also to have a meaningful impact on daily life. Fortunately for those of us trained first as literature scholars in the New Critical perspective, Ottmar Ette's calls for reconceptualizing our work's relationship to lived experience have provided a useful vision for maintaining such skills as close, careful reading of the "literary" (however one defines that category), but not solely for the purposes of aesthetic analysis. Urges Ette: "For literary criticism and critical theory, knowledge for living is intrinsic to the very process of knowing: it is part of the object of study and of the subject's (the scholar's) individual life contexts" ("Literature," 987). Ette argues that such a vision for the literary scholar moves us from feeling we should "confront the natural sciences" to "initiat[ing] a serious dialogue," one that, by including "literary and cultural knowledge," will enable "a more complex understanding of life and of the humanities as part of the *sciences for living*" (983, emphasis in original). In setting up the cross-disciplinary conversations around media coverage of the Ebola outbreak as potentially illuminated through (re)engagement with Camus's philosophical novel, the collaborative "Contagion" programming I described above was seeking just such a "serious dialogue" toward a "sciences for living," in Ette's terms.

In this book project and within the civic engagement programs I've joined across my academic career, two other scholarly frameworks play a key role: American Studies and studies of communities of practice in education. In the first case, I affiliate with the longstanding commitment of American Studies Association presidents such as Paul Lauter, Mary Helen Washington, and Karen Halttunen to partnering with K-12 educators and community activists. Further, I embrace mandates such as Barbara Tomlinson and George Lipsitz's to enact an "American Studies as Accompaniment," so that, in collaborating with colleagues from different backgrounds than our own, we position ourselves for "traveling the road with them," while learning "to listen" and craft "more cosmopolitan and critical conversations" (27). Accordingly, the historical case studies I present here all involve women rhetors who were also activist educators in their own day, capitalizing on connections to learning communities they helped construct and nurture. From those networks of narrative inquiry in action, shared stories emerged. On a parallel front, my analysis of contemporary applications of those women leaders' past stories will show how the heirs of their work are constructing new communities of practice in day-to-day and project-based teaching.[18] Networks of educators sharing praxis-based knowledge, with the National Writing Project's interconnected local communities and nationwide programming being a prime example, offer compelling evidence of the efficacy in such collaborations. My own involvement, for over a decade, in helping build the Kennesaw Mountain Writing Project in metro Atlanta has certainly had an impact on my scholarship and on communities of teachers and learners there.

Studies of women's educational rhetoric in action invite a mixed methodology, given the need to examine the original context of textual production as well as later transmissions and reconfigurations. Therefore, in this book, I begin each historical case study by recovering particular instances of archive-building through stories of teaching practice and then shift to tracing ways that twenty-first-century educators have used those textual legacies to guide their own work. My method is "text-based," with my analysis grounded in cultural records—some inscribed, some performed, some enacted in conversations. This focus on textual records of learning as a social resource is one feature of my project that aligns it with traditional scholarship in the humanities, including cultural rhetoric's studies of narrative writing as an activist genre. But I also hope to expand the way we conceptualize such archives to embrace texts that are often excluded, to encourage strategies of interpretation that are under-utilized, and to apply archival resources to our own social agency today. To clarify this goal, which links my methodological commitment to aspirations for how others may be able to use my work, I will now explicate several of this book's key terms.

Counter-Narratives as Resistance

One concept essential to this project is *counter-narrative*, a politicized discursive strategy: when marginalized people are denied full access to social agency, they sometimes construct stories that push back against a constraining ideology's textual power. As my English Department colleague Richard Enos suggested in an email after reading this introduction: "counter-narratives figure prominently in social movements," partly because "they are used to provide a (counter/alternative) view of reality." They are also useful in cross-cultural storytelling "because they provide diachronic accounts of issues centering on value and preference."[19]

In particular, the counter-narratives at the heart of the upcoming chapters are inscribed and/or enacted stories strategically constructed to claim agency by mimicking some features of dominant narratives while simultaneously resisting other features of expected generic form and the belief system shaping it.[20] In that sense, Molly Andrews has defined counter-narratives as "stories which people tell and live" in order to "offer resistance, either implicitly or explicitly, to dominant cultural narratives" ("Opening," 1). Andrews describes the interrelationship between dominant (or master) narratives and the resistant texts that sometimes emerge in response: "master narratives" express "what is assumed to be a normative experience," so that "such storylines serve as a blueprint" for understanding ourselves and social practices in the world around us. Accordingly, she argues, "the power of master narratives derives from [our] internalisation," as "we become the stories we know, and the master narrative is reproduced." However, Andrews suggests, particularly among members of marginalized groups, alternative visions may develop. In such cases, individuals who see themselves as outside the dominant pattern may choose to create "personal stories which go against the social grain," and, through that process, generate "new possibilities" available to others as well. Andrews argues that such narrative-making has particular appeal for those outside the mainstream, whose perspective has been undervalued or even ignored. Self-consciously positioning their alternative stories on the margins, individuals who generate counter-narratives also do an important service for others, as the new storylines can eventually be adopted by larger communities (1–2). If dominant narratives offer maps reflecting "the social construction of normalcy," with related patterns of "inclusion and exclusion" creating "pressures of social expectation" (3), counter-narratives open up alternative possibilities based on resistance to those constraining norms.[21]

Andrews does offer this vital caution: "Counter-narratives exist in relation to master narratives, but they are not necessarily dichotomous entities" (2). Thus, though operating in tension with dominant narratives in a culture, and basically from an oppositional stance, this genre does not always respond from an entirely resistant position and, in fact, may participate in some ways with discursive features that mark a more dominant form. For example, in this book's treatment of writings by Native students who themselves became teachers in White-run boarding schools for Indigenous pupils, I'll take note of ways that an author like Zitkala-Ša or S. Alice Callahan could invoke features of the familiar "uplifting savages" narrative as part of an overall strategy for undermining that very position.

The major counter-narratives recovered and interpreted here emerged from collaborations that enacted communal more than individual agency. For instance, stories that Jane Addams and her Hull-House colleagues wrote about settlement house work deemphasized individual leadership and, in its place, asserted shared endeavors as a means toward social change. In doing so, these counter-narratives offered an antidote to the rhetorical model of individual heroic influence, on the one hand, and the seeming erasure of personal agency from detached "scientific" analyses of social problems, on the other. Indeed, one trait the progressive educators whose writings are highlighted here share is a persistent investment in narrative itself as a knowledge-making process, particularly through stories grounded in everyday experience.[22] Recovering and interpreting examples of such stories in action is a crucial step to asserting the humanities (and the liberal arts more broadly) as a meaningful route to knowledge today. And, through that process, an expansive concept of the archive and a multilayered Archive emerges.

Archives as Resources

In this project on learning legacies, I use "archive" to refer to a specific collection of artifacts and/or observable practices associated with an identifi-

Figure 1.1. A youthful Jane Addams at her writing desk at Hull-House. Hull-House Photograph Collection (JAMC_0000_0005_0019). Courtesy of the University of Illinois at Chicago, Richard J. Daley Library Special Collections and University Archives.

able community, historical movement, or site of inquiry—as in "I worked in an archive" of, say, periodical publications or public records or personal letters at a community-affiliated research site, or "I gathered an archive of oral histories" from a particular group of people. I use "Archive," in contrast, for the multilayered set of cultural resources that accrue, over time, through assembling, saving, and *sustained, culture-making use* of texts and social practices linked to communities' shared agendas. In particular, this project explores how an archive of learning legacies, over time, can grow into an Archive.

In general, whereas I see *counter*-narratives as basically *oppositional* responses to dominant ones, I propose that the "archives" we analyze to understand learning legacies represent an *expansion* (not a rejection) of traditional meanings of the term. I aim to apply the kind of careful cataloging and analyzing associated with studying traditional archival documents to an expanded range of materials and records of social practices so as to surface their cultural meanings, in past historical moments and today. Thus, given the wide readership I hope to reach with this project, it's necessary to explain my own use of the term.

Explication of the term *archives* by the Society of American Archivists (SAA) on its website points to some areas of agreement around the term, but also variations, including ongoing shifts in meaning within different informal, vernacular uses.[23] The SAA's first-given meaning for "archives" (which they denote in plural) is "materials created or received by a person, family, or organization, public or private, in the conduct of their affairs and preserved because of the enduring value contained in the information they contain or as evidence of the functions and responsibilities of their creator, especially those materials maintained using the principles of provenance, original order, and collective control; permanent records."

My use of "archive" here does represent a discursive intervention, of sorts, into ideas about what "counts" as archival cultural resources, who assembles them and why, and how they are used. That is, I affirm long-recognized commitments to stewardship of resources such as official public documents. But my application of the term "archive" here also operates as a logical extension of prior scholarship by members of marginalized groups who have already done important work to expand our understandings of its meaning and purview. In terms of archival research techniques, I honor methodological guidance from longtime leaders of archival studies such as T. R. Schellenberg, who emphasized the need for attentive care in assembling and managing archives, and whose in-service training of staff members working in the National Archives, along with his influential 1954 series of lectures in Australia as a Fulbright fellow, helped establish the field's professional identity in the context of preserving official public records. Schellenberg's commitment to organized method arose in part, I suspect, from his realization that archives play a crucial role in the stewardship of culture. Thus, in honoring Schellenberg's foundational vision, I affirm an insightful assessment by his Australian colleague H. L. White in an appreciative forward to *Modern Archives*: that a society's commitment to maintaining archives "is a measure of our faith in the future."[24]

Schellenberg's *Modern Archives*, which brought together principles and techniques from his Fulbright lectures, initially approached his subject from the perspective of someone striving to establish the value of the National Archives both as a support for governmental efficiency and as a keeper of cultural resources, a role which, at that point, he argued could be fulfilled only by the government. That is, if the archive was made up of public documents produced by the government, then only a public agency could maintain them: "The care of valuable public records," he averred, "is a public obligation" (8).

In a second book, *The Management of Archives*, originally published in 1965, Schellenberg would revise his definition of archives "on the assumption that the principles and techniques now applied to public records may be applied also, with some modification, to private records, especially to private manuscript material of recent origin." [25] But he continued to distinguish between what he called "records for research use" (which he classified as "archival") and items intended for "current use," which would not be (xxix). Thus, though his definition by then incorporated private as well as public materials, and though he included "textual, cartographic, and pictorial" materials (xxx) and not only government documents in the narrowest sense, Schellenberg's framework, at least in the context of this project, ultimately envisions a relatively limited conception of "archive" on two counts. First, it fails to assert, specifically, a potential value for materials and practices from outside the mainstream. (Like Jennifer Sinor, who recovered a family member's writing and applied techniques of archival analysis to that text, I join other feminists in recognizing that official archives have been dominated by male figures' records, both in content and in documentation approaches; like Francisco Jiménez, whose frustrated search for signs of his own Mexican-American heritage in a range of formal "permanent records" (to use the SAA's terms) underscored patterns of exclusion—I call for a vision of "archive," in the kind of collaborative enterprise I promote here, that extends beyond the materials already safely tucked away and carefully catalogued in a sanctioned and professionally managed collection.)[26] Second, it falls short of encompassing the new and emerging materials that are now generating cultural resources every day, that is, the textual products and practices that Schellenberg could not have anticipated in his own time. (For instance, the archives I study now could include blog postings about the Spelman College Founders Day; or an audio recording available, via touch screen, as part of an exhibit at the Jane Addams Hull-House Museum; or a YouTube video record of a powwow dance; or a sequence of associated comments posted by web visitors who viewed that event online.)

Similarly, for this project, which calls for imagining archive-making as a widely participatory social action, a traditional perspective on the term is too restrictive when it explicitly or implicitly isolates archival resources from lived experiences that make meaningful use of cultural resources. In this context, for instance, several of the definitions proffered by the SAA would be too limiting if held as the only operant meaning: one by envisioning an archive as a "division within an organization responsible for maintaining the organization's records of enduring value," since this would assume an archive must have an institutional affiliation; a second for seeing an archive as a "building (or portion thereof) housing archival collections," since this meaning would locate "archive" in a particular physical location; and a third for casting an archive as a "published collection of scholarly papers, especially in a periodical," as this meaning assumes public circulation. Because I argue here for a concept of "archives" that emphasizes active culture-making through ongoing, communal cultural work, I favor a more generative vision for my use of the term.

That said, in previous projects and for this book, I have certainly done extensive work in traditional archives.[27] On one very basic level, for each of the case studies presented here, I have researched literal archives like those designated by the SAA's first definition, outlined above, namely, materials that have been preserved because of their "enduring value." Diana Taylor has offered up a relevant catalogue of examples of what such an archive might incorporate, materially speaking: "'Archival' memory exists as documents, maps, literary texts, letters, archaeological remains, bones, videos, films, CDs, all those items supposedly resistant to change" (*Archive/Repertoire*, 19). In this sense, the historical "archive" that undergirds this particular project is a set of tangible records bequeathed to us by women (and men) who used their teaching to enact a vision of social justice in their own day. For example, when Sophia Packard and Harriet Giles journeyed from New England to the postbellum South to found what became Spelman College, they had a clear view of the potential benefits to be derived from documenting their work—and enabling students to contribute to that narrative—in print stories aimed at cultivating a network of stakeholders. That archival record, represented in part as a periodical named the *Spelman Messenger*, today exists in material form in the Spelman College library, as a retrievable account of institutional history.

However, this archive is actually only one part of a multilayered Archive of cultural resources going back to the liberal arts knowledge Packard and Giles brought with them from their own previous schooling, a heritage they would redesign for (and with) their African American women students, through iterations of a legacy both celebrated and revised strategically in the pages of the student-and-teacher made publication. And within the *Spelman Messenger* stories (many of them covert and some of them overt counter-narratives), later generations of students and their teachers have found authoritative resources for identity-shaping performances of that institutional history in an annual Founders' Day celebration. Those very performances, in turn, have become part of a larger Archive of ever-adjusting cultural resources that promote gendered and race-based agency for Spelman community members today.

For Diana Taylor, such performances represent part of a rich cultural repertoire that enables social change across time. As she notes, an individual performance, drawn from and/or shaped by an available archive, "enacts embodied memory: performances, gestures, orality, movement, dance, singing—in short, all those acts usually thought of as ephemeral" actually produce knowledge through the doing. Meanwhile, an adaptable, archive-based repertoire of cultural forms also "allows for individual agency," partly because it "requires presence: people participate in the production and reproduction of knowledge by 'being there,' being a part of the transmission" (*Archive/Repertoire*, 20).

Within the framework of my own project, therefore, while one meaning of "the archive" invokes literal textual records from the past, another is more layered, interactive and evolving. This Archive constitutes a growing body of cultural resources continually reshaped through use—and also, even now, through my own interpretations. As Carolyn Steedman has pointed out in *Dust: The Archive and Cultural History*, archives are places from which a "resurrectionist historian creates the past that [s]he purports to restore." Steedman argues that an archive "is made from selected and consciously chosen documentation from the past," but that without the researcher's work, "it just sits there until it is read, and used, and *narrativised*" (38, 68, my emphasis). Scholar-activists, my project assumes, want to draw from and transform archives into Archives of agency or at least to study how others have done so.

In the Spelman College documents under review here, the initial archive of stories made for the *Messenger* embodied a positive force that, in turn, generated new layers of a socially enabling Archive. That shared cultural memory both evolved over time and maintained a strong, purposeful connection to communal history. From Spelman's original counter-narratives resisting the marginalization of African American women, a powerful learning legacy continues to operate, illustrating both the pragmatic and the aspirational potential of humanistic study. So, in the case of the learning legacy examined in chapter 2, we can see how the gradual accretion of stories in this Archive helped contribute to and, over time, strengthen the institution. That is, we might argue that the institution of Spelman, which still operates and continues to refine itself and its mission today, was socially constructed from counter-narratives—or, to be more precise, counter-narratives that eventually became this college's empowering dominant narrative.

To track this process of making and using learning legacies, chapter 2 will combine analysis of counter-narratives from the early *Spelman Messenger* with a parallel reading of the college's Founders' Day performances in our own time. Reuse of Spelman's shared stories about itself as an institution reaffirms its identity to its community members. In addition, consistent with the way liberal arts learning can happen through study of cultural resources, others can actually draw on that heritage to do additional cultural work. To suggest how this expanded Archive provides cultural resources extending beyond groups like the yearly pageant participants themselves, I will also revisit my own experiences as a learner encountering Spelman's recurring stories through collaborative study and, I hope, as a teacher now positioned to pass those narratives on productively and respectfully to others from a stance of still-learning student. In other words, by generating a story of my own earlier learning and current teaching about Spelman's counter-narrative heritage, I will show how that Archive has expanded its cultural force beyond the institution's insider audience (Spelman's own students and alumnae) to others (like me) eager to draw from its example. These stories of women learning to claim socially significant agency exemplify the ability of humanistic study to cross cultural boundaries (for instance, in my case, racial identity) and to encourage affiliations fostering shared value systems for leadership in the public sphere. In other words, one aim of revisiting my own learning about the *Spelman Messenger*'s early counter-narratives, as well as their reconfigurations for contemporary audiences more recently, will be to document how these learning legacies have had an impact on my own worldview, enabling me to teach with enhanced intercultural awareness.

Cross-Cultural Storytelling

Chapter 3's analysis of counter-narratives created by Jane Addams and her colleagues at Hull-House offers a similarly positive account of women moving from marginalized positions to social agency through collaboration. Like Packard and Giles (Spelman's women founders), Addams benefited from access to liberal arts traditions herself—specifically through attendance at Rockford Seminary. She self-consciously drew on that learning legacy when developing educational opportunities that the settlement made available to its middle-class residents and the Hull-House immigrant "neighbors" who joined its reading groups, enrolled in its creative array of courses, and participated in its public projects. From building playgrounds and launching kindergarten programs to organizing political debates and operating a coffee house that provided healthy foods for working-class families, Hull-House transitioned early on from a hierarchical enterprise seeking to transmit cultural training to a far more participatory—even reciprocal—endeavor. Ultimately, the settlement neighborhood's community members increasingly guided Hull-House's arts- and humanities-oriented learning activities themselves. Addams herself focused more and more on the creation of stories about the settlement as a democratic educational program that could enable similar enterprises beyond that particular site. To extend that history forward, chapter 3 outlines ways in which the multidimensional legacy of cultural rhetoric from Addams's leadership-through-writing (grounded in collaborative learning) still offers up efficacious guidance for civic engagement projects today.

As my analysis will establish, Hull-House produced, and is still producing, a vibrant Archive of stories in multiple genres. Addams and the others living at the Chicago settlement, like the well-to-do men residing at London's Toynbee Hall (her role model for the settlement), were white, college-educated, and well-connected members of a highly privileged social class who might have been expected to place as much social distance as possible between themselves and the city's burgeoning immigrant population. Instead, adapting the London example of Canon Samuel Barnett and his wife Henrietta in England, Addams and Ellen Gates Starr turned the former Hull mansion into a magnet of proactive learning programs that eventually spread all along Halsted Street and beyond, as Hull-House became the United States' national model for settlement work.

Small wonder, perhaps, that Addams and her colleagues generated such a rich archive of published and unpublished accounts of the Hull-House program. Addams's own individual writing archive is vast. Though for a long time *Twenty Years at Hull-House* was virtually the only one of her many books to glean much scholarly attention, editions of additional texts she penned across the many years of her life have become available for study through both print projects allied with the feminist recovery movement and digitization efforts involving many institutional entities. Chapter 3 takes advantage of this enhanced accessibility to Addams's published oeuvre by focusing, in part, on one underinterpreted text, *My Friend, Julia Lathrop*. My analysis of this late-career narrative by Addams complements archival research I've done in the Special Collections of the University of Illinois at Chicago (UIC). There, I've retrieved such records as stories associated with Addams's own education at Rockford Seminary; letters she exchanged with Henrietta Barnett, cofounder of Toynbee Hall; and scrapbooks where Addams built a hybrid account of settlement history from others' newspaper and magazine clippings on Hull-House. Here, I place this individual archive of writing in dialogue with the multifaceted Archive of the settlement's longstanding cross-cultural teaching (including copies of the *Hull-House Bulletin*, memoirs by residents like Alice Hamilton and "neighbors" like Hilda Satt Polacheck, and material culture items such as photographs and everyday objects).

Addams's individual archive remains at the heart of this Archive. Casting her numerous publications on settlement programs as stories accessible to a broad readership, she produced a deeply reflective record of cross-cultural work that resisted many of the conventions for Progressive-Era writing affiliated with academic discourse in the emerging social sciences. As such, her personal record of teaching represents a counter-narrative that exalts both the reciprocal learning of daily settlement life and the residents and neighbors whose ongoing engagement with urban social issues she foregrounded in her storytelling. That is, by subsuming her own identity into an overarching counter-narrative of collaborative learning, Addams generated an archive of adaptable stories. For instance, because she consistently positioned her self-depictions within a "we" context of shared action rather than in a first-person singular, heroic-type voice, readers seeking a similar social leadership role could draw upon her narratives about teaching without being overwhelmed by a disempowering sense of her individual celebrity status. Further, in supporting the writing of other women at the settlement, as well as storytelling by her immigrant neighbors (such as the theater performances at the settlement, the political debates, and their arts and crafts), Addams helped expand the archive of her individual oeuvre into a constantly enriched Archive of progressive education in action.

A tireless fundraiser and network-builder, Addams used her writing talents to tell compelling stories of Hull-House's projects while also nurturing the reporting skills of other residents and the "neighbors" themselves. Over and over, whether through speaking engagements of her own or in accounts crafted for settlement-sponsored publications like the printed yearbook; whether in public performances by Hull-House dramatic clubs or in presentations at the Labor Museum showcasing crafts from neighbors' home countries—whatever the particular form taken, Addams's texts from the settlement's teaching programs emphasized their cross-cultural community-building.[28]

Given this longstanding focus on making connections across cultural divides, the Chicago settlement's historical record has engendered an increasingly substantial body of scholarship, encouraged in part by the ways in which current social issues echo those of Addams's time. From sociologists to rhetoricians, theater studies specialists to literature scholars, women's studies researchers to educational historians, Hull-House's determined reach across boundaries during Addams's lifetime continues to invite exploration. A good deal of recent feminist scholarship on Addams and the settlement has sought to correct previously limited interpretations of her social role.[29] My own analysis joins this effort. As chapter 3 will explain, over the initial decades after her death in 1935, Addams's narrative approach for recording settlement activities led many scholars to downplay her role as a theorist. This view typically cast university-authorized academic men like John Dewey (who himself lived at the settlement for a time) as the primary, definitive commentators on the Progressive Era. Now, however, reconsiderations of the settlement legacy by activist researchers, like the staff of the Jane Addams Hull-House Museum (JAHHM) as revitalized by Lisa Lee's directorship, have revised that portrait. By reanimating the space of the museum to reinterpret Hull-House's stories, the JAHHM cultural curators began generating an expanded Archive for applying settlement house lessons in our own time.

To illuminate this ongoing process, chapter 3 blends textual analysis of previously underexamined writings by Addams and her colleagues with observation- and interview-informed accounts of cultural work by intellectual heirs. Besides the cadre of women at JAHHM, another team self-consciously adapting resources from the settlement Archive includes professors and students from the English Education program at the University of Illinois, Chicago, the very institution whose launch, ironically, wiped away most of the architectural archive of Hull-House in the 1960s. Underscoring ways in which women educator-authors' legacy is increasingly being recognized by thoughtful men involved in civic leadership, chapter 3 also celebrates the Addams-inspired counter-narrative energy evident in Professors David Schaafsma and Todd DeStigter's mentoring of teacher-writers for their *Jane Addams in the Classroom* project.

Unlike Spelman, still a very visible institutional presence as a black women's college prominently situated within the cluster of affiliates making up Atlanta University Center,[30] Hull-House has shrunk to a small remnant of its original identity as a multistructure settlement originally stretched proudly along Halsted Street in downtown Chicago. So, whereas one narrative thread for chapter 2 traces the institutional history of Spelman as growing, fed by its storytelling, from a dark, damp church basement to a multifacility college campus, chapter 3 must present a different kind of overarching narrative. In terms of recovering the Hull-House Archive, we must acknowledge substantial loss of material space and educational activity, and thus, to some extent, a displaced identity. Though the original Hull home and a restored version of the dining hall remain, positioned somewhat precariously on the edge of the campus for the University of Illinois at Chicago as the Jane Addams Hull-House Museum, the more accessible legacy of Hull-House, today, is inscribed in the virtually countless narratives that make up its rhetorical heritage. These stories, now, do help maintain a living legacy for the settlement, as they continually beget more humanistic, artistic, and educational resources for collaborative use by students, teachers, scholars, activists, and community members who hope to learn from Addams's and her colleagues' work. Accordingly, chapter 3 posits an argument about communal writing itself, broadly conceived, as a learning legacy shaping cultural practices. Here, then, is a question addressed by this chapter: if the ongoing stories by and about Spelman provide an adaptable framework for institution-building and associated cultural maintenance, what do the inscribed counter-narratives from Hull-House's evolving learning legacy offer us as teaching texts modeling civic engagement approaches that are not institution-dependent or even institutionally situated, but rather transportable through intercultural/interpersonal partnerships?

Though each is distinctive, as noted above, the learning legacies of Spelman and Hull-House are both basically positive. Like chapter 2's examination of an Archive's ongoing cultural stewardship by the Spelman community, chapter 3 also affirms the utility of constructive humanities-oriented collaborations from the past and traces processes that are carrying such learning legacies forward. In both cases, we find adaptable models in counter-narratives originally created by women educators and learners in an era that often sought to constrain their agency. However, if aspirational legacies like those located through the stories of Spelman and Hull-House are to be trustworthy as maps to social action, they cannot be touted as indicators that every Archive straightforwardly facilitates agency. Hence, the second part of *Learning Legacies* addresses a far more problematic heritage from narratives developed originally to support assimilationist education of Indigenous American students.

Mining a Negative Archive through Empathy

Archives are not always sources of positive inspiration. Therefore, recognizing the "Negative Archive" as a cultural force inviting humanistic inquiry that incorporates critique along with resistance is equally important to my project. As noted above, one especially significant Archive emerging during the same decades as the Spelman and Hull-House stories has Indigenous roots. This complex cross-cultural resource surfaces from records of the boarding school enterprise infamously envisioned to "kill the Indian" through a comprehensive, white-run educational program. Like the textual legacies of other genocidal and soul-attacking enterprises—such as memoirs of Holocaust survivors—stories arising from the assimilationist education movement and related, more overt assaults like Wounded Knee serve today as potent warnings against atrocity rather than as aspirational models to emulate. As such, these Archives must be approached with humility and care by members of dominant/majority groups, like me, who hope to enact responsive, responsible teaching from an empathetic stance.

In the later chapters (4 and 5), I engage with the Negative Archive linked to the heritage of Carlisle-based assimilation programs aimed at Native Americans. This Negative Archive—promoting a vision of teaching and learning that suppresses difference and aims for mono-culturalism—still operates today. We need to recognize and track that ongoing power, even as we study examples of narratives resisting its force. In chapter 4, therefore, I first identify examples of dominant narratives that helped construct the Negative Archive advocating assimilationist education. Then I interpret a cluster of oppositional texts and social practices that arose across diffuse communal networks to resist its force, even in an era when American Indians' access to institution-building opportunities of their own was extremely limited. In chapter 5, I position learning legacies from Indigenous/First Nations educators themselves in the context of institutional spaces where they have been able to claim notable agency—through strategic entry into publishing sites (some of them white-managed), in the

National Museum of the American Indian, and in universities and other instructional settings where Native intellectuals are now exercising leadership as scholar-teachers.

Read as a unit, chapters 4 and 5 address hermeneutic challenges associated with transforming this Negative Archive, a process which necessitates confronting such documents as white cultural arbiters' propaganda promoting the assimilationist education program as a "civilizing" process, but also the rightly privileged narrative responses to their personal experiences created by Native students themselves. In reading these counter-narratives, which express a notable diversity of views, I must confront my own race- and class-based interpretive limitations. If I want to earn an ally-type status with colleagues whose identities bring an epistemic privilege for interpreting such Negative Archives today, I need to make my own learning process one object of scrutiny.

Overall, I seek to develop what scholars in education often term a "critical consciousness" to guide my teaching of these texts, including the specific stories of individuals' encounters with oppressive learning situations.[31] Pierre Bourdieu's *Practical Reason: On the Theory of Action* is helpful in this context. Bourdieu explains that "the mechanism of scholastic reproduction" is derived from groups that already hold high capital (both cultural and economic) in a society; using discourse to complement their other political tools, these power figures strive to sustain "the preexisting order" (20). Through the sorting and containing processes inherent in educational systems, he indicates, "social borders" are constructed and maintained (21). Thus, to interpret these enterprises—which may claim to be dispensing education for the common good—"true epistemological questioning" must be exercised (36). Only if we cultivate such a stance—one attuned to the regulatory force of instructional agendas managed by members of the dominant culture—can we achieve a clear view of how "symbolic capital" dispensed through education systems becomes the site, means, and "concentration and exercise of symbolic power" (47).

On one hand, in line with Bourdieu's framework, my project underscores and resists power-claiming social interactions within dominant education programs. On another hand, when examining the experiences and responses of students within such systems, I aim for a self-critical empathetic stance supporting principled rhetorical analyses in historical context. That is, when interpreting the textual archive associated with assimilationist education, I strive for intense awareness of my own social position of privilege. That recognition of privilege is crucial for making my standpoint another tool contributing to, more than impeding, my efforts to create ethical knowledge.

Most of all, chapter 4's encounter with the Negative Archive of the assimilationist education program honors, as a rich cultural resource, the counter-narratives deployed by a range of Native intellectual leaders who have written in response to that otherwise disempowering legacy. An essential step in this process entails revisiting the very dominant narratives that sought to justify oppressive instructional practices based on constructing the Indian as a "problem" and an uncivilized Other. I highlight power-accruing strategies embedded in stories by figures ranging from Carlisle founder Richard Henry Pratt to white women authors whose accounts of teaching helped validate his program. For instance, in the Negative Archive of texts by Marianna Burgess and the admittedly more complicated figure of Elaine Goodale Eastman, I point to genre features which, in Bourdieu's terms, discursively enforced the borders of the existing social order of racial hierarchies. I also highlight the strategic cultural rhetoric in Native counter-narratives of that time. Consistent with Molly Andrews's explanation above, some of these blend echoes of master narratives with subversive subtexts. These personal accounts may read like mixed messages today, but in their own time they were surely aligned with Steven Mailloux's concept of rhetorical pragmatism: they sought an avenue for resistance within a constrained space. Zitkala-Ša (Gertrude Bonnin) claims a central position in this configuration of counter-narratives.

Extending the legacy of critique by Indian writers from that earlier era, an impressive array of Native scholar/teacher authors has produced their own new counter-narratives to undermine that negative legacy's power. Thus, also in chapter 4, I salute poets like Laura Tohe and Esther Belin, who effectively reconfigure language from assimilationist narratives into their own reformative responses. And in N. Scott Momaday's dramatic renderings of the boarding school ethos (via *The Indolent Boys* and *The Moon in Two Windows*), I demonstrate how counter-narratives overtly critiquing that agenda's heritage perform essential cross-cultural work. Drawing on my training in close reading as a literature scholar, I outline how Momaday uses plot, characterization, theme, and tone to overturn a Negative Archive. Where Spelman's annual Founders' Day performances celebrate an educational history so as to provide models for black women's learning today, Momaday's bitter and poignant dramas call for continued resistance. If accounts of the Hull-House theater's productions, grounded in positive cross-cultural exchange, suggest possibilities for new intercultural resource-making via performances in our own time, Momaday's plays remind us that today's Native teachers are endowed with epistemic privilege as the most authorized voices to counter past cultural histories.[32] Ultimately, therefore, chapter 4's analysis of Native counter-narratives rejecting the assimilationist agenda calls for members of the dominant culture, myself included, to cultivate a version of empathy that moves beyond *feeling sorry for* or *wanting to "help"* members of a marginalized group to ceding social authority to its members. This stance, ultimately, may earn the role of ally. Since self-critical empathy requires cultivating a humble eagerness to be guided rather than to lead, a story like mine here, which has been supported by interpersonal connections, is actually collaboratively constructed, even when conventions associated with academic writing (as for this book) present the rhetorical product under one name.

From Archive to Collaborative Action

Acting on their knowledge-making authority while justly claiming a corrective agenda, today's Native educators might be expected to counter the legacy of assimilation schooling's Negative Archive with confrontational teaching cast as cultural payback. As indicated in chapter 5's accounts of nurturing teachers reaching out from Indian Country to share their knowledge, however, a far different strategy is evident these days in multiple Native-managed educational activities. Gifted and generous, Native teachers are promoting resilient, restorative intercultural learning. Ranging from individual classrooms led by Native instructors to large-scale cultural events welcoming diverse audiences, these reclaimed spaces of social interaction are strategically extending an Indian-made Archive of positive teaching approaches linked to Indigenous cultural values. As chapter 5 chronicles, this aspirational Archive is retrievable in diverse texts from both the past and present, crafted to convey proactive Indigenous education practices. Chapter 5's focus on such counter-narrative teaching within Native societies, but also for other cultural groups, encourages readers to engage with this Archive as a transformative resource.

One strategy I used to identity texts to highlight for this chapter has uncovered a genealogy of Native teachers who emerged from within the narrow pedagogical spaces of the boarding school movement itself. Building on a foundation established by past cultural brokers such as Ruth Muskrat Bronson and Esther Burnett Horne, later generations of Native educators gradually acquired enhanced control over curriculum. One line in this Native teaching heritage, I'd suggest, extends back to such early appropriations of white print culture as the *Cherokee Phoenix*, which in pre-Removal days rhetorically embodied the potential for cross-cultural exchanges by way of a bilingual periodical.[33] In a similar strategy, women writer-educators like S. Alice Callahan (*Wynema: A Child of the Forest*) and Ella Cara Deloria (*Waterlily*) offered subtle, double-voiced, counter-narrative approaches for intercultural teaching pitched to address white audiences. Depicting teaching models guided by Native tenets, these texts sought to reform whites' pedagogical practices. This counter-narrative tradition anticipated the ways in which a number of Native educators now situated in relatively empowered institutional settings are transmitting Indigenous value systems to members of the majority culture. In their classrooms and in writing about such principles as rhetorical sovereignty, scholars like Malea Powell and Lisa King are productively extending this strategy of positive counter-narratives. As chapter 5's interviews with several Native educator-writers indicate, the growing Archive of their teaching stories offers a hopeful alternative to the Negative Archive of White-over-Red assimilationist programs.

Meanwhile, on a larger and even more expansive institutional level, chapter 5 posits, the National Museum of the American Indian (NMAI) has assumed a vital educational role in cross-cultural education, authorized by no less an arbiter of social capital than the Smithsonian Institution (SI). In that context, like the Jane Addams Hull-House Museum, the NMAI is purposefully using counter-narratives and other New Museology techniques such as community curation. However, if the JAHHM's on-location exhibits, community outreach activities, and representations of settlement-linked stories on their website have communicated a revitalized resource from Addams's prior cultural work, the NMAI has an even more extensive Archive to call upon for public pedagogy. Whereas JAHHM digs deep into the legacy of Addams-led settlement education to cultivate an updated focus for urban learning, the NMAI's mandate extends across the heritage of all Native peoples in the Americas. This broad reach provides its leaders with a wealth of potential resources, but also presents challenges associated with such debates as how to determine genuine Indian identity (for tribal groups associated with a "national" museum as well as for individuals).

Hence, this flourishing Smithsonian-affiliated teaching space has (perhaps unavoidably) bred its own share of critique, from both Native and non-Native assessors, as chapter 5's treatment of the NMAI duly notes.[34] However, when viewed in the context of this book's learning legacies framework, the museum's already-realized and still-evolving potential as, itself, a counter-narrative addressing multiple audiences comes to the foreground. In that vein, Jolene Rickard, Tuscarora artist/designer and guest curator for one of the NMAI's initial exhibits, *Our Peoples*, invoked a concept of corrective narrative when describing her work. For Rickard, creating an NMAI exhibit brought "an opportunity in the collection to recapture Indigenous history with the very objects that represented our capture'" via "'an intervention on the framing of Native cultures within a metanarrative of the West.'"[35]

Now in its second decade, the museum seems to be growing even more deliberate in deploying a proactive blend of resistant counter-narratives and restorative collaborations. Associate Director David W. Penney describes "collaborative and participatory scholarship" as a major strategy the NMAI is utilizing to "change perceptions about American history" through exhibits like *Nation to Nation: Treaties Between the United States and American Indian Nations*. He outlines the NMAI's efforts to develop "new curriculum content available online as part of our National Education initiative" and, in doing so, to partner with Native community groups in public programs transmitting "the most accurate and up-to-date information about . . . Native culture and history" ("Scholarship for Leadership," 12). Asserting that, for the NMAI, "Knowledge creation is a collective endeavor benefiting from the broadest range of input," Penney articulates a vision for the museum's mission as more than a remedial response to views of "American Indians as peripheral to the mainstream of American history"; additionally, he explains, this Native teaching space is constructing an activist, communal narrative conveying "experiences that are relevant, useful and true" (12).

A crucial element in the NMAI's teaching entails nurturing the cultural authority of Native peoples themselves, as chapter 5 establishes. To cite one example here, I'd point to the language in calls for applicants to the Artist Leadership Program (ALP) in spring 2015. The project's website describes its goals in terms that envision links between archival study and enhanced artistic authority: "The National Museum of the American Indian's (NMAI) Artist Leadership Program (ALP) for Individual Artists enables indigenous artists to research, document, and network in Washington, D.C., then return home empowered with new artistic insights, skills, and techniques to share with their communities and the general public the value of Native knowledge through art." Via a commitment "to rebuild cultural self-confidence, challenge personal boundaries, and foster cultural continuity while reflecting artistic diversity," the ALP provides an opportunity for Native artists, when working in the NMAI's archive, to "meet and consult with staff at SI and other arts organizations; participate in a public art panel discussion, speaking as voices of authority on their art; break down stereotypes about indigenous art; and, through a personal artistic narrative, speak to social justice issues and current events important to indigenous communities." Secondarily, the ALP strives to position "young artists in collaboration with elders," building networks "to share ideas and resources" and to "affirm that indigenous arts hold value and knowledge" that can "offer communities a means for healing and new ways to exchange cultural information."[36] Overall, the ALP both draws upon and makes Indigenous Archives.

Interestingly, in this context of affirming Indigenous knowledge as already present in the culture, one of the controversial aspects of the NMAI's day-to-day practice (as examined by Kristine Ronan) is its use of Native interpreters within the museum space. Ronan points out that one view of the placement of staff on site "to connect visitors daily with Native people" sees this practice as an opportunity for genuine cross-cultural exchange. Yet she notes how another perspective critiques the approach as rendering those same Native people into colonized pseudo-interpreters ("Native Empowerment," 136). While affirming the complexity of such identity-related issues—perhaps an inescapable point of debate in the NMAI's educational work—I address this topic more fully in chapter 5, in part through interviews with Indian educators there such as Dennis Zotigh and Renée Gokey, who use rhetorical engagement with identity as a proactive teaching tool.

Like previous sections of the book, chapter 5 raises standpoint-related questions about how my own identity both enables and constrains my ability to report on a specific learning legacy. As one way of addressing these issues within the context of longstanding critiques of whites' appropriating Native knowledge, I fold in several location-specific descriptions of my interactions with Native teachers who mentored my work. Thus, I join Native scholar Andrea M. Riley Mukavetz in asking: "How can we draw attention to the complexity of moving across and participating with cultural communities?" To follow her authorial lead, I make visible ways that "the roles of the researcher and the participant are fluid" for "intercultural researchers," as the Native teachers who "share space" with me to support my learning also share knowledge-making ("Towards a Cultural Rhetoric," 120). Along the way, I strive to give respectful credit to multifaceted collaborations, by presenting this chapter, like my others, as a first-person account of my learning, and I accept responsibility for shortcomings and errors.

Significantly, as for other sections, the collaborations that enabled chapter 5 took different forms in different locations and situations. For instance, my online and in-person interviews with scholars like Malea Powell, Lisa King, and Kimberli Lee weave in references to research they have published themselves within the dominant culture's network of academic knowledge-making. In contrast, stories I share from visits with on-site NMAI guides draw primarily on other epistemological pathways, including social practices such as powwows and oral story-making. These differing routes to my own text-making for the chapter should not be viewed as hierarchical, however, and neither should they be seen as dichotomous. The NMAI is part of the Smithsonian, after all, and the knowledge-bearers there have as much cultural authority as a university-based scholar. Indeed, many of those who work at the NMAI are academically trained researchers, and all are skilled cultural mediators.

Furthermore, among the university-based mentors who contributed teaching stories for this chapter, there were also variations in how our collaborations played out on different occasions. For instance, I recorded one interview with Malea Powell during a meal break at a conference sponsored by the Society for the Study of American Women Writers (SSAWW), when our dialogue zeroed in on sometimes-frustrating traits we had both observed in professional organizations' networks; that day, the shared experience of thinking about our scholarly work in such terms framed the conversation's content around gender and academic professional class roles, alongside points about Native knowledge-making. At another meal, actually several years later, we addressed specific questions about revision of this manuscript after I had received readers' reports from the University of Michigan Press. For that more recent occasion, when we were joined by Lisa King, our talk shifted back and forth between my asking questions about updating chapter 5's content and my seeking more general advice on revision processes for the entire manuscript. Around that second topic, the three of us brainstormed particular revision strategies in line with our then attending a convention under the auspices of the Conference on College Composition and Communication ("the Cs"), which also sponsors special interest groups aligned with both Native studies and cultural rhetoric. Now, when I reread my notes from these two different occasions of sharing food and sharing ideas, I can see how intersectionality has come into play to direct collaboration differently at different times, even within the same multiyear partnership.[37] Via these diverse paths, both in this introduction and in later chapters, even if overt signs of Malea's and Lisa's influence on my revisions are not easily traceable in the text that you, my readers, are encountering here, I know that their wise counsel has made this writing an example of what I call *research with* more than of *research on*.

Thus, in this "monograph" project, partners who've guided my work should be viewed as carrying out different kinds of collaboration than when a team of people prepares a "coauthored" product or plans for an event that they present to the public together somehow (such as a theatrical performance, say, or a video or website for which everyone writes text and takes pictures). In honoring these perhaps-not-fully-visible contributions, I affirm the attentive approach to cultural rhetorics methodology articulated by Riley-Mukavetz in her description of collaborative talking circles with Odawa women from Lansing, Michigan. As in her example, I seek to enact "relational accountability" and to "challenge disciplinary and professional practices that emphasize strict categorization and demarcation" when doing intercultural research ("Towards a Cultural Rhetorics," 113–14).

As Riley-Mukavetz admits, affiliating simultaneously with academic institutions whose professional frameworks privilege individual productivity does mean we have a complicated rhetorical dance to do, one requiring the use of traditional scholarly discourse conventions too. I hope my readers will take note, therefore, of my efforts to craft a hybrid text, blending essential markers of careful scholarship like a formal bibliography of others' research with equally important (even if less formal) collaborations. For instance, chapter 2 cites multiple illustrations of partners aiding my research on Spelman; these examples appear both within the core text and in the endnotes. I name colleagues who made content suggestions, identify specific conversations around their recommendations, and describe informal written feedback they gave to various drafts. Adding another textual layer of collaborative knowledge-building and writing, chapter 3's treatment of diverse composing enterprises linked to Hull-House's legacy— including Jane Addams's own accounts of her work *with* settlement residents to "story" their way to theory—also signals that writing emerging from project-oriented teaching practice is never single-authored, even when published under one name, as in the individual chapters within the *Jane Addams in the Classroom* collection of essays. Along the way, therefore, chapter 3 makes the case rhetorically for forms of scholarship that are possible to achieve only through shared cultural work.

Consistent with this project's core concept of "learning legacies," as authors working in such multilayered humanities traditions, we are always, in fact, drawing on cultural resources that we did not create on our own. In that vein, Phil Bratta and Malea Powell aver: "knowledge is never built by individuals but is, instead, accumulated through collective practices within specific communities" ("Introduction," paragraph 11). Just so, *Learning Legacies* maintains that we need stories of multifaceted, diverse, and community-based collaborations. These stories must recognize how uneven power relations come into play anytime people from differing backgrounds work together, seeking to carry out meaningful cultural interventions through partnerships. But our stories of praxis can also carry out a teaching agenda of their own by attentively noting those power relations in action; by using language itself to expand avenues of community-building; and by blending our steps to delve into cultural resources together with efforts to create new ones, inviting and available to others for their own use.

Embracing Aspirational Scholarship

To sum up this approach to teaching and scholarship, a framework also providing structures for the chapters that follow, let me reiterate the core vision this book advocates. *Learning Legacies* demonstrates, through multiple historical cases, how narrative Archives of intercultural exchange operate within public culture for broad communal use. Integrating rhetorical analyses of archival (and Archival) resources from the past with accounts of their application in community-building enterprises today, this project calls for narrative knowledge-making at the intersection of the humanities, the arts, and education. To illustrate, I celebrate intercultural work (at Spelman, through Hull-House, and extending out from the NMAI, as in other Native-led teaching enterprises) that have been tapping into such archives as avenues to social empowerment, for themselves and *with* others. These examples show how strategic teacher-learners in diverse educational settings can draw creatively from diverse cultural resources, can extend those Archives by generating purposeful counter-narratives of their own today, and can disseminate their own new stories as pathways to pragmatic civic action.

Meanwhile, by documenting my own processes of reflection on archival materials and their potential social usefulness today, I highlight the value of such resources for sustained cross-cultural education. By using first-person narration to revisit others' archive-based teaching and to evaluate my own learning, I resist reducing cross-cultural study to quantifiable measures. At the same time, I call for spaces in public scholarship where we can share our personalized learning legacies to help make and shape cultural memory. Along the way, in stressing collaborative epistemology's value to social justice goals, I stake a claim for the humanities as a privileged site of agency, particularly when linked to public scholarship that also engages with the arts and education.

How can individual teachers foster the kind of collaborative endeavors *Learning Legacies* advocates? Throughout this book, I weave in references to my own teaching practice as illustrations, not to provide a set blueprint, but rather, consistent with the historical case studies here, to situate praxis within a flexible conceptual framework for teaching grounded in open-ended inquiry and storytelling. In a coda chapter that closes the book, I lay out more specific portraits of work I am doing now in teaching and in scholarship aligned with that framework, and I also offer up suggestions for future applications of ideas here that others may want to undertake in their own community-building projects.

The most productive among such collaborations, this book maintains, extend in a relatively open-ended fashion over time. Studying the past, then imagining, listening, and sharing together, we can narrate our way to new knowledge—in the classroom, in our communities, and in our writing. These learning experiences can't always be counted in numbers or represented in a clear-cut set of statistics. They reside and continue to grow in our shared stories. So we should facilitate occasions, formal and informal, to affirm the intercultural learning processes that arise from narratives and counter-narratives. Let me cite one example, a retrospective meal and conversation I shared with Renée Gokey and Dennis Zotigh at the Mitsitam Café in the NMAI, after creating a first full draft of this manuscript. As we looked ahead to eventual publication, we also looked back at previous dialogues and events we'd participated in together. Renée and Dennis updated me on some of their own new teaching initiatives at the museum; certainly several of those specific anecdotes are now incorporated into this book. But I hope, even more, that the spirit behind them and the staying power of these colleagues' examples—like those of archivist Taronda Spencer at Spelman and the gifted museum curators I connected with at Hull-House—are also infused throughout the manuscript. When sharing learning legacies, collaboration also resides in the stories we carry forward, through our words and our actions, in our hearts as well as our minds. Whenever, in the process of beginning a new teaching endeavor, I call up memories of such past conversations and projects carried out with colleagues like these, they remain part of an ongoing Archive-making collaboration based in shared knowing and doing.

Achieving social justice, on a large scale or even around a particular issue, will always remain elusive. But stories of how we've cultivated that goal through shared public work nonetheless merit telling. In that spirit, even while acknowledging the many shortcomings associated with the community reading project that I described at the start of this introduction, I'll close by pointing to patterns of learning there that I hope to build upon in the future. For one thing, the enterprise brought together a range of participants whose usual conversations are held within tight disciplinary boundaries. Directly affirming this border-crossing, clinical veterinarian and public health educator Katherine Fogelberg commented online in one of her early postings: "Looking forward to reading further—both with Camus and with this community!" Later, responding to details in Katherine's post, one undergraduate participant wrote: "I'm only halfway done with Part II of *The Plague*, but . . . . issues like this force individuals to stop their day to day lives and consider serious questions: How do we confront our own mortality? Like Katherine noted, why do we feel so affronted when tragedy strikes in our home? How do we respond to the pain and suffering of others?"[38]

However moderately, we bridged cultural boundaries between disciplines, between the professorate and undergraduates, between university insiders and alumni off-campus. A project like this is certainly not as significant as the journey Packard and Giles made from New England to found a seminary along with black women in the postbellum South, or as visionary as creating a settlement house in an urban ghetto, or as challenging as a Native teacher carving out a space of subversive pedagogy at a white-run assimilationist school. But small collaborative acts that lead us to asking questions together—to shared reflection promoting new learning communities—represent a worthwhile first step.[39] So, too, by engaging with others' counter-narratives and the challenges they record, we stand to enrich our own lived experiences, and we begin, in at least a tentative way, to move from archive to action.

CHAPTER TWO

"That my work may speak well for Spelman"

Messengers *Recording History and Performing Uplift*

"I am not going this way again. I must say what I have to say now."
—Emma DeLamotta, *Spelman Messenger*, November 1903

"We know where we're going, and we know where we've been."
—Student Performer, Spelman Founders Day, April 2011

Fostering Community Connections

This chapter revisits connections linking a curriculum development initiative funded primarily by the National Endowment for the Humanities (NEH), subsequent research I've done to extend my scholarship and teaching around one of that project's key themes, and ways in which both those endeavors (in the archive and in the classroom) have benefited from collegial, cross-racial support. Readers will find many examples here of previously published research that has supported my own. But in this case, I will also highlight the personal guidance of two mentors—a schoolteacher and an archivist. Their contributions to this chapter, each illustrating multiple strategies for collaborative leadership, represent the kind of "behind-the-scenes" support for shared narrative knowledge-making that, far too often, goes under-acknowledged. So, here at the start, let me salute Deborah Mitchell and Taronda Spencer, who together, as servant leaders enacting sustained Spelman traditions, led me to relate what we can learn in the archives to the ongoing project of nurturing future educational leaders, learners, and citizens.

I begin with a memory of Deborah's classroom. In the spring of 2001, I drove from the northern suburbs of Atlanta, through the heavy traffic on our city's skyscraper-lined downtown "connector" of I-75/I-85, to Slater Elementary School. I had a late-afternoon appointment with Deborah, an inspirational elementary school teacher and participant in the multi-year humanities project, Keeping and Creating American Communities (KCAC). I could hardly wait to reach Deborah's school: I knew she'd have stories to tell about an artifacts-and-family-history project her young students were completing. The previous summer, during an institute on the Kennesaw State campus near Marietta, Georgia, Deborah had taken on a leadership role for one of the project's curriculum-building teams. She had been a pivotal voice in identifying the particular local topic we'd begun exploring under the umbrella of one of our KCAC themes, "Educating for Citizenship." A proud graduate of Spelman, Deborah had urged us to dig into the college's archive.

Over the years, she had learned much about the institution's founding. She easily invoked stories of how students, teachers, and members of Atlanta's black pastoral network overcame economic, political, and ideological challenges to launch what evolved into the women's college of today. These affirming narratives circulate continually among Spelman community members, but they had also come to her through cross-generational family accounts. However, Deborah had not, at that point, fully investigated Spelman's early history in a more formal "academic" way. Like many a K-12 educator, she had been constrained time-wise from such work, but this NEH-funded project brought opportunities for collaborative scholarship.[1] From the outset, one KCAC project aim was to explore how having K-12 educators actually *do* interdisciplinary inquiry would make it easier for them to teach such processes to students. An important related premise was the idea that community-based research topics would matter to learners. With this context in mind, Deborah had suggested that having one teacher-scholar team focus on Spelman would produce resources of value to many US classrooms.[2] This chapter, accordingly, grows out of place-based inquiry initially carried out by a group of educators who themselves crossed cultures of disciplinary training, race, teaching "level" (elementary through university), and neighborhood in a sprawling metropolitan area. My writing here about Spelman students' and others' longstanding engagement with its history has been seeded and nurtured with the wisdom and energy of team members involved in that project, which originated well over a decade ago.[3]

"Educating for Citizenship" was one of several themes identified by the core group of K-12 teachers who had helped write our proposal to NEH.

This particular topic resonated powerfully for our team members. Living in a metro area so closely associated with questions about access to civic participation—Atlanta, after all, being home to Rev. Martin Luther King Jr. and other civil rights leaders—our region was also facing intensely debated questions about citizenship for an exploding immigrant population. "Educating for Citizenship" was a topic rooted in Atlanta's past and highly relevant for our own time.

KCAC's structure called for each subgroup of teachers to spend much of our first summer, as well as the following academic year, in interdisciplinary inquiry around one of our community-focused themes.[4] For our original proposal to NEH,[5] we had chosen community studies themes we hoped could be adapted to any US region. Besides "Educating for Citizenship," we adopted these other topics, with our own local applications for each: "Reclaiming Displaced Heritages" (for us in Georgia, the Cherokee Removal); "Cultivating Homelands" (studying early twentieth-century rural life in our area); "Building Cities" (an examination of Atlanta's transformation to an international city); and "Shifting Landscapes, Converging Peoples" (suburban life in our own time). Deborah's advocacy of Spelman's learning legacy as a local application for the "Educating for Citizenship" theme was especially promising for its transportability. How racial identity has interacted with debates about appropriate learning agendas, how women might serve as leaders in educational movements, how teaching enterprises forging new paths can best gather community support, and how a specific institutional vision can best interact with larger issues of social justice—these were just a few of the questions we began to investigate together, through the lens of Spelman's archive.

By 2001, as KCAC-affiliated classes across metro Atlanta (including mine at Kennesaw State) studied Spelman's founding era, we were all asking related questions about our own institutions' histories and current values. For many of our students, whatever their grade level, this was their first experience engaging directly with archival materials, so we were tracking what most attracted their interest, and how. One learning legacy to emerge for classroom teaching was in the *Spelman Messenger*, which started publishing early in the college's life.[6] Experimenting with that resource, Journalism and American Studies teacher Dave Winter of Grady High School had begun using Spelman student-writers' texts to engage his classes in interdisciplinary inquiry of their own.[7] Thus, I arrived at Slater Elementary eager for dialogue about classroom projects linked to archival research—in this case, in an elementary school. Deborah's students, like

Dave's and mine, had been inspired by reading the *Spelman Messenger* to dig into other archives, including personal and familial ones.

Our access to the *Messenger*'s pages had come through the gifted, hard-working archivist who had become an unofficial member of the KCAC project—Taronda Spencer. From the very first visit we'd made to the Spelman archive, Taronda had welcomed us. She embraced our program as an avenue for disseminating knowledge about the college's past to new audiences. She worked alongside the "Educating for Citizenship" group on Spelman's campus.[8] She came to Kennesaw State the next summer to lead a workshop on archival research. Across many years after the KCAC project's funded phase ended, she mentored my own follow-up research at the college; read drafts of my writing; invited me to Founders Day; and hosted my participation there. This chapter's analysis of counter-narratives emerging from Spelman in its early days, and continuing today, was possible to develop only because Taronda, along with other Spelman alumnae like Deborah, took on the role of guide.[9] As I typed out this chapter years later, in what grammarians would call a first-person voice, my words came from prior collaboration, with each of my colleagues enabling this process in different ways. So my "speaking" voice here is actually a plural one, supported indirectly by their affiliation with a broader network of alumnae that safeguards Spelman's learning legacies. My readers will find other signs of collaboration undergirding this chapter's story woven throughout its endnotes, which, besides traditional citations, also include comments from generous African American women scholars who have read and responded to drafts. In making visible some of the personal interactions that gradually deepened my own commitment to Spelman's legacy-making stories, I hope to demonstrate how multifaceted collaborations can enrich archival research as well as community network-building today. In particular, to highlight how stakeholders' engagement with archives from Spelman's past enables active learning and social action in our own time, this chapter addresses multiple counter-narratives. These include texts created by Spelman's founders and their students, as well as more recent storytelling enabled by those artifacts to help today's community at the college connect to that heritage.

Making History through Collaboration

On Wednesday, April 11, 1888, students, teachers, and alumnae gathered in one of Spelman Seminary's sunlit new buildings to commemorate the school's founding, seven years before, in the basement of Atlanta's Friendship Baptist Church. There was much to celebrate, including enrollment growth, steady increases in funding from loyal supporters, and the advancement to seminary status. But nostalgia for the early days reigned as well. And proud former students led that retrospective storytelling.

We can participate vicariously in that springtime occasion—foreshadowing the annual Founders Day event at the college in our own time—because writers for the school's thriving periodical, the *Spelman Messenger*, recorded it in front-page anecdotes from founding students such as Emma DeLamotta and Mary Ann Brooks. Their accounts brim with details about their inaugural 1881 classes—a time of both trials and vision-shaping. Thus, in her recollection, DeLamotta "told of her years of prayer that God would sometime give her the opportunity to go to school and learn to read her Bible." She recounted how "with joy she hailed the coming of Miss [Sophia] Packard and Miss [Harriet] Giles as God's own messengers to her." In praising the arrival of the northern teachers who collaborated with minister Frank Quarles to open "their little school in the basement of Friendship church," DeLamotta affirmed the role that she and other first-generation students played in establishing what would become Spelman: "She studied with all her might when it was light enough to see the letters; the basement was but dimly lighted at best, and in cloudy weather it was often too dark to study; but it was never too dark to pray." Echoing DeLamotta, other speakers all confirmed their original determination "to make their future lives useful . . . and by their works to prove their gratitude for their privileges at Spelman" ("Spelman's Birthday," May 1888, 1–2). Grounded in documents like these, we can track how the learning legacies from Spelman's earliest students established an institutional commitment to education for servant leadership. We can also see how such counter-narratives resisted dominant discourse that might otherwise have limited those authors' access to social agency. Exercising an astute rhetorical pragmatism, attuned to both constraints and possibilities, Spelman's first teachers and students produced a still-generative cultural resource. In records from these early years, we find valuable examples of black women students' own counter-narratives. The early *Messenger* and its associated Archive—the layers of multifaceted cultural resources developed over time by tapping into that original archive's narrative power—offer a welcome affirmation of African Americans' cross-generational and cross-race collaborations in liberal arts learning. Leaders at the college today clearly convey this message to students, as well as to alumnae and other supporters. Here,

I will describe Spelman's ongoing strategies for telling stories about itself and its mission; these are models for others committed to liberal arts learning with a community-oriented focus.

Revisiting the *Spelman Messenger* also reveals a counter-narrative correcting oversimplified versions of post-Civil War southern educational history—one that has important implications today for programs constructed as "service learning" and "community outreach." Hopefully, disseminating a counter-history of the leadership behind this postbellum institution's development as, actually, cross-racially collaborative will affirm a framework also emerging in some other university-community partnerships, in place of more "benevolent helping" approaches.

For too long the prevailing narrative of learning by freed people and their children credited whites from the North as saviors, traveling south to rescue helpless blacks from slavery-induced ignorance. The stereotype of the Yankee schoolmarm—whether idealized as a selfless angel[10] or excoriated for her racist and/or regionalist sense of social hierarchy[11]—dominated accounts both literary and scholarly. And certainly these women played a crucial part. Two from the post-Reconstruction generation, Sophia B. Packard and Harriet E. Giles, were at the forefront of Spelman's founding, as Emma DeLamotta's account above noted. However, long before the migration of such northern educators to southern classrooms, blacks had been drawing on every means imaginable to help each other secure access to literacy and its pathway to social agency.[12] That heritage and local leaders committed to it were essential to Packard and Giles's imagining they could open a new school for black women in Atlanta in the early 1880s.[13]

In accounts of the Reconstruction era before Spelman's founding, we can see some hesitancy in prior scholarship to spotlight the leadership of African Americans themselves—like Harriet Jacobs in Alexandria, Virginia, or William and Ellen Craft in coastal Georgia.[14] Resisting this gap, historian James Anderson cites the *Loyal Georgian* to illustrate how black leaders honored their colleagues from the North, but at the same time urged these supporters to get over "any vain reliance on their [supposedly] superior gifts . . . [of] intelligence or benevolence . . ." (*Education of Blacks*, 12). What the New England influx clearly did bring to economically impoverished freed people was resources, both materials (books, buildings) and people. In the decade after the war ended, organizations like the church-supported American Missionary Association (AMA) and the self-consciously secular New England Freedmen's Aid Society (NEFAS) worked in concert with the Freedmen's Bureau to set up schools across the South. For several years, the roster of schoolhouses and students grew exponentially, along with the number of Yankee teachers (mostly white women) seeking to teach there. While some certainly held racist biases, initially viewing their students as inherently less capable, their private journals and correspondence suggest that positive shifts in attitude often developed through ongoing contact with pupils. And many of the northern teachers, as letters from individuals sponsored by NEFAS demonstrate, were dedicated to racial equality.[15] Packard and Giles certainly represented such a stance.

In contrast to the majority pattern, some northern teachers were free blacks eager to uplift their own race, both by serving in the classroom and by promoting the enterprise in their writing. Published accounts like Charlotte Forten's *Atlantic Monthly* portrait of her work in Port Royal, and like those by white teachers writing for the *Freedmen's Record* of the NEFAS,[16] stoked interest in the North. But, perhaps predictably, northerners' commitment waned over time. Donations dropped. Politically, as Reconstruction came to an official end, federal troops pulled out of southern communities, making it increasingly dangerous for northern white women—typically shunned by local members of their own race—to keep schools running, particularly in remote rural places. In Columbus, Georgia, for instance, one small group of NEFAS teachers clung desperately to their school, even in the face of overt intimidation from night riders; they wrote heart-wrenching letters to lead administrator Ednah Cheney back in Boston, begging for continued funding, but eventually had to shut down when the society could no longer provide resources. "Cause fatigue" had set in among many northerners.

Fortunately, however, locally based coalitions of African Americans continued the effort to lift up the newly freed people through education. Black-run schools faced intense danger after Reconstruction. Yet opposition to African American learning was nothing new, as reflected in Frances Harper's 1869 novel *Minnie's Sacrifice*, where the heroine is murdered by whites hoping to halt learning in her community. Ronald E. Butchart has documented that, even during the period when federal troops provided some protection, and clearly in the decades after Reconstruction's official close, "the unrelenting terrorism targeting teachers, school-houses and students" continually "reinforced the black community's folk knowledge . . . that while whites might tolerate a small cadre of educated blacks, any broader educational movement would reawaken the beast of white terrorism" ("Black Hope, White Power," 37). But a people who had generations of experience eavesdropping on white children's lessons in plantation homes, holding night classes in the woods, or hiding literacy acquisition as in Frances Harper's poem on Aunt Chloe "Learning to Read" (Foster, *Brighter*, 205)—such a determined community was not going to stop seeking education.

This precarious context faced white educators Packard and Giles when they arrived in Atlanta in 1881, hoping to open a school for black women. They had already taught together for years at various New England institutions, and Packard had been working, most recently, as secretary for the Woman's American Baptist Home Mission Society (WABHMS) in Boston.[17] With a personal history that included having been shunted aside from leadership at a prestigious academy after conflict with a new male head of school, they came in part from an altruistic impulse and in part seeking self-advancement at a time when women's administrative skills were easy to dismiss.[18] The coalition that produced Spelman was thus an alliance joining people from different backgrounds who shared past frustrations of having been marginalized, but who also shared the confidence, capabilities, and energy to move forward through collaboration.

Thus, one story that Packard, Giles, and their students would repeatedly tell in the *Spelman Messenger* was about the efficacy of blacks' and women's leadership in education. So, a prerequisite for unpacking the rhetorical force of the *Spelman Messenger* and its present-day heirs is revisiting the cross-racial, cross-gender, and cross-region partnership that enabled the school's founding despite the structural forces aligned against them.[19]

Reverend Frank Quarles, minister of the appropriately named Friendship Baptist Church, was one of many African Americans who had been striving to advance southern blacks' education. Among his great skills was collaboration with whites. Quarles found vital allies in Packard and Giles. Reverend Quarles opened the basement of his church to launch the school for Christian girls and women. The enterprise began modestly enough with just under a dozen students on April 11, 1881. A key factor promoting a soon-burgeoning enrollment was Quarles's leadership, which included drumming up funds and students from other black ministries in Atlanta. He even intervened when a misunderstanding between the Yankee teachers and their sponsoring group of Boston women threatened the new school's fiscal viability. Quarles was on a funds-seeking and fence-mending trip to the North, in fact, when he tragically became ill and died. Though he didn't live to see the phenomenal growth of the enterprise that began in his church basement, the pattern of collaboration he established with Packard and Giles—not to mention the entrée he provided for them into

Figure 2.1. Sophia Packard and Harriet Giles, founding teacher-administrators at Spelman. Courtesy of the Spelman College Archives.

black community groups—was essential to Spelman's success.

Affirming that contribution, Spelman saluted Quarles's essential leadership in an article for the spring 2012 version of the *Spelman Messenger*. The story reprinted a speech delivered at the Founders Day Convocation in Sisters Chapel on April 10 of that year by Muriel Ketchum Yarbrough, class of 1949. The great-granddaughter of Father Quarles, Yarbrough had been given Spelman's Spirit Award. In the context of that honor, this "Fifth Generation" print account included a family tree tracing eight alumnae's ties back to their shared ancestor, Father Quarles.[20]

Other alumnae I've spoken with about Spelman's early days can describe Quarles's foundational role. Indeed, I first heard about "Father Quarles" from Deborah Mitchell, during the KCAC project, as noted above. Deborah herself interviewed "Aunt Ruth" (as the family called her) in March of

2001. According to Deborah's vivid notes from that conversation: "There was no stopping Aunt Ruth" on the subject of Quarles's leadership and its connections with previous work his family had already done to promote African American education post-Emancipation.[21]

Yet scholars have been somewhat less inclined to highlight Quarles.[22] Some accounts refer exclusively to Packard and Giles as the founders.[23] In contrast, Florence Read, herself one of Spelman's presidents (1927–53),[24] headlines Quarles's importance to Spelman's history. Noting their immediate efforts to make contact with potential allies upon arriving in Atlanta on April 1, 1881, Read recounts how Packard and Giles were told that the "most important person in Atlanta . . . to see . . . was the Rev. Frank Quarles," since he "was regarded as the most influential colored preacher in the state," leading a congregation of 1,500 at his Friendship Church (*Story of Spelman*, 42). Read further reports that Quarles welcomed the two women as sent by God in answer to his prayers for "teachers for the Baptist women and girls of Georgia" (43). In line with this view, the figure of Quarles appeared prominently on stage during the Founders Day performance I attended in April of 2011.

Similarly, Spelman has a longstanding tradition of honoring its first alumnae as educational leaders themselves. And rightly so, since, as archivist Taronda Spencer pointed out to me in several personal notes, many of the earliest students "were older women," so that their relationship with Packard and Giles was more collegial than we see in the stereotyped images of postbellum white motherly teachers with black child learners.[25] One of Taronda's clarifying margin comments to this effect appeared on a flyer she sent me while I was first drafting this chapter—a printed advertisement originally distributed on April 6, 1881, to announce the upcoming opening of the new school "in the basement of Friendship Baptist church," where "Instruction, pervaded by religious principle" was to "be given in all the usual branches." Taronda stressed that the significant prior life experiences that Spelman's first women students brought to the school left an indelible mark.[26] Possessing mature goals, these first students eagerly looked past the rather humble basement setting to the race uplift they would be empowered to deliver from the learning legacy nurtured there.

One of Packard's many handwritten letters to supporters from this period underscored this pattern. This missive enthusiastically profiled student "Mrs. Mary Ann Brooks," as "a widow whose husband died very many years ago." Packard admitted that Brooks's studies represented "up-hill work" at times. Yet however challenging the formal curriculum might be, Packard insisted, "Brooks [had] a heart full of our Savior's spirit, which makes her long to 'uplift the fallen.'" In line with that aim, Packard reported, Brooks had herself "established a little school for street waifs." Like many later Spelman students, Brooks began teaching while still herself a student. So, Packard recounted, Brooks arrived "every morning to Spelman's Primary Department as a pupil there," unabashed that, at "forty years old," she was among the oldest pupils. Always "very attentive not only to what is taught, but also to the manner in which it [was] taught," Brooks would then, "in the afternoon," move "to her own little school" "to repeat the lessons she had learned in the morning," Packard explained. Thus, through Mary Ann Brooks, the pioneering enterprise in Father Quarles's church basement was already reaching "scores of boys," who were acquiring "respect and confidence" from their teacher, as she "rouse[d] aspirations for true nobility of character" among her pupils.[27] Packard's story of Brooks's desire to blend student and teacher roles should remind us how much work remains to be done to reconstruct a full history of postbellum black women's education and related learning legacies for today. Indeed, despite the centrality of Spelman itself as one of the Historically Black Colleges and Universities (HBCUs) of great historical importance, the extensive archive of Packard's personal correspondence held in the college's archive represents an as-yet under-accessed resource. Although I hope that others will provide more extensive contextualized analysis of these semipublic texts,[28] by drawing on my own preliminary readings, I can point to striking counter-narrative features there.

First of all, Packard's epistolary records of her years in Atlanta repeatedly highlighted the cross-racial partnerships crucial to launching Spelman. A key dimension of that networking involved convincing white male leaders (whose vision for "New South" politics was then coalescing) that educating black women would contribute to the economic advancement of postwar southern communities. As a persistent promoter of black women's social agency, Packard would use her own writing to bridge between local black and white leaders, as well as between the Atlanta institution's day-to-day needs and the women (and men) back in the North whose financial support could ensure its growth. Central to this complex rhetorical networking, meanwhile, was the discursive construction of a counter-narrative portrait of black womanhood itself—or, more precisely, of mature, educated Christian black womanhood—as a resource for the nation as a whole.[29]

The claims Packard made for women like Brooks—for their capabilities, commitment, and influence—are not surprising now, in an age when black women's leadership has become so visible in American culture.[30] However, in the 1880s, in the supposedly "New" South, far less positive characterizations dominated. This presuffrage and Jim Crow time period was particularly tenuous for African American women. As Anne Gere and I noted in "Gendered Literacy in Black and White," black women's forays into print culture then often took on a corrective stance, asserting their commendable literacy practices, intelligence, and their "moral character" (664). Similarly, Packard and Giles's cultivation of support for Spelman among whites in both the South and the North required nonstop rhetorical intervention in public as well as personal writing. Paradoxically, the central vehicle for that effort would be created through funding from white male power structures.

Sending Out the *Messenger*

Only a few years after Spelman's founding, Packard and her colleagues secured an ideal avenue for circulating counter-narratives to promote the institution's agenda by establishing a print shop where students and teachers produced their own in-house periodical, the *Spelman Messenger*.[31] Atticus Haygood, an influential local white leader, called Spelman to the attention of the Slater Fund, which was established by the industrialist John F. Slater in 1882 to help educate formerly enslaved peoples and their descendants. Already enrolling well over five hundred students by the mid-1880s, Spelman was a logical site for Slater's support. Slater Fund donations to Spelman backed course work in such practical skills as dressmaking, millinery, and basic nursing techniques. One Slater donation purchased a printing press and supplies so that Spelman students could learn typesetting. For cultural arbiters like the Slater Fund's managers, the *Spelman Messenger* would have been viewed as an organ of industrial education—providing practice in a job skill—not a site for advancing what today would be called critical literacy,[32] and not a means for assisting Spelman's creative navigation of the developing battle between industrial education and liberal arts learning for African Americans.[33] However, consistent with the ambitious institutional vision shared by Quarles, Packard, and Giles; supported by the careful management of its teacher-editors; and, most of all, articulated through the voices of student writers, the *Spelman Messenger* carved out an intricate counter-narrative embodying women's advanced, yet pragmatic, learning.[34]

As the fulcrum for that balancing act, the *Spelman Messenger* would, over time, blend celebration of experiential job skills training with demonstrations of higher-order liberal arts learning. Accordingly, on one page of the June 1891 issue, a report of an "annual entertainment" of literary recitation was juxtaposed with an announcement of a new "proficiency" certificate in advanced printing skills—a credential that, the *Messenger* indicated, had already enabled "[s]everal of our compositors" to garner regular employment "in other offices" beyond campus (June 1891, 4). On the *Messenger's* pages themselves, meanwhile, type set by Spelman's pupils would facilitate the continued dissemination of other brands of knowledge.

Mentored by Spelman's archivist Taronda Spencer, I've read the issues of the *Messenger* from its inaugural number through the turn of the twentieth century. (A version of the publication still exists today, with its core audience now alumnae.) Here, I'm focusing on the first decades of the publication's history, 1885–1909, because during this period the seminary (later college) was most vulnerable and thus the most dependent on effective communication with supporters. These years also match the administrative tenures of Packard and Giles, each of whom served as the school's leader, with Packard passing away in 1891 and Giles in 1909. This period represented both a decisive phase in Spelman's maturation process and a challenging stage in the broader efforts by African American women to resist post-Reconstruction attacks on their identity.

In that vein, as Frances Smith Foster chronicles in *Written By Herself*, the history of African American women's authorship in this period has coalesced around well-educated practitioners like Anna Julia Cooper, Frances Harper, and Ida B. Wells. Through their work, in Foster's formulation, we see a race-based tradition wherein literature became "one of the tools they employed to bring into being the new world order they envisioned" (179). And, as Foster says, combining political uplift with aesthetic productivity often entailed blending "the secular and the spiritual" by linking "religious imperatives" with other themes (178). Spelman's periodical is part of this tradition. Joining with the sustained efforts of publications like the *Woman's Era* (the influential print publication led by clubwoman Josephine Ruffin),[35] the early *Spelman Messenger's* counter-narratives creatively addressed the oppressive context of Jim Crow. Strategically, the *Messenger* of this period laid the foundations for rhetorical pragmatism still evident today in venues like Founders Day, which itself has been faithfully celebrated, from the first issue forward, in the periodical's pages.

By reading through springtime issues of the early *Messenger* still retrievable in the Spelman archive today, we can retrace the mutually reinforcing relationship between African American print culture, across decades, and the annual Spelman Founders Day celebrations. That is, yearly accounts in the *Messenger* repeatedly signaled the importance of Founders Day to the Spelman community, while also allowing those unable to attend in person to participate through reading about it afterwards. Meanwhile, on a parallel track, regular preview and post-event stories in the *Atlanta Daily World* have marked the importance of the tradition to the larger Atlanta black community, reiterating the central position of Spelman as a beacon of race pride.[36] Even now, a legacy-enhancing tradition of race-based storytelling continues through an interactive network of the original *Messenger*'s print archive, layered reiterations of its themes in texts published later, and annual on-campus performances drawing on all these resources.

To characterize this learning legacy in its initial stage, I will highlight two of the recurring features of the early *Messenger*—also unmistakably emphasized in the Founders Day celebration of Spelman's 130th anniversary, which I attended in 2011. First, the publication repeatedly presented student writing and alumnae portraits exalting the learning Spelman women were achieving. Second, the periodical told—and retold—the institution's history to reinforce Spelman's significance and sustainability.

Addressing External Audiences

As we'd expect from skilled rhetoricians like Packard and Giles, anticipated readership for the periodical shaped its depictions of Spelman women in their day. One audience was potential white supporters inside and outside Georgia. Therefore, the turn-of-century *Messenger* carefully balanced assertions of black women's race-based progress with characterizations cast to reassure white readers. Portrayals of both the curriculum and student learning often aligned more with religious/spiritual and "industrial" goals than intellectual or political ones. That is, while affirming that the products of a Spelman education could be counted on to advance their race, *Messenger* stories concurrently suggested that the brand of uplift being achieved would not undermine the traditional social order. In line with Molly Andrews's characterization of counter-narratives as often incorporating language from the dominant culture (see chapter 1), rather than presenting a straightforwardly resistant rhetoric, texts in the *Messenger* during these years navigated cautiously. Some echoed the accommodationist language of Booker T. Washington's controversial "Atlanta Compromise" speech, delivered at the Cotton Exposition of 1895.[37] Simultaneously, though, in foregrounding (former) students' engagement with the liberal arts and the advanced

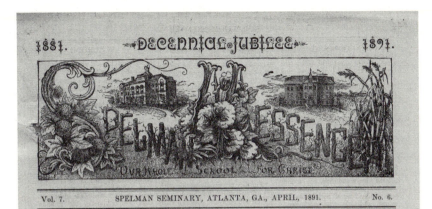

1881. ·DECENNIAL·JUBILEE· 1891.

SPELMAN MESSENGER

"OUR WHOLE SCHOOL FOR CHRIST"

Vol. 7. SPELMAN SEMINARY, ATLANTA, GA., APRIL, 1891. No. 6.

BASEMENT OF FRIENDSHIP BAPTIST CHURCH, ATLANTA, GEORGIA.

SPELMAN, DECEMBER, 1882.

"Class, recite in concert! *loud!* LOUDER!!" was the direction occasionally given to one of the classes in the basement.

At the desk was Miss Packard with her advanced classes of Fourth Reader, Fractions, and Green's Grammar. The pupils recited to be *heard;* what they lacked in knowledge was made up in volume.

At her right, near the window, Miss Giles' class was seated on three sides of a hollow square formed of the movable benches. The water from the muddy street oozing through the wall glistened in the uncertain light, thoughtful pupils brought pieces of carpet that their teacher's feet might be protected from the dampness. This class vied with the first in energy of recitation. The illustration above shows this corner.

In the opposite corner was another class arranged in the same form, a hollow square; here the words —"*loud!* LOUDER!!" were spoken, as the only hope, at times, of hearing a recitation, was by excelling in tone the other classes. The surprised faces turned towards the transgressing class and the enforced silence of the others was an immense satisfaction and a tribute to superior vocal powers. The desired result being attained, recitations were peacefully resumed until another lapse would necessitate a repetition of the stratagem.

In the coal-room, Miss Champney held gentle sway with open door to let in light and heat. We well understood the hint when the door was seen to close, that the peace of the little room was disturbed.

Precious memories cling to basement days—days of trial and of gladness—memories of the tender sympathy of pupils, their faithful friendship, their words of comfort falling with gentle healing upon sorer hearts than they knew. Their faith finds recompense in the Spelman of to-day. Most precious of all memories,—the prayer-meeting,

Figure 2.2. Masthead of the *Spelman Messenger*, April 1891. Courtesy of the Spelman College Archives.

literacy skills they were using to disseminate that knowledge, the publication affiliated as well with W. E. B. DuBois's "talented tenth" concept.[38]

Descriptions of Spelman's curriculum in the very first issue of the *Messenger* established this complex pattern. Invoking quantitative measures, this overview announced: "Last year there were enrolled five hundred and eighteen; to-day, there are enrolled over five hundred and seventy. From two teachers the faculty has increased to sixteen, but twenty or more are needed." Blending documentation of growth with a related call for enhanced resources, this inaugural *Messenger* also justified requests for supporters' aid by positioning the curriculum to appeal to white northern and "New South" cultural arbiters: "The Industrial Department receives special attention. The girls are taught cooking, sewing in all its branches, general house-work, and laundry-work. A printing office has recently been added—a gift from the Slater Fund—in the use of which the girls can be taught to set type thus opening another avenue for earning an honest livelihood."[39] Ignoring the direct evidence of the *Messenger*'s other content—student accounts of learning through arts and humanities study—this narrative incorporated a then-dominant narrative for African American women's education, even as, on later pages, the same issue verified pupils' mastery of deep reading and polished writing. To finesse this contradiction, the *Messenger*'s front-page story moved from touting "Industrial," job-skills-based learning to remind potential donors that black women did require advanced curricular content, for the good of the larger society: "But while the aim is to make their education practical, their spiritual welfare is first in the minds of the teachers. . . . The very success of the school creates a demand for means and better facilities for carrying on the work. The work is imperative, and must be done. Educate and Christianize the women, and you save the race" ("Spelman Seminary," March 1885, 1).

Here the institution-level authorial voice (presumably Packard, Giles, and/or other teachers) called upon arguments that had been successfully used earlier in the nineteenth century to justify advanced learning for white, middle-class women.[40] Having taught at several New England institutions whose curricula benefited from this same "educate-the-mothers" argument, the Yankee women shepherding Spelman's progress knew how to apply this gendered rhetoric, leavened with a race-based focus on "Industrial" training. In these early *Messenger* stories, therefore, the publication was already creating learning legacies by providing access to agency for individual students via a rationale of benefiting society as a whole.

To maintain this both/and stance, the *Messenger* astutely incorporated a rhetorical device quite familiar to readers of prior African American writing—the testimonial. Echoing whites' endorsements of antebellum texts by and about African American women,[41] consistent with reports by teachers affirming pupils' successes during Reconstruction,[42] and in line with other publications by Spelman supporters like Atticus Haygood,[43] prominent white voices in the *Messenger* testified to Spelman's social efficacy. Sometimes the *Messenger* presented these endorsements indirectly via praise for supporters, as in an 1891 tenth anniversary-of-school invocation of "Hon. John D. Rockefeller and family" as "ever . . . dear to the colored people of the south," due to "the generosity that has never failed to respond to our appeal for money" (April 1891, 3). Similarly, in such salutes as one confirming that "the very title of our institution calls to mind the honored parents of Mrs. Rockefeller" (that is, the Spelmans), *Messenger* invocations of the main donors' generosity aimed to attract still more dollars from the magnate himself and others.[44] Similarly, the *Messenger* thanked the "Hon. Sidney Root of Atlanta," who, "very indifferent at first, became a warm friend."[45]

Spelman's leaders also incorporated direct testimonials from influential white leaders, as in a May 1887 reprint of a *Harper's Weekly* article by Charles Dudley Warner praising the seminary.[46] Occasionally, stories like these in the periodical might be complemented by a free-standing flyer, such as one printed in December of 1887, with an endorsement by Atticus Haygood (by then secretary of the Slater Fund). Calling Spelman "this phenomenally successful and useful school," Haygood credited Packard and Giles with having "wrought steadily and wisely, with firm faith in God and abiding compassion for the poor and needy of the colored race." Haygood intoned: "No investment known to me shows better results than the money and labor laid out in the work of Spelman Seminary." He urged readers to donate too, since "[t]his needed money will yield very large dividends."[47]

The thank-you and testimonial genres remind us that the *Messenger* had complex layers of authorship. Just as donors to educational institutions today can exert influence, the financial sources that Spelman depended upon shaped the publication's content.[48] Cultural arbiters such as Haygood generated both literal and ideological intrusions into the early *Messenger*—with these interventions carrying all the more weight since they simultaneously stood in for white male power brokers like New South spokesman Henry Grady looming just outside the institution's gates. In that vein, the effusive reprint of Charles Dudley Warner's story from *Harper's*, referenced above, transitioned from complimenting the core curriculum to say, "it is of its industrial department that I wish to speak" (Warner, "Colored Schools," May 1887, 1). If, to his credit, Warner closed his paean to the program's training in cooking, laundering, and sewing with praise for the new nursing division—a more innovative curriculum at that time than that for domestic workers—even here he imagined graduates doing subservient gendered work: "gentle, patient, dexterous" when "in the sick-chamber." On balance, however supportive comments like Haygood's and Warner's may be, their statements also verify the influence white male leaders then exerted over the school and the skill with which the *Messenger* managed these relationships.

White women were also a crucial audience. One recipient of repeated thanks within the *Messenger* was the WABHMS, which for years subsidized teacher salaries. This Boston-based group had an occasionally rocky relationship with Packard, Giles, and their colleagues, partly because the team situated in Atlanta sometimes resisted directives from the North. As mentioned earlier, Reverend Quarles had played a peacemaking role during one of this uneasy alliance's tussles. Packard, for her part, tried valiantly via personal correspondence to cultivate the male-run American Baptist Home Mission Society in New York, then led by corresponding secretary Henry L. Morehouse (for whom Morehouse College, Spelman's male counterpart institution nearby, would be renamed in 1913). In part due to careful writing in the *Messenger*, Packard made gradual progress at fence-mending with the women's auxiliary group. A strong attachment with the WABHMS was vital—both to maintain salary support and to legitimize Spelman's commitment to Protestant Christian affiliation.[49] In a broader sense, linking to the then-dominant social narrative of Protestantism was essential for student recruitment as well. Small wonder, then, that the masthead of the *Messenger* proclaimed this school motto: "Our Whole School for Christ."

In contrast to these conventional elements, the rhetoric of the *Messenger* increasingly fostered a counter-narrative of groundbreaking black women's education. Counterbalancing the testimonials and thank-you pieces directed to conservative white (male) supporters, other stories described visits to the school by innovative women educators who thereby burnished Spelman's progressive image. In December 1895, for example, the *Messenger* reported that "Miss A. M. Ely and Miss Lucy M. Salmon, professors at Vassar College," had, when in town for the Atlanta Exposition, "paid a visit to Spelman. 'The Vassar of the South' gladly welcomed representatives of

Vassar in the North. Come again, sisters" (*Messenger*, December 1895, 4).[50] Similarly, an enthusiastic feature noted Frances E. W. Harper's trip to the school during one of her lecture tours (December 1889, 6). Forecasting parallel presentations of distinguished women leaders at future Founders Day events, these stories in the early *Messenger* established such connections as an ongoing rhetorical strategy.

Spelman's Own Celebrities

Messenger-enacted rhetorical moves to bond with figures such as author Frances Harper and Vassar professors Ely and Salmon reaffirmed Spelman's gendered pedigree. Perhaps even more important to defining the institution's distinctive identity in the long run, though, were stories of student role models for women-led race-based uplift. As pointed counternarratives to resist negative stereotypes of African American women, these accounts did important cultural work. Accordingly, this subgenre, which I call *Spelman story-portraits*, actually claimed the most space in the *Messenger*'s first decades. Through these accounts, over time, the qualities of a Spelman woman took hold around the capacities for social action that she attained through study and then applied to the larger benefit of her race.

In the Packard-Giles leadership era, accounts by and about the founding students drew special attention. These voices repeatedly chronicled Spelman's progress from the oft-invoked basement days. Personal stories balanced details about the challenging first site with claims that those same struggles had molded students' character and, by extension, Spelman's. Such stories played a central role in each anniversary issue; later, as these women grew older and gradually passed away, obituaries positioning their lives within Spelman's larger history combined memorials with reaffirmations of institutional vision. An article on Emma S. DeLamotta in 1903 stands out in this regard. In a quote from DeLamotta herself, the *Messenger* shared her observation about acquiring a voice through Spelman-sponsored learning: "I am not going this way again: I must say what I have to say now" (November 1903, 1). Through this founding student's unassuming yet telling declaration of agency, the *Messenger* urged others to follow her example. The periodical thus honored her legacy and reasserted its power as a model.

Students from the "basement days" had originally brought limited literacy skills to their schooling, leading to a modest curriculum at first. Yet Packard and Giles (like their founding partner Quarles) had strong aspirations for advanced liberal arts teaching. Hence, *Messenger* stories gradually presented more emphatic narratives touting the higher-level liberal arts access being provided to Spelman students and its benefits to the larger society. Two early graduates—Carrie Walls and Nora Gordon—embody this message. Both wrote for the *Messenger* as students and became model graduates.[51]

While still enrolled, Walls, originally from Columbus, Georgia, created her own regular feature, the "Children's Exchange." These letter-narratives emphasized a major learning outcome of a Spelman liberal arts education—being able to teach others. Walls enacted this role on multiple levels: by serving as a schoolmarm herself during vacations; by writing about her teaching experiences and thus instructing child readers; and by demonstrating, within her *Messenger* stories, that Spelman students were ideal candidates for uplifting the race. In this combination of classroom-based instruction with storytelling as itself a form of teaching, Walls provided an example for later Spelman graduates, even as she also created a textual learning legacy that we can still draw upon today.

In one "Children's Exchange" piece, for example, she crafted an astute narrative describing a rural school where she taught younger learners:

My Dear Little Folks of the North and South:

I think you will like to hear about the summer school of a Spelman girl, and I always like to please the little folks. My school was in Rock Fence, one hundred and forty-two miles east from Atlanta, and fourteen miles in the country from Elberton, the shiretown of the county. I have taught there two terms. My schoolhouse, a rude log hut, fifteen by ten, also serves as the church of the district. It stands in a beautiful pine grove and has a very large pleasant playground. The school this year numbered forty-two, thirty of them being boys. The reason there are so few girls is, many of the parents think it useless to educate their daughters so do not send them. I opened school every morning at eight o'clock with the Lord's Prayer which the pupils repeated after me. In this way many of them learned it. We next repeated a passage of Scripture in the same way, after which I explained it as well as I could. This exercise was followed by singing; then came the recitations which continued until five o'clock in the afternoon (November 1886, 6).

When we apply a counter-narrative lens to Walls's epistolary story to-day, we can see its strategic blending of conservative and resistant arguments. The salutation in Walls's letter signaled her wished-for audience as located in both "the North and South," signifying her awareness that the Atlanta school was actually a cross-regional enterprise, still in need of northern supporters. In hailing "little folks," she envisioned young readers, of course, but also, by extension, their parents, who themselves could come to understand the value of Spelman as a source of Christian teachers. Walls's narrative also offered an implicit plea for African American girls to have access to education. She made this tradition-resistant case both in a critique of "parents [who] think it useless to educate their daughters" (offered as an explanation of the gender disparity in her summer school classroom)[52] and, indirectly, through her self-presentation as able to provide spiritual and intellectual training, even in "a rude log hut," based on her own education at Spelman.[53]

Walls's description of her rural schoolhouse was surely pitched to echo the "basement days" of Spelman's own first students. Underscoring the literal constraints of her current teaching space, she nonetheless proclaimed her ability to pass along the legacy of her own advanced learning. She declared: "While teaching in these log huts we were very much troubled when the summer storms came up, because when the rain poured, we could scarcely find a dry place in the house; but if the wind came with the rain we were much worse off. When it blew from the south I crowded my scholars into the north side of the room; if from the north, we went to the south side; thus we traveled till the rain was over. Sometimes the rain seemed to come in on all sides, then I raised my umbrella and did the best I could" (6).[54] Like her foremothers in Spelman's first days, however, Walls and her young students determinedly overcame these constraints, putting in a full day's work. Meanwhile, Walls depicted her teaching as a natural extension of her studies at Spelman: "During our vacation, when we are away from our pleasant home (Spelman) we not only teach but try to live by the text, 'Freely ye have received, freely give.' As our dear teachers give us from their store of knowledge so we try to give to those who have less advantages" (6).[55]

The headnote to Walls's story invited her young readers to write back to her, in line with the "Exchange" title. Many were doing so. Within the January 1887 installment, she printed responses to some of their questions, such as a "May Woolridge" query about Santa Claus and another's request for information about Walls's Sabbath school. This installment ended with a letter to "Cousin Carrie" (Walls's regular signature) from Rosa Stanly, a "little friend" in Wild Cat, Georgia. Rosa explained: "I know you are wondering how I learned of you in this far-off corner, but I saw a Messenger that my teacher had and read the column for little folks. I knew you would like to hear from me even if I was so far in the country" ("Children's Exchange," January 1887, 6). In the January 1888 installment, Walls's correspondents ranged from children attending Spelman's laboratory school on campus and others from around Georgia to Josie M. Freeman, who wrote all the way from Salem, Massachusetts, that she had "read quite a number of Spelman *Messengers*, and liked them very much" ("Children's Exchange," January 1887, 6). In an earlier feature, a report on Spelman's lab school, Walls encouraged her correspondents to keep writing her: "How glad I was to hear from so many this month; your letters are a proof of your interest in the Children's Exchange" ("Children's Exchange," February 1886, 6). Walls's repeated moves to engage directly with young readers helped the *Messenger* promote a network of far-flung participation in the Spelman enterprise. Belying stereotypes of rural black culture as cut off from the larger world, and consistent with Benedict Anderson's conception of imagined affiliations facilitated through print-based exchange, Walls and her periodical stories built community across otherwise-separate social spaces.[56]

Walls's multifaceted and cross-regional teaching continued after she graduated in 1888 with the highest honors in her class. In the next year, she taught school in Belton, South Carolina. She married another educator, Mark H. Gassaway, and they both taught from 1890 until 1919 at the Greeley Institute in Anderson, South Carolina. In 1919, the Gassaways moved to Cleveland, where Carrie's husband pursued a career in manufacturing. Carrie remained active as learner and teacher. She took summer courses at the Cheyney Institute in Pennsylvania one year and at Case Western Reserve another. She taught handicrafts at a settlement house in Cleveland. Meanwhile, the Gassaways had seven children, two of whom attended Morehouse. Carrie herself maintained strong ties with Spelman, making donations and corresponding with institutional leaders until her death in Cleveland in 1935.[57]

Like Walls, Nora Gordon regularly contributed to the *Messenger*. And, like Walls, Gordon crafted vivid chronicles of her own Spelman-enabled teaching. For one article framed as a "Dear Messenger" letter, Gordon described herself as "truly glad to get back to my dear Spelman home" when a new term began, but also eager to "give you a description of Victoria, the place where I taught last summer." Again echoing Walls, Gordon portrayed her school as remote—set in a "rude little country town . . . about fifty miles northwest of Chattanooga." Gordon admitted, "As a rule, the people of this part of Tennessee have had very few advantages[;] hence they care very little about Christianity and education." Yet, she reported, her teaching had made a difference, as "many have promised to begin life anew" (December 1887, 2). Anticipating future Founders Day performances by today's students, these stories by Gordon emphasized how Spelman's social impact reached far beyond its Atlanta home.

Gordon wrote poetry for the *Messenger* as well. The November 1886 issue contained one of her lyrics, celebrating the fall reopening of school (1). Her subsequent "Emancipation Poem" avowed: "In ignorance and wickedness / We must not now remain," but instead press on to "cleanse our race." The poem asked God to "Aid us to help our brother up, / In Afric's heathen land, / Till all our people, taught of Thee, / Rejoice a ransomed band" (February 1887, 5). By imagining a global, pan-African learning community, this text also marked a new learning legacy of the *Messenger*'s student authors and anticipated Gordon's own upcoming role as a missionary in the Congo.

The early *Messenger*'s incorporation of such poetic voices claimed a distinctive rhetorical agency for its student writing as both popular and literary, both gendered and race-oriented. Many late nineteenth-century periodicals were circulating poetry as a popular form, aimed at broader audiences than we would tend to envision for the genre today. Furthermore, as Paula Bennett's extensive archival recovery of poems from diverse nineteenth-century periodicals has shown, women poets of this period regularly engaged in serious social issues.[58] Given the still-pervasive stereotypes depicting black women as unrefined, the *Messenger*'s frequent use of student lyrics employing poetic conventions also positioned its authors in a tradition of women's aesthetic productivity linked to a cultured racial identity.[59] Decades earlier, as referenced above, Phillis Wheatley's lyrics had been greeted with both enthusiasm and some disbelief in her authorship because the idea of a well-educated black woman poet was then surprising.[60] By the time the first *Messenger* poems were appearing, however, Frances E. W. Harper had more confidently claimed a free black poetic voice associated both with African American causes and a refined personal identity.[61] Thus, the young women composing poems for the *Spelman Messenger*, and the teachers who encouraged this cultural work, would have seen their compositions as accruing valuable symbolic capital—for the authors and for the school.

Figure 2.3. Nora Gordon, early Spelman graduate and missionary to the Congo. Courtesy of the Spelman College Archives.

Enabling Communal Agency

On the front page of the *Messenger's* April 1885 second issue, a poem signed by "A Student" spoke directly to readers and commended the periodical itself for reaching out with news of the institution:

> I know you will be happy
> To have the "Messenger" come,
> And tell you the news of Spelman,
> And the good that's being done.

Personifying the *Messenger* as a womanly speaker who would be "bearing the news to all," this brief lyric promised that the periodical would share stories "From the early start of Spelman, / E'en from the very fount," along with up-to-date accounts of how the school was preparing students to serve "our people, / Who are ignorant and rude / . . . To teach them to be good" ("The Messenger," April 1885, 1).

We'd hope that this text's characterization of black recipients of Spelman graduates' teaching as otherwise "ignorant and rude" would not appear in an American publication today.[62] Still, we should acknowledge the rhetorical role of such portraits for the original *Messenger* readership, which included so many powerful whites eager to maintain social hierarchies. Similarly, aesthetic tastes of today might lead us to cringe at the sing-song rhyme and meter in poems like this one. However, shifts in how we now judge lyric excellence should not obscure the efficacy—the rhetorical pragmatism—of the periodical's presenting early Spelman students like this one as skilled poets by the standards of their own time.[63]

However we respond now to these poems' techniques, the *Messenger's* constant retelling of institutional history may be easier to appreciate as an astute rhetorical enterprise. By regularly revisiting its church basement past, but also chronicling ongoing stages in Spelman's growth, the periodical set up recurring counter-narrative themes to show that Spelman had survived challenges; had always been allied with powerful supporters; and had steadily expanded in size, infrastructure, and cultural capital. Thus, this subgenre forcefully resisted stereotyped portrayals of blacks and their institutions as unstable in the face of pressures based on racial identity.

From the periodical's inception in March 1885, history-telling in the *Spelman Messenger* would support the institution's long-term health.[64] An "Our Needs" article on page one of the first issue trumpeted growth:

"Our buildings are literally overflowing. . . . Our membership is 575 and promises to reach 600 before the term closes. . . . The dining room is so crowded that the students sit shoulder to shoulder, and back to back." A nearby front-page announcement explained: "Board and tuition are $7.00 per month; instrumental music, $2.00 extra." Such details reiterated the literal value of this learning opportunity and implicitly reminded readers of the institution's being attentively managed. Meanwhile, in each retelling across the Packard-Giles leadership years, the foundational story served as a launching pad for outlining current needs. By linking past history to in-the-moment fundraising, the *Messenger* dignified the process of donor cultivation and aligned giving dollars to Spelman with promoting the entire African American race. A theme of continual curricular development, linked repeatedly to calls for enhancing the institution's physical and human infrastructure, was embodied in the visual rhetoric of a redesigned 1892 masthead. Images of two new buildings appeared along with a rendering of the publication's name designed to connote an ever-organic identity.

Accounts characterizing Spelman's curriculum emphasized its Christian promotion of servant leadership. Thus, the April 1891 issue took as its theme the school's tenth anniversary and that milestone's implications. In "Our First Decade," Mrs. T. M. Woodward, class of 1890, described her experience at Spelman in these terms: "Among the many things for which we have to be thankful are spiritual growth, spiritual salvation, being taught how to reach the highest end of life" (2). She contended that the foundation for a life of service was set in place during her Spelman years, which she directly connected to the previous inspirational generation of students who labored "in the basement." In invoking both the original church basement site and the institution's commitment to spiritual teaching, Woodward positioned herself and Spelman as Christian leaders. She applauded how graduates had "been promoted to high positions." But she leavened this claim of individual success with an emphasis on service: Spelman graduates "have gone out into the world to raise fallen humanity, to lift up the downcast, to bind up the bruised and pour in the oil of consolation" (2). Comparing this ever-widening servant leadership to the example of "two good Christian women who came from the North, seeking the poor and humble that they might receive good from their liberal hands" (i.e., Packard and Giles), Woodward also pointed to familiar alumnae role models— the "Two [who] are in Africa expounding to those poor heathen, the gospel taught them ten years ago in the basement of Friendship Church."

The graduates exalted by Woodward were Nora Gordon and her friend

Clara Howard, both of whom by 1891 were teaching in Baptist mission schools in the Congo. Reports on their work kept readers of the *Messenger* informed about how these two were extending the influence of their alma mater. In addition, while overseas, Gordon wrote for white northern Baptist mission periodicals. Addressing a mixed-race audience, Gordon joined a literacy network nested within the massive American foreign mission enterprise, then claiming an even larger cohort of US women supporters than either the suffrage or temperance movements. For instance, in an 1892 piece entitled "Africa. The Congo Mission," appearing in *The Baptist Missionary Magazine*, Gordon recounted the contributions she and Clara Howard were making by using their Spelman-acquired abilities:

> I help Miss Howard in the afternoon station school, and have charge of the printing. We are now getting out a circular letter for the churches and schools. In this letter the people are urged upon to support their own schools, native teachers, etc. We have many reasons to believe that they will do this most heartily. (January 1892, 26)

When we read this brief, seemingly straightforward account in light of Gordon's personal learning history and Spelman's institutional context, we see how she was employing both the typesetting "industrial" skills and the rhetorically sophisticated writing abilities, honed back in Atlanta, to address a transnational audience.

In transferring her Spelman-based learning legacy to a new global context, Gordon affirmed not only the socially constructed nature of her identity but also her individual agency. In this way, she demonstrated how early student writing for the *Messenger*, though guided by white teachers, had also facilitated her race-based life choices. Indeed, if we make oversimplified assumptions about teacher-editor control of such writing, we deny authors like Gordon and Carrie Walls the very agency they worked so hard to attain through education. After all, we have come a long way from the period when Jean Yellin had to press for recognition of the authorial agency of a figure like Harriet Jacobs.[65] Still, the impact of white-controlled cultural forces on black writing remains a point of intense examination.[66] On the one hand, textual products associated with whites' teaching of black students have been convincingly critiqued as embodying a mental and thus identity-shaping "colonizing" process, as Ngũgĩ wa Thiong'o points out in texts such as *Decolonising the Mind*, forcefully critiquing colonial educational programs like he experienced in Kenya.

On the other hand, as Ryan Dunch and others such as Lamin Sanneh and Ngũgĩ himself have argued, in an even broader comparative context, we must recognize that colonized learners in such cross-cultural contact zones are perfectly capable of choosing which aspects of a white-directed curriculum, cast within a Christian mission context, to adopt.[67] In the case of the early *Messenger*, life choices made by many Spelman alumnae, including their continued submissions to the publication after graduation, suggest that they embraced the institution and the community-made periodical touting its work as promoting both personal growth and race uplift along with a Christian capacity for servant leadership. White teachers and other sponsors certainly guided the overall framework and even individual texts within the *Messenger* in its first decades.[68] But black student authors chose to come to Spelman and chose to stay. And the black alumnae who continued to write for the publication long after graduation affirmed that their learning there had generated a race-oriented vision of what women could do for black communities beyond the campus itself. Through texts by, for, and about African American women, therefore, the early *Messenger* helped produce an empowered race-and-gender-linked network while expanding the social influence available to alumnae. As such, we can view the *Messenger* as a location of ongoing collaboration that helped maintain a community of women learners; they, in turn, helped sustain a shared legacy through their reading and writing.

A letter submitted by a former Spelman student for the May 1888 *Messenger* issue offers a case in point. Writing from Stilesboro, Georgia, where she was continuing her own independent studies of "Moral Philosophy" and "Bible History" while managing a school with "104 pupils enrolled" and "a daily average of over 80," Sarah H. Lay described her work "teach[ing] arithmetic, geography, and grammar." She also outlined her introduction of a new subject into the curriculum. "When I began, there was no writing done in the school; I now have a class of twenty, doing nicely." She envisioned sending some of her own students to Spelman, where, following in her footsteps, they could "go and prepare for future usefulness." For herself, her main hope was "trying to do my duty that I may please Christ and the people and that my work may speak well for Spelman" (6). Significantly, because she still had access to the Spelman network represented in the *Messenger*'s pages, Sarah Lay could send writing about her ongoing teaching back into that literacy community, so that her print storytelling itself, like that of Carrie Walls and other *Messenger* authors, enacted another form of sisterly instruction.

Performing History

The postgraduate experiences of *Messenger* writers like Carrie Walls, Nora Gordon, and Sarah Lay point to the positive long-term personal impact of their study at Spelman and their storytelling about it. But there remains another question to ask about these learning legacies. In what ways have the narratives generated by such past students provided cultural resources for those enrolled at Spelman more recently? Are the counter-narratives recorded in the *Messenger*, supplemented with new story layers over time and passed across generations, really enabling other women's agency today? Based upon the Founders Day performance I attended as one example, I'd shout out "yes." Spelman's April 7, 2011, Founders Day, "The Sustaining Vision: 130 Years and Leading," heralded a distinctive anniversary while also underscoring how the college continues to access its learning legacies, including those from the early *Messenger*. By reflecting on one year's performance and its echoes of the archive I've studied, we can also see the event as a model for strategically marshaling the liberal arts to build solidarity around a progressive educational vision. Thus, as an example of how purposeful cultural rhetoric can enable collaborative social agency today, the yearly Spelman Founders Day holds significance far beyond its particular institutional setting.

An analysis of the annual event at Spelman as rhetorical pragmatism in action requires us to recognize each annual text as both a unique performance shaped by a given year's participants and a recurring genre self-consciously invoking (and reconstituting) a shared cultural memory. Accordingly, my account below of one year's celebration exemplifies how each annual performance participates in multiple layers of history-making and transdisciplinary storytelling, while simultaneously extending that ongoing process. Every performance draws on a rich narrative Archive, creating a unique new individual record that adds to the continued layering of cultural capital available to future community members. That is, each Founders Day marshals the resources of prior texts such as the *Messenger* and previous performances, then blends those materials with new contributions from Spelman's current students and supporters. Through this collaborative textual production, the annual event reaffirms the school's connections with an institutional past (retold in new narratives) and a commitment to continual growth consistent with the original vision, as well as new exigencies. In this way, the counter-narratives from Spelman's past become, for institutional insiders and supporters, its dominant narrative.

Both annually and over time, and in concert with the learning legacies of Spelman women's prior self-representations, Founders Day also taps into the race-based heritage of African American performances aimed at social agency. As outlined by Daphne Brooks in *Bodies in Dissent*, her study of *Spectacular Performances of Race and Freedom, 1850–1910*, African Americans can point back to and presumably capitalize on race-based approaches for "translating alienation into self-actualizing performance" as part of a strong "literary tradition" facilitating positive "identity formation" (3). Brooks explores what she calls a "motley crew" (6) of transatlantic African American performers—figures ranging from Henry Box Brown to Adah Isaacs Menken to Aida Overton Walker—and subgenres ranging from whole-troupe song and dance performances to scenic panoramas and highly individualized characterizations. Brooks uses a different chronological framework and geographic range than I have here, and her cases are drawn from cross-racial rather than intraracial performances like those currently enacted in the college's chapel each year. Her study nonetheless suggests how African American performance texts from the past (whether in print or embodied, as on a stage) have laid the groundwork for the performances still going on at Spelman every spring. In both contexts, as in Founders Day events in other HBCU settings,[69] we find "aesthetic experimentalism" countering what might otherwise be "political marginalization"; with purposeful and sustained "cultural innovation," all these race-oriented performances have "envisioned a way to transform the uncertainties of (black) self-knowledge directly into literal and figurative acts of self-affirmation" (Brooks, 3).

So, using Brooks's model to complement my focus on counter-narrative formations, we can highlight continuities between the storytelling in the early *Messenger* (nurturing both institution-wide and individual agency) and the yearly performances rearticulating that cultural work. Specifically, performances for Founders Day in the year I attended clearly positioned the singular institutional history of Spelman as a counter-narrative resisting the dominant pattern of white-oriented higher education in US culture, which tends to erase racial identity as a constructive learning force. Accordingly, in revisiting the 2011 performance text below, I will spotlight that year's rhetorically pragmatic remix of specific narrative elements from the *Messenger*-archived stories of Spelman's founding students with current-day reaffirmations of their relevance as learning legacies resisting black women's political marginalization. Celebrating these legacies together, in a spirit my TCU English Department colleague Professor Stacie McCormick has aptly compared to "the black church where performances were designed to promote a sense of communal celebration and intimacy,"[70] the insider audience members at a Spelman Founders Day event both claim their past heritage and envision a shared future of social agency.

Founders Day for April 2011, like all the annual performances over the years, took place in Sisters Chapel. The printed program signaled the event's identity-affirming goals in a visual design with a double-opening fold-over format. Lifting the flap on the left side (which on the outside read "Spelman" and "The Sustaining Vision") revealed a picture of Packard and Giles above a brief account of their collaboration with Quarles to open a school "in the church basement with 11 students, some of whom were not far removed from slavery, and all eager to learn." Opening the flap on the right side (where "College" appeared above "130 Years and Leading") uncovered a short biography of "Honorary Degree Recipient Tina McElroy Ansa," a role model from the Spelman class of 1971. In its visual rhetoric, with its left panel hearkening back to the "Vision" of the founding women and their original community partners, and its right panel suggesting how "130 Years and Leading" were embodied in the example of Ansa, the printed program recalled discursive strategies already evident in *Messenger* accounts of the earliest Founders Day celebrations. In both cases, the original alumnae from "the church basement" appeared alongside stories of the institution's continuing cultural work.

Like the Packard-Giles and Ansa profiles, the center-section listings for various elements in the performance itself also echoed details in Founders Day accounts from Spelman's first decades. Reminiscent of the first teachers' intentional valuing of student authorship in the early *Messenger*'s pages, numerous segments of the program carried such designations as "Written by Ebonee Holyfield, C'2010" for a scene entitled "The Gates" and "Written and Performed by" a group of then-current students for "Great Firsts." The tradition of bringing alumnae back to campus—both to honor their contributions and to provide inspiring examples—reappeared in the names and graduation years for various performers, from Ansa to "Cynthia Jackson, C '81" and "Adrienne Joi Johnson, C '85." Once the performances began, learning legacies from the *Messenger* and other sources became even more evident. As in the earliest institutional anniversaries, music merged with testimonials: backward-looking vignettes revisited key moments in the institution's history, including the meeting of the Packard-Giles duo with Father Quarles, the shift from school to seminary to college, and a series of "Great Firsts" (specific institutional and individual achievements linked to Spelman's identity).

Due to the chapel's limited space, only seniors, freshmen, and special guests attended; others could watch on closed-circuit television, and students with whom I spoke during a postperformance picnic had certainly done so. From the processional of upper-class women in the robes they would soon wear for graduation to the march-in of their younger "sisters," wearing white dresses, to the closing recessional, the packed student audience participated actively, joining in songs and frequently shouting out in response to appealing scenes.

Several vignettes made direct reference to the institution's heritage, while along the way recapitulating rhetorical moves evident in early *Messenger* anniversary stories. For instance, "Spelman Testimony" presented two singers and four speakers representing "The Granddaughters Club," whose speeches underscored the practice of legacy-making. A duet opened the segment, with the singers urging the audience, "Look at me. I am a testimony." Then, the four speakers avowed, in sequence, "I am a testimony. Every Spelman student is a testimony," "Every alumna is a testimony," and "This ritual is a testimony." Saluting their own "testimony of prayers answered," they echoed the language of both founding figure Quarles and the original students, who had so often cited the opening of the school in 1881 as the result of prayer. Further relating this theme of "testimony" to spiritual practices, later elements in this ensemble averred that Spelman's early students' learning built special capacities for "service," just as Carrie Walls had argued in her *Messenger* stories.[71] Directly recalling the founding moment after emancipation, the quartet declared: "I want my children to be educated." By positioning such phrases in dialogue with scriptural language, this segment grounded Spelman's origin in spiritual and intellectual principles still guiding the college while articulating a black counterpoint to the white-voiced testimonials necessary to the early *Messenger*.

The scene with Packard, Giles, and Quarles reconfirmed these themes. This exchange resonated with Brooks's view that African American performances of the past sought to "transform the uncertainties of (black) self-knowledge directly into literal and figurative acts of self-affirmation" (3); the white bodies of Packard and Giles themselves underwent a "literal" transformation, as two black Spelman students took on the roles of the white women cofounders. Having hurried down the aisle from the back of the chapel, suitcase in hand, the two teacher figures met up with a black male actor, Lummba Seegers, playing Quarles. Dressed in period costume, the women introduced themselves as on "a mission" (Packard), since "God . . . told us," according to the Giles character, to "educate his people." In yet another echo of early *Messenger* accounts, Quarles responded: "There is a basement in the church, and you are welcome to use it." Gazing out toward the audience, Packard asked: "Can you see it, Harriet? The Atlanta Baptist Female Seminary." Through this reference to the "seminary" name, adopted originally to signal their school's advanced curriculum, the performers invited the audience's reconnection with Spelman's foundational commitment to liberal arts learning, despite the admission, in dialogue just before, that American society had not made "provision" then for the education of black women. "I can see it," the Harriet character predicted. "One day there will be hundreds of colored women making an impact on the world."

Along related lines, Brooks's astute analysis of the significance of dance and music in nineteenth-century black performance culture provides a useful framework for embracing, as the audience did, a later scene in the 2011 pageant: a cluster of students-playing-students in a jaunty ragtime-evocative dance. Textbooks in hand, smiling exuberantly as they circled the stage, this dancing troupe might have seemed tonally at odds with the preceding scenes' serious recapitulation of foundational history. Yet, as Brooks has explained, traveling troupes of black musical performers like those putting on the *In Dahomey* show during the Gilded Age used just such high-spirited dancing to reconfigure outworn stereotypes of black minstrelsy into new forms combining "black entertainment culture and racial uplift politics" (*Bodies*, 215). As such, this scene provided an apt transition to others, when contemporary music would celebrate Spelman's engagement with social needs today.

Soon after the dance scenes, a brief transition elicited shouts and applause when the audience saw a set of symbolic gates brought onstage, set up to mirror the actual gates now standing as a local landmark at the college entrance. Packard and Giles having passed through and then offstage, a Spelman woman of today entered and recited a cross-generational story of opening "Spelman's historical gates" to leadership. This commitment, the student-actress declared, belonged to her entire family, since their time at Spelman always became a stepping stone to social agency: "immense and endless service." Through her studies, she too would "leave behind the words" that had, in the past, "cursed the very essence" of black woman-hood. She would replace those constraints with a limitless range of possible identities, "walking into a legacy of Spelman women," a legacy conferring "permission to create her own world."

Consistent with this vision, a parade of students enacting various role models followed, accompanied by triumphant music. This march of student actresses portrayed each as claiming a different identity (e.g., physician, teacher, nurse) with its own pathway to agency.[72] Significantly, the women's costumes crossed historical periods. Reenacting learning legacies across time, the performers collectively embodied a Spelman Archive of continuous agency. To underscore this connection, the final figure who came onstage wore the white dress of current underclassmen and repeatedly invoked the "Spelman legacy." She acknowledged the other actresses as, each one, a "first" (e.g., "the first black registered nurse" and "the first African American woman to pass the bar in Mississippi"). So, through story portraits reminiscent of early *Messenger* alumnae stories, this scene touted the college's unique ability to prepare black women "to change the world."

A series of songs, dances, and individual story-portraits then demonstrated the power of Spelman's women to be world-class leaders. One of these segments recalled the artistic contributions of alumna Varnette P. Honeywood, whose colorful paintings flashed on a screen until one came alive in a dance with current students echoing figures in the painting, then positioning themselves within a large frame they carried onto the stage, a performative story portrait as vivid as the narratives about alumnae in the *Messenger*'s early decades. Students who had recently studied or done volunteer work abroad, in Africa and the Caribbean, also presented accounts of global learning and servant leadership recalling first-generation alumna Clara Howard, whose mission service had earlier been saluted as one of Spelman's many "firsts."[73]

One of these reports closed with a poem celebrating both the speaker's experiences in Panama and the ways Spelman prepared her to excel there. Echoing sentiments in lyrics from the early *Messenger*, she asserted: "we know where we're going, / And we know where we've been." By the time a choral reading led by Atlanta's True Colors Theatre leader Kenny Leon[74] and several recent alumnae claimed the stage, audience members had seen an array of success stories, all linked to Spelman's learning legacies and their current reiterations. A final soaring anthem by guest artist Jennifer Holliday urged all to make a "Choice to Change the World."

Figure 2.4. Story-portrait from the 130th anniversary Founders Day performance in 2011. Courtesy of the Spelman College Archives.

Spelman's Storytelling in Current Context

While each year's Founders Day brings its own topical focus,[75] recurring themes emerge through the historical legacy of past Spelman women, as Beverly Daniel Tatum has noted. Near the end of her own presidential service in spring 2015, Tatum reflected on a question many had asked her: "What is your legacy?" She identified "milestones of progress, like more students traveling abroad or doing undergraduate research, more faculty positions," and "a new and improved Read Hall." However, she suggested, the "legacy" query also encouraged her to reconnect with Spelman's first women leaders: "Sometimes I imagine how Spelman founders Sophia B. Packard and Harriet E. Giles might answer that question. They said they were building for 100 years, and they did." Tatum speculated that the college's founders would cite Spelman's "pioneers in every field imaginable," more than its historic buildings and other marks of progress. As examples, she catalogued successful alumnae, beginning with Nora Gordon and including the "first Black female physicians . . . in Georgia," as well as "military leaders like Marcelite Harris Jordan, C'64," and social "activists like Marian Wright Edelman, C'60, and Sarah Thompson, C'2006." Tatum continued, "I think Sophia Packard and Harriet Giles would say that women like these were their legacy, their gift to the future," since "an educator's most important legacy" can best be framed with this query: "Who takes action because of the experience that has been provided? Who truly makes a choice to change the world?" Looking ahead, Tatum saluted the about-to-graduate class of 2015, 70 percent of whom had donated to a safety net for "their younger sisters" through an "emergency scholarship" fund. Said Tatum: "If I have a legacy to claim, I want it to be that one—that the women of Spelman have fully embraced their responsibility to support Spelman College and its future—the students who come after them—so that our living legacy will endure forever."[76]

I suspect Packard and Giles would smile if they could indeed see themselves cited in a twenty-first century president's personal narrative. They might commiserate on the subject of fundraising as never-ending, pausing ruefully, perhaps, over the echoes of their own constant call for resources. But I think they would also cheer how Spelman's own women are moving to the forefront of donors to be cultivated. What a distance this detail marks between the institution's early years, when their own and their students' rhetoric of progress had to take into account a far different social hierarchy. Then, black women's leadership had to be positioned as an unexpected counter-narrative rather than the norm, despite the many ways they did, in fact, already lead.

This contrast suggests one rationale behind what one of my academic colleagues, after hearing a presentation based on this chapter, characterized as "over-the-top" content in the annual Founders Day pageant. There is, frankly, much to celebrate, not only in the accomplishments of Spelman's individual women but also in how far they've come, as a group, in claiming access to agency. And Founders Day, as staged for an insider audience of the college's own community members, serves a crucial function of preparing both performers and those witnessing their testimony in any given year to face the far less supportive audiences for black women's would-be agency beyond the gates of the college.[77] This identity-affirming dimension of the event's cultural rhetoric acknowledges that so many of the same challenges facing black women (and men) of the founding generation remain in force.

Agency for African Americans is still clearly constrained by identity-associated discourse constantly reiterated in dominant narratives across our culture. In the weeks when I was drafting these very paragraphs, protests against racially linked assaults by police on black American citizens in multiple cities conveyed a stark reminder that we are not living in a postracial society. Michelle Alexander's compelling study of *The New Jim Crow* provides a potent academic counterpart to the "body-cam" and bystander videos of black bodies placed in terrifying jeopardy. These seemingly never-ending events also help us understand the thoughtful, often poignant, responses of black scholars resisting Kenneth Warren's provocative suggestion, in *What Was African American Literature?*, that the Jim Crow era's white hegemony came to an end decades ago, so that a distinctive literary category's cultural intervention is no longer needed.[78]

Indeed, at the intersection of race and gender, research by feminist scholars from a range of disciplines confirms the staying power of negative images embedded in the narratives of black womanhood still evident throughout our society.[79] What are effective pedagogical strategies for resisting these persistent narratives? One involves incorporating a comparative, global perspective to put the challenges facing African American women in dialogue with others' experiences.[80] Along those lines, back in 1996, Beverly Guy-Sheftall and Kimberly Wallace-Sanders reported on a Spelman delegation's participation in an international women's conference in Beijing. Guy-Sheftall and Wallace-Sanders reflected on the need to "better prepare our Black women students for the global, multicultural

world of the future in which people of color and women are the majority."
They speculated that developing such a global perspective might counter
the ongoing "negativity directed at African-American women" which could
otherwise leave "Spelman students . . . overwhelmed" ("Educating," 212).
After hearing similar "reports from feminist media-watch organizations"
all over the world, the Spelman team was struck by the potential efficacy
of studying negative representations comparatively, both to better understand phenomena like violence against women as transcultural and to forge
networks of global leadership.[81] By 2011, in the Founders Day presentations of student texts on "Global Experience" and the musical composition
"Choice to Change the World," I could see their commitment was bearing
fruit.[82] Meanwhile, on the domestic front, the gender-based solidarity represented by Spelman's response to the charges cast against Bill Cosby by
women from a range of backgrounds—specifically, the College's suspension
of the William and Camille Olivia Hanks Cosby Endowed Professorship—
offered another striking example of the institution's commitment to wom-
en's agency. Coming soon after the *New York* magazine July/August 2015
cover featuring thirty-five of Cosby's accusers, along with an empty chair
suggesting the potential of other, as-yet unheard stories, Spelman's decision to cut ties with Cosby reaffirmed its recognition that gender, as well as
race, places black women's bodies, and thus their spirits, in jeopardy.

In that vein, work by black feminist scholars like Tatum, Guy-Sheftall,
and Wallace-Sanders also implicitly suggests a productive pathway for
white teacher-scholars like me to support our black colleagues in cross-
cultural, social justice-oriented efforts associated with the learning legacies
explored in this chapter. For one thing, our identity position in the classroom gives us a potentially useful standpoint-based position from which
to teach counter-narratives resisting the still-actively pernicious narratives
depicting black women. As members of the (current) majority culture,
when we teach cultural interventions like those of the early Spelman students writing for the *Messenger* and of performers revisiting that heritage
in the Founders Day pageant, we acknowledge how value systems operate
in a culture over time, but also how they can be resisted and revised. As a
white educator, I cannot be accused of self-interestedly promoting my own
racial identity when I affirm the cultural value of black texts by foregrounding them in my classroom. Rather, my inclusion of stories like those in
the *Messenger* makes a different kind of value statement about them—one
asserting literary merit, rhetorical complexity, and historical significance

beyond the personal. On another pedagogical front, I can draw on gender affiliation, particularly if I underscore intersectionality in the interpretations I encourage my students to produce.

I also have a potentially helpful role to play around extra-literary questions of social power. Similar to serving as a heterosexual ally promoting rights for students in the LGBTQ community by simple steps like posting a "Safe Space" flyer on my office door, or more complex ones like modeling inclusive language in my classroom, I can help build a more welcoming community for students of color at majority-white institutions like Kennesaw State and TCU. By teaching the learning legacies of Spelman's heritage from a stance of appreciation, I affirm the position of black students in my classroom as belonging there. And these efforts are equally important for their hoped-for impact on white students. To illustrate in the concrete terms of syllabus construction—a site of action clearly available to all faculty—I make a value statement to all my students by positioning narratives from the Spelman Archive of this chapter next to the 1895 *Texas Poems* by Ida Jarvis, one of TCU's early white women educators. And I extend the impact of that localized canon-making choice by thinking critically about *how* I can teach those texts comparatively, including highlighting white privilege inherent in the TCU-based woman writer of the same era as the *Messenger* authors. Emphasizing intersectionality, when juxtaposing poetry from early *Spelman Messenger* writers with Jarvis's, I can counterbalance contrasts between the two settings based on racial differences with similarities in their authorial contexts, such as the self-conscious invocation of Christian identity in both places, as well as a parallel sense of gender boundaries being crossed in a progressive institutional setting.[83]

Further, by making sure that the Spelman-created texts are far from the only ones by women writers of color on my syllabus, I seek to avoid mere tokenism.[84] I also invite guest lecturers into my classroom, colleagues whose epistemic privilege for speaking about women writers of color is stronger than my own. This move simultaneously asserts the multifaceted authority—the "belonging in place"—of such colleagues. Taken together, these admittedly small steps in the space of a single classroom will not, of course, make for big change. But I hope they help ensure that the intellectual and sociopolitical agency of women of color is embraced as a given, even at a majority-white institution, not a point of contention. Then my students, whatever their own racial/ethnic identity, will be better prepared to take on leadership in future projects like my colleague Deborah Mitchell surely aspired to promote when she urged our KCAC team to study Spelman's learning legacies in the first place.

Archive-Inspired Community Projects

Valuable as single-classroom and single-course pedagogical counter-narratives may be, positioning our work in larger community frameworks grounded in collaborative archival recovery can have a more widespread public impact. Take, for instance, the potential reach of a project like the Civil Rights Digital Library, which also draws on the complex archive of southern race relations through such artifacts as unedited news footage from television stations in Spelman's Georgia home. Providing access to such resources invites teachers and community members in the Internet's expansive community to create new learning legacies around civil rights history. Or consider the multiyear teaching enterprise of the Harriet Wilson Project. Its groundbreaking collection of multidisciplinary essays won critical acclaim for counter-narrative moves to correct the cultural record around Wilson's place in New England culture. That collaboration has also reached out to nonacademic audiences by sponsoring statewide readership of Wilson's own writing and creating a memorial statue in Milford, New Hampshire. Thus, as Eric Gardner has noted in *Unexpected Places*, the project has modeled how "a new regionalist approach to early African American literature can work to transform communities" while giving the field itself "a larger public presence."[85] Similarly, housed at my second institutional home of TCU and led by historian Max Krochmal, the "Civil Rights History in Black and Brown" project is creating a counter-narrative of multiracial collaboration by gathering oral histories to complicate versions of a movement so often cast straightforwardly as a black/white conflict.

Public endeavors like these and KCAC's "Educating for Citizenship" have benefited from grant budgets that, once they disappear, may leave participants sorely pressed to continue working at a broad community level. The websites and books originally generated during a funded phase of collaboration still endure, of course, providing resources that are just a click or a library checkout away. But the networks that initially collaborated to build those resources are themselves fragile communities, so that maintaining connections to produce more knowledge and facilitate sustained public activity together becomes more difficult over time. In that context, I've been glad that writing this chapter led me to revisit the website for Slater Elementary in Atlanta, and to find Deborah Mitchell now serving as an instructional coach for other teachers, a more formal leadership role than when we first worked together in Spelman's archive. Reconnecting with Deborah by phone, I was excited to hear about her work today, but also about ways our prior collaboration still contributes to it. Similarly, in the decade since Dave Winter wrote about his classes' study of early *Messenger* authors, students mentored by him at Atlanta's Grady High School earned numerous journalism honors—and Dave himself, now teaching in Texas, claimed well-earned awards for nurturing student publications. The leadership of K-12 teachers like Mitchell and Winter, who have devoted such productive careers to fostering the capabilities of so many students of color, is building another culture-shaping Archive enhanced by collaborations like those that founded Spelman.

Individually, even after moving from Georgia to Texas myself, I continued to engage with Spelman's on-campus archive—in large part because Taronda Spencer advocated for my doing the additional research for this chapter. She pushed me to return to the college on multiple occasions; encouraged me to stretch my study of primary texts beyond the *Messenger* to a deeper reading of Packard's personal papers; tracked down key documents to send me; and celebrated with me when I uncovered more writing by Nora Gordon in the archive of the American Board of Commissioners of Foreign Missions in Boston. When I suggested that Taronda herself should write about Packard, Giles, and the early Spelman students, she laughed and explained why she preferred being the finder, steward, and distributor of materials, leaving most of the writing to others.[86]

I say "most of" because Taronda did write to me.

She is gone now, like so many other Spelman alumnae referenced here, though certainly long before we would have hoped. She passed away suddenly at only fifty-four years of age. A heart attack took her with no warning in the spring of 2013, during that busy, hopeful season that every year included her excitement over Founders Day bringing Spelman history to life again, just as she was preparing to support the inevitable summer visits of scholars from all over the world to the ever-growing archive on the campus.

There is some small comfort in knowing I thanked her many times for her guidance. I particularly treasure a set of handwritten notes I made during one extended conversation on a late afternoon when we were alone in the archive. Taronda was explaining the rationale she saw behind the original choice to name Spelman's in-house periodical the *"Messenger"*—how that designation surely held an aspirational connotation envisioning particular black audiences I hadn't thought of at first, fixated as I was initially on its function as a persuasive fundraising pipeline to white supporters. No, Taronda clarified, an even more important audience, from the start, was in rural black communities where future Spelman students lived, young girls like those attending schools taught by Carrie Walls and Nora Gordon in between their Spelman terms.

"Let me tell you what that really says," I wrote at the top of this sheet of notes, as a quote with Taronda's name beside the comment, to remind myself that there are always gaps in my tentative readings of individual archives and layered Archives of cross-cultural relationships, gaps I can only begin to fill when working collaboratively. Taronda's "Let me tell you" comment reconfirmed my own limits as an interpreter and gently insisted that I listen attentively to voices speaking of experiences beyond my own. To collaborate most effectively, Taronda taught me, includes accepting that we bring different tools and understandings to shared work—and that we should embrace those differences if we want to make the most efficacious new knowledge possible together.

When I turn through pages in the file folder that bears Taronda's name, I see typed, official-looking communiques on Spelman letterhead, giving various permissions across multiple years of shared scholarship. But I also find friendly emails identifying secondary sources I should consult, and Xeroxed artifacts she sent to me when she came across (or even sought out and then forwarded) specific items linked to this research. There's a flyer that, her notation says, was "sent by Rev. Quarles & Baptist ministers" to recruit students for the original school opening in 1881. There's another advertisement, giving the cost of enrolling in the early seminary as fifty cents, and half that price "for children under twelve." Taronda's notation this time directs me to notice that the "First students were older women and girls," so that "partnership between Founders & students" was "in some cases on peer level."

I hope she thought of our connection as something of a partnership. I know it was surely not "on peer level," because I could never achieve her quantity and nuance of knowledge about Spelman. But I am grateful indeed that she shared so much of it. And I hope my efforts to pass that learning legacy on here are worthy of her, and worthy of *Messengers* like Sarah Lay, who expressed a wish I have truly come to share: "That my work may speak well for Spelman," its Archive, and all its students aspire to do.

CHAPTER THREE

Collaborative Writing as
Jane Addams's Hull-House Legacy

"What would Jane do?"
—Todd DeStigter, *Jane Addams in the Classroom*, p. 27

"We see ourselves as a connecting agent in the city."
—Lisa Junkin Lopez, Jane Addams Hull-House Museum
(JAHHM) interview

"One evening, as I entered the reception room, Miss Addams called
me into the residents' sitting room and asked me to join a class in
English composition. . . ."
—Hilda Satt Polacheck, *I Came a Stranger*, p. 77

Writing as Teaching

Hull-House as a social settlement on Halsted Street in Chicago—as led
by Jane Addams and her numerous partners in progressive education—
shut its doors long ago.[1] But Hull-House as an aspirational model, as a
practice of democratic vision, still thrives. It lives now, primarily, through
writing as a form of teaching and a pathway to learning. Addams's own
writings about the settlement, along with many other texts documenting
its work in her day, embody and thus promote collaborative storytelling about activism. This chapter revisits that legacy of communal writing about Hull-House and demonstrates how self-conscious heirs to that
heritage are following its lead.

For Addams herself, some settlement compositions involved group research and reporting, with coauthorship directly designated, as in the *Hull-*

79

House Maps and Papers.[2] Sometimes, though, we must look within narrative descriptions to find details of a collaboration that, over time, produced stories for a communal archive. As one example, in "Women's Conscience and Social Amelioration," Addams described how a determined band of Hull-House Woman's Club members spent months investigating the high death rate of children in their neighborhood. Club members divided up their ward into sections and documented cases where the city's refuse department was failing to pick up garbage. They compared those findings with figures on death and disease, then disseminated that data to campaign for enhanced sanitation service. This was a memorable case, Addams noted, of group commitment to "moral vigor and civic determination" succeeding via "not very pleasant" on-site research three times per week, followed by political action (fixing the garbage pick-up shortcomings) that was achievable only through team effort (257). Addams's characterization of the club's shared research-and-writing project in this case was affirmed more broadly by one of its most enthusiastic immigrant members, Hilda Satt Polacheck, who wrote in her autobiography that "the Hull-House Woman's Club was Jane Addams's pet activity," carried out as "a real venture in democracy" by virtue of its ongoing collaborations (Polacheck, *I Came*, 101).

Along related lines, Addams often described specific elements in the settlement's educational program as reciprocal endeavors, providing as much learning for the middle-class "residents" of Hull-House (herself included) as for their immigrant "neighbors." Such stories presented evolving settlement projects as cross-cultural bridge-building, thereby deemphasizing whatever individual leadership role she might have played to enable a program. So, for instance, over several pages in her best-selling *Twenty Years at Hull-House*, Addams recalled a particular moment of reflection that led her to the concept for the Labor Museum, but she then identified, as more crucial to its launch, the contributions of "a Syrian woman, a Greek, an Italian, a Russian, and an Irishwoman." In her claim that "we prize it [the Labor Museum] because it so often puts the immigrants into the position of teachers" (140), Addams not only marked the need to recognize collaborations behind her print-text story; she also underscored how visitors to the settlement often learned the most about its work through interchanges with those immigrants-turned-educators.[3] If Addams herself was admittedly the guiding light for Hull-House in her day, her framing of this anecdote suggested that she nonetheless wanted readers to recognize its shared energy and, implicitly, to see all its community members as settlement program coauthors.

Yet the precise learning legacies of Hull-House, cast in such terms, remain difficult to codify. Why? For one thing, the settlement's original projects—its reading clubs and citizenship classes, its political interventions around labor issues and its innovative outdoor playground-building, its coffee house and its summer camps—formed such a diverse array of activities that to articulate a unifying vision becomes challenging, even for Addams herself. Similarly, Hull-House's stories have been told through so many voices, representing so many different perspectives, that the very capaciousness so treasured by Addams and her contemporaries has at times obscured the shared features of its diverse collaborations. What, overall, did Hull-House aim to teach? How can we best apply its lessons? Given the rich complexity of the Hull-House enterprise across the decades of Addams's 1889–1935 personal leadership, I aim in this chapter to follow her lead by foregrounding *writing*, broadly conceived, and supported by shared civic engagement, as the main Archive of the settlement's learning legacy and a means to extend its teachings into social action today.

To claim that writing, and especially collaborative writing, held a privileged place in the work of Hull-House is, on one level, easy to do, given the sheer quantity of texts produced by Addams and her colleagues to form an interconnected web of discourse. Chapters in *The Autobiography of Florence Kelley*, for instance, echo Addams's repeated invocation of settlement colleagues in her own publications to underscore how all stories about the Chicago settlement can, and probably should, be viewed as collaborative. Still, in the context of my *Learning Legacies* project here, merely to follow verbal threads across these narratives is not sufficient. After all, an assertion that Hull-House writings embody a heritage of shared composing has significant implications for teaching in the liberal arts today, leading us, for instance, to consider how and when to structure collaborations among our students, particularly those involving production of text. Similarly, if we emphasize Addams's efforts to build community connections as a key element in her education program, what are ways we can borrow from her example to create productive partnerships today? What does the Hull-House Archive, in these terms, demonstrate about the benefits of storytelling itself, done collaboratively or at least informed by collaborations? And what unfinished business of the settlement should we try to address through these interconnected strategies of cultural pragmatism?

To address these questions, I have needed both to revisit my own original connections with Hull-House and to put that earlier inquiry in dialogue with more recent study. Doing so has led me to examine my evolving standpoint as a white woman scholar-teacher immersed in Addams's authorial archive and in the cultural work of Chicago-based educators who've been drawing on her example in their own work.

My starting point for this chapter's study of Addams and Hull-House coincided with my own transition from K-12 schoolteacher to university-based teacher-scholar. I first visited Hull-House in the early 1990s, while doing dissertation research in the Jane Addams Memorial Collection at the University of Illinois at Chicago (UIC). The museum seemed an essential stop for a pilgrimage to supplement the hours I was spending in the archive—turning creaky microfilm reels and squinting at Addams's tough-to-decipher handwriting. Crossing the campus, I set out to explore what remained of the original home base for her work: one lone relic from what had been a conglomerate of bustling settlement spaces. To help make room for the urban university at UIC, almost all of Hull-House's buildings had been sacrificed.[4] Decades earlier, Hull-House had included everything from a gym to a theater, from meeting rooms for clubs and a kindergarten to an art gallery, as well as living quarters for both college-educated residents and working girls. But in the early 1990s, the home Charles Hull had built in the 1850s was all that remained open from what had been America's premier settlement. The single "house" where Jane Addams and Ellen Gates Starr had launched their progressive experiment had been maintained, so their visible legacy had not been erased entirely. Yet, clinging to the edge of the sprawling urban campus, that constricted version of the previously vibrant settlement conveyed only limited appreciation of their work.

During my initial 1992 research trip, I could see that the university library's preservation of the Jane Addams Papers did signal a wish to honor her. Yet scholars' patient recovery process, which would eventually lead to numerous editions of her writings and analyses of her influence, had not yet borne substantial fruit.[5] And the museum at the other end of the campus seemed more a poignant memorial than an active affirmation of her heritage. Wandering through the quiet facility, at first the only visitor, I was eventually joined by a slender, elderly man who spoke wistfully about his own youthful experiences as an immigrant taking part in Hull-House clubs. We chatted briefly about how he had benefited from those settlement-sponsored classes. But our talk felt more melancholy than invigorating, since the museum presented itself, on that occasion, as more static landmark than living legacy. In the built environment of its surroundings, in the distant-seeming verbiage of its display labels, and in the very absence of communal activity on site, this space spoke a tale of loss: lost energy, lost voices, lost stories.[6]

So my stay at the museum then was brief, because I didn't sense much of Addams's presence there. A better source for delving into her teaching seemed, at that point, to be in the textual archive held in the special collections. I pored over her scrapbooks, looking not only at what she had clipped and saved from decades of periodical articles but also her margin notations. I scoured the handwritten narratives she'd crafted to describe her own learning experiences at Rockford Seminary. I reviewed the many pieces of publication-related correspondence—ranging from brief notes sent by different publishers who rejected "A Modern Lear" as too incendiary, on one extreme, to effusive "fan-mail" letters from appreciative readers, on the other. I waded through stacks of photographs, still only loosely catalogued. I read copies of the bulletins, seeking Addams's own voice at a remove in the careful third-person language advertising for classes across a range of topics (like literature, politics, and history) and skills (such as cooking, sewing). That early archival research helped me identify continuities between her self-conscious collaborations with other students at Rockford Seminary and her partnerships with Hull-House residents later. Yet I didn't then know enough about the rich impact of Addams's multidecade publication enterprise to see how her writing processes—particularly her continual repurposings of texts for different venues—interacted with her cultivation of interpersonal relationships to support her own and others' learning. Thus, though I frequently taught *Twenty Years at Hull-House* (in American literature classes; in courses on immigrant life) and occasionally ventured into using other publications (such as *Peace and Bread in Time of War* and her women's college speeches in Gender Studies courses), I held back from producing additional scholarship on Addams. Her deepest thought on teaching and her most strategic use of rhetoric were too elusive to capture. She was a role model whose influence I constantly felt but could never adequately explain.

Finally, for this *Learning Legacies* project, I simply could not leave Hull-House out of the picture. So, intrigued by signs of curators' substantial engagement with her writing when I dipped into the Jane Addams Hull-House Museum website, and called to rereading Addams by conversations with UIC-based teacher educators, I reimmersed. The collaborative writing I saw coming out of both these enterprises—the revitalized museum and the gradually developing essays being shepherded by Dave Schaafsma and Todd DeStigter for *Jane Addams in the Classroom*—led me to distin-

guish, at last, Addams's productive use of counter-narrative rhetoric. I finally grasped how she employed a communal vision of that genre to engage with ever-unfinished business, forge collaborative connections across
cultural divides, and embrace story as a mode of writing-to-learn and
writing-to-teach about the settlement. So this chapter represents both my
new appreciation of Addams in a cultural rhetorics framework and an invitation to others to extend application of her Archive. Understanding Addams, I'd now maintain, requires us to examine her own and her settlement
contemporaries' writings as purposefully interconnected to do shared cultural work. And understanding Addams-linked writings as a learning legacy
also demands that we take into account the ways scholar-educators today
are utilizing Hull-House texts (broadly conceived to include an array of
expressive forms) to address current social issues.[7]

Revisiting Hull-House Heritage

In my second, 2012 visit to the Hull-House site, twenty years after the
first, I found much had changed. The settlement's vision and productivity
had been recuperated through new cultural work at the museum, by then
clearly reconnected to its heritage. The Jane Addams Hull-House Museum
had again become a pulsing hive of activity informed by research and reflection conjoined to civic engagement. The museum itself had been re-
made, as forecast by the description I had seen on its website:

> The Jane Addams Hull-House Museum serves as a dynamic me-
> morial to social reformer Jane Addams, the first American woman
> to receive the Nobel Peace Prize, and her colleagues whose work
> changed the lives of their immigrant neighbors as well as national
> and international public policy. The Museum preserves and devel-
> ops the original Hull-House site for the interpretation and continu-
> ation of the historic settlement house vision, linking research, edu-
> cation, and social engagement.[8]

In the interim since my own first foray into Addams's archive, traditional
print research on the settlement leader herself had also exploded. Multiple
biographies had appeared.[9] Scholars from diverse disciplines had claimed
Addams for an array of purposes. Treatments of Addams ranged from recovering her role in the formation of social work as a field to repositioning
her intellectual relationship with John Dewey as an educational theorist;

from tracking her views on the settlement movement across decades of authorship to examining her role in Progressive Era political agendas, including immigrant acculturation and juvenile justice projects, and labor union and peace movement organizing. Researchers had been revisiting everything from Hull-House's gendered programs and intensely personal relationships to its theater productions' playful, purposeful aesthetics.[10] Multiple factors have stimulated this escalating interest in Addams and the settlement: feminist recovery efforts; a reenergized commitment, at universities, to public history and community partnerships; an impulse to seek strategies for responding to our current wave of immigration; and an awareness that, more broadly, issues of urban life addressed by the Progressive movement still need our attention.[11]

Assessments of Addams during her lifetime reflected drastically different perspectives across time (from "Saint Jane" characterizations in the settlement's early years to excoriations during Addams's peace movement connections, to a reassertion of positive views after her receipt of the Nobel Peace Prize). The twenty years between my original exploration of Addams and my new research for this chapter witnessed similar shifts. If some treatments as part of an initial recovery stage of women's history were overly enthusiastic, then a backlash of sorts, reflecting emphasis on white women's relatively more powerful social positions in American culture, may have overcompensated. At least, research by twenty-first-century biographers such as Jean Bethke Elshtain has suggested as much. For example, in oral histories Elshtain gathered for her influential *Jane Addams and the Dream of American Democracy*, she found strong indicators that some of the Hull-House immigrant "neighbors" had grown quite tired of critiques of Addams as patronizing and of settlement programming as imposing dominant culture values.[12]

Accordingly, Elshtain's report of a four-hour conversation she held with Ruby Jane Delicandro (née Gorglione) and Marie Thalos (née Bagnola) emphasizes their intense appreciation of Addams and the settlement's middle-class residents, who, they insisted, "'treated us on an equal basis'" and provided "'a rich environment'" in which Delicandro and Thalos freely chose to participate (9). Further, Elshtain says they declared, "Hull-House enlarged but did not supplant the world of their immigrant community," since activities at the settlement purposefully honored their home cultures while offering up a range of cross-cultural opportunities (10). Thus, Elshtain argues, evaluations of Hull-House need to honor perspectives like these. They paint, she notes, a portrait of Addams as having "'respected people's traditions'" rather than inculcating simplistic assimilation (11) and as opening up countless prospects for personal growth among Hull-House neighbors that would otherwise have been unavailable (12–13). These benefits included cross-ethnic exchanges that, said Ruby and Marie, "'taught us to respect each other's traditions'" (13). Elshtain herself has clearly been persuaded by such informants that a more balanced assessment of Addams and her work is needed. Therefore, she calls on her own readers to eschew "a stance of condescension or ahistorical present-mindedness" that can actually impede productive "civic culture" work today. Instead, she asks interpreters to cultivate "keen, responsible criticism" (14), acknowledging Addams's commitment to "human empathy" as expansive enough "to welcome" to Hull-House "[a]ll those who were, in one way or another, alien or foreign" (254).

This newer body of research like Elshtain's certainly informed the Hull-House museum's revitalization in the early 2000s.[13] Creative leadership by museum director Lisa Yun Lee and her colleagues—acting themselves as self-conscious feminist educators—reformulated its activities and associated public discourse, just as I was returning to Hull-House study myself. That is, both in the writing they did to present Addams to the public (in display objects and labels, on the website, and, more broadly, in their exhibit concepts and designs), as well as in their published writings *about* their work as curators, the Lee-led team worked to pass along Addams's learning legacy from a stance of critical empathy. I credit much of my own enhanced understanding of Hull-House's heritage to connecting, beginning in 2012, with the museum educators then guiding the JAHHM's community-building agenda. By visiting with the staff and collaborating with exhibition curator Heather Radke to prepare conference presentations, for example, I gleaned energizing insights into the group's practice and their self-conscious study of the settlement's rich archive.

On a parallel track, I was tracing the generative process of Addams-informed activist scholarship led by teacher education faculty at UIC, which now virtually surrounds the Hull-House museum site. David Schaafsma, Todd DeStigter, and their teacher-researcher colleagues carried out a sustained reading of Addams's published legacy. Then they extended their inquiry through collaborative writing about their applications of her example in diverse classrooms around the country. In turn, by studying storytelling within these sometimes-overlapping projects—the re-presentation of Hull-House at the JAHHM and the creation of *Jane Addams in the Classroom*—I have identified core strategies from Addams's collaborative teaching practice that are still applicable today. In this chapter, I am setting this storytelling by museum leaders and teacher educators in dialogue with the archive of Addams's own writing, particularly from late in her career. As in other learning legacies throughout this book, when we dig into this Archive, we find that women educators' counter-narratives from the past can continue to do relevant intercultural work for our current time. Like the Spelman founders' archive as it is maintained now at the Atlanta college, Hull-House's counter-narratives offer a pathway to inquiry into past cultural interventions, and that inquiry produces resources for cross-cultural community-building today. Crucial among these adaptable tools, in Addams's case, are several themes: embracing learning and associated social justice interventions as perpetually "unfinished business"; cultivating interpersonal relationships and shared authority as avenues to knowledge; and storytelling itself as a method for doing intercultural work and for reporting on that process.

Jane Addams's Stories of Learning

From her early days as a student at Rockford Seminary (which became a college just in time for her to claim a full-fledged degree), Addams had an intense awareness of her capacity to mine cultural resources and then to disseminate that knowledge. She was virtually obsessed, while a student, with maintaining records of her own liberal-arts-oriented learning, as if confident, even in youth, that her personal archive would have long-term value. Thus, in the UIC Special Collections Library, generations of scholars, myself included, have been able to revisit her notes from school debates on the relative importance of women's literary authorship versus their sponsorship of social activism; pore over her essays for Rockford's student newspaper; and reread her commencement speech on graduates' becoming "Breadgivers" through gendered leadership, not just bread-makers within the home. Addams would continue this practice of saving records of learning throughout her career. She would also draw on that ever-growing personal archive as a source for writing about the settlement's educational agenda. Accordingly, by turning the pages of scrapbooks holding newspaper stories about Hull-House, it's possible to identify recurring ideas (such as women's civic housekeeping as a rightful extension of domesticity) in quotes she gave reporters. We can catch echoes of those same terms in internal settlement publications and in her speeches; see her invocations of those same phrases in periodicals ranging from *Ladies Home Journal* to the *Century*; and track still more reiterations in longer narratives like *Twenty Years at Hull-House*. Skilled at crafting what today we'd call a "sound bite" when being interviewed, Addams was equally adept at remixing her own reflective commentary back into various internal settlement texts. She would then recirculate those stories to broader readerships. Multifaceted in its venues and in the audiences she addressed, the vast body of Addams's own writing—along with the parallel texts she helped other settlement women create—forms a uniquely rich archive aimed from its very inception at shaping future generations.

One feature cutting across all these texts is a commitment to *story* as an avenue to teaching.[14] For Addams, such a text-making approach represented a conscious counter-narrative strategy, since her publications appeared at a time when university and corporate emphases on "hard" sciences, professionalized male leadership of social enterprises (including obsession with efficiency as measured via the "Taylorism" model), and expository discourse reflecting scientific methods all flourished.[15] Now, through recovery of her learning legacy, we can resist the restrictive epistemologies and exclusionary language often dominating scholarly writing in our own time. That is, adopting these same principles can open an avenue (back) to a humanistic framework too often undervalued in the current climate that overemphasizes (seemingly) quantifiable measurements of learning and reductive versions of teaching content.[16] Therefore, in retracing my own efforts to reconnect with Hull-House's heritage, I will highlight how the themes of unfinished business, collaboration, and storytelling for knowledge-making have been reanimated, for me, in story-making by JAHHM staff and by the *Jane Addams in the Classroom* project. To explicate these connections, I'll now revisit collaborative writing from the settlement itself and afterwards underscore links between those narrative practices and the more recent reinvigorations of its heritage.

To illustrate Addams's own rhetorical model, which embedded teaching within storytelling discourse, we need to carry out an intertextual reading of her last book, *My Friend, Julia Lathrop*. So far, this biography has garnered limited scholarly attention,[17] partly because of the enduring appeal of *Twenty Years at Hull-House*. Significantly, however, these two narratives share notable rhetorical features. One trait evident in both is Addams's choice to craft an accessible story addressing a broad audience rather than the increasingly discipline-oriented academic readers of her time.[18] In *My Friend, Julia Lathrop*, one subtle vehicle for signaling this affiliation with storytelling for general readers emerges through a reference to Lathrop herself. Specifically, Addams recalls one of her friend's many speeches for the National Conference of Social Work. Says Addams of Lathrop: "She deplored that, while the Government statistical material is basic, it is unfortunate that the art of popularizing has not seemed of equal importance" (87). Though by this time Addams's penchant for addressing general readers was well established, she was aware that her commitment to broad audiences was distancing her authorial cachet from the increasingly specialized academic texts of university colleagues like John Dewey. So her choice to present Lathrop's defense of "the art of popularizing" was likely aimed as much at asserting her own writer's status as her friend's.

If the legacy of her authorship was understandably on Addams's mind while composing her final book, she was even more intent on affirming the settlement's shared vision than on seeking individual credit.[19] Thus, another trait evident in *My Friend, Julia Lathrop*, consistent with her earlier writing, is Addams's insistent foregrounding of the Hull-House community over her own role as its leader. Addams relegated herself, in *Twenty Years* and its *Forty Years* sequel, to a self-deprecating subtitle: *with Autobiographical Notes*. Similarly, to underscore her commitment to shared authority, Addams often wrote in first-person plural, rather than singular.[20] She depicted projects as sustained collaborative endeavors, more than individually conceptualized or led.[21] And, significantly, instead of writing in an assertive argumentative mode, she took her readers along, through reflection, to revisit past experience, conveyed in story.[22] Via this last strategy, her texts embodied a counter-narrative rhetoric simply by presenting themselves *as* narratives in an era when expository forms used for scientific, discipline-based study had gained a strong foothold as the authoritative discourse for making knowledge.

Addams drafted *My Friend* with full awareness that her own life was nearing its end. Though driven by the recent death of Lathrop, one of Hull-House's central figures, the book narrates ways of *living* in the settlement as a communal experiment in democratic learning. *My Friend*, in line with its title, repeatedly emphasizes relationships. Along the way, while chronicling reciprocity in action, the text stresses Addams's narrative approach to ever-unfinished, collaborative knowledge-making. Through individual anecdotes accruing cumulative narrative force, the book also portrays a model of cross-cultural learning for others to follow. Reading Addams's narrative from a participatory stance, we can follow her example of shared civic engagement and her strategies for crafting stories about such work.

Like so many of Addams's books, the *My Friend* biography evolved from

Figure 3.1. Julia Lathrop. Hull-House Photograph Collection. JAMC
0000 0267 0411. Courtesy of the University of Illinois at Chicago, Richard
J. Daley Library Special Collections and University Archives.

a periodical starting point. In this case, we can trace the text's genesis back to Addams's "A Great Public Servant, Julia C. Lathrop" essay, which appeared in *Social Service Review* in 1932. Here, Addams introduced themes she would develop more fully for the book, including anecdotes from Lathrop's various social justice projects to illustrate Hull-House methods in action. For one example of this indirect but purposeful rhetoric, we need look no further than that 1932 essay's first sentence, which would reappear in an early paragraph of the biography's fourth chapter: "My earliest impressions of Hull-House include Julia Lathrop."[23] In linking Lathrop with the settlement, Addams suggested that, to narrate a history of Hull-House, one must focus on its women leaders. Also, in beginning with "My earliest impressions," Addams connected Lathrop's ties to Hull-House with her own. After all, "Earliest Impressions" had also been the title for the first chapter of *Twenty Years*, so astute readers could catch the allusion. Additionally, within *My Friend, Julia Lathrop*, as was typical in Addams's writing, she would revisit "impressions" arising from shared experience—from sustained personal relationships—to assemble a narrative conveying larger principles. So, many of the text's anecdotes recalled collaborative activities, including animated conversations between Addams and Lathrop about their gendered network in action.

What drove me to reread this text, in fact, was a vague memory of its engaging dialogic moments—a memory stirred up through interviews with the Hull-House museum staff beginning in 2012. Over and over, they referenced conversations with each other as guiding their practice, and they situated those discussions in a kind of imaginative exchange with Addams and other women in her circle. I had long known about the role that the community of women residents and other Hull-House supporters played in the settlement's success.[24] But I came to better understand the centrality of these bonds by hearing staff members like Lisa Lee, Lisa Junkin Lopez, and Heather Radke describe their own frequent conversations about Addams and her colleagues.

For example, in one dialogue about her role as exhibition coordinator, Radke referenced how the interpersonal network of the settlement in Addams's day had been shaping her museum projects, quite literally:[25]

One of the things I think that is most important [about Hull-House] is that it's not just Addams' work. It's actually the work of many reformers and also the immigrant neighbors. And actually in this room right behind you there's . . . an exhibit about Florence Kelley and

Ellen Gates Starr and [other] women who were here at this place. (Radke, "Interview")

Describing another exhibit, Radke reflected:

One of my personal interests is in the history of domesticity and the intimate moments of domestic life, and the old feminist trope of the personal is the political. I feel like Hull-House is actually such an interesting example of that because it was about the entirety of these people's lives. It wasn't like they went to work and then came home. . . . They lived here. Their relationships with each other were as much a part of their work as going out into the neighborhood. And their relationships with the neighbors also. (Radke, "Interview")

Lisa Lee, leading the JAHHM at the time of my first interview with Radke, expanded upon the notion of the settlement's cultivating interpersonal relationships to include the larger community. This emphasis on cross-class and cross-ethnic relations, she said, had carried over into museum programming under her directorship:

There's an effort these days [in museum practice] toward, what people call shared authority, and for us, it's one which is so familiar just from looking at Hull-House history. I think its roots are in a notion of solidarity, and the notion that the settlement house movement itself was built in [that]. . . . To sum it up in a nutshell, [the principle] is that you're not going to be from the ivory tower, standing afar, trying to figure out what the issues are and then coming up with solutions, but you're going to settle in the neighborhood, figure out the problems and solutions with the people that you are purporting to help. And then, also, you acknowledge that you will probably be as transformed as those people, and so it's never a stance of service. It is always one of solidarity. (Lee, "Interview")

To nurture that sense of solidarity, both Lee and Radke explained, entailed engaging in imaginative dialogue with the archive as a starting point. That is, these museum-based teachers would hearken back to Addams's own language to recapture her vision. Further, they would make material objects through which Addams and the other residents engaged in daily life a direct source of inspiration to guide new partnerships with community members and new exhibits inviting such connections. Words and objects originally embedded in Addams's story-making practice could thereby be reanimated through empathetic recovery and dissemination via new stories.

Those dialogues with Addams and her settlement's learning legacies had a clear and purposefully managed parallel among members of the UIC English Education writing team, I discovered. Having the chance to read drafts for *Jane Addams in the Classroom* (*JAC*) as they were being crafted gave me a window into that collegial writing process as an echo of the Hull-House residents' and neighbors' shared inquiry. Several of the essays in *JAC*, being revised collaboratively around the same time when I was revisiting the JAMHH, depict the various authors as holding imaginative dialogues with the Hull-House leader. Perhaps the most striking of these is Ruth Vinz's "Afterword," which repeatedly locates its author as evoking Addams's own voice, as self-positioning back into Addams's life, and as metaphorically sharing spaces and thoughts with the settlement leader.

Traces of that cross-era connecting also emerged in language from online interviews I carried out with several of the contributors to the *JAC* volume, who, I noted with some initial surprise, had taken to referencing Addams herself as "Jane." "WWJD? (What would Jane do?)" had become a shared question among this energetic group of educators—a mantra to guide both their teaching and their writing.[26] Todd DeStigter memorably invoked this conversational affiliation by using the "WWJD" question as a header for the final section of his "In Good Company" essay (27). He then answered it in a vivid passage I'd later set in dialogue, myself, with commentary by Native American scholar-writer Diane Glancy on the importance of place visits and analysis of material objects for taking up activist agendas through archival research (see Coda in this book). Here is DeStigter's anecdote on finding Addams's grave during a site visit to Cedarville:

> Jane's headstone lay at my feet. . . . I knelt and ran my fingers over the letters. Scattered on the headstone were thirty-four pennies—a nod, I guessed, to the admiration for Lincoln that Jane had inherited from her father.
>
> As much as I was enjoying the moment of reverent solitude, I couldn't help wondering why I was out there all by myself. I should have been surrounded by admirers and activists. . . . Where were the busloads of progressive pilgrims? By all rights, I should have had to buy a ticket and nudge my way through a crowd to get a glimpse of the final resting place of such an historic figure. . . . Still,

the more I thought about it, the more it made sense that I was out there alone, for anyone who cares enough about Jane Addams to visit her gravesite doesn't likely have time to linger in homage for long. There's just too much to be done. Back in Chicago, I knew, were neighborhoods struggling with poverty and violence, streets where thousands of homeless people eat and sleep, and high schools where only about half of the students graduate. I rested for a while in the shade, took some pictures, got on my bike, and headed for home and work. I think it's what Jane would have done. (DeStigter, "In Good Company," 28–29)

Years ago, Todd and I shared an office during graduate studies at the University of Michigan,[27] so I can hear his voice in the text, and I can see him, a visible textual presence, in his self-description at Addams's gravesite. At the same time, partly because we've now both read so much of Addams's writing, I recognize traces of her counter-narrative theory-making in passages like the one above, and in other essays for *Jane Addams in the Classroom*. In this story, for instance, Todd sets up a subtle verbal interplay between Addams's grave and his bicycle. Addams's grave marker, like the Lincoln-evoking pennies scattered over it, prompts his reflections on the meaning of her career. Then, he moves from contemplating the material culture archival resource of Addams's simply inscribed nameplate ("Jane Addams of Hull House and the International League for Peace and Freedom") to pedaling back to the city and purposeful civic engagement there. Reading an historical marker prompts a return to action.

As readers, we come to this scene and its implied theorizing through Todd's storytelling. We should note that he crafted the words later, capitalizing on moments of empathetic analysis to revisit the actual experience of his on-site research and thereby to position his readers, too, *within* his narrative as cointerpreters of Addams's richly layered life. Imaginatively visiting the locale with him, we are invited to recall both the powerful mentoring from her father, cast as a Lincolnesque figure in her *Twenty Years* autobiography, and the centrality of her gendered experience working with other women leaders in enterprises like the League for Peace. But it's in the culminating image of this scene, where DeStigter forecasts the work that awaits him back in Chicago, that we make the most intense contact with "Jane," as Todd depicts himself headed into action, biking back to Chicago. In narration that invites empathy with them both, he affiliates his own commitments with projects like hers: "I think that's what Jane would have done."

In *writing* as well as *doing* like Jane, Todd runs the risk of having some readers miss the deeply theorized argument contained within such a story. But he gains a potential pathway of imaginative affiliation, particularly among those who have schooled themselves in the inductive approaches to learning through narrative accretion—a route to *lived understanding* where the arts and humanities excel as epistemological systems. In illustrating his knowledge-building through the daily practice of reflecting, teaching, and writing like "Jane would have done," Todd also urges us, as readers, to carry out the patient, inquiry-based search for knowledge that learning legacies like hers can enable. Taking a cue from Todd and his *JAC* coauthors, throughout the rest of this chapter I'll weave together narratives about *Jane Addams in the Classroom* and the JAHHM as led by Lee, along with analysis of "Jane's" storytelling about Julia Lathrop and others, to illuminate the settlement's Archive. Having tried to enter these narratives by way of self-critical and empathetic connections myself, I can now call on my own readers to join a participatory analysis.

Jane/J.A. and Julia

The regular invocation of "Jane" by the UIC English Education writing team actually has a telling textual parallel within *My Friend, Julia Lathrop*. There, one rhetorical tactic Addams used to underscore the closeness of her ties to her subject was by recreating conversations where Lathrop playfully references Addams with the nickname "J.A."[28] Though told in past tense, these scenes bring readers to a participatory sense of shared experience like that in DeStigter's story, referenced above. Addams's reconstructed dialogues often include a forceful (if deft) questioning on Lathrop's part of the settlement's agenda. Sometimes this challenge involves self-criticism; sometimes it pushes Addams herself to reconsider a particular activity; sometimes it becomes a collaborative evaluation, through conversation, by Addams and her longtime colleague, together.[29] Within such anecdotes, Addams casts herself as the familiar "J.A." friend of "J. Lathrop" rather than as the revered Nobel laureate or the icon of Progressive Era politics. Individually and together, the anecdotes illustrate how a collaboration bolstered by mutual trust can (and should) include convivial critique. In revisiting her colleague's leadership as part of a sisterly network that

Lathrop herself called "our precious H.-H. society," Addams shows how the gendered work of the settlement operated.[30]

In a 2014 updating of his earlier work on autoethnography as knowledge-making strategy, Norman Denzin emphasized that all biographical narratives require a particularly alert reading stance. Denzin stressed that narrative revisiting of a life always entails reshaping, that rather than being empirically verifiable records of an individual's or a group's lived experiences, such texts "are only fictional statements with varying degrees of 'truth' about 'real' lives." Thus, he asserted, although they "provide framing devices" for understanding "the lives that we study," biographical narratives are always "*incomplete* literary productions"; they are "*narrative arrangements of reality*" that give only a partial account of a life, organized to align with a writer's value system and rhetorical goals (14–15, emphases in original). Such is certainly the case in Addams's account of Lathrop's life and its Hull-House connections. To read (as to write) such a narrative calls for self-aware empathy that fills in gaps and positions the story within Addams's implied theoretical framework, noting still-unfinished agendas and her own place in the storytelling. Addams invites this type of a participatory stance by bringing her readers into an intimate friendship, revisiting recollections of shared experiences.

Actually, Addams's *My Friend, Julia Lathrop* was "incomplete" in more ways than Denzin's description of all life stories would immediately suggest. "J.A." did not live long enough to revise and edit the text for publication. Finalized by another of Addams's associates, Alice Hamilton, this last publication itself thereby symbolized the settlement's ongoing commitment to doing unfinished business through collaboration that takes on multiple forms.

In a brief note appended to Addams's "Preface," longtime colleague and, in this case, editor Alice Hamilton outlines how the portrait of former settlement resident Julia Lathrop has been prepared for readers: "After Miss Addams' death the manuscript for this book was found to be practically ready for publication although she had not yet made the final revision. It has fallen to me to do this and I have carried out the task with scrupulous care, making as few changes as possible. The book is therefore not quite as she would have made it but at least it bears no imprint of any hand but her own."[31]

On first reading, that last sentence seems contradictory. How could the book be "not quite as she would have made it" yet, nonetheless, "bear[ing] no imprint of any hand but her own"? The answer lies in the narrative's

Figure 3.2. Alice Hamilton. Hull-House Photograph Collection. JAMC
0000 0258 0399. Courtesy of the University of Illinois at Chicago, Richard
J. Daley Library Special Collections and University Archives.

insistent depiction of Addams *at work along with* Lathrop. Though neither sought credit for her leadership of Progressive causes, both left learning legacies for others to access—a heritage which, Hamilton asserts, we may not be capable of duplicating "quite as [Addams] would have made it," but which still enables worthwhile cultural stewardship. Hamilton herself shows she has internalized this lesson of how the Hull-House community functioned at its best: foregrounding the work itself, not the leaders making it possible. Self-effacing in this description of her own editorial task, Hamilton positions the book on Lathrop as Addams's own writing while forecasting one of the text's core themes: that Hull-House women addressed social problems and made new knowledge collaboratively, eschewing personal credit in favor of achieving results.

Hamilton, a central figure in the Hull-House circle of friends-in-action,[32] grasped the importance that the biography of Lathrop held for Addams. Hence, Hamilton's willingness to prepare an unfinished project for publication, one "practically ready," on the one hand, but admittedly not yet fully revised. She assured readers that the text was indeed Addams's own work (an ironic point, given the constant commitment of "J.A." to crediting others). So, Hamilton described her own process as "carr[ying] out the task with scrupulous care, making as few changes as possible." Ultimately, Hamilton presented the book's readers with a narrative on Julia Lathrop both *by* and *about* Jane Addams—providing entry into the Hull-House visionary's retrospective reflections in a summing up that would never have a "final revision" ("Preface," *My Friend*, 4). Hamilton's taking on this task was, meanwhile, entirely consistent with the view of settlement life as she would express it a decade later in her own autobiography: "Hull-House is not an episode of the past; its influence still lives, and it deserves a tribute from one of its devoutest followers" (*Exploring/Autobiography*, 16).

Reading *My Friend, Julia Lathrop* for the first time just over twenty years ago, I found Addams's efforts to honor her longtime compatriot commendable—endearing even. But it was only more recently, when *re*-reading the account to research *Learning Legacies*, that I reached a deeper understanding of Addams's more veiled personal goals for this slim volume. In writing on Addams for my 1990s' dissertation, I had duly noted her choice to frame *Twenty Years at Hull-House* as more about the various enterprises of the settlement than about herself. Along related lines, my only previous freestanding publication on Addams, a journal article examining her time at Rockford College as useful preparation for Hull-House, underscored connections between the gendered network of learners she had helped lead as young student and the similar modes of action that she would undertake at the settlement.[33] In that essay, I interpreted the archival record of her school-based literacy practices to establish that Addams, while still a student, had adopted what I termed a "sororal" brand of leadership (Robbins, "Rereading," 42). From her days at Rockford, as evidenced in her personal texts from that time, on through her decades-long leadership of Hull-House, Addams used shared literacy practices to guide her thinking and her activism.[34] Through this self-conscious approach, she developed an empathetic stance toward others' ideas—whether conveyed in print text, conversation, or other expressive forms. Thus, over time, the Hull-House book clubs, which may have initially smacked of imposing high-art texts on neighbors with different interests than the college women running them, morphed into a more expansive version of productive social literacies, including theater, debate clubs, music, and crafts. On a parallel track, Addams and her colleagues learned to welcome wide variations in viewpoint, so that the settlement could "house" dialogues around the most radical political positions alongside far more conservative ones. In the *My Friend* text, accordingly, with the help of both Lathrop (in remembered dialogues) and Hamilton (as editor) Addams inscribed a closing salute to sisterly relationships shaping shared work.

Reading to Write

Like her interpersonal connections, the imaginative ones Addams forged through reading were a source of knowledge for learning and teaching. For Addams herself, print text remained a special source of pleasure, inspiration, and even day-to-day direction. Writers like George Eliot and Leo Tolstoy represented far more than a pastime: they also provided pragmatic guidance. Books by the women with whom she worked were especially valuable to Addams and the settlement movement. On one hand, and consistent with Deborah Brandt's concept of "Sponsors of Literacy," Addams and the Hull-House network can be said to have "sponsored" a number of influential publications over the years—from the *Hull-House Maps and Papers* (1895) to the *Hull-House Bulletin*'s collaborative reporting, to the autobiographies of Florence Kelley and Alice Hamilton, to texts by Julia Lathrop herself on work with the Children's Bureau.[35] Meanwhile, Addams's constant reading of others' writings and her attention to their composing processes directly supported her own writing-to-teach.

One example of this communal literacy engagement was pivotal in my own recent rereading of *My Friend, Julia Lathrop*. As important as her US-based women's network was to Addams's career, her transatlantic friendship with Dame Henrietta Barnett held a particularly crucial place in the American writer's settlement leadership and publishing practices. Addams cultivated a multidecade literacy-linked relationship with Barnett, co-founder with her husband, Canon Samuel Barnett, of the Toynbee Hall London settlement that inspired Hull-House in the first place. Elsewhere, I've tracked the various articulations of this friendship in both personal and public writings by Addams and Barnett.[36] Here, I want to show how my own "reading" of that relationship led me to a fuller recognition of Addams's storytelling-to-teach approach in *My Friend, Julia Lathrop*. Specifically, by *reading Addams's reading* of both Henrietta Barnett, herself, and of Barnett's principal publication—a biography of her husband, Canon Barnett—I identified purposeful elements I had previously missed in the Lathrop biography. Then, by resituating *My Friend, Julia Lathrop* within a multivalent textual archive of writing, reading, and interpersonal relations from across Addams's career, I could finally recover this seemingly simple narrative's strategic call for progressive social action through empathetic collaboration. Like Henrietta Barnett's use of a biography of her husband to tell her own story, Addams crafted a book about her lifelong friend Julia Lathrop to offer their would-be intellectual heirs a path to follow.

From early on in the text, Addams links *My Friend* with the story of Hull-House and thus, implicitly, with a retrospective account of her own life's work. While admitting that Lathrop "did not come to live in the settlement the first year," Addams insists that her colleague's "sympathetic understanding of its purposes and her co-operating spirit in all its activities . . . became an integral part of it, from the very day of its opening in the autumn of 1889" (16). In attributing both "sympathetic understanding" and a "cooperating spirit" to the young Lathrop, whom she had known since they grew up in Rockford, Illinois, Addams begins to lay out two traits (empathy and collaboration) that she invokes throughout the book to show how Lathrop embodied Hull-House's vision. At the same time, Addams uses anecdotes revisiting particular occasions of Lathrop's leadership—very often set within accounts of the two women collaborating—to celebrate the narrative's purported main subject (Lathrop), while illustrating the settlement's communal approach. Addams's strategy here imitates a model she had read quite carefully: *Canon Barnett*, the biography that Dame Henrietta had published to honor her husband, the founder of Toynbee Hall, and, at the same time, to claim a role for herself, beyond

loyal helpmate, in settlement leadership. Addams had described her attentive, appreciative reading of that biography in a letter to Barnett in early
winter of 1920, soon after its publication: "I have been asked to review it
for various magazines and have accepted the Atlantic and the Yale Review.
It has had very favorable notices thruout the country. . . ."[37]

That Addams regularly used her personal reading to feed her own
writing is clear from many examples. In "A Modern Lear," for instance,
she set up a parallel between Shakespeare's troubled protagonist and
George Pullman's misdirected strike-inducing behaviors in 1894. In her
introduction for 1902's *Democracy and Social Ethics*, she associated her understanding of lived experience with a brand of empathy gleaned from
reading, especially literary texts.[38] And in numerous passages within
Twenty Years at Hull-House, she used references to reading to elucidate
everyday life at the settlement.[39]

As Barbara Sicherman has explained in *Well-Read Lives*, "For Addams . . . literature was—or at least could be—a kind of experience rather
than a substitute for it" (187). In defending the "reading parties and clubs"
that were part of Hull-House from its earliest days, and which, Sicherman
admits, have sometimes been deemed an "attempt to impose elite culture
on those who did not seek or want it" (174), *Well-Read Lives* characterizes
Addams's personal approach to authors like Charles Dickens and Emile
Zola as mining textual resources to develop her own writing skills (187–88).
Therefore, Sicherman suggests, when America's best-known settlement
storyteller describes the powerful impact a particular book by Israel Zangwill (*Children of the Ghetto*) has had on readers' ability to grasp his complex
subject, "Addams could be describing her own goals and literary practice"
(187). Sicherman focuses on how Addams drew on compelling texts to address an "educated audience" and "interpret" for them "the needs and out-
looks of her neighbors," by promoting "imaginative engagement" through
reading (Sicherman, 189). Extending this framework, I have tracked how
Addams used the content and rhetorical stance of *Canon Barnett* as a model
for *My Friend, Julia Lathrop*.

Addams's reading of Barnett's book built on a gendered bond similar
to those grounded in Hull-House collaborations and, like the relationship
with Lathrop, enduring for many decades. Addams's relationship with Barnett had its seeds in the young American's early pilgrimages to Toynbee
Hall and her initial moves to envision a Chicago-based settlement inspired
by the London example.[40] Although the friendship began with Henrietta
Barnett very much a mentor, over time their connection became more

collegial, and in the later stages each of the two women repeatedly drew on the other for intellectual as well as emotional sustenance. This was a friendship—like so many others in Addams's life—both professional and personal. And one dimension of this sustained transatlantic networking (fed by visits back and forth and maintained through correspondence) rested in each woman's regularly reading and critiquing the other's writings in private communications and in published reviews. With these two friends holding major leadership positions in the best-known settlement houses within their respective nations, and with both regularly publishing accounts of their work, it was perhaps predictable that each would frequently reference the other's oeuvre. And, within this ongoing intertextual exchange, the parallels between *Canon Barnett* and *My Friend, Julia Lathrop* are especially notable.

Dame Henrietta's 1919 biography of Samuel Barnett predated Addams's account of Lathrop's life by more than a decade, but the two books clearly took on parallel rhetorical tasks. If the stance Barnett adopted to portray the relationship between herself and her husband had the effect of downplaying her own crucial leadership role at Toynbee, we might well speculate that she was taking a proverbial page from her friend Addams's 1910 *Twenty Years at Hull-House*. Further, between the initial publication of Addams's bestselling memoir and the early 1930s release of the Lathrop narrative, the American settlement leader had experienced a dramatic downturn in her reputation that her British counterpart had sought to mitigate through writing in Addams's defense. Specifically, Addams had gone from being renowned as a Progressive Era heroine to being vilified as a traitor to her country. That shift in the popular perception of Addams can be traced to her trip to The Hague as a peace movement supporter and an address that she gave in New York in 1915, where she cast World War I soldiers in the trenches as reluctant combatants.[41] This bold overstepping of feminine boundaries led, Sherry Shepler and Anne Mattina report, to a rash of verbal assaults in venues like the *New York Times*, countered by Henrietta Barnett's depiction of Addams in a number of published defenses, including within the *Canon Barnett* biography of Samuel.[42] Small wonder, then, that Addams provided emotional support during Barnett's initial widowhood and, after the release of *Canon Barnett*, helped promote the biography, even assisting with arrangements for Dame Henrietta's book-tour-type visit to the United States.

Ever the astute reader, Addams clearly appreciated the rhetorical sophistication of *Canon Barnett*. Addams was well aware of Dame Henrietta's significant influence on Toynbee and the larger settlement movement, as evidenced in the American woman's references to Henrietta in publications and in their private correspondence. But she also understood the British woman's choice to downplay her own role while highlighting her husband's. Indeed, this was the same strategy Addams had used over the years when writing about Hull-House. Thus, in reading Henrietta Barnett's account of her spouse as both a celebration of his life and a retrospective analysis of the project they had actually *co*-led, Addams would have recognized a viable strategy for conveying her ultimate vision of her Chicago settlement at the end of her career. Accordingly, echoing *Canon Barnett*, and in a more focused way than for her earlier *Twenty Years* memoir, *My Friend, Julia Lathrop* used story to show readers that the heart of the Hull-House program lay in interpersonal relationships, that those bonds enabled shared social action, and that there was still unfinished business from the settlement movement for readers to address.

My Friend Storytelling as Teaching Text

Despite an outpouring of celebratory occasions honoring Addams in the wake of her death, *My Friend, Julia Lathrop*, her last testament on Hull-House, did not garner the broad-based readership of the *Twenty Years* text. An unsigned June 1936 assessment of the later book in *Social Service Review*, the same periodical that had earlier published Addams's seed essay for the biography, may reveal why. While praising both Lathrop and Addams personally, the reviewer took Addams to task as a biographer:

> Miss Addams, by the fact of their mutual comfort and aid, on account of their united front against sloth and stupidity, by reason of their common objectives and their common will to press forward to their goals, naturally took Julia Lathrop more for granted than did others more remote from their friendship might be inclined to do. In her biography of Miss Lathrop, accordingly, we have the record of the woman—a thing of infinite value of course—but not the drama of the woman battling against vested interests, social indifference, and emotional lethargy.[43]

Rose C. Feld—who wrote regularly for the *New York Times*, *The New Yorker*, and the *Herald Tribune*—did offer a more appreciative view. Feld praised key features in the biography as I've interpreted it here, that is, as indicative of the settlement's shared values and of Addams's propensity for locating its story within networks of empathetic collaboration. Arguing that "[n]ever did a title more successfully give the essence of the contents of a book," Feld touted the narrative's focus on "the relationship of author to subject" and on "mutual labor in the same field of service." Feld shared several anecdotes from the biography to illustrate Addams's portrait of Lathrop's engaging wit; to underscore the author's linkage between Lathrop's model of "disinterested virtue" and their shared commitment to social justice; and to assert the important legacy both women had left behind. Feld opened her review by saying, "The last thing that Jane Addams did before her death was to write the final pages" of her book on Lathrop, and Feld's closing paragraph declares, "The world is a richer and better place for having held these two women." By framing her assessment of the book as an evaluation of both their lives, Feld invited her own readers to view this text as a record of collaborative endeavors in life and an admirable ongoing legacy ("Jane Addams, Wrote," BR 4).

Turning to the text itself, we can find multiple examples of how *My Friend, Julia Lathrop* purposefully performs a rhetorical double-duty: celebrating Lathrop while coupling her self-effacing version of leadership with Addams's, thereby providing an adaptable collaborative model. Repeatedly, *My Friend* depicts Lathrop's commitment to social justice through stories that illustrate what Addams dubs "disinterested virtue," or "the refusal to nurse a private destiny,'" and instead to cultivate "'a complete freedom from egocentric preoccupations'" (36). One compelling example—seen both in Lathrop's approach to leadership and Addams's mode of storytelling about it—depicts a shipboard intervention by Lathrop into the treatment of steerage-class passengers during a transatlantic voyage. This episode, appearing in both the original 1932 *Social Science Review* article ("A Great Public Servant") and in chapter 9 of the book, recounts how Lathrop advocated for the "many immigrants" on board a ship she and Addams were taking from France to the United States. The "coarse black bread which was given the immigrant passengers" three times a day "had become filled with green mould," and was therefore "unpalatable and probably dangerous" (104). Their pleas ignored by the captain, these fellow travelers found an ally in Lathrop, who "secured the promise from the Captain himself that fresh bread should be baked for the immigrants every day" (105).

As the memoir progresses, Addams's linkage of Lathrop's portrait with her other Hull-House compatriots establishes the individual biography as, actually, depicting the settlement community. For instance, in the chapter entitled "Friendship with Florence Kelley," Addams quotes at length from an article that "Julia Lathrop wrote for *The Survey* only a few weeks before her own death, revealing as to both of these good friends" (90). Utilizing letters that Lathrop had written to Kelley across multiple decades, Addams's citation of this article on Kelley prompts readers to see the Lathrop-Kelley intimate friendship's expressions of mutual support as a model of sustained collaboration. Addams directly alerts her readers that the *My Friend* reprinting of Lathrop's 1832 essay is intended to highlight both the designated subject—Kelley—and the original author—Lathrop—by saying that the text is about both "these two brilliant women" at once (90). Accordingly, when Addams presents Lathrop's assessment of Kelley—"always doing whatever came to her hand, studying, writing, teaching, speaking, always stimulating"—we should also see that Addams is bringing another self-presentation into play: her own. By casting Lathrop's account of Kelley as being, in fact, about both—"praising and stimulating others, asking nothing for herself"—Addams signals that her profile of Lathrop can be read as autobiography. Like her two Hull-House colleagues, Addams implicitly admits, she "gave herself" to "friends," so that each of the Hull-House women led "a nobly rich and generous life," exerting "influence" "far beyond her day" (92).

Along related lines, the final shared project Addams treats in the biography aptly exemplifies the Hull-House practice of accepting that some social justice work will likely go unfinished and will need to be taken up by others. In a chapter entitled "The Last Decade," *My Friend* describes Lathrop's campaign against capital punishment. Addams revisits Lathrop's support for Russell McWilliams, who had been condemned to electrocution for murder during a 1931 robbery. Addams's account of a conversation, during the "last time I saw Julia Lathrop," emphasizes her colleague's assertion that, by claiming it served as a deterrent, capital punishment advocates actually violated "the findings of science." Echoing Lathrop's point, Addams reiterates in her own voice that "the findings of scientific inquiries" refute such views (*My Friend*, 152).

Addams's wrap-up for the chapter then reports that, in April 1933, McWilliams's sentence was finally commuted to 99 years, "a year after Julia Lathrop's death . . . on April 15, 1932" (153)—illustrating how campaigns for social justice often seem to end, unfinished, but may eventually bear fruit. To underscore that many of the battles they had fought together would have to be won by later generations, Addams presents a Coda of published tributes to Lathrop. Addams notes that the last of these "emphasizes the pioneer aspect of her activities" (156). She compares Lathrop's leadership to women such as Anna Howard Shaw and Susan B. Anthony, who had passed on before achieving their generation's goals. And she calls on readers to become "a new race of pioneers" building on that example (156). Casting both Lathrop and Addams as leaders in their day (from "the gay nineties" through "fifty years" of "spiritual zeal that never flagged"), this accolade again yokes Lathrop's life with her biographer's and portrays both women as leaving work unfinished. Overall, Addams's closing commentary indicates that her own time is also drawing to a close, and that she, too, must look ahead to visionary heirs.

Sponsoring Immigrant Authorship

As noted above, the interactive relationship between Jane Addams's authorship and that of other well-educated middle-class women who lived at Hull-House and wrote about their experiences can be retraced by reading their publications intertextually. That process garners support from research documenting Addams's longstanding practice of learning from her peers, even as she influenced others as thinkers, activists, and writers.[44] Equally (if not more) important to this *Learning Legacies* project, though, is the increasing trend in scholarship to highlight how Addams supported the growth and agency of working-class women. As Maurice Hamington has noted in "Community Organizing," an essay in *Feminist Interpretations of Jane Addams*, there is still a need to remedy the tendency to depict Addams and Hull-House as "well meaning," yet "patronizing" in their interactions with working-class and immigrant community members (256). Hamington traces this stereotype to "blatant condescension and sexism" in views of Addams circulated by later male community organizers such as Saul Alinsky. Indeed, Hamington argues, to cast Hull-House and Addams in such terms misrepresents her approach, since "she vehemently contended that settlements were intended to facilitate education and connection, not charity" (263).

Aligned with Hamington's view, Karen Pastorello points to the example of Bessie Abramowitz Hillman, whose connection with "the community of women reformers at Chicago's premier settlement transformed" her from "novice working-class" political figure to skilled "labor leader" (98–99). Recalling that Abamowitz and other leaders of the strike against Hart, Schaffner, and Marx "affectionately began to refer to [Hull-House] as the 'House of Labor,'" Pastorello locates her recovery of Abramowitz's story in the context of a larger process. She critiques some historians' suggestions that all "middle-class 'allies' [of labor groups] were merely patronizing the so-called 'girls' as they pushed their own agendas," and insists such a stance did not apply at Hull-House (99). She relates Addams's more supportive position to work by Florence Kelley and Julia Lathrop in the Halsted Street neighborhood. Pastorello also spotlights such writings by Addams as "Trade Unions and Public Duty" and her facilitation of the Jane Club's founding to provide "cooperative living arrangements to young working women" (104) as forecasting the settlement leader's active support of Abramowitz during the 1910 strike. Pastorello even traces Abramowitz's later development as a pro-suffrage writer and speaker back to Addams's respectful tutelage: Abramowitz, Pastorello indicates, "modeled her skills after Addams, whose clear and confident public speaking demeanor often drew praise" (111). In all, Pastorello maintains, the relationship between Addams and Bessie Abramowitz Hillman should be viewed as exemplifying reciprocal, cross-class learning—a clear indicator that the Hull-House founding figure moved well beyond her initial naïve views about how to make the settlement a site of democratic energy.

Sadly, retrieval of what could be many individual archives growing out of such relationships is unlikely to yield a volume of text equivalent to that created by Hull-House women residents, whose enhanced access to advanced education and professional training gave them far greater ability to publish their writings. Much of the settlement-based authorship of women neighbors in Addams's day took on ephemeral forms, such as in performance pieces for the theater or compositions created in their evening classes. Fortunately, though, through the strong authorial identity of one such Hull-House student, further supported by her daughter's determined archival recovery, we have the so-far unique publication *I Came a Stranger: The Story of a Hull-House Girl*, by Hilda Satt Polacheck, edited by Dena J. Polacheck Epstein.

Polacheck's autobiography is doubly interesting as a learning legacy, for it retraces her personal growth from student to accomplished writer and offers up vivid examples of Addams's respectful teaching. As such, *I Came a Stranger* enacts a counter-narrative response to overgeneralized critiques of "benevolent" teaching interventions associated with Progressive Era settlements.[45] Hilda Satt (later Polacheck) offers up plenty of specific examples of Addams's attentive mentoring, which gradually but persistently led the young Russian Jewish immigrant to a new self-image, mainly by way of writing- and conversation-enhanced educational opportunities. After feeling trapped in the monotony of sweatshop labor sewing cuffs all day, at Hull-House Polacheck found that she "came in contact with people from all over the world" (89). For Hilda, Hull-House became an "Oasis in the Desert" (68) of urban life, as she studied poetry and Shakespeare with Harriet Monroe, worked at the Labor Museum, attended lectures by celebrity speakers, and dined at the coffee house (76, 69–70, 66). "For ten years," she reports, "I spent most of my evenings at Hull-House," and interactions with Addams were a highlight of that time. Addams, Polacheck avers, "was never condescending to anyone. She never made one feel that she was a 'lady bountiful.' She never made one feel that she was doling out charity. When she did something for you, you felt she owed it to you or that she was making a loan that you could pay back" (74–75).

In one anecdote, for example, Polacheck describes Addams's gentle but irresistible pressure to enroll in a new writing course being offered by Henry Porter Chandler. Though a timid Hilda demurs initially, saying "that I had never written anything," Addams insists, and Hilda begins a learning journey that becomes one of the major strands in her autobiography (77). Proudly presenting her first composition for this course ("The Ghetto Marker") in *I Came a Stranger*, Polacheck takes her own readers along through an empowering series of literacy sponsorship experiences facilitated by Addams. Thus, we see Hilda soon enrolling at the University of Chicago, with Addams having secured the funding to make this momentous event possible (87). Declares Polacheck, in retrospect: "That term at the University of Chicago opened a new life to me," as "reading the assigned books became a tonic to my soul," and honing her writing abilities prepared her for new opportunities at Hull-House (88). Then, in the summer after her magical, if relatively brief, time of university study, Polacheck finds herself teaching a Hull-House English class for other immigrants (89). Proud to report that, in later offerings, her "class was always crowded and the people seemed to make good progress," Polacheck is equally thrilled when Addams approvingly visits the class (91). Polacheck shares affirming memories of teaching, including having a Greek immigrant who had been a professor in his home country take her course, developing creative pedagogical techniques such as using the Declaration of Independence as an instructional text, and successfully preparing her pupils for the naturalization test (91).

Addams's mentoring of Hilda Satt Polacheck extended well beyond the Hull-House walls. Seeking ways to expand her own learning beyond that miracle university term Addams had made possible, Hilda later benefited from the settlement leader's "letter of introduction" that led to employment at "A. C. McClurg & Co., a publishing house and at the time the largest bookstore in Chicago" (93). Still devoting most evenings to Hull-House, Polacheck, with Addams's backing, soon organized a new "social and liter-ary" group, the Ariadne Club (94). Alternating social events like dancing one week with reading/writing activities the next, Ariadne Club members first generated a wide range of papers on a various social issues and then moved to sponsoring debates and the sharing of book reviews. Under the auspices of the club, Hilda recalls, she read *Uncle Tom's Cabin* and wrote a review that generated such intense responses during the group's discussion session that it spilled over into a second week. Before long, the club even branched out into producing plays, with Hilda enthusiastically immers-ing in yet another Hull-House-sponsored learning avenue that, she remi-nisces, was truly "a preparation for life" (95).

Polacheck's look back at the importance of the Hull-House theater takes on special resonance in the context of learning legacies because this connection provided yet another opportunity for her writing. Addams, in-viting Hilda to turn Leroy Scott's *The Walking Delegate* into a play, coupled that commission with advice on how to earn enough money with a summer waitress job that would allow plenty of off-duty time for working on the adaptation. Once Polacheck had prepared and revised the script under the guidance of the Hull-House Players' director, preparations for the perfor-mances began. Polacheck's pride in this occasion's significance—for herself and for Hull-House—is clear in her description of the audience's "shouts of 'Author!'" as "the curtain came down on the last act." Onstage in that self-affirming moment, "there I stood bowing, my heart just too full to say a word" (125–26).

Although the period of the play's production also marked the time when Hilda Satt married Bill Polacheck and moved to Milwaukee, this transi-tion did not end her commitment to authorship, so effectively nurtured by Addams and Hull-House already. As later sections of her autobiography recount, her married life incorporated writing in a range of public genres. These subsequent experiences included periodical publications such as her reviews of plays for the *Milwaukee Leader* and, in the 1930s, a series of texts for the WPA Folklore Project.[46]

Given her wide-ranging writing history, Hilda Polacheck was likely dis-appointed when she was unable to find a publisher for her autobiography. She left multiple versions of the narrative behind at the time of her death in 1967. In a rightful affirmation of the role Hull-House and Addams had played in her writing life, family members gathered to hold their memorial in what remained of the settlement's physical space, where they read excerpts from Hilda's manuscript to honor her. Dena J. Polacheck Epstein took up the task of editing the manuscript years later. Using diaries and letters, along with literary and historical sleuthing, Epstein prepared an edition that intermingles personal memory with thoughtful analysis. A crucial contribution to the Archive of Hull-House teaching, especially given its repeated validations of Addams's efforts to nurture public voices from those too often marginalized, *I Came a Stranger* calls upon readers to listen attentively to such stories. Though "unfinished" at the time of her death, Hilda Satt Polacheck's narrative—thanks to her daughter's dedicated cultural stewardship—now stands as a rich learning legacy in its own right.

Museum Enactments of Addams's Legacy

As the primary interlocutor of Hull-House's many programs, Jane Addams knew well that its work would always be "unfinished," calling for the kind of "scrupulous care" Alice Hamilton exercised as textual mediator for *My Friend, Julia Lathrop* (4). More recently, a parallel conviction that much of Addams's vision still remains to be addressed reemerged at the Hull-House Museum. If studying Addams's archive of writings has led me to reassert the relevance of the settlement's mission, much credit should go to the museum's educators during Lisa Lee's tenure.[47] Actively shaping exhibits and social programs, they also collaborated with communities beyond the landmark itself to reinvigorate its promotion of social justice. By reanimating Hull-House through what museum leaders Lee and Lisa Junkin Lopez termed "radical empathy,"[48] the network of cultural workers there crafted an active teaching site for civic engagement. In drawing on Hull-House's archive to guide their cultural interventions, the staff, under Lee's leadership, self-consciously demonstrated how aesthetic and political learning legacies can operate together—and how public scholarship can revitalize those stories.

Though I use past tense in this section of my chapter, I do not mean to imply that, since Lee's move to a different role at UIC, followed by Radke's and Junkin Lopez's relocations to different cities, the JAHHM has abandoned the principles these colleagues brought to the museum's work. Rather, I want to suggest that the *ethnographic moment* of my multiple visits to the site during Lee's tenure, and the specific conversations I held with staff members, represent a particular archive of social action. Such archives of collaborative practice are necessarily fluid—adaptable to shifting circumstances, such as a new museum director. Understandably, with different leadership now in place, adjustments in emphasis may occur, including some reflected in the disappearance of several texts from the museum's website as indicative of teaching practices during my on-site research. Perhaps, in a book exploring the seemingly stable archives held in facilities such as library collections, but also the more layered and evolving Archive of cultural resources around social agency, to bring two such bodies of material together in one chapter is quite appropriate. Like Addams, Lathrop, and Hamilton from earlier settlement days, Lee and her colleagues Lopez and Radke have left a written record of their own Hull-House practices, as well as material culture markers and conversational accounts of their engagement with the site. In doing so, these new archive-makers built a flexible foundation that others can now extend, continuing to address the ever-unfinished business of cross-cultural teaching.

Thus, my interpretation of a particular group of women museum leaders' counter-narratives, enacted over several years, also aligns with multiple texts from the larger settlement Archive. These include Addams's own published writings and personal artifacts, but also elements such as the built environment of Hull-House itself (in Addams's day and more recently); records of work by participants in the settlement's daily life (such as Edith de Nancrede, Ellen Gates Starr, and Julia Lathrop);[49] commentaries such as newspaper accounts and magazine features in Addams's day; and research by other scholars. My major sources for this analysis, however, are colleagues who worked in, and wrote about, the museum over several years of Lee's leadership.

Those dialogues confirmed that the JAHHM began a major renaissance under Lee's guidance, from 2006 to 2013, when she became director of UIC's School of Art and Art History. In this same period, Lisa Junkin Lopez served first as an education coordinator and, after Lee's shift in positions at UIC, as interim and then associate director, until moving on to the Juliette Gordon Low Birthplace in Savannah.[50] Exhibition coordinator Heather Radke, meanwhile, joined Lee and Lopez as team members whose generative interpersonal approach clearly echoed the feminist network of women from Hull-House's earlier days.[51] Radke's transition to MFA studies at Columbia University in New York in the fall of 2015 and her selection as a 2016–17 PAGE fellow for Imagining America echoed Florence Kelley's transition from the Chicago settlement to New York-based work in that previous generation. Overall, therefore, we could say that the twenty-first-century Hull-House network led by Lee followed the pattern of their predecessors, leaving unfinished business to do on Halsted Street but also useful roadmaps for others to follow. Likewise, as illustrated by Lopez's self-descriptions in an interview after her relocation to Savannah, the experiences these educators shared at the JAHHM have remained accessible to them individually as concepts guiding their current work, with Lopez's vision for new projects at the Low Birthplace (discussed in more detail in the Coda) being just one case in point.

Aiming for the kind of reading-to-listen that Dave Schaafsma, editor of *Jane Addams in the Classroom*, has identified as one of Addams's own goals,[52] I've repeatedly studied transcriptions of my interviews with these three staff members about their time at the JAHHM. I've drawn as well on published accounts by Lee, Lopez, and Radke, all of whom followed the lead of settlement women authors like Hamilton, Kelley, and Addams by writing about their social justice projects. My intertextual review of these museum educators' publications and their practices-in-action has revealed a productive interplay between Addams's strategies for settlement-based teaching and what Lee termed "a form of rhetorical pragmatic discourse" in JAHHM's work.[53]

Among all three of these creative cultural stewards, I've identified several interconnected curatorial approaches in line with Michel de Certeau's framework for purposeful use of available space—extending both storytelling and social action beyond the museum walls, partly by bringing *into* the JAHHM new voices, expressive acts, and shared activities. De Certeau's formulations for doing productive cultural work within constrained spaces are especially relevant here since, as noted above, the Hull-House of our own time operates in a far more limited physical space than the settlement had during its heyday. As de Certeau has noted in *The Practice of Everyday Life*, our available sites of social action are often constrained ones. At a literal/material level, the reduction of space represented in Hull-House's diminished physical presence at the edge of the UIC campus is one example. Still, following de Certeau, purposeful deployment of language can exercise a liberatory power. Thus, he argues, "ways of using the constraining order of the place" can emerge in our application of words or collaborative activities or even by adjusting a built environment like a street or classroom, allowing "users [to] carry out operations of their own," despite the constraints they face. Accordingly, "[w]ithout leaving the place where [they have] no choice but to live and which lays down its law," astute adapters of place generate "plurality and creativity." De Certeau explains that, through this artful manipulation—this purposeful "re-use" of any available room for maneuvering in tight quarters—creative practitioners of every-day life can produce "unexpected results" from an otherwise limiting situation (*Practice*, 30–31). In that context, with keen awareness of collaborative storytelling as a powerful strategy for countering these limits, Lee and her colleagues positioned their educational initiatives both within and beyond the current Hull-House site. This reclamation of place through strategic use of language at the museum reanimated Addams's original agenda to promote social justice.

The museum staff's arrangement of their physical workspace as it was organized during my first interview sessions there in July 2012 embodied their commitment to enacting Addams-informed collaboration through management of physical and discursive space. Perched in a shared office on the second floor of the restored Hull-House dining hall, the team's cluster of desks formed a circle for conversational planning. Although then-director Lee's small office was set just to the side of this main beehive of activity, she clearly had an open-door approach. Later, through their interview comments' echoes of each other, the group repeatedly demonstrated how their ongoing dialogue mined archive-based resources for JAHHM's execution of its mission. That is, in conversations reminiscent of those Addams, Lathrop, and Hamilton revisited in the *My Friend* text, this new cluster of Hull-House women was similarly using dialogue to enact and critique their shared praxis.

Consistent with trends in many heritage museums today, the JAHHM under Lee shifted its emphasis from memorializing to community engagement through shared curation. This vision had a sustained impact on everything from topics addressed to the rhetorical pragmatism the museum used to document its work. To capitalize on Addams's narrative heritage, JAHHM staff purposefully invoked her language to characterize their practices. Therefore, staff members reported, the mission under Lee's guidance involved reconnecting with the "Unfinished Business" of the settlement, affirming its interpersonal dimensions of knowledge-making, and using storytelling as both art and social intervention.

A recurring theme under Lee's directorship, "Unfinished Business" was articulated rhetorically in exhibits and in staff members' written reports about their work. So, for instance, in an interview describing her role as an exhibition coordinator, Radke referenced an "Unfinished Business" project on arts education to exemplify the museum's commitment "to link the history of Hull-House and the history of the Progressive Era with contemporary issues." Radke further described the exhibit as "an advocacy piece," encouraging visitors to go beyond "learn[ing] the history and what's happening today in a particular subject area" to embracing "an opportunity for engagement and activism around that" (Radke interview).

Similarly, in their essay for the Schaafsma-edited *JAC* collection, Lee and Lopez reiterated the team's commitment to "Addams's most fundamental educational beliefs about the impact of culture in the practice of democracy and furthering social change" ("Participating," 175). Lee and Lopez directly echoed Radke's explanation of the "rotating exhibition space" as "devoted to making connections between Hull-House history and contemporary issues while also seeking to unleash our radical imaginations about our collective futures." Intended to honor ways that "much progress has been made on the issues that Jane Addams and the reformers cared about," they noted, these projects also underscored how "there is still more to accomplish," since "the work of creating a more just society continues" (175). For Lee and Lopez, this stance required the museum team to embrace the concept of cultural institutions as "permanently impermanent" ("Participating," 170).

One example of this principle emerged in a collaboration between the Tamms Year Ten program and the JAHHM to engage museum visitors as supporters of prisoners in solitary confinement.[54] When asked how people outside prison walls could provide solidarity-oriented support, one suggestion prisoners made was to *send poems*. In response, by setting up a writing station at Hull-House, the JAHHM generated postcard poems from over five thousand museum visitors in 2011–12—a vibrant example of "radical empathy" linked to Hull-House's legacy. As Lee and Lopez noted, this strategy engaged visitors through "observation, empathy, critical thinking, and participation." Such projects affirmed "the possibility to participate in history, rather than simply be subject to it," as visitors became "part of the making of a better world" ("Participating," 177).

Radke's leadership in development of another "Unfinished Business" project—on "21st-Century Home Economics"—led to a Brooking Prize from the American Alliance of Museums. In an essay about that exhibition's execution, Radke explained how interdisciplinary inquiry into historical archives can focus as much on absence as on presence—and how critical engagement with a legacy from the past can both deepen our understanding of history and open up possibilities for social action today:

> "Unfinished Business: 21st Century Home Economics" . . . transformed a historic house museum into a vibrant space of inquiry about a pressing contemporary issue, while simultaneously maintaining a

commitment to transformation of the visitor, the community, the nature of an exhibition and institutional structures. This exhibition challenged our most basic conceptions about museum practices, including those around curatorial authority, how to write an effective object label and what makes for a relevant, resonant artifact. It also expanded the horizon of our imaginations and aspirations for the potential impact of an exhibition on social change. (Radke, "Unfinished Business/Economics")

As Radke indicated, research behind this exhibit included rethinking domestic labor's role in the original settlement. Specifically, the museum staff realized, the leadership of women like Alice Hamilton, Florence Kelly, and Ellen Gates Starr has long been celebrated. But who was doing the household chores that enabled those well-educated and privileged women to become social leaders? To make the contributions of housekeeper Mary Keyser visible, the JAHHM exhibit emphasized elements in the Hull-House story too long under-acknowledged. In Radke's words:

Until her death, Keyser ran the household . . . so that other residents could do a wide range of work that made Hull-House a crucial space for democracy. Keyser also actively participated in helping to organize other domestic workers as the head of the Labor Bureau for Women, working as both a domestic servant and social reformer. She made crucial connections in the neighborhood surrounding Hull-House, and brought her knowledge of the needs and lives of the immigrant neighbors into the settlement house project. She was so beloved by the community that upon her death, her obituary ran in several newspapers and hundreds of people attended her funeral. (Radke, "Unfinished Business")

By spotlighting Keyser, "21st-century Home Economics" extended the historical record of women's work at Hull-House during Addams's day. Keyser's contributions to the Hull-House enterprise were different than those of the residents, a number of whom held jobs off-site during the day and gave time to settlement programs at night—perhaps by teaching classes or supporting clubs—in exchange for room, board, and the chance to participate in an innovative experiment. This exhibit's recuperation of Keyser's legacy affirmed the settlement's practice of enabling a range of collaborative connections to its work, all valuable, if in different ways.

Cultivating Collaboration

Like the "Unfinished Business" of revisiting Hull-House's learning legacies through a critical lens, a related agenda of the museum leaders I interviewed blended curatorial vision with collaborative social action, as in
the Tamms Year Ten project referenced above. Along related lines, for the
home economics project, the JAHHM partnered with the Chicago Coalition for Household Workers to investigate issues associated with domestic
work today and to promote solidarity and activism.

Still, as Radke acknowledged in her Brooking-award essay, establishing a meaningful collaboration through community curation—a growing
trend in the cultural work of museums[55]—can itself be challenging. "One
difficulty that can come from community curation," she noted, "is a false
sense of reciprocity." While community members' contributions to a particular exhibit—whether personal artifacts or commentary—can give a
museum's presentation a heightened sense of authenticity, ethical practice
requires the institution to ask what community partners actually gain from
their involvement. As Radke observed: "The process can feel like the re-
inscription of a colonialist project of plundering artifacts from a community group so that the museum can display them safely within the sanitized
gallery space" ("Unfinished Business"). Decontextualized from actual lived
experience, stories presented by community partners may seem more like
tokenism than a true partnership.

One resource the Lee-led JAHHM educators used as a model for cultivating reciprocal partnerships was the Hull-House Labor Museum's
engagement with community members during Addams's time. That turn-
of-the-century program was popular with both middle-class visitors and
Hull-House neighbors serving as what we'd call community curators today.
However, as Lee and Lopez reported in their "Participating in History" essay for *Jane Addams in the Classroom*, some scholars have raised questions
about the degree to which the Labor Museum was coopting the experiences of workers for displays that may have honored their skill at crafts
but admittedly did not lead to radical changes in the often-demoralizing
factory labor at the time. Nonetheless, Lee and Lopez maintained, the Labor Museum enacted cross-class collaborations meriting our attention. For
one thing, as they indicated in their review of Hilda Satt Polacheck's autobiography, the Labor Museum helped some participants view their own
daily work more positively. Setting factory labor within a longer history,
the Labor Museum invited participants (visitors and community curators

alike) to make connections between the tasks of daily industry and a craft heritage.[56] For another, Lee and Lopez suggested, although today we might undervalue the Labor Museum's affiliation with the Arts and Crafts Movement, for Addams and other settlement leaders—both at Hull-House and at its model Toynbee Hall in London—access to artistic production and appreciation was a right as worthy of advocacy as political action.[57] Thus, rather than oversimplifying the recruitment of community docents for the Labor Museum then (or the 21st-Century Home Economics exhibit more recently) as patronizing, we should recognize that such partnerships can be both ethical and enabling, with shared cultural rights being honored on a par with (and potentially even contributing to) political rights.[58] Along those lines, Lee and Lopez have advocated viewing the Labor Museum within a larger context of arts-based learning at Hull-House to make the case for both programs as inclusive and empowering: "Through the Labor Museum and art classes, Hull-House encouraged all people to see themselves as creative and emotive beings and to claim their right to such notions as beauty and truth" (170).

Another rhetorical space Lee's team utilized to embody this stance was the World Wide Web. Over several years of research, I noted how web-based stories about exhibits and programming enabled off-site access to the museum's cultural work. "Check It Out," for instance, a story on the arts lending program, displayed an online description of that initiative, including images of art works that could be borrowed from the museum for three months at a time, through a partnership with Threewalls art center in Chicago. By scrolling through images of art available for checkout, a website visitor could imaginatively associate with the original conception of this project—potentially making a connection between these objects becoming accessible online now and the efforts of the settlement's Butler Art Gallery (like the Hull-House theater) to locate aesthetic activity within a democratic, broadly accessible space.

So, too, even after the "21st-Century Home Economics" exhibit ended its run at the museum, it had a digital afterlife through a YouTube video, including images of the original exhibit and an explanation of its goals. Also on this page, web visitors could find an audiotape commentary from "Julia O'Grady, a food service worker at the Academy for Global Citizenship, a charter school on Chicago's southwest side dedicated to a dynamic food curriculum and healthy cafeteria food for all students." Explaining to listeners that "I don't like when people call me a 'lunch lady'" rather than the more appropriate title of "lunchroom manager," O'Grady's renaming of her own social position reinforced the original exhibit's incorporation of marginalized voices into curatorial conversations.[59] As such, her brief but engaging audio story reasserted the museum's commitment to multivocal storytelling enabled by community curation.

Hull-House-affiliated programs, both in Addams's era and under Lee's mentoring, created opportunities for new voices telling stories to broader audiences. In that context, web-based exhibitions sponsored by the museum applied de Certeau's call for creative resistance against spatial constraints—in this case, the limited ability of any museum to have people visit a site in person. And "Look at It This Way," an online-only exhibit created by students enrolled in a fall 2013 UIC course entitled "Collecting from the Margins," exemplified another advantage of digital curation: providing extra space for display of artifacts along with interpretive context. These students, in fact, were empowered to address questions long reserved only for museum managers: "What makes an object an artifact? Why do we save some things and not others? What can we learn from the things we save?"[60] In response, they created labels (in museum parlance) for such artifacts as a copy of a George Eliot novel (*Romola*) frequently studied in a Hull-House book club and a milk bottle evoking the settlement's campaigns for food safety.

Overall, JAHHM's ongoing use of digitization for teaching reinforced the settlement's original commitment to democratizing knowledge. Like the Labor Museum and the Hull-House theater in Addams's day, and in line with her writing for popular venues, the museum's development of online resources affirmed Hull-House's vision of education as a public act expanding networks of engagement. Thus, though not every online "story" of community curation that I've reviewed remains available through the JAHHM's website, a number of these collaborations have left other public traces through partners' online records, thereby illustrating how even the most tenuous of archives may sometimes have compelling afterlives.[61]

Closely aligned with the museum's collaborative methodology under Lee was a goal of cultivating conviviality and hospitality reminiscent of Addams's own stance at Hull-House. As Lopez explained in one of our conversations, JAHHM staff sought to "open the doors" to grassroots organizations (Lopez, "Interview," 2012). For example, one partnership revitalized the settlement's longstanding work around "Unfinished Business–Juvenile Justice." This project accentuated connections between Hull-House's leadership in the founding of the nation's first juvenile court in 1899 (which Addams chronicled in chapter 9 of *My Friend, Julia Lath-*

rop) and the museum's commitment to juvenile justice and prison reform today. This exhibit fostered new dialogues on site, and the partnership also reached into the community in locations such as the Chicago Freedom School. The extra-museum activities were both socially and artistically generative, as seen in an e-zine graphic narrative series representing girls' experiences within the juvenile justice system today.[62] This project invited readers' empathetic identification with the authors, thereby merging art with community-building.

Interestingly, UIC itself has been tapping into the settlement's historical legacy as well. For example, like the Hull-House-affiliated labor organizers of the settlement era, in 2013 the lowest-paid workers at UIC garnered support for a unionizing movement by involving faculty. When over a year passed without a contract negotiated, where did the leaders of this campaign gather to strategize? As Deanna Issacs reported in an online essay for *Chicago Reader*: "in the campus's historic Hull-House Residents' Dining Hall, where the spirit of Jane Addams is as palpable as the wood-paneled walls, the union held a half-day teach-in. The standing-room-only crowd got a crash course on labor activism, along with a free lunch of homemade soup and bread" ("Crunch Time"). And in spring 2014, when full-time faculty at UIC joined the campaign to raise the pay for adjuncts, the Hull-House dining room served as a meeting place. In fostering intellectual, affective, and political solidarity, these gatherings reaffirmed the settlement's original aspirations for labor equity. More broadly, by opening its spaces to dialogue and collaboration, the museum affiliated with the original settlement's commitment to community connections.

Reanimating Hull-House's Stories

Though Lee is no longer directly responsible for guiding the museum, her written accounts of JAHHM teaching remain a valuable archive for others seeking to do similar cultural work. Along with scholarly stories on curation by Radke and Lopez, Lee's narratives of practice echo Addams's own writings and add to the settlement's Archive. An example relevant to this study's focus on using story to theorize, Lee's "Peering into the Bedroom" essay reflects on decision-making behind two pivotal exhibits. One of these highlighted the portrait of Mary Rozet Smith along with a participatory space for visitors to propose and counter-propose labeling to best represent Addams's relationship with Smith. Although their partnership has often been downplayed—sometimes even suppressed—in histories of

Addams and Hull-House, Lee's counter-narrative argues that encouraging guests to address different possibilities for explicating their bond renders museum practice itself into a participatory ethics. Our own moment carries reminders that terms for describing a life partnership like Addams and Smith cultivated, as well as socially sanctioned avenues for expressing their relationship in public, were often limited in their day.[63] So, Lee's essay asks, how can a cultural steward like the JAHHM convey the centrality of their connection in Addams's lifetime, an era far removed from contexts such as the recent US Supreme Court decision on gay marriage? By inviting visitors to address such questions, Lee notes, a multivocal labeling exercise also raised questions about responsible truth-telling, including what the International Coalition of Sites of Conscience terms "restorative truth" (176). For Lee, a tool for confronting such issues resides in the archive: "Drawing inspiration from the history" of the settlement, "where dialogue, dissent and discussion fostered a participatory democracy," she avers, this alternative labeling exhibit "address[ed] visitors as citizens engaged in the process of creating meaning" (180).

Similarly, in describing the staff's plans for an exhibit of Addams's bedroom—including mounting Smith's portrait on the wall where it hung during their lifetimes—Lee calls for resisting "the bonds of normative distinctions between the private and the public" (182) while honoring Addams's efforts toward "making the world more just" (184). In explaining curatorial choices she admits could meet with public resistance, Lee affiliates with the tactic of *Jane Addams in the Classroom* by wondering: "What would Jane do?" In both cases, we see the empowering efficacy of using principles derived from Addams's own archive as ethical guides for public work today.

So, too, in "Hungry for Peace," Lee invokes Hull-House's history of activism to tell a story of "the literal and metaphorical ways that bread manifests itself in different aspects of Jane Addams's life and work." The particular public program that Lee revisits in this account is "Re-thinking Soup," "a modern day soup kitchen, democratic forum, laboratory space, and museum exhibit" that attracted participants to the dining hall once a week to share food and learning.[64] Like the original settlement residents, Lee says, those attending "Re-thinking Soup" programs enjoyed "a collective dining experience that [fed] people's minds and bellies as well as their hunger for community" (63). Given this learning legacy, it is fitting that the restored dining room is one of only two structures now in place from the previously extensive complex of buildings on Halsted Street.

After all, shared foodways played a central part at Hull-House in Ad-

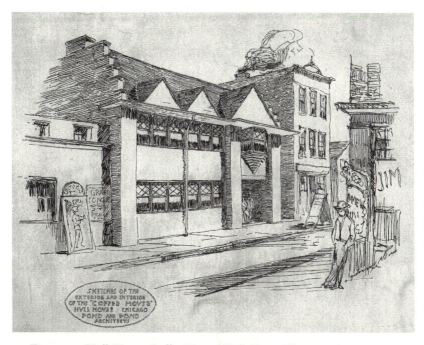

Figure 3.3. Hull-House Coffee House. Hull-House Photograph Collection. JAMC 0000 0138 0608. Courtesy of the University of Illinois at Chicago, Richard J. Daley Library Special Collections and University Archives.

dams's day. In line with that tradition, during Lee's tenure the museum staff utilized the dining room as a staging area for multiple programs (including "Re-thinking Soup") consistent with the settlement's conjoining of physical and moral sustenance. For example, during my July 2012 visit, a group of K-12 educators attended an early evening dialogue. After discussing photographs suggestive of a range of social issues, these visitors enjoyed a meal prepared in JAHMM's kitchen. As the group discussed social justice issues like those Hull-House residents explored at their own group meals, echoes of earlier dialogues reverberated through the wood-paneled hall.[65] With fresh loaves at their tables linking sociable dining and productive dialogue, this meal alerted all of us to a metaphor recurring throughout Addams's archive: bread as communally significant and figurative "bread-giving" education as cultural work.

In that vein, Lee's "Hungry for Peace" essay underscores her embrace of Addams's storytelling approach to explicating pedagogical practice. This essay's account of the launch of the settlement's Coffee House in July of 1893 is a case in point.

To convey the philosophy behind the Coffee House, Lee (channeling Addams's writing method) shares an anecdote:

> Addams borrowed the money from Mary Rozet Smith's father to start the Hull-House Coffee House. . . . Julia Lathrop, a Hull-House resident . . . , oversaw it. In addition to being one of the foremost advocates for the health and well-being of mothers and children, and becoming the first head of the Children's Bureau in 1912, Lathrop was also known as a fabulous cook who made delicious omelets and brown butter oysters at midnight for the other residents. (70–71)

Like Addams in *Twenty Years*, *My Friend, Julia Lathrop*, and so many other texts, Lee begins with narrative detail that helps readers see the actual day-to-day work of the Coffee House first. Meantime, Lee adds clarifying brushstrokes to her portrait of Lathrop—whom she has cast as both an administrator of unusual skill and a "fabulous cook"—to show how the invitational stance of sharing food represented a larger social value system of communal knowledge-making. Lee argues that the Coffee House marked a crucial shift away from earlier approaches the settlement had tried for "changing the food habits of immigrants and the working class." Through "the Diet Kitchen and New England Kitchen (NEK)" earlier in the decade, Lee suggests, the settlement had mistakenly tried to persuade neighbors to "give up avgolemono, pierogi, or ciabatta for flax seed tea, corn starch gruel, mutton broth or Case's health bread," items that came out of a home economics movement (69). In shifting to hospitality and shared dining through the Coffee House, "The goal became providing wholesome, hot food to people who lived under conditions where cooking was out of the question," such as "nearby tenement house dwellers, who might be living without running water and/or heat." Other patrons, Lee notes, were "the Hull-House Residents who were engaged in the democratic experiment of communal and collective living" (71). Open daily "from six in the morning until 10 at night," as Lee documents by way of an ad from the Hull-House archive, the Coffee House embodied "artful" collaboration in a "cozy space where people dined, communed, nourished, and sustained themselves and each other" (71–72).

Lee's story ably adopts Addams's narrate-to-theorize method for elucidating the settlement to external audiences. Through that approach,

"Hungry for Peace" also enacts a compelling example of moving from archive to action today. Describing "Re-thinking Soup" as grounded in study of the Hull-House Coffee House, Lee's look back at the museum staff's progression from scholarly retrieval of Addams's model to creation of a current-day program serves up an adaptable civic engagement recipe:

> When we decided to re-open the kitchen and the Residents' Dining Hall in the Jane Addams Hull-House Museum in 2008, we drew upon the "domestic revolution" begun by Progressive Era reformers, re-interpreted for our own day. We started to sift through special collection folders about the kitchen and Coffee House and were inspired by an advertisement for a coffee, bread, and soup program offered by Hull-House to local factory workers. . . . We decided to start a modern-day soup kitchen in the Residents' Dining Hall. (74)

Lee recounts how the dining hall had originally welcomed such diverse visitors as "Susan B. Anthony, Ida B. Wells Barnett, W. E. B. Du Bois, [and] Eleanor Roosevelt." Thus, she places her own readers in the historical space where "they met to share meals and ideals, debate one another, and conspire to change the world." For instance, she recalls, "Upton Sinclair came to eat supper every night at Hull-House while he was writing *The Jungle*" (74). Such images prompt readers to participate imaginatively in the rich conversations that must have gone on at his table every evening. Through these anecdotes, Lee prepares her current-day audience to appreciate the museum's "Re-thinking Soup" program, which entailed "a series of community conversations on contemporary issues" including addressing "food as a social issue."

For "Re-thinking" attendees, Lee's story shows, "Hull-House history" became "a point of departure" for engaging such current issues as "women's rights, labor, [and] poverty" (75). Further, for those reading now, narration blended with analysis enables a form of indirect participation, just as the audiences Addams herself cultivated in her own "popularizing" stories could imaginatively come to the settlement through her texts. Using story to depict and explicate cross-cultural teaching practices, both Addams and Lee encourage what I call *participatory reading*.[66] That is, both writers use story to bring readers into the lived experience of Hull-House collaboration. They ask readers to pay attention to narrative illustration as an entryway into theory that affirms inclusive community welfare over individual credit-seeking.

Figure 3.4. Hull-House Dining Room (with Jane Addams far right, top table). Hull-House Photograph Collection. JAMC 0000 0310 0445. Courtesy of the University of Illinois at Chicago, Richard J. Daley Library Special Collections and University Archives.

Just so, across the pages of *My Friend*, Addams marshals narrative examples of Lathrop's "disinterested virtue" to support her own contention that this trait enabled her friend to achieve a communal moral sense—an empathy free of egoism (36). Addams repeatedly returns to this idea, underscoring specific examples of Lathrop's ceding credit to others for "accomplishments she herself inspired" (45) and giving generously of her time to social groups like Hull-House's Everyday Club of "forty civic minded women" who met regularly to strategize approaches for addressing public issues (118).[67] As readers, then, we come to view "disinterested virtue" as a life goal through imaginative participation with these anecdotal illustrations more than through abstract theorizing.

A "Sex in the Museum" essay by Lisa Junkin Lopez, Lee's museum colleague, invites a similar stance of participatory reading—in this case linked to storytelling carried out *along with* a too-often-excluded counterpublic. By taking readers along through narrative to revisit a Sex Positive Documentary Film Series, Lopez, like Lee, stresses their shared commitment "to reframe our understanding of the relationship between historic house museums and the public" (137). She characterizes this project as bringing "diverse communities into conversation and collective action" around a controversial subject. She admits that, in a parallel to scholars' and teachers' hesitancy to address Addams's own deeply significant same-sex relationships, "Counterpublics are rarely considered to be legitimate audiences by museums and other institutions, and so their needs largely go ignored. This means that museums, as so-called neutral institutions and agents of 'truth' are often complicit in marginalizing the very publics they should be serving" (141). Resisting such limits on their spaces and programs, Lopez argues, today's museums should tell previously suppressed stories and welcome more diverse narrators into their spheres of action. This cause, she says, should be a self-conscious goal of the JAHHM, which "centers its values within the legacy of our site" (143).

To embrace this mandate, as this story of the Sex Positive project shows, entails challenges—including the need to avoid an uncritical stance toward Addams herself. In other words, just as Addams determinedly opened the doors of Hull-House to immigrant neighbors' visits, and just as she boldly welcomed widely divergent political views in settlement-sponsored political debate, so, too, should today's stewards of that learning legacy open up examination of Addams and her era to topics even she was un-ready to address. Therefore, the documentary series presented during the "Sex in the Museum" project considered how and why Addams's most profound personal relationships have often been veiled in treatments of her life. But this project also invited critique of the Hull-House founder's own staunchly conservative positions around topics such as prostitution (articulated in *A New Conscience and an Ancient Evil*), as opposed to the sex positive movement's recognition that, for some, sex work can be a valid choice (143). Therefore, Junkin [Lopez]'s narrative itself invites us to see how fully applying Addams's vision can create "a more inclusive, more relevant and just museum" (147).[68]

Through participatory critical reading of the Hull-House Archive like Lee's and Lopez's writing advocates, we can take real steps toward social action. And, if we also adopt the stance of "disinterested virtue" Addams herself attributed to her friend Lathrop (*My Friend*, 36), we may, like those two self-effacing women leaders, achieve a genuine "capacity [for] humaniz[ing] every social situation" (*My Friend*, 118).

Storytelling for *Jane Addams in the Classroom*

In a knowledge-making endeavor grounded in shared reflection, a group of colleagues affiliated with UIC's English Education program carried out an Addams-inspired collaboration in line with JAHHM's approaches. Through reading, writing, and research on their own teaching as seen through an Addams-oriented lens, this team, led by professors David Schaafsma and Todd DeStigter, has reconfirmed how vital her legacy can be to teachers today. Indeed, one key element of *Jane Addams in the Classroom* has been to reclaim, for Addams herself, a leadership role as an educator and pedagogical theorist. Noted DeStigter in an interview:

> It's no exaggeration to say that my "take away" from this project is that I think Jane has a more nuanced understanding of what it means to work for social justice and democracy than any theorist or activist I've ever read. Why? Because her philosophical understanding of the work she was doing was deliberately shaped by experience. Even John Dewey—as brilliant as he was—never came close to the level of day-to-day engagement with people and problems as Jane did. Her work is, quite literally, the best example of praxis I know. (DeStigter, "Interview")

For DeStigter, the value of Addams's learning legacy is also tied up with her commitment to social action. "She has renewed my faith in American pragmatism and progressivism," he explained. Unlike "current educational policies . . . driven by classical liberalism's emphasis on individualism and competition and by neoliberalism's application of the logic of the marketplace to all aspects of human interaction (including education)," DeStigter maintained, "Jane was different." Addams, in DeStigter's view, realized that "in order to understand problems and ameliorate them, you have to operate across a huge range of human interactions. You have to cultivate face-to-face relationships with people, listen to them, enter into reciprocal understandings and courses of action with them." But, he noted, Addams cultivated such collaborations while also "operat[ing] at a political and economic level" (DeStigter, "Interview").

Schaafsma made a similar case for Addams in a separate interview:

> I came actually to think of Jane as a better theorist of progressive practice than Dewey. It might have something to do with the fact

that Dewey's a philosopher and writes like a philosopher. There are whole sections of books that Dewey's written that nobody talks about really. The long working out of an argument the way that a philosopher does.

For Schaafsma, in fact, one insight that emerged through multi-year collaborative study of Addams was a deep appreciation for her writing—its accessibility for today's teachers, but also its relevance, achieved through her use of story:

> [H]er way of coming to an issue through story immediately appealed to me. English educators are story lovers and storytellers by and large. When I wrote my dissertation, I did not call it narrative inquiry. . . . I didn't have a niche to put it in. We called it ethnography. Technically speaking, it wasn't really. Todd DeStigter wrote *Citizen Teacher*, called it an ethnography. . . . But these are stories about the classroom and educational practice that imbed theory into the stories. And I thought that's the thing she does so well is "story" ideas. In a way that makes them understandable, possible, portable. I thought people need to know about this. (Schaafsma, "Interview")[69]

Intriguingly, however, as DeStigter and Schaafsma have reported, both in their interviews with me and in their book's "Introduction" (2–3), they came to collaborative work on Addams in part by an accident of place. Teaching in the English Department at UIC, with the Hull-House Museum nearby, they nonetheless were only loosely familiar with Addams's career until Todd happened upon a flyer for a talk biographer Jean Bethke Elshtain was giving on campus. Having attended, he began to colead a reading group with Schaafsma, exploring the settlement educator's own writings. They started with an eclectic cluster of graduate students "who were eager to engage in conversations about how Addams's life and work illustrate and advance some of [their] priorities as teachers" ("Introduction," 3). This group—a fitting echo of the reading clubs Hull-House itself had sponsored—eventually inspired a graduate course taught by Dave. Later, adding new essays to extensions of several papers originally produced for that class, *Jane Addams in the Classroom* evolved as a communal publication. One strength of the collection is the institutional border-crossing represented by its contributors' list, which includes two of the Hull-House Museum's educators (Lee and Lopez), a previous manager of the Jane Addams Children's Book Award (Susan C. Griffith), and scholars of narrative inquiry (Ruth Vinz of Teachers College, Columbia University, and Petra Hendry of Louisiana State University).

The core of the book is the learning site designated within its title—the classroom. In stories reminiscent of Addams's own rhetoric, the coauthors take readers inside today's diverse classroom communities. Following Addams's lead—as seen in their repeated engagement with her publications—the contributors offer more than teacher-voiced action research (though this, too, is a valuable contribution): they also exemplify the power of linking a rich humanistic archive to pragmatic pedagogical storytelling.

Professional connections with Dave and Todd through the Joint Program in English and Education at the University of Michigan provided me with a window into their multiyear writing project. While Dave preceded my time in the doctoral program, Todd's enrollment there overlapped with mine. Interestingly, however, even though all three of us share histories in K-12 school teaching, as well as post-doc work in teacher education through national-level grants, we had never worked together on Addams. Dave and Todd knew of my long interest in Hull-House, though, and they had recommended my previous work on Addams to their doctoral students. When initially envisioning their book, they approached me about contributing. Though I was overcommitted to other projects, I sought regular updates. And once I began *Learning Legacies*, I reached out to get a fuller picture of their progress. Within those conversations I found another sign of how Addams's archive could drive significant social action today.

What fascinated me, early on, was the group's genuinely communal method of knowledge-making, which embraced both the spirit of Addams's educational practice and her narrative rhetoric. Having participated in several collaborative writing experiences with K-12 teachers in the past,[70] I was aware of such benefits as exchanging drafts and staging presentation occasions to spur texts along. But what seemed unique about this collaboration was its self-conscious engagement with the content of a particular archive—Addams's learning legacy—as a path to public writing.

To illustrate, let me cite the "'To Learn from Life Itself'" essay by Bridget O'Rourke, associate professor at Elmhurst College, outside Chicago. Her argument affirms a theme that has run throughout this chapter, indeed this book—that boundary-crossing work done in the past has left a learning legacy held in cultural memory, available for transformative use today. Thus, O'Rourke declares: "Jane Addams insisted that . . . institutional accomplishments did not define the settlement's mission. Addams came to define the value of the settlement in terms of the form of its activities—the ongoing expression of a reciprocal social relationship." So, O'Rourke asserts: "Addams was less concerned with the settlement's success at having achieved a predetermined end (such as economic unity) than the character of its activity, the collaborative process of its making and remaking that gave rise to diverse and unpredictable forms of expression" ("To Learn," 33). O'Rourke places Addams's commitment to community-building in dialogue with current emphases on university-community partnerships, bringing to the analysis a cautious optimism that nonetheless avoids easy conflations between the history of Hull-House and today's civic engagement agendas. Her organizational sequence of starting with a description of the settlement's practice and then shifting to potential applications envisions, on the surface, a seemingly straightforward progression from archive to social action. But the careful interrogation of Addams's ideas in the essay's closing pages, where O'Rourke emphasizes ways in which Hull-House "put knowledge at the service of the community" rather than exploiting partners as sources of data (40), achieves a nuanced application of *JAC*'s repeated question: what *would* Jane do? Stressing that a worthy enactment of Addams's legacy would aim at "transforming the conflicts and mistakes of the past into *meaningful collective action*" (41, emphasis mine), O'Rourke echoes Addams's own calls for *shared* learning toward democratic ideals. With O'Rourke's deft guidance, we are drawn into a participatory reading of the *JAC* collection as attempting a "reciprocal social relationship."

As O'Rourke suggests, the particular classroom-based projects revisited in *JAC* explicitly affiliate with Addams's praxis. Furthermore, the group's shared writing process and the narrative mode they employ also follow her lead. Collection editor Schaafsma has freely admitted that such collaborative projects, appropriate as they are for responding to the settlement's knowledge-making role model, do not carry the same cachet in academic circles as the monograph genre—even though anyone who has shepherded such a publication to fruition will testify that the process can be as complex and challenging as writing "alone." Yet, Schaafsma also opines, a collection, assembling a wide range of voices and perspectives, "It's what Jane would have done" ("Interview"). If such an assertion seems, at first, to ignore Addams's own success as writer of many single-author books, it nonetheless rightly affiliates the *JAC* project with the overarching commitment she made to collaboration, with the pluralistic rhetorical methods adopted even in her sole-author narratives, and with the many other publications and productions (such as the settlement's theatrical events) that affirmed shared composing as essential.

As *Jane Addams in the Classroom* demonstrates via its diverse list of contributors and the varying, yet cohesive, ways in which they applied their study of Addams's own work, her stories of settlement-based learning can helpfully guide the daily intercultural work of teachers now. Schaafsma and DeStigter themselves observe, "We see the legacy of Addams for education not only in the things that she says directly about her schooling; her value to us as educators lies also in the example she set through her actions at Hull-House and in the disposition that inclined and enabled her to enter into new modes of fellowship and action with other people" ("Introduction," 3). In this regard, it's worth noting that, too often these days, teachers themselves are being cast as "Others" and classrooms as colonized spaces governed by forces ranging from the standardized testing industry to political figures eager to point fingers at educators, as if such large-scale problems as economic disparity, racism, and learning achievement gaps were somehow the fault of, rather than social challenges being faced by, schools and colleges.[71] In coming together to create *JAC*, the contributors drew strength from their sustained engagement with Addams's writing—generating intellectual energy and a mutual theoretical vision for dealing with constraints. Consistent with de Certeau's mandate for managing what he calls "the practice of everyday life" (de Certeau, *Practice*, title/cover), they used language (in this case guided by Addams's model) to resist the inhibiting spaces where they teach. Shared study of Addams's archive enabled them to push back against the isolation and frustration classroom teachers confront in the face of underfunded, misguided mandates and public misperceptions about their quotidian professional lives. In stories analyzing the unfinished business of their own work, they followed Addams's lead by giving readers an entryway into the enterprises going on within their classroom practice, making it public and available for others to analyze and adapt.

Let me cite a few more specific examples from *JAC* before reporting on several interviews with contributors about the impact of this project on their work. Chapters affiliating with Addams's commitment to the unfinished business of social justice issues include Lanette Grate's account of her college composition students' engagement with cases of wrongful imprisonment (60–75) and Jennifer Krikava's description of balancing mandates for standardized testing with students' other learning needs in her public high school (112–26). Similarly, Darren Tuggle analyzes the multifaceted collaboration between his students at Kelvyn Park High (an "open-enrollment, neighborhood school," with "approximately 90 percent Latino" population) and preservice teachers from Todd DeStigter's classes at UIC ("Scaling Fences," 100). Tuggle draws a parallel between Addams's account of her postcollege ennui, followed by the epiphany that led her to founding Hull-House, and his own gradual embrace of a teaching vocation. He calls for curriculum that addresses both "objective" and "subjective" needs of learning (102), in line with Addams's explanations of Hull-House programs in those same terms.

Like the commitment to unfinished business and collaboration that they clearly share with Addams and with her heirs at the Hull-House Museum, the teacher-writers of *JAC* are united in their vision for—and skill in—storytelling. For these writers, like Addams, story creates counterpublics joined in cooperative cultural work. Just so, Erin Vail's "Surveying the Territory" chapter "stories" (to invoke Schaafsma's verb form) her quest to reconcile private school teaching at Chicago's Marist High School with public work: "where," she wonders, do privileged "middle-class students fit into the notion of educational democracy. In other words, what role do they have in promoting equality and social justice?" Capitalizing on her careful study of Addams's exploring "a similar disconnect in the 'snare of preparation,'" and, by implication, Addams's awareness of her own class-based privilege (127), Vail's story demonstrates how her teaching of films like *The Pursuit of Happyness* is informed by the settlement author's efforts to balance the family and the social claim. Invoking such resources as Addams's "A Modern Lear" application of Shakespeare to situate a public battle within a domestic frame (131), Vail follows Addams's model of imbedding analysis within storytelling.

Beth Steffen adds yet another layer to the *JAC* collection's demonstration of how Addams-inspired storytelling can enable teacher-scholars' examination of classroom life. In "Student Stories and Jane Addams," Steffen references *Democracy and Social Ethics* to advocate for empathetic, reciprocal learning in public school classrooms like hers in urban Wisconsin (80–82). She taps *The Long Road of Woman's Memory* to call for students' right to teach each other (and their teachers) via concrete experience (89), and she reads *Peace and Bread in a Time of War* to find hope that such society-wide challenges as racism can one day be overcome (97). By describing how she scaffolds students' narrative-writing and by excerpting vibrant passages from their compositions, Steffen foregrounds their personal storytelling,[72] just as Addams placed the cultural productions of neighbors at the heart of her accounts of settlement pedagogy.

In academic publishing, once we hold a book in our hands, we're too often already so deeply immersed in the next project that the particular strategies we've employed to create our hard-earned knowledge may fade from memory. For the multiple authors involved in *JAC*, however, learning from Addams and from their collaborative processes is still unfinished business. Like the community curators who enthusiastically described their personal takeaways from collaborative Hull-House work, participants in the *JAC* project are still reflecting on ways that studying Addams's work and writing about it together continue to guide their praxis. Steffen, for instance, says she draws on Addams's example to navigate discouraging contexts of public education today, including assumptions that good teaching can be "quantified" and packaged. For Steffen,

> Addams's perspectives—on working with immigrants, their families, bureaucrats, managers, political radicals, the poor, benignly-intentioned and civically-aware business people and philanthropists, educated reformers—reveal the complexity of human systems. . . . Working with students, I am more effective when the complexity of human experience is acknowledged and brought to bear in our reading, writing, and talking. Addams has helped me there. (Steffen, "Interview")

Bridget O'Rourke suggested in an online interview that her study of Addams has made her hopeful about her future writing and reinforced many of her long-held values as a teacher, while also setting a high bar for cultivating a professional identity. O'Rourke avers, "I don't feel like I live up to Addams's model, if anyone ever could. Like Todd DeStigter, I've often asked myself, 'WWJD?' ('What would Jane do?'). I lack the moral courage to live up to her example." Still, O'Rourke finds solace in Addams's propensity to learn from failed experiments and to embrace uncertainty:

> The Jane Addams I love is not the beloved Jane Addams (though she is lovable); it's the despised Jane Addams (post-Bayonet speech).[73] When she wrote that her isolation made her begin to question whether she was right, my heart could just burst. I love her for her willingness to engage with the perplexity of her being, of her knowing, as subjective and conditioned. (O'Rourke, "Interview")

For the primary facilitators of *JAC*, meanwhile, Addams's example as teacher, writer, and community-builder sustains them. For both DeStigter and Schaafsma, doing work on Addams has heightened their awareness of the complicated identity politics within cross-cultural collaboration. But it has also given them hope. As DeStigter notes:

> One of the reasons Jane has such potential to be useful to contemporary educators is that I think so many of us see aspects of ourselves in her. According to the most recent statistics, the overwhelming majority of teachers are still white and female and at least middle-class. Also, like Jane, I think we educators are driven by some desire to reach out to other people and to use our gifts and experience to do some good in this world. But what I love about Jane most is that she's a wonderful model of how—almost despite herself—she had to learn that in order to do this, she had to change the nature of her relationships with other people (make them more reciprocal, mutually influential) and she had to be ready to tackle problems in the political and economic spheres. (DeStigter, "Interview")

In that context, reflecting on his decision to take on the book project, Schaafsma admits:

> I had some hesitations at first because I thought most of the best work was being done by feminists. And I found it a little bit funny that Todd and I were two boys who would take this work on. But I came to like that. It's usually African American scholars that talk about African Americans; you know, women talk about women. [But] I finally came to think that [my leading a project on Addams] was all right. That it was important. . . . We should all be part of the process of honoring her work, to learn from it.

Schaafsma feels one factor enabling him to assume that role is Addams herself. "She said," Schaafsma recalls, "I want to hear from everyone here. We're going to have a conversation here. . . . We're going to listen." For Schaafsma, listening to everyone was "possibly her best attribute," a strategy that he now carries forward in all his work to promote civic literacy (Schaafsma, "Interview").

Choral Coda

Through my own listening to this chapter's range of voices appreciating Addams and her settlement's learning legacy, I can't help but tweak the *JAC* team's recurring question to ask: what would "J.A./Jane" herself *say*, if she could return to Hull-House for a visit herself, to see the rotating exhibits, and to dialogue with visitors, staff, and community partners? And how would she respond to the compelling accounts of activist teaching in *Jane Addams in the Classroom*? What aspects of the "unfinished business" of Progressive Era reform would she most push us to tackle? What new opportunities for collaboration would she recommend? What stories would she urge us to tell? I think she would welcome whatever choices we made for projects to develop, as long as we committed to a reciprocal stance and found ways to represent our resultant learning as a communal experience. Thus, I suspect she would direct us to enact one of her own most famous descriptions of the settlement's brand of collaborative civic engagement:

In a thousand voices singing the Hallelujah Chorus in Handel's "Messiah," it is possible to distinguish the leading voices, but the differences of training and cultivation between them and the voices in the chorus, are lost in the unity of purpose and in the fact that they are all human voices lifted by a high motive. This is a weak illustration of what a Settlement attempts to do. It aims, in a measure, to develop whatever of social life its neighborhood may afford, to focus and give form to that life, to bring to bear upon it the results of cultivation and training; but it receives in exchange for the music of isolated voices the volume and strength of the chorus. (Addams, *Twenty Years*, 125–26)

CHAPTER FOUR

Reclaiming Voices from
Indian Boarding School Narratives

Pratt: It was a transformation, you must admit. When you first
 came to the school, you were . . . .
Luther Standing Bear: A savage?
Pratt: You were . . . unschooled, unsophisticated. You were an
 Indian.
Luther: I still am. Imagine.
 —N. Scott Momaday, *The Moon in Two Windows*

"Your quotation, 'Kill the Indian, save the man,' binds you to the
attitudes that were already in place in your time, attitudes that
would subject Indian people to cultural genocide. . . . I voice this
letter to you now because I speak for me, no longer invisible, and
no longer relegated to the quiet margins of American culture. . . .
Writing is a way for me to claim my voice, my heritage, my stories,
my culture, my people, and my history."
 —Laura Tohe, "Introduction: Letter to General Pratt,"
 No Parole Today

Learning to Listen Across Cultures

On Wednesday, April 6, 2011, I attended a half-day workshop at the national convention for the Conference on College Composition and Communication (CCCC), a division of the National Council of Teachers of
English. Facilitated by a group of Native scholar-teachers, the program introduced attendees to resources for teaching writing, rhetoric, and culture
from a perspective honoring American Indian communities. The presentation team embodied the rich diversity among Indian nations while communicating shared value systems to inform the teaching of participants,
most of whom (like me) were white Euro-Americans.

Part of what drew me to the session was its title: "Standing Peachtree: Trading Ideas about American Indian Rhetorical Texts with 'All Our Relations.'" The ending words referenced the conference theme, selected by Malea Powell (mixed Miami/Shawnee/Euro-American),[1] that year's conference director/organizer. The opening terms, meanwhile, combined a "Peachtree" allusion that resonated for me as a former Atlanta resident, aware of the city's many Peachtree streets and avenues, with a reminder that before white Georgians settled in the region, the area had been the longstanding home of Native Americans.[2] While a faculty member at Kennesaw State, before moving to Texas, I had devoted a good deal of energy to teaching about these earlier residents, the Cherokee who had also lived (and still live) in my own original home state of North Carolina. For example, the Keeping and Creating American Communities (KCAC) grant-funded program, referenced in chapter 2, included study of Cherokee history and literature. That project had made me eager to learn more, especially about approaches that would encourage students to connect with Native people today, rather than thinking of Indian Country as only a culture long "removed."

My first moments in the workshop were disconcerting, I admit. I slipped in after the session had already begun, since my plane from Dallas/Fort Worth arrived late. The packed room percolated with unfamiliar language. Professor Qwo-Li Driskill had immersed everyone in a lively introduction to Cherokee vocabulary. As s/he circled the tables, s/he prompted dialogue through repetition.[3] I had trouble joining in the conversation. Having missed the first example exchanges, I strained to listen. I stumbled over words. Though a veteran of foreign language immersion courses in both French and Italian, I found the Cherokee sound sequences difficult to process.

My struggle to understand reminded me how hard it must have been for Indian boarding school students when they first arrived at unfamiliar places where only English was spoken. At the same time, I realized that the nods and smiles from Professor Driskill, reinforced by an openness to the occasional question in English, represented a far cry from the brutal approach to "English only" employed in settings like Carlisle Indian School in the late nineteenth century. Here, in this supportive workshop, there were no suggestions that our lack of knowledge of the new language marked us as uncivilized, no associated requirements that we change our familiar clothing, or give up home-taught social practices, as part of a cross-cultural curriculum. The contrast was striking, even as the good-natured efforts of my fellow students, being gently corrected by our teacher, underscored the value of honoring a language we would never master ourselves.[4]

Unlike students at assimilation-oriented boarding schools "for" Native Americans, I have never been pressed to give up my home language completely. The closest I've ever come to that experience hardly compares as an assault on my self-image. As a teacher just moved to mid-Michigan from coastal Georgia years earlier, I had sat nervously through a principal's debriefing after his first observation of my middle school classroom. I was relieved that he had nothing but praise to share—until he issued a seemingly nonnegotiable closing directive: "You need to lose that southern accent right away. The kids and parents will never respect you if you go on sounding like that."

Reluctant to resist overtly, I commiserated at home that night with my husband, also a southerner, who had been warned repeatedly that his career in television news required him to develop a Midwestern nonaccent accent. Somehow, I argued, I couldn't see the harm in asking my Michigan students to listen to a Carolina voice. Flashing back to that memory in the midst of lively Cherokee language sounds circulating around the room, I called up a more pleasant classroom scene than that painful assessment from my former school administrator. At another Michigan school several years later, in a more welcoming multicultural environment, several of my students regularly teased me on Monday mornings. "You've been talking to your sister again, on the phone, over the weekend; your accent is always more pronounced on Mondays."

Native American students who were placed in boarding school settings in the late nineteenth and early twentieth centuries didn't get to talk with their families on the weekend. They didn't get to reconnect regularly with their home cultures. For long stretches of time, sometimes for years, even, they were cut off from their families, discouraged or even forbidden to return home in the summers. Reconnecting with home, after all, would get in the way of assimilation.

In that context, this chapter turns to a more vexed, and highly punitive, approach to cross-cultural teaching than those examined up to now, to consider the legacy wrought by the culture-suppressing curricular program carried out in residential schools aimed at young Native Americans. The teaching sites at the heart of the previous two chapters—Spelman and Hull-House—were both implicated in debates about the best ways to educate the students they served. In both cases, we can point to ways in which white social power shaped the content, guided the instructional strategies, and affected the resources available for cross-cultural teaching. But in both those other cases collaboration across racial, ethnic, regional, and generational lines supported educational aims shared by all participants, by white teachers and minority students alike, even during their nineteenth-century founding years. In addition, from the start, both these institutions, Spelman and Hull-House, served learners who *chose* to attend.

In contrast, the foundational site for defining the Indian assimilation agenda—Carlisle—could hardly be described as fostering collaborative learning or as building a supportive community. The Indian assimilation program embodied in Carlisle, and extended to its many imitators, was *imposed* on Native students as part of a large-scale, national-level effort to address the so-called Indian problem through cultural erasure. Further, although some Native parents "chose" to send their students to residential schools, they did so in response to overwhelming material and political pressures that had deprived tribal communities of land, resources for sustaining daily life (including basics such as food, clothing, and housing), and self-governance. Thus, the cross-cultural teaching situation represented by the Indian boarding school movement was, at its core, purposefully destructive. This stance is clearly signaled in the infamous statement by the founder of Carlisle, Richard Henry Pratt, to whom Laura Tohe's "letter," excerpted at the head of this chapter, is addressed. The learning legacy of Indian boarding schools like Carlisle, therefore, exemplifies what my introduction termed a "Negative Archive." And yet, ironically, this legacy has been a highly generative one, producing two distinctive brands of counternarratives.

Through the history of assimilationist boarding schools aimed at Native Americans, we can trace both the power of dominant narratives shaping those programs and the growing force, over time, of counter-narratives resisting that movement. The dominant narrative—including related beliefs about "savage" Indian identity and supposedly limited learning capacities—was not always articulated in an explicitly suppressive form. Similarly, resistant responses were (and still are) expressed in mixed messages as well as forceful, overt defiance. As such, the counter-narratives opposing the residential school movement's agenda have also come in multiple forms, ranging from attacks on the abuses linked to the program to the presentation of alternative positive models for cross-cultural teaching.

Both elements in this two-pronged rhetorical engagement with the Negative Archive of boarding schools—generating critique and offering positive alternatives—can align with a strategy for Native intellectual leadership outlined by Robert Allen Warrior in *Tribal Secrets*. Warrior argues for a Native commitment to seeking intellectual sovereignty by drawing from both Indian and Euro-American resources. Part of that process, he suggests, involves using the tools of the oppressor's own education system (which, in the context of this chapter, is embodied in the assimilationist boarding school movement) to build "technical and critical knowledge of how the society that dominates us works." This stance, he notes, results in "critical knowledge of what has happened in this history of that dominating society that helps explain the situations in which we find ourselves." Adopting such an approach to knowledge building (and associated social power), Warrior suggests, does not translate to accommodation or an uncritical assimilation. Instead, by avoiding the false dichotomy of either "abandoning ourselves to the intellectual strategies and categories of white, European thought" or "declaring that we need nothing outside of ourselves and our cultures in order to understand the world and our place in it," true intellectual sovereignty combines knowledge-making systems from the white world with situated practices from Native cultures.[5]

Accordingly, this chapter and the next recognize the ongoing narrative/counter-narrative interplay between Euro-American/settler/dominant education systems and Native visions for learning across cultures. Chapter 4 will demonstrate how Native writers have forcefully critiqued the boarding school system and its heritage, sometimes by applying Euro-American analytical tools to revise its history, thereby reconfiguring a Negative Archive. Chapter 5 will focus on alternative educational models for cross-cultural instruction grounded in Native practices of cultural transmission: more than a rejection of the oppressive heritage of the assimilationist boarding school program, this creative Archive presents its own positive vision for teaching and learning. In chapter 4, the counter-narratives under review generally assume a resistant stance somewhat similar to those used by chapter 2's African American women writers seeking to "counter" the negative discursive power of demeaning representations and longstanding social policies directed against them. Often located within institutional settings shaped (and constrained) by white values, these learning legacies have frequently constructed self-consciously hybrid voices. In chapter 5, somewhat parallel to the distinctive social practices imported into settlement education programs by immigrants themselves, as referenced in chapter 3, I celebrate alternative knowledge systems and associated teaching models drawn from Indigenous traditions to offer up alternative pathways for cross-cultural learning.

In both chapter 4 and chapter 5, I assume a position of learner rather than expert. Thus, in chapter 4 I review powerful critiques of boarding school ideology mounted by Indian writers in the assimilation era and more recently, and I point to the layered legacies of these critiques as an Archive applying strategies of rhetorical pragmatism that other marginalized peoples can tap into when seeking their own educational sovereignty. In chapter 5, I affirm both the vision and particular practices of teaching as modeled by Native educators from the past and today. Embracing this rich legacy's focus on story-based knowledge-making, and on empathetic listening and dialogue to build community across cultures, I call for a related revitalization of American education, overall.

Two figures will stand out in this chapter as writers and as teachers: Zitkala-Ša and Elaine Goodale Eastman. Starting from contrasting perspectives, each of these women produced widely read accounts of the program enacted at Carlisle Indian School, the most influential site of assimilation teaching of its day. Each author published significant narratives responding to Carlisle-inspired agendas. Zitkala-Ša, a Yankton Sioux whose career included acclaimed musical performances and community leadership as well as print-based authorship, generated numerous counter-narratives invoking blends of the rhetorical approaches described above. She attacked the abuses of assimilation-based teaching, on the one hand, and provided adaptable alternative models, on the other. Her impact on other Native women writers has been so extensive that Laura L. Terrance describes Zitkala-Ša as an "intellectual ancestor" and asserts: "As Native feminists we are her descendants" ("Resisting Colonial Education," 625). Elaine Goodale Eastman, who may be best known today for her writing partnership with her husband, Charles (Ohiseya) Eastman (Santee Sioux),[6] also published her own writing, some of it promoting a complex brand of assimilation education both linked to and resisting the Carlisle model. Although her impassioned attacks on the military assault at Wounded Knee and other pro-Indian writings prompted intense criticism from whites during her own lifetime,[7] Goodale Eastman's texts, overall, reflect the internal struggles among many self-anointed "friends of the Indian" who fell far short of fully empathetic intercultural awareness. Juxtaposing these two teacher-authors, we gain a heightened sense of the practical and rhetorical challenges facing all those involved in Indian education during that pivotal era.

With writings by Zitkala-Ša and Elaine Goodale Eastman as key examples, this chapter will focus on Natives' and others' critiques of (and resistance against) dominant narratives linked to assimilationist boarding schools. In my own teaching, I've come to recognize the power of analyzing negative examples. A professional development exercise often assigned to both preservice and current teachers today asks them to articulate a philosophy by writing out a description of classroom activities and linking it to an associated value system. Once I started using this technique in my methods classes for future teachers, or when facilitating sessions with practitioners, I noticed that their "visioning" texts frequently revisited their most painful experiences as learners—a "bad" teacher, unsupportive school, or inflexible, constraining curriculum. At first I found this pattern puzzling. Gradually, I grasped the efficacy of the negative example as a tool for reflection and future action. Although "majority" students and teachers would very rarely, if ever, have a past history with abusive education comparable to Indian residential school settings, their reevaluations of problematic moments in their learning histories can still be a powerful tool for projecting forward to future teaching. In this sense, the Indian boarding school movement provides striking negative cases from which we all can learn. Thus, an important body of writing to examine within the context of this book's project is the still-growing set of narratives condemning the many abusive elements in assimilationist education. Through this Archive, despite its origins in pain, we can find adaptable ways to resist oppressive teaching—whether a particular classroom tactic such as silencing minority views through micro-aggressions; or a larger strategy such as suppressing inquiry-based teaching by overvaluing standardized assessments; or a pervasive political agenda pushing refugees from "outlier" homelands to erase their home cultures (as, say, seen in a headscarf or observed in a type of prayer or practices via key foodways) from public school classrooms.

Boarding Schools' Enforced Assimilation

The troubling history of boarding schools for Native American youth has been well documented, but it certainly merits summarizing here, both in terms of its starkly abusive elements and as a site that did empower some students as individuals and as members of a Pan-Indian community.[8] Overall, the assimilation program for Native education evolved within a larger framework of US-Indian relations.

In *Education for Extinction*, David Wallace Adams connects the initial impetus to educate Indians to government policy seeking "civilization" of Native peoples, as articulated in early nineteenth-century writing by Thomas Jefferson and enacted legislatively soon afterwards via an 1819 congressional appropriation for a "Civilization Fund."[9] Adams indicates that this "civilization" phase of Indian education by US whites was "carried out mainly by missionary societies," whose (at least partially) altruistic efforts were often undermined by land-hungry white settlers (6). The next stages were far more aggressive and more directly linked to military conquest. Through the 1870s, Adams suggests, *subjugation* replaced *civilization* as the overarching goal of whites to address what was frequently dubbed the "Indian problem." On the one hand, well-meaning (if politically limited) white reformers like Helen Hunt Jackson sought to advocate for Native peoples.[10] On the other hand, once Indian nations had been contained militarily, government policy shifted to ensuring long-term control through an aggressive enterprise pressuring Native youth to reject their own culture.

Significantly, the federally funded, government-run version of the assimilation movement arose at a time when debates about the best educational programs for African Americans had led some leaders to promote "industrial" or vocational curricular models as a preferable alternative to providing blacks with access to liberal arts learning, as outlined in chapter 2. Parallel to such institutions as Booker T. Washington's Tuskegee, the curriculum developed in many federally sponsored boarding schools for Native Americans emphasized "training" for manual labor—such as farming skills for boys/men and bourgeois homemaking ones for girls/women. Even in its most benign forms, such as those touted by Washington's famous Atlanta Exposition speech, this curriculum carried with it inherent limits. In line with racial ideology of the period, to focus exclusively on industrial training presupposes the incapability of minority students to attain higher levels of intellectual achievement.

At the same time, whatever the specific content of an "industrial" curriculum, these schools operated under the assumption that the values and social practices associated with white "civilization" were so obviously superior that students would—sooner or later—embrace white ways and reject their own racial identities.[11] The recurring use of "before and after" photographs to convey a contrast between African Americans and Natives who had not completed such a schooling process, versus those who had, constantly reinscribed this ideology for the public. For just one example, we can look to the photographs in the Hampton Album of Frances B. Johnston.[12]

The two groups targeted for industrial education—African Americans and Indians—actually came together at Hampton Normal and Agricultural

Institute, which was established with a goal of serving African Americans but began enrolling Indians in 1878. General Samuel Chapman Armstrong (1839–93), a child of missionary parents who had worked for the American Board of Commissioners of Foreign Missions (ABCFM) in Hawai'i, was the influential principal of Hampton. As a Yankee officer during the Civil War, Armstrong had volunteered to lead one of the first contingents of black soldiers. After the war, he drew on his missionary impulses and his army leadership skills (including a stint as head of a local Freedmen's Bureau) to preside over a new school for the freedmen in Hampton, Virginia, which opened in 1868.

The motivation behind the expansion of the Hampton student body to include Native Americans was an alliance between Armstrong and Richard Henry Pratt, who would soon adapt the Hampton program to found a separate institution, Carlisle Indian Industrial School, in Pennsylvania. Armstrong's rationale for expanding Hampton to serve two racial minorities was both idealistic and pragmatic. "Armstrong firmly believed that his philosophy at Hampton could be applied to all 'backward races,'" says biographer Robert Francis Engs, who suggests a link between Armstrong's conflation of Hawaiian and African American racial identities and the assumption that the Hampton curriculum would be equally appropriate for blacks and Native Americans. The decision to bring Indians to Hampton was also grounded in the very practical benefit of generating income. Lacking an endowment, Armstrong was always on the lookout for funds. Being able to charge the government for Indian students helped Hampton's bottom line.[13]

If Armstrong was ambitious for Hampton, Pratt had his own craving for a national-level leadership role addressing the "Indian problem." Accordingly, just as Hampton became the template for a number of other institutions offering African Americans industrial/vocational education, Pratt's Carlisle would play an influential (and pernicious) part in shaping other Indian boarding schools.

That Pratt's initial efforts at Native American "education" originated in his being the jailer for prisoners captured during Western Indian wars is, of course, telling, given the ways that his eventual leadership of Carlisle would take on a military-cum-incarceration tone. Charged in the spring of 1875 with transporting a band of defeated warriors to Fort Marion in coastal Florida, Pratt soon attracted the attention of wealthy, prominent white vacationers in the area by experimenting with a combination of military drills, basic literacy instruction, and work assignments outside the fort for his charges. By 1877, Pratt had used his growing network of supporters to gain access to Hampton for a number of his prisoner-students, and, in alliance with Armstrong, had convinced officials in Washington to approve government funding for Indian students, with Pratt himself heading west into Dakota Territory to recruit a cohort.

Before long, it was clear to many at Hampton (including Booker T. Washington, then serving as a "house father" in one Indian dormitory) that the two groups of students had very different needs, as seen in everything from varying food preferences to the contrasts in language backgrounds. Thus, although Indians continued to be enrolled at Hampton, and government subsidies for that purpose continued until 1912, Pratt pressed for a separate school in Carlisle, in what had been a military barracks. Carlisle opened in 1879, with Pratt himself at the helm until 1904, by which time attendance had risen to over 1,000. Having been promised additional funding for more than the 150 students with whom he began, assuming the experiment showed signs of success (from the perspective of white political leaders, that is), Pratt was highly vested in demonstrating the efficacy of his curriculum. As for its forerunner at Hampton, therefore, the public relations enterprise for Carlisle was crucial to its growth—as well as to replicating the industrial training program at other boarding schools founded in succeeding years across the West.[14] From this need, the dominant narrative of assimilationist Indian education emerged.

The figure of Pratt himself was at the center of this public relations campaign, which convinced government leaders to support increased appropriations, including a supplement to Pratt's own military salary. Expansion at Carlisle and implementation at other institutions in the East (Pratt's preference) lost ground, however, once the actual dollar cost that would be required to educate all Indian youth in facilities far from their Western homes began to sink in among political leaders. Philosophical differences also played a part in the gradual decline of Pratt's influence. Even as they continued to praise Pratt for his work, leaders like John Oberly (an Indian commissioner under Grover Cleveland) argued that on-reservation schools would be more efficient than institutions in the East. Commissioner Thomas Jefferson Morgan (under President Benjamin Harrison) also advocated on-reservation day and boarding schools. Predictably, Pratt opposed such moves, arguing that residential schools far from the reservation were essential to ensuring full assimilation.[15]

Pratt's intense, uncompromising, and aggressive personality also played a part in the increasingly conflicted relationships with government officials that eventually led to his being removed from leadership at Carlisle in 1904.[16] By then, however, the Carlisle model had already spread to numerous other institutions. More importantly, perhaps, the ideology driving Pratt's program had taken hold in the larger culture in ways that would constrain American Indians' access to intellectual sovereignty and political agency—as well as delimit whites' perceptions of Native people—for generations.

Documenting Boarding Schools' Impact

Many scholars have underscored the debilitating effects assimilationist boarding schools had on Native students and their families. Caskey Russell (Tlingit, Alaska), for example, has chronicled ways in which "Indians are still haunted by the boarding school legacy"; he notes that the oppressive practices of the system have left "today's Indian children with a strong distrust of the American education system," impeding their opportunities to succeed academically even now.[17] In *Education for Extinction*, David Wallace Adams casts the residential schooling system as a horrific extension of the efforts to eradicate Indian culture on Western battlefields:

> For tribal elders who had witnessed the catastrophic developments of the nineteenth century—the bloody warfare, the near-extinction of the bison, the scourge of disease and starvation, the shrinking of the tribal land base, the indignities of reservation life, the invasion of missionaries and white settlers—there seemed to be no end to the cruelties perpetrated by whites. And after all this, the schools. After all this, the white man had concluded that the only way to save Indians was to destroy them, that the last great Indian war should be waged against children. They were coming for the children. (336–37)

Similarly, Ward Churchill's *Kill the Indian, Save the Man*, which draws on Pratt's own language for its title, chronicles what its subtitle characterizes as *The Genocidal Impact of American Indian Residential Schools*.[18] As noted in George Tinker's introductory essay, Churchill shows "that the Indian schools were consciously designed as part of the colonizers' imperial project" ("Preface," xiii). David H. Dejong has called attention to the many health issues associated with boarding schools. Having documented various manual labor situations (such as "steam-filled laundries") as particularly harmful, he points out that "[s]ome schools became synonymous with death and disease," with epidemics of tuberculosis and smallpox only made worse by the push to boost enrollments. Along with overcrowding, he notes, unhealthy diets contributed to many students' ill health, as did such draconian practices as nailing windows shut to discourage runaways.[19]

Much of the criticism of boarding schools has focused on the programs' undermining of home-based (both parental and tribal) teaching of children, as well as the brutality evident in the forcible round-ups that were frequently a part of the so-called recruitment of students. Thus, Ward Churchill has argued: "There can be no question whether the transfer of children upon which the residential school system depended was coercive, that it was resisted by indigenous parents and others adults—and often, to the extent that they were able, by the youngsters themselves—or that physical force was used to overcome that resistance" (*Kill the Indian*, 16). Charles L. Glenn's review of scholarship on residential schools in both Canada and the United States stresses the "damage to the relationships between Indian children and their parents, their ancestral culture, and their ability to function as members of their tribal societies."[20]

Consistent with Glenn's move to address both US and Canadian settings, recurring themes in the scholarly critiques of the boarding school programs—whether run as religious or secular enterprises—echo much postcolonial writing about settings beyond North America.[21] For example, in both fiction and nonfiction texts, African author Ngũgĩ Wa Thiong'o has mounted vigorous depictions of colonizers using schools to support an agenda of conquest in places like his native Kenya.[22] Similarly, scholars have traced telling parallels between the enforced round-ups and residential teaching of Aboriginal children in Australia and those in the United States.[23] Rauna Kuokkanen has identified connections linking writing by Indigenous women resisting the colonial educational enterprises in two seemingly diverse contexts: one in Shirley Sterling's *My Name is Seepeetza* (1992), grounded in experiences of First Nations Salish students, and a counter-narrative by Kerttu Vuolab emanating from faraway Finland.[24] Native writer-teachers are drawing on similar parallels in their own curricula, as Esther Belin outlines in describing her work on the reservation in Torreon, where she linked Native Americans' experiences of colonization to those addressed by Trinh T. Minh-ha, bell hooks, and Gloria Anzaldúa.[25]

Some studies of Indian boarding schools have suggested that the shared experience of attending a residential school did promote cross-tribal solidarity, thereby enhancing the ability of Native students—eventually as adult leaders—to battle white domination politically. Glenn balances his description of residential schools' negative impact with reports from Cherokee anthropologist R. K. Thomas and Devon Mihesuah's historical study of the Cherokee Female Seminary (*Cultivating the Rosebuds*), both of which indicate some students capitalized on boarding school experiences in positive ways (Glenn, 81–82). Tsianina Lomawaima's interviews with alumni of a residential school in Oklahoma for *They Called It Prairie Light* establish that some students nurtured interpersonal ties and fostered community through such tactics as forming gangs based on tribal affiliations.[26]

Rather than view this research as undermining rightful critiques of the residential schooling enterprise, I propose starting with these assumptions:

- that core goals of assimilationist boarding school programs were unethical;
- that some students' maneuvering strategically toward an individual agency and group solidarity does not affirm the underlying aims of the assimilation movement;
- that some individual schools did not (fully) fit the dominant pattern associated with Pratt's Carlisle model;
- that individual teachers (some of them, increasingly over the years, themselves Indians) labored to counteract the worst dimensions of assimilationist practice even while acting, officially, as agents of those institutions.

Along those lines, scholars are underscoring the variations across individual schools, as well as different teachers' and students' experiences.[27] Brenda J. Child's *Boarding School Seasons* employs letters from students and their family members that she uncovered in government archives to survey the responses of Ojibwe students to schools like Carlisle, Haskell, and Flandreau. Taking the full range of this correspondence into account, Child notes that assimilation-oriented schools "dismantled the economies of self-sufficient people who had for generations successfully educated their children in the cultural knowledge, values and economic tradition best suited to the integrity of the woodland environment"; she describes the coercive tactics used to recruit and isolate students, including withholding rations from parents who resisted having their children taken away.[28] But Child's research has also revealed that some twentieth-century Indian students chose residential schooling as a preferable alternative to public schools where they tended to be victimized by racism (22); that clusters of siblings and cousins at the same school developed ways to maintain a strong sense of family (23); that some students found boarding schools "useful" when their families faced personal crises or economic pressures (24); and that the schools did provide access to skills that might enable students to earn a living (24).[29]

Pipestone, a memoir published in 2010, exemplifies how some students effectively navigated the boarding school experience. Adam Fortunate Eagle finds features to celebrate in revisiting his decade (1935–45) at Pipestone Indian Training School. *Pipestone* includes scholar Laurence Hauptman's "Afterword" analysis of the lead author's narrative. Hauptman argues that Fortunate Eagle's account "challenges some of our long-held assumptions about federal Indian educational policies and young children's experiences at these boarding schools" (171). Hauptman goes so far as to suggest that the Native writer's leadership of the Alcatraz Island takeover in the 1970s, his powerful abilities as a speaker in support of Indian rights (including his successful cultivation of humor as a teaching tool), and his influence on Native American Studies curriculum all have roots in boarding school attendance (172–74). This argument contextualizes Fortunate Eagle's student experience within a broader history that stresses how curricular programs and teaching practices did evolve over time (rather than maintaining a "pure" vision of a Pratt-like agenda). Hauptman additionally points to individual "administrators and teachers with varying educational philosophies" approaching their work differently in diverse institutional settings that, he believes, have erroneously been overgeneralized (175–76). Thus, while acknowledging Fortunate Eagle's own portrayal of the negative dimensions of Pipestone, including its marginalizing curriculum, Hauptman urges readers to see this first-person narrative as a corrective demonstrating how a leader like Pipestone superintendent J. W. Balmer "was no Pratt," how positive changes in policies around Native language use reflected a major shift in philosophy, and how, by the Depression-era time period, in this school, students were not isolated but instead encouraged to connect with the outside world while maintaining strong tribal affiliation (176–78). Significantly too, Hauptman asserts, "the existence and roles of Indian employees" at numerous residential schools have been underexamined, so that their influence on students, the institutions themselves, and society's views about educating Native learners has been underappreciated (178).

Implicit in Hauptman's analysis of Fortunate Eagle's memoir is an affirmation of Native peoples' active agency in educational settings. Whether as students or teachers, Indians involved in boarding school culture sought ways to claim as much control as possible over their experiences and, thus, to have an impact on individual institutional settings as well as the larger social framework driving such programs. A key avenue to cultural agency was (and is) through the creation of texts resisting the ideology, teaching practices, and history associated with assimilation education. And an essential context for appreciating the rhetorical pragmatism and sophistication of such texts lies in the dominant storyline embodied in Carlisle.

Propaganda for Indian Boarding Schools

Pratt's determined efforts to cast himself and Carlisle as "killing" Indians in order to "save" them drew rhetorical energy from familiar portrayals of Native peoples as *needing* to be saved—as frightening savages or hapless victims, incapable of transitioning on their own to a more "civilized" white-dominated world. Mass media, a growing presence in American life at the turn of the twentieth century, played a major role in strengthening such stereotypes.[30] After all, as Philip J. Deloria has pointed out in *Playing Indian*, by the late nineteenth century, images of Indians were already firmly ingrained in the national consciousness in ways that served whites' self-images and their visions of US identity.[31]

In *The Newspaper Indian*, John M. Coward has shown how popular periodicals reflected and shaped the way that many nineteenth-century readers viewed Native Americans and, as a result, how whites responded to various attempts at solving the "Indian problem." As Coward indicates, mass-market representations of Indians invoked stereotypes. Coward further suggests that many nineteenth-century portrayals of Indian violence capitalized on whites' need to demonize communities like Sioux, Cheyennes, and Utes as perpetrators of events like the Battle of the Little Bighorn (198). In contrast to this trend, as the Indian Reform movement gained steam, an alternative stereotype of Indians as helpless, innocent victims of exploitation began to circulate. One thing these two overgeneralized versions of Native people had in common was portraying "Indians as a large but coherent race, not as individuals" (201). Depictions drawn from both of these patterns helped marshal support for the boarding school movement.

Carlisle had an especially sophisticated approach to public relations— techniques for managing the assimilation narrative that simultaneously accrued symbolic capital for similar institutions as well. Utilizing both internally produced publications and savvy self-presentation for external media, Carlisle generated texts that drew on the stereotypes Coward has tracked across the late nineteenth century. Several rhetorical patterns in this campaign—such as photographs of transformed students embodying social values like hard work and well-groomed cleanliness—can be traced back to equally well-organized presentations of Hampton Institute for white middle-class audiences.[32] However, other elements selling Carlisle's program used prevalent ideas about Native Americans, in particular, such as the supposed necessity to constrain their otherwise "savage" natures through strict, regimented learning.

Consistent across all publication sites, portraits of Carlisle's program emphasize a "before and after" plotline and an implied benefit to the larger society achieved through Indian assimilation.[33] As Amelia Katanski explains in Learning to Write "Indian," "to make it appear that the schools did succeed in their mission of cultural genocide, Pratt and his cohorts needed to shape representations of their students" to embody "total transformation."[34] Internally produced publications designed for dissemination beyond Carlisle reiterated this message, often using what Katanski has called a "ventriloquized" Indian voice in the school's newspaper, initially Indian Helper (1885–1900), renamed Red Man and Helper in 1900.[35] Katanski shows how Carlisle's public relations managers, especially head of publications Marianna Burgess, appropriated student writing and thereby created "paper Indians" to broadcast the school's message to readers, including congressmen whose legislative support was essential (47ff). On a larger scale, these publications also garnered support for imitator programs.

On one level, such publications paralleled the cultural work of institution-produced periodicals like the Spelman Messenger and the Hull-House Bulletin, as outlined in chapters 2 and 3. A big difference between those publishing programs and Carlisle's, however, was the latter's being tied to a federally mandated policy of assimilation aimed, ultimately, at the eradication of its students' personal identities. Spelman and its publication grew out of a shared commitment involving African American leaders like Father Quarles as well as white partners like Packard and Giles, at an institution dedicated to collaborative race uplift. Georgia's black women community leaders helped shape the curriculum and its promotional narrative. Similarly, though Jane Addams opened Hull-House and launched its programs out of a sense of noblesse oblige, over time she developed a more collaborative spirit and strategy for community education grounded in reciprocal learning. The public relations campaign for Carlisle, in contrast, consistently reinscribed a "natural" racial hierarchy to justify ongoing suppression of Native culture.

Accordingly, Jessica Enoch has noted the important role that Carlisle's two periodicals, *Indian Helper* and *Red Man and Helper*, played in spreading its message. "Through these newspapers, Pratt created his own aggressive system of propaganda, which articulated and disseminated Carlisle's master narrative by convincing readers of both the necessity and the good of the work done at the off-reservation school." As Enoch observes, these publications actually had two audiences: Indian students, teachers, and alumni, on the one hand, and potential white supporters, on the other. Internally, Enoch suggests, one recurring character in the periodicals, the "Man-on-the-band-stand," continually reiterated surveillance—reminding students that it was impossible to escape the omnipresent scrutiny of the institution. For white readers, meanwhile, the publications justified the curriculum and rebutted its opponents via success stories.[36]

Stiya, a novel by Carlisle teacher and publications manager Marianna Burgess (writing as "Embe"), recycles many arguments evident in the periodicals being printed at the school. Originally published in 1891, *Stiya* imagines a Pueblo girl returning home from Carlisle and struggling to maintain the new identity she had developed in the East. Besides being handed out to students who were about to leave school, thereby supposedly preparing them for what might be a challenging transition,[37] *Stiya* also served as propaganda for white readers.[38] To counter assertions that Carlisle alumni often went "back to the blanket," the novel offered a fictional narrative complement to the many official school reports and newspaper accounts touting assimilation. Having adopted white ways, ranging from her clothing and language use to her eating habits and ideas about acceptable home furnishings, Stiya was appalled by her Pueblo family's behavior. Gradually, however, she won them over. Her father moved from what Stiya viewed as shiftless laziness to job-seeking provider; her mother (though still wearing Indian dress) now "kept her home and the dishes nice and clean." When two of her Carlisle teachers came to visit, Stiya was proud to show off Anglo-type furnishings in her home and a newly acquired sewing machine. Spreading her influence to include young cousins, Stiya had become a model alumna, ready to advise others: "If every returned girl could resist the first efforts of her home friends to drag her back into the old Indian ways and make them feel in a kind but decided way that they were no longer right for her, she would eventually enjoy untold satisfaction and happiness."[39]

Managing Public Perceptions

In publications like the *Indian Helper* and *Stiya*, officials at Carlisle reached out to audiences beyond the school. These texts had relatively limited circulation, though.[40] Granted, Pratt was astutely sending copies to such prominent supporters as Thaddeus Coleman Pound, who, Scott Laderman reports, "became a legislative champion of the early off-reservation boarding school movement in the House," and of Carlisle in particular. Bombarding influential figures like Pound with rhetorical ammunition, Laderman explains, Pratt's persistent publicity campaign enabled other leaders' efforts to cast the assimilation agenda as humanitarian, masking its connections with such imperial enterprises as expanded white settlement of the West.[41] Yet Pratt was wise enough to know that even larger audiences needed to be cultivated; congressmen, after all, listen to the voices of their constituents, so additional political networks had to be addressed too.

As one example, we can cite a technique also regularly employed at Hampton: inviting potential supporters to visit and then to write about the school. In *Twenty-two Years' Work of the Hampton Normal and Agricultural Institute*, Armstrong and others acknowledged the importance of "its open doors to the visitors who come in increasing numbers—hundreds during each year—to see its work for themselves" (iii). Pratt emulated (and collaborated with) his mentor Armstrong in this public relations effort, as illustrated by an enthusiastic essay Woman's Christian Temperance Union (WCTU) president Frances E. Willard wrote in 1889 for *The Chautauquan* after touring Carlisle.[42]

Similarly, Jonathan Baxter Harrison drew on his visits in a publication commissioned by the *Boston Herald*. In his 1887 book, *The Latest Studies of Indian Reservations*, Harrison repeatedly strayed from his announced assignment to report on reservation life in the West and focused, instead, on the assimilation curriculum. For instance, Harrison asserted, "There is no adequate justification for the Western hostility to the Eastern Indian Schools. . . . [T]heir work is still indispensable. Their influence as *advertisements* of the general Indian problem and situation would, alone, amply justify their existence and cost."[43] Though he recommended increased use of day schools on the reservations, Harrison insisted that the basic model for teaching Native children should be based on Carlisle. To support that assessment, Harrison described tracking down former students of Carlisle and Hampton during his reservation visit and finding them working, consistent with their training, as "tin-smiths, harness-makers, carpenters, etc."

(149). In cases where alumni of the Eastern assimilation programs had, instead, become "pathetic cases," he opined that these situations arose from the limited "employment for educated young Indians on the reservations," made worse by "a general prejudice . . . against the young men who have returned from the Eastern schools" (149). For Harrison, this situation, rather than highlighting problems with the assimilation curriculum, instead could be remedied by alumni remaining in (or returning to) the East, rather than "wasting their years to no worthy end" on the reservation (150).

Elaine Goodale (later Eastman) became a reliable contributor to Carlisle's public relations campaign. Goodale was already well known for having published collections of poetry in a precocious childhood voice long before she began work at Hampton in 1883. She was also a stalwart supporter of assimilationist education. She disagreed with Pratt on several major fronts, however. For one, she favored Hampton's initial approach of allowing Indian students to blend English-language learning with use of their mother tongues—a practice later forbidden by government mandate.[44] Second, having followed up her time at Hampton with a stint in Dakota Territory—first on a six-week learning tour arranged by Armstrong and funded through periodical feature-writing, then as a day school instructor for the Sioux, and later as a government inspector of other schools and an in-service leader—Goodale advocated reservation-located teaching to maintain strong familial and tribal ties. A related distinction between her own teaching approach and Carlisle's is evidenced by her efforts to immerse in tribal culture, including traveling during the summer with her Dakota neighbors, as well as learning the Dakota language.[45]

Despite their differences on some issues, Goodale and Pratt shared affiliation with the Indian Rights Association, which sponsored an eight-page pamphlet tracing (and praising) the history of Carlisle in 1886, before Goodale took on her supervisory position in the West. With Helen W. Ludlow (a colleague at Hampton who had also written a history of that institution), Goodale cowrote the pamphlet, full of accolades for Carlisle and for Pratt himself. Ludlow's section offered a romanticized version of Pratt's time in Saint Augustine as a seemingly beneficent jailer for Indian warriors, some of whom eventually became students at Hampton. Goodale followed up that report with a glowing description of Carlisle. Celebrating "the four hundred dark faces and bright uniforms, the industrious labor, the accurate drill, the vigorous teaching, the perfect discipline," she also touted the outing system that assigned students to work for white Pennsylvania farmers. Navigating the complex terrain of racial hierarchy endemic to the curriculum, she noted: "We are struck at once with the fact that the minimum of allowance is made here for the Indian boys and girls as Indians. They are expected to do well as a matter of course, without any consideration at all! Their labor is put right into competition with white labor." At the same time, she intoned: "The Indian youth is not, on the face of it, the equal of the Anglo-Saxon youth," yet simultaneously asserted that if we "will only tell him that he is, and tell everybody else that he is," then "the chances are that you will make him pretty nearly so!"[46]

Pratt continued to cultivate Goodale, recognizing her value as an advocate. After wedding Charles (Ohiseya) Eastman, she had the added rhetorical authority of being married to a much-admired "assimilated" Indian. Furthermore, she was a tireless and prolific writer. Both before and after her marriage, she generated essays and feature stories for Eastern periodicals whose readership was crucial to Pratt's agenda.[47] During a period when her husband held a position lobbying for Indian causes in Washington, for example, some of her proassimilation texts folded accolades for Carlisle within feature stories summarizing activities in Congress for publications like the *New York Evangelist* and *The Advance*. Other pieces focused specifically on Carlisle, as in "A New Method of Indian Education," which described the "outing" program to readers of *Outlook*, or her report on the 1900 commencement ceremonies, entitled "A New Day for the Indian."[48]

Goodale Eastman was under no illusions about Pratt himself being a volatile lighting rod whose personality repelled many potential supporters; on a personal level, she clearly preferred her mentor Armstrong.[49] Nonetheless, she wrote a book-length biography of Pratt in the 1930s. Becoming increasingly conservative in her own views on white-Indian relations, she was by then opposing changes in federal policies on Indian education that could undermine the assimilation programs. Thus, a strident essay like her 1934 "Collier Indian Plan a Backward Step" and a letter to the *New York Times* in the same year, written to oppose "Reviving Indian Customs," were consistent with her moves to cast the Carlisle founder as an heroic figure in *Pratt: The Red Man's Moses*. To some extent, Goodale Eastman was likely responding to the powerful mythology that had already grown up around Pratt, similar to the phenomenon Michael A. Elliott, in *Custerology*, has astutely described as developing (and still operating) around George Armstrong Custer in the years after Little Bighorn (2).

So, in her "Foreword," Goodale Eastman struggled to paint a balanced portrait acknowledging both the enormity of Pratt's character and the controversies associated with his educational agenda.[50] She termed him "a crusader, an idealist, a man of compelling personality," but she also noted that his work "for the first Americans" garnered "reproach" as well as praise. Characterizing him as both "visionary and fanatic" (7), she admitted that many found him "temperamentally extreme and intransigent" (10). Similarly, though she praised Pratt for affirming Indians' capacities for learning and for citizenship "at a period when red men were almost universally despised as an 'inferior race,' and hated as dangerous enemies" (8), she also observed that he was "influenced by the dominant social and political philosophy of his time" (10), and in some ways she distanced herself from him. Still, choosing such an affirmative subtitle for her book as *The Red Man's Moses* marked an affiliative stance in line with the Eastman family's relocation to New England and the schooling of her own children there. The many positive elements in her narrative also underscored how powerful Pratt's persona remained, even in the mid-1930s, a decade after his 1924 death. Her biography's continued endorsement of enforced assimilation, meanwhile, demonstrated the dominant narrative's tight hold on so many white leaders of her day—even someone who, at other times, had written passionate critiques of the military's assaults on Native people (at Wounded Knee and elsewhere) and equally insistent assertions of Indians' distinct cultural values. Thus, in a *New York Times* review of the biography soon after its 1935 release, we encounter an assessment suggesting that, in regard to assimilation's overarching goals, both Pratt and Goodale Eastman were in tune with their times.[51]

Painting a Periodical Portrait

The persistence of such positive images for Pratt and Carlisle well into the twentieth century can be traced back to astute media management in the early days of the institution's history. One telling example of the ongoing rhetoric Carlisle's public relations effort funneled into mass circulation venues appeared in an 1884 issue of *Frank Leslie's Illustrated Magazine*, in an article entitled "Indian Education." I want to devote close attention to this text not only as a sign of Pratt's successful promotion of Carlisle but also as a foundation for tracking discursive patterns in subsequent counternarratives from Native authors like Zitkala-Ša and her rhetorical heirs.

The article's first paragraph situates its subject within ongoing conversations about Indian education and makes clear that the author views assimilation as beneficent:

The subject of Indian education is just now attracting an unwonted degree of attention from public men and the country at large. The sentiment that it is cheaper—as it is certainly more humane—to educate and civilize these "wards" of the nation than to exterminate them by ball and cartridge, is everywhere growing, and the liveliest interest is beginning to be felt in the experiments which are being made at Hampton, Va. and Carlisle, Pa., in the education of Indian youth. So far as now appears, these experiments have more than realized the expectations of those who instituted them.[52]

Identifying Native Americans as "'wards' of the nation" invokes the familiar stereotype of Indians as child-like figures in need of white guidance and ignores the sovereignty of Indian nations. Linking "educate and civilize" as coordinate terms, similarly, positions both the assimilation program at Carlisle and its rationale in a framework appealing to "public men and the country at large." Contrasting that agenda with what's cast as the only alternative available (that is, "to exterminate") positions the Carlisle curriculum as "certainly more humane," thereby suppressing any impulse readers might have to consider the residential program as itself inhumane.

After having characterized the Carlisle program as "successful" under guidance by "Captain R. H. Pratt, U.S.A.," the report offers a history of the institution that is actually a narrative of Pratt's personal leadership "in behalf of the down-trodden race," dating back to his 1875 supervision of prisoners at Florida's Fort Marion. To de-emphasize the incarceration context for that "industrial training . . . experiment," the article quickly shifts its historical overview to Pratt's having taken "seventeen Indian pupils to General Armstrong at Hampton Institute, in Virginia" and then to "the old historic military barracks at Carlisle" in 1879, where Pratt's own program had its "auspicious beginning." The narrative then focuses on Carlisle's continued growth, via the data point of its enrolling "433 pupils, representing thirty-six different Indian tribes" at the time of the article's 1884 publication. A catalogue of tribal groups follows, including "the Sioux, Navajos, Apaches, Utes, Kiowas, Comanches, Arapahoes, Crows, Shoshones, and Pawnees." The report then recalibrates its stereotyping strategy from the earlier "wards of the nation" image to another representation of Native youth then familiar to *Frank Leslie's* readers: these "young Indians," notes the story, are from the "most troublesome" tribes. "Veritable savages the young pupils are, upon their first arrival at the school." Descriptive details support this assessment of their "before" status, which is then, the article avers, undone through assimilationist teaching:

> It is only with great difficulty that they can be induced to sleep in a bed; and teaching them the use of the knife and fork at table is one of the first signal triumphs of civilization. But the rapidity with which they adapt themselves to their new surroundings, the eagerness and intelligence with which they absorb the instruction afforded them, are extraordinary and touching. The improvement is physical as well as mental; and the bright, intelligent, well-mannered and altogether fine boys and girls which these young Indians become after an astonishingly short period of training furnish living refutation of the slanders heaped upon the race.

Here, the *Frank Leslie's* writer melds a complex pair of characterizations. Before Carlisle enrollment, these Indian youth are "wild," their habits "uncivilized," as marked by their attire. In contrast, after "an astonishingly short period of training," they become "living refutation of the slanders heaped upon the race." The catalyst for this transformation is Carlisle itself, which the article portrays as inculcating "mastery of the English language" along with basic academic subjects (such as "reading, geography, arithmetic, grammar and writing") and "industrial education" that will eventually enable "self-support." The reporter touts training for the boys in such practical skills as blacksmithing, wagon-building, carpentry, tinsmithing, shoe-making, tailoring, and print-shop work, as well as farming. The account also extols how the girls become both "tidy and industrious" through their own gendered skills development. Noting the "importance of the careful training which the Indian girls receive," the writer asserts, in line with Burgess's *Stiya*, that "with the Indians, as with other peoples, the home influence is the prevailing one. No real progress was made until girls as well as boys received civilized training." By claiming that the young female students actually "choose what suits them best at the start" from such work options as sewing, cooking, and doing laundry, and that they "seldom" change to different options later, the author short-circuits any questions about the girls being taken advantage of as unpaid laborers. Overall, the enthused journalist praises the industry of Carlisle boys and girls: "they work with a will, and the products turned out from the various workshops are of the very best quality."

In line with Katanski's analysis of student writing being used to garner support for assimilation education, this *Frank Leslie's* piece describes "a neat eight-page monthly" that is written and printed by students. By citing letters from alumni, parents, and other relatives of students, the story maintains "that there is an awakening among the Indians in favor of education, and that they heartily appreciate the benefits of industrial training for their young." Indeed, says this reporter, "Those who have returned to the agencies [i.e., the reservations] from the school are industrious and efficient workers, doing whatever they can to earn money and help themselves to independence; and they are of great service to the Government and to their people, in that they urge others of their tribe to follow the white man's example and learn to take care of themselves."

Additional details in the article praise the "influence of education and contact with civilized surroundings" as the mediating factor between the *before* characterizations ascribed to the Indian children—wild savages, with one "pretty little girl," even, having arrived with a "human scalp" memento as well as "bows and arrows"—and the *after* portrait of re-formed "Carlisle schoolchildren" as "well-behaved and gentle creatures." Central to this story of "the transformations wrought at Carlisle" is another implicit contrast—one between this supposedly remarkable educational program and any teaching they would have received in their tribal communities, via acculturation that apparently would only have reinforced *uncivilized* tendencies. After all, when they first arrive at Carlisle, "To them a house is a prison." They eschew knives and forks, and they sleep not in beds but on the ground in a savage "wigwam life."

Illustrations associated with this affirming narrative about Carlisle's curriculum reinscribe the article's themes.[53] A before-and-after pair of pictures at the top of the page contrasts a group of "Indians Just Arrived" with the same "Group in School Dress Two Years Later." Whereas the first image shows so-called blanket Indians, the second presents neatly uniformed students consistent with Carlisle's military ethos. Additional illustrations show lines of "Pupils on the Way to Supper," two male students working "In the Saddlery" and another pair "In the Tin Shop." (References to several images are included within the article. For instance, the story approvingly highlights the illustration documenting "the boys and girls in their simple and neat clothes, marching across the yard to supper.") At the bottom of this page, one image depicts girls seated at table, "At Prayer" before a meal; another limns "The Dawn of Civilization—An Indian Belle at Her Toilet" (as, standing at a mirror framed by a bow and arrows, she

Figure 4.1. "Educating the Indians—Scenes at the Government Training School at Carlisle, Pa.—From Photographs and Sketches by Joseph Becker," *Frank Leslie's Illustrated Newspaper* (March 15, 1884). Courtesy of the Library Company of Philadelphia. **Per L, Mar. 15, 1884, #1.

braids her long hair). A third represents a classroom scene. Taken together, these ties between print and visual descriptions reinforce the article's praise of assimilation education.

The classroom scene at the bottom of the full page of images is particularly telling. Three young Indian students face a white woman teacher, who holds a book in her hand and prepares to write on a chalkboard at the front of the classroom. Already on the blackboard is a command to "stand up," and above that is a framed inscription: "My sheep hear my voice and they follow me." Bound up with the religious language of the motto is an equation of the students with "sheep" who need to follow the leadership of whites, adopting such mandates as the order to "stand up" and follow directions. The figure of the white female teacher here both underscores and obscures the racial hierarchies at work in the illustration and within the curriculum. Standing tall herself above her young male Indian students, the white woman holds sway over them; at the same time, with the tool of her dominance objectified as a book (rather than a more overtly coercive weapon like a gun), the violence of forced acculturation that would be so incisively critiqued in future counter-narratives by Native writers is rendered into a seemingly gentle cross-cultural intervention. Overall, packagings of the assimilationist teaching agenda like the story-plus-images blend of this 1884 *Frank Leslie's* text gradually assembled an archive of white-managed promotional literature gaining more rhetorical power with each new iteration.

Zitkala-Ša's Boarding School Counter-narrative

Individually and collectively, dominant narratives like the *Frank Leslie's* article summarized above promoted an agenda of assimilationist education consistent with the enthusiastic reports penned by Elaine Goodale Eastman. Missing from such texts were the direct, unfiltered accounts of Native students and teachers themselves. They might appear in passing as characters reinforcing the normative storyline, as in Goodale Eastman's "From Washington" *Advance* column of 1898, where she notes: "Among the teachers, by the way, we noted three young women of Indian blood, one of them a graduate of Carlisle and of the Custer Normal School. I remember reading of Miss Simmons, who is from White's Institute, that she carried off the prize in an intercollegiate oratorical contest, not very long ago" (356). However, Natives' own critiques of boarding school programs did not reach many white readers during this period—at least not until the early months of 1900, when that same "Miss Simmons," now writing under a self-assigned Indian name of Zitkala-Ša, burst onto the literary scene and into the politics of assimilation education in the august pages of *Atlantic Monthly*.[54]

In 1884, the year of the *Frank Leslie's* "Indian Education" accolades for Carlisle, Gertrude Simmons was attending boarding school herself, at White's Manual Labor Institute, a Quaker mission school in Wabash, Indiana, where she enrolled for three years. After a year and a half back home with her mother, she moved to another boarding school on the Santee Reservation, where she remained until 1890. By 1891, she was back at White's, a decision biographer Doreen Rappaport attributes to Zitkala-Ša's love of learning—including the opportunity for music instruction—outweighing the many factors that would have discouraged her from reenrolling.[55] After graduation in 1895, she began classes at Earlham College, where she excelled at oratory, as she would later recount in her *Atlantic* series. She was unable to complete her course work due to illness, but after a period of recuperation, she accepted a teaching position at Carlisle in 1897. She resigned in 1899 to study music at the New England Conservatory of Music, where her expenses were initially covered by a white Quaker patron. The loss of her patron left the young woman with few avenues for self-support. Fortunately for many readers then and since, she chose a route parallel to Goodale Eastman, who during this same period was also writing about Indian issues as a way of generating income, in the latter's case to help support a growing family.

In her 1900 *Atlantic Monthly* narratives, Zitkala-Ša confronted Anglo-American middle-class readers with a disturbing portrait of the assimilationist teaching they had long been encouraged to support. Over three months, she presented an indignant memoir of her own experience within that brutal system in "Impressions of an Indian Childhood" (January), "The School Days of an Indian Girl" (February), and "An Indian Teacher among Indians" (March). Through this series, she planted the seeds for a sustained, strategic counter-narrative response to oppressive education of Native peoples.

Zitkala-Ša was not the only Native author of her era to confront the boarding school experience in texts aimed at white readers. But her work claims close attention for several reasons. For one, the *Atlantic Monthly* was a particularly influential publication at the cusp of the twentieth century, when her stories appeared, so we can trust that the original audience represented just the kind of readers an Indian advocate would be most eager

Figure 4.2. Zitkala-Ša (Gertrude Simmons). Gertrude Kasebier Collection, Division of Culture & the Arts, National Museum of American History, Smithsonian Institution.

to reach. More recently, the compelling nature of Zitkala-Ša's narrative—its intense images and righteously angry tone—has helped claim a secure position for her serialized memoir in American literature curricula, particularly since an expanded canon has brought minority writers' counternarratives to such venues as the Heath, Bedford, and Norton anthologies.[56] The middle essay in this series, "School Days of an Indian Girl," focused most specifically on the author's boarding school experience: she vividly described such cruel and identity-threatening practices as having her hair forcibly cut, being punished for failing to speak English, and being cast into a rigid daily routine at odds with her upbringing. This middle essay and a closing section of the first story, which depicts her journey to the boarding school, have also drawn extensive scholarly attention, adding layers of interpretive resources to her learning legacy.[57]

Elements in Zitkala-Ša's "School Days" offer an uncannily direct response to the *Frank Leslie's* story summarized above. For example, as a counterpoint to the depiction of young girls enthusiastically embracing work in the laundry or kitchen, Zitkala-Ša describes one of her own kitchen assignments: to "mash turnips for dinner," a hot and difficult task allotted to her, not as a learning experience but as punishment for "disregard[ing] a rule which seemed . . . very needlessly binding" (*AIS*, 93). In place of the image of a patient white woman teacher nurturing several students' reading skills in a classroom setting, in Zitkala-Ša's narrative we see "a paleface woman" infuriated by the young girl's purposefully overmashing the turnips. Similar anecdotes emphasize the power of the white teachers over their charges, as well as physical abuse linked to pupils' difficulties with the unfamiliar English language (a brutal "whipping" of Zitkala-Ša's friend Thowin [93]). Whereas the *Frank Leslie's* story presents instruction in English in a brief reference along with other basic academic subjects, Zitkala-Ša's account stresses how the sudden immersion into a setting where one's own language is forbidden leads to fear, punishments, and cultural dislocation (93). Similarly, whereas the *Frank Leslie's* writer approvingly describes a scene of "boys and girls in their simple and neat clothes, marching across the yard to supper," the "School Days" account laments the "Iron Routine" of "cold winter mornings," with "a small hand bell . . . vigorously rung for roll call," as individuals are reduced to lists of names to be checked off, so that Zitkala-Ša found herself "actively testing the chains which tightly bound my individuality like a mummy for burial" (97). In place of "the little coal-black heads reverently bowed for a moment, while grace is said" in the 1884 periodical portrait, the 1900 *Atlantic* essayist recalls how confused and frightened she was at her first dining hall meal: having "marched in," she responded to a ringing bell by sitting down, only to find that all the others remained standing. When a man's booming voice recited puzzling words, while "all the others hung their heads over their plates," Zitkala-Ša "caught the eyes of a paleface woman" staring so disapprovingly that, in retrospect, the Native writer remembers "crying instead" of eating, feeling fear instead of the sweet devotion the *Frank Leslie's* reporter had seen (90). In place of the *Leslie's* article describing new arrivals as needing to be taught how to use a "knife and fork at table" so as to achieve "one of the first signal triumphs of civilization" (59), Zitkala-Ša's counter-narrative makes clear that she certainly knew how to use those instruments, but hesitated because of timidity, exhaustion, and embarrassment (90). Similarly, where the full-page illustrations for the 1884 story included the pleasing image of an "Indian belle" combing her long hair in front of a mirror, Zitkala-Ša's memoir presents the appalling "Cutting of My Long Hair" (89) as an assault with "cold blades of the scissors against my neck" as they "gnaw off" her treasured "thick braids" (91).

As a central dimension of the assimilationist agenda being advocated in the *Frank Leslie's* narrative, that author had confidently asserted how Indian relatives, back at the reservations from which Carlisle students came, "heartily appreciate[d] the benefits of industrial training for their young." The 1884 article also posited how, after this purportedly forward-looking educational experience, former students "returned to the agencies from the school" well prepared to be "industrious and efficient workers," achieving individual "independence" while also providing "great service to the Government and to their people, in that they urge others of their tribe to follow the white man's example and learn to take care of themselves" (59). In contrast to this enthusiastic description, in a section entitled "Four Strange Summers," Zitkala-Ša's middle essay characterizes the dislocation students face when they return to their families. Despondent and unable to feel at home there now, Zitkala-Ša bemoans her mother's ineffectual efforts to offer comfort—a cycle that leads to the older woman's own sorrowful weeping. Overall, in place of the celebratory tone in the pro-Carlisle reportage, what readers encountered in Zitkala-Ša's "School Days" counter-narrative was an overriding mood of frustration, loss, suffering, and despair.

Continuing Counter-narratives as Protest

The personal anger and communal sorrow embodied in Zitkala-Ša's 1900 memoir has had compelling counterparts in more recent literary responses

Figure 4.3. Female Student at Carlisle Visits Home at Pine Ridge Agency, from *Frank Leslie's Illustrated Newspaper* (March 15, 1884). Courtesy of the Library Company of Philadelphia. **Per L, 3/15/4, p. 49.

to the boarding schools' Negative Archive. Native writers have made effective use of diverse literary forms to echo and reinforce her resistant rhetorical patterns. Plotlines, characterizations, and recurring imagery tied to the schools' past have coalesced in a body of texts that, taken together, achieve a powerful corrective to flawed prior histories. Key themes include running away to escape, abuses of authority by teachers and administrators, conflicts over language use (including renamings of students and suppression of Native language and individual voices), and contests over cultural memory-making.[58]

Counter-narrative rhetoric by several Native women poets is illustrative. Louise Erdrich's compelling 2003 poem "Indian Boarding School: The Runaways" invokes several recurring critiques while depicting a failed escape. The first-person speakers in this poem are students who tried desperately to reverse the direction of their earlier trip via train to school by stealing aboard a boxcar. Recaptured, they are brought back and punished for the attempt to go home, "the place we head for in our sleep" still, even after being assigned "shameful work" as punishment.[59]

Poet Esther G. Belin has poignantly addressed the oppressive learning legacy of boarding school culture even among today's urban Indians. For Belin, whose 1999 *From the Belly of My Beauty* explores Native life through the lens of personal reflection, the assimilation curriculum experienced by her older family members has left its mark on her own sense of self. Though "[r]aised urban among Los Angeles skyscrapers, Mexican gangs, Vietnamese refugees," she is self-consciously Indian, "eating frybread and beans." But being Indian also means being shaped by those family members' experiences in the United States' "Federal Indian Relocation Policy," which her prose poem says

> placed them in boarding schools away from the rez. Five-Year Program at Sherman Institute, Riverside, California. Goal: annihilation of savage tendencies characteristic of indigenous peoples. New language. New clothes. New food. New identity. Learn to use a washing machine. Learn to silence your native tongue, voice, being. . . . Learn new ways to survive. ("In the Cycle of the Whirl," *From the Belly*, 68)

Belin censures the cross-generational impact of the residential schools' assimilation agenda. For instance, she confronts the paradoxical situation of being admitted to the elite University of California at Berkeley, yet still being an outsider, by contrasting her own educational access with her mother's constrained economic situation, just one of many long-term results of industrial training as a curriculum: "I was awarded grant money to read literature and analyze theories of Manifest Destiny while my mother worked two jobs.[60] The irony always silenced me" (78). Trying to overcome that silence, Belin's narrative persona signals ways in which the University's bureaucratic culture limits political pressure from the very minorities so proudly recruited and admitted (9). On one side, she herself "questioned [her] presence in that institution of higher learning" and her status as a Native at a very different kind of school than her ancestors had been forced to attend (77). On another, she tries to speak out, to advocate for curriculum and student services responsive to the small but growing minority population at Berkeley, even though she "didn't know where to begin," since "[e]very time I shed tears, re-awakening old wounds, in an almost-prayer of thanks for those sacrificed" (77).

Laura Tohe's 1999 collection of poems, *No Parole Today*, begins with a direct assault on the figure of Carlisle's leader himself, in an "Introduction: Letter to General Pratt." Like Belin, Tohe also strives to honor those who suffered through assimilation education programs. Dedicated "to all those who survived Indian schools everywhere," Tohe's book devotes texts in Part I to vivid portrayals of the abusive boarding school setting, with Part II's examination of social problems within the Native community today implicitly presented as the result of that heritage.

In the opening letter to Pratt, Tohe uses his own words from an 1883 speech to convict the Carlisle founder of "colonialist efforts," while stressing that his influence spread well beyond the school he founded to others and past his own time to the present moment: "The assimilation policies you put in place to turn Indian people into *civilized* white American citizens, who would . . . hold the values of the dominant culture, still affect us today" (ix, emphasis in original). Describing herself as "a survivor, as my parents' and grandparents' generations were, of the legacy you established," Tohe lays the groundwork for additional poems that reiterate her theme. These include "Prologue: Once You Were Signed Up," a reflection on boarding school life by her grandmother presented "in Diné storytelling fashion" (xiii); a narrative on her own first-grade experience of the "taking of our language" through "Dick and Jane books" that would "*Subdue the Diné*" (2–3); "The Names" poem comparing Indian children's hearing the school-based imposition of Anglo names to immigrants "waiting for the names that obliterate the past" (4); and a series of imaginary letters depicting survival strategies developed by students in such settings.

Comparing boarding school life with "serving a sentence," Tohe underscores the incarceration theme that will recur later in her text in portraits of Indians who are today trapped within the literal confines of US prisons. "While some of us survived these schools," she declares, "others ran away or died trying. . . . A cemetery adjoined almost every Indian school" (ix). Reemphasizing how a brand of cultural genocide has been achieved in part through linguistic erasure, Tohe asserts: "The most crippling legacy of boarding schools is the devastation of our native languages and culture" (x). Personally, she resists that legacy by using Native terms for herself and her tribe: "Although outsiders gave us the name Navajo, we call ourselves Diné, *The People*. I prefer to call myself the name my ancestor gave us because I am trying to de-colonize myself."[61]

Erdrich, Belin, and Tohe are certainly not alone in mourning, but also drawing paradoxical literary productivity, from the heritage of past loss linked to assimilation programs. Delving into even deeper realms of oppression, the 2009 novel *Porcupines and China Dolls* confronts the sexual abuse that has long been erased from boarding school histories. Set in a present-day moment when alumni of residential programs are grappling with suppressed personal histories of victimhood, this stark narrative connects social problems often associated with Indians' lives today—such as alcohol abuse, low expectations for employment, and challenges with interpersonal relationships (including parenting)—to one of the most troubling, yet underacknowledged facts of boarding school life: white authority figures becoming sexual predators.

The novel's central characters, James and Jake, have struggled in silence with memories of that abuse. When they finally open up to the larger community about their nightmare experiences, they seek retribution for individual but also for communal suffering. The plot line offers no false resolution, but it does end with some hope that confronting the darkest elements of this past history may bring at least a limited sense of peace to the Native community where the story is set, in Canada's Northwest Territories. To underscore the historical backdrop for this account, author Robert Arthur Alexie, a former chief of the TeetI'it Gwich'in, begins his narrative with an extended flashback to the 1920s when the Canadian government began placing children of his community (including Alexie himself) in residential mission schools. In a chapter entitled "The First Generation," Alexie presents powerful descriptions of the fear-filled arrival at school and subsequent immersion into a culture completely foreign to the young students. Details here—such as the pupils having their hair suddenly cut short and their clothing replaced, a delousing imposed without explanation, and a quick line-up that inaugurates the military-like routine—recall Zitkala-Ša's 1900 narrative. Alexie introduces a strikingly discordant new comparison: in their new uniforms, the students "look like porcupines: well-dressed porcupines" (9–10).

To stress the stifling sense of isolation these First Nation children feel even in their barracks-like sleeping chamber, Robert Alexie first describes a frightened young boy's "low and muffled" cries, which sound "like a million porcupines crying in the dark." Soon, however, for most of the boys, "the cries are silent. They'll always be silent" (11). Silence becomes a strategy for managing pain, for suppressing abuse too dark to name: "they'll try not to remember. They'll block out everything bad that happens to them and others in those hallowed halls. They'll remember only the good things, and those will be few" (12). The pressure of this silence is doubly debilitating, however, as "He'll learn how to hide his emotions and will rarely smile. He'll never laugh" (13).

By using vague "they" and "he" pronouns, Alexie suggests that the story, which in later chapters will focus on James, applies to many former students. Thus, memories this unnamed figure struggles to tamp down become communal more than individual:

> He'll remember the fear, the hunger, the hits, the slaps, the straps, the tweaks, the work and the loneliness. He'll remember a lot of what went on in that place, but he'll talk only about the good things. He'll try to forget the not-so-good things, but he'll never be able to do it. . . . He's never going to forgive those who lied to him and those who abused him. He'll never say it out loud. He can't. They cut his tongue out, and he can't talk about it." (15)

Within the wounded world of Robert Alexie's novel, this up-to-now concealed history of boarding school life finally breaks silence, finds voice, and seeks healing. If there is hope to be gleaned from this painful process, it lives within the story-based recapturing and deployment of a more honest memory, one facing and naming the abuses of a system from which so many still carry scars.

Dramatizing a Communal Heritage

N. Scott Momaday's *The Indolent Boys* stages a passionate critique of the assimilationist agenda within a time frame comparable to Zitkala-Ša's *Atlantic* accounts, even as the play also imagines how reclaimed historical memory can play a constructive role in community life for later generations. Momaday's "About the Play" overview unabashedly classifies the events being portrayed as "a tragedy."[62] Grounded in the actual case of three Native boys caught in a winter storm when running away from the Kiowa Boarding School, the drama depicts both abusive practices at the school itself and determined resistance by the Kiowa community.[63]

For Momaday, this counter-narrative is, ironically, a shared tribal resource. "I have heard the story of the boys who froze to death from the time I was a child," he explains. "It is deeply and ever more dimly embedded in Kiowa tradition" (5). Accordingly, Momaday declares, his text, crafted to "commemorate" the boys, actually represents a collaborative writing process: "I was greatly aided in the process by my Kiowa kinsmen, by others who knew of the story, and by the staff of the Oklahoma Historical Society and of the National Archives" (5–6). Signaling both the important place of this story in Kiowa culture and an assertive move to place official, white-oriented institutions like the historical society and the federal archives in service of this revised history, Momaday's introduction simultaneously provides a cultural context for audiences beyond his own tribe. He reminds us that governmental institutions still bear responsibility for the past. Recovering the darkest elements in that troubled heritage is, therefore, an ethical duty. At the same time, Momaday positions himself as a story-bearer serving his community—a role he achieves by facilitating a reformative collaboration between Native and white memory-keepers. While insisting that authorship of this new narrative is communal, even if published under his sole name, he also imagines a healing process with aspirations extending outward to include others. By dedicating his play to "the numberless souls whose stories have fallen beyond reach," Momaday shows that some awful debts can never be truly repaid, but that a communal counter-narrative record of such tragedies may bear lasting fruit. As such, his storytelling establishes the social justice potential in oral and performative dissemination of a communal Archive, which is moved to action both in his own playwriting and in the hoped-for audience response.

Within the play itself, Momaday uses a small cast to stand in for the "numberless" victims of assimilationist policy as well as the perpetrators. Recognizing that motivations driving individual whites' involvement were often quite complex, he uses three figures to convey a shifting, nuanced range of perspectives among the staff at the Kiowa boarding school, whose history is framed both as one particular case and a representative site. Accordingly, whereas Barton Wherritt, one of the school's teachers, spouts Pratt-like rhetoric justifying the school's program in stereotyped terms, Carrie, a young white woman teacher, seems at first to embody a more sympathetic view. Dialogue between Wherritt and school superintendent G. P. Gregory gradually builds a picture of personal and official complicity in the abuses of boarding school education, including its commitment to strict "discipline." Thus, Wherritt first describes to Superintendent Gregory a vision of teaching as bound up with (white-led) national destiny:

I want to make them [the Indian students] fit in their heads and hands. I want to teach them to think, as far as they are able, to read and write, to know and respect the law of the land, to figure and keep accounts, to buy and sell. I want them to earn a decent living, earn it, I say. I want to teach them to paint and carpenter and husband and farm. I want them to be, by God, Americans. . . . It is our time, America's time. . . . Why can't they see it? Why do they resist that glorious destiny? (20)

Gregory and Wherritt commiserate about the difficulty of achieving these goals. After all, Wherritt exclaims, the Indians (and here they clearly mean all Indians, not merely the missing students) "are *children*" (21). Affirming both the aims originally driving Wherritt to the school and "the reality of the situation," Gregory invokes the wisdom of "The United States Government" as the rightful guide for their enterprise (22–23). Wherritt thereafter slides into a less flowery (and notably more cynical) assessment:

Isn't the object of teaching these children to convert them, therefore to save them? . . . Wasn't that Mr. Pratt's idea of Fort Marion? Shackle the cream of the warrior crop, the poor beaten bastards, stuff them in a train, scare the shit out of them, then, in mercy, let them live in a prison that was called a hotel, give them ledger books and colored pencils, give them sticks and string to make bows and arrows, and allow them to sell their charming, primitive arts and crafts to benevolent, curious sightseers for money, honest-to-God coin of the realm. Give them the English language, Christian names, and gainful employment. Inform them politely that their gods have forsaken them and that their way of life is unacceptable, *uncivilized*, and poof!—the transformation. (22)

Momaday's counter-narrative here sarcastically invokes the theme of "transformation" (and associated public relations images) used by assimilationist advocates.[64] To undercut the Carlisle-based dominant narrative, this speech distances Wherritt and Gregory from their own previous, more idealistic frame of "missionary zeal" for their work (21). Thus, even for audiences previously unfamiliar with the oppressive underpinnings of these institutions, the white men's dialogue ironically justifies the missing students' escape.

By characterizing these two school leaders in inconsistent language, while avoiding the tempting option of casting them as overly flattened villains, Momaday prepares his audience for a more complex portrait of Carrie, a white woman teacher whose tendency to honor her students' cultural values draws criticism from Wherritt and Gregory. Wherritt notes how she has made a Kiowa "medicine wheel" the object of study in her class, after the "grandfather of one of her pupils brought it to her" (14). He complains that "[w]ith her it is sometimes difficult to tell who teaches and who is taught." Wherritt also contrasts his own commitment to serving as a "disciplinarian" with Carrie's tendency toward gentler, more sentimental (that is, feminized) teaching strategies (15).[65] Wherritt further stresses the necessity of forcefully punishing any misbehavior, since "[i]t is our duty" to do so (17). And through this self-justification, another contrast emerges: one between "troublemaker" students whom Wherritt has disciplined and model pupils like John Pai, "the best student this school has ever had," one "soon to be apostle to the Indians, the Kiowa messiah" (18–19).

With consummate skill, Momaday soon complicates our expectations concerning the characters of Carrie and John Pai, however. In a monologue at the beginning of scene 2, John Pai addresses a portrait of Lincoln, using an imagined conversation to undo the certainty with which Wherritt and Gregory presented this student as a future advocate of white values in his community. Declares John: "School here, Mr. Lincoln, is a camp where memory is killed.[66] We must forget our past. Our existence begins with the cutting of our hair and the taking of a Christian name. Here at the Kiowa Boarding School . . . I am taught not to remember but to *dis*member myself" (24). Referencing a sexual attraction to "Miss Carrie," John Pai surfaces complicated elements in the relationships between white woman teacher and Native student—relationships whose intricate interactions around multiple power axes were certainly never addressed directly by the public relations machines supporting the boarding schools' program.

When the audience hears Carrie herself speak, we are forced to confront the contradictory goals and needs behind white women's teaching of young Natives. However seemingly open she is to cross-cultural exchange in the classroom, we see that a large part of Carrie's motivation for her work is self-aggrandizing. She tells John Pai: "It's just that I wanted for so long to find a student who, who could make use of me, total use, whose mind and sensitivity I could shape and sharpen, who would justify and fulfill me, who would confirm me in my purpose . . . in my person and . . . vocation" (29, ellipses in original). Carrie's effusive self-description here, along with its undertones of personal (including sexual?) needs, is in line with a recurring pattern of cross-racial relationships that emerged at institutions like Hampton and Carlisle and which, Katherine Ellinghaus has pointed out, were actually being encouraged by a number of assimilationist leaders on political grounds. With increasing numbers of white women drawing on the ideology of feminized purity, piety, and morality to claim positions as teachers and missionaries, these individuals also accrued strong female moral authority that could then supposedly be deployed to help civilize Native American men through marriage, thereby simultaneously positioning such women back in the domestic sphere (to the benefit of the nation). As Ellinghaus observes, positive responses to such pairings affirmed their potential value to the larger society, as in an 1891 speech by President Seelye of Smith College and in reports on the marriage of Elaine Goodale with Charles Eastman, one of which described their union as "a 'Solution to the Indian problem.'"[67]

In this case, Momaday limns the Indian half of any would-be union as ambivalent about, perhaps even resistant against, his own feelings of attraction toward Carrie and what she represents. We see this complicated identity politics at play in the character's strong identification with the runaways, despite Momaday's making other aspects of Pai's portrayal reminiscent of "model" acculturated figures such as Eastman, Francis La Flesche, and Carlos Montezuma.[68] John Pai, clearly troubled by the larger implications of the runaways' attempted escape, verbally assails his mentor (and would-be mate?) with barbed critiques of the school, which he dubs a "conversion factory." Repeatedly asking if he will be "whipped," John Pai rejects Carrie's attempts to describe a previous punishment of one of the runaways as merited discipline. Carrie expresses hope that the boys will be found, despite the brutal weather, but John Pai repeatedly shifts their conversation to the punitive features of the institution that led to their running away in the first place. He then shocks her by confessing that he once ran away himself—and that he "was disciplined" afterwards to be "made an example" (33). He stresses that the "pain of humiliation" was more brutal than the whipping, so that he forces Carrie (and through her, the audience) to face her own complicity in cultural genocide.

Like the opening of the play, this key scene has focused on those still at the school rather than depicting the runaways themselves. Rendered memorably present by their very absence from the stage,[69] these figures gradually take on a mythic quality, enabling them to stand in for all "the numberless souls whose stories have fallen beyond reach" that Momaday had honored in his preface. By the time we finally see the boys in scene 4 of act 1, their inability to speak for themselves (since, presumably, they have already died in the storm) does not actually render them voiceless. Momaday depicts Kiowa community members speaking to and about them in an imaginative conversation that includes the sleeping John Pai. Mother Goodeye and Emdotah (father of one of the boys and a Kiowa leader) pay tribute to the snow-sleeping runaways by saying their Native names over them, linking their personal stories with tribal lore, and imagining a better future for them, now that they "have gone away, into the darkness." There, they can reconnect with tribal elders who have gone before. Explaining that he wishes "to place my words upon you now," Emdotah uses Native language to reclaim the boys for the Kiowa community. Thus, he asserts their deaths represent a subtle victory (39). The quiet, dignified speech of these two figures, Emdotah and Goodeye, offers a marked contrast to the self-serving ranting earlier by Gregory and Wherritt.

Act 2 examines the aftermath of the boys' deaths, which have prompted much self-questioning for John Pai, as well as frantic efforts by Gregory and Wherritt to justify their harsh disciplinary practices. In a tense exchange, Carrie turns down a proposal from Wherritt, whose jealousy of John Pai seethes. Fearing both reprisals from the Kiowa people and, at least, a reprimand from the federal agent in charge of the area, Wherritt and Gregory are relieved to avoid repercussions on both counts. For the Kiowa, however, as a closing commentary by Mother Goodeye makes clear, more suffering lies ahead. An outbreak of measles will, ironically, lead school administrators to send children back to their tribal home—where the illness will spread rapidly throughout the community. At the same time, though, even in the face of this new tragedy, the Kiowa will call on the resources of storytelling to help safeguard who they are, as Emdotah says, "a tribe of dreamers" (29). Accordingly, together with John Pai and Mother Goodeye, Emdotah reconstructs the escape of Seta and his companions Mosatse and Koi-khan-hodle (no longer designated by white school names) in a narrative celebrating their bravery. This scene's vision of the children's final hours avows that they reacquired their true identities in the end, singing "a song at last, a death song, the song of a warrior," for themselves and for their community. Momaday's powerful counter-narrative play thereby closes with a touch of hope, implicitly imagining the cultural work his own performative story song can do. Through the shared Archive of tribal cultural memory, and in collaboration with other community members who have helped recover and revise their history, the "boys" of Momaday's play can now perform a restorative task.

Teaching about Survivance

Texts that present corrective histories are crucial to study in today's cross-cultural classrooms. For one thing, these counter-narratives push members of the dominant culture to confront past abuses that we would generally prefer to forget. There's a danger, however, to limiting our engagement with counter-narratives to stories revisiting oppression. Doing so may send an inadvertent message to students, leading them to stereotype as helpless victims the very people whose experiences and associated wisdom we need to honor. In such cases, pathways to productive, self-critical empathy can be sidetracked into pity that denies current and future agency to the very people whose histories have been marginalized and oversimplified in the past.

During the Keeping and Creating American Communities (KCAC) project I referenced in chapter 2, we sometimes encountered just such a response from students when studying the Cherokee Removal. Fortunately, though, we had support from a gifted Native scholar-writer, Diane Glancy (herself Cherokee), as we sought, over the multiple years of the KCAC program, to refine our cross-cultural teaching. Both her writing and her teaching about the Removal served as models we tried to adapt.

One narrative we used to reexamine Removal history was Glancy's own compelling multivocal novel, *Pushing the Bear: A Novel of the Trail of Tears*. Glancy generously visited one of our summer institutes for K-12 teachers, and her ideas for teaching the book and its historical context soon carried over into area classrooms. In one productive exercise, she had us freewrite about the Removal, as it happened in the nineteenth century, in the first-person voice of someone who had not been fully represented in her novel. Some wrote as children on the journey; others as empathetic bystanders witnessing the travelers' trek and struggling with how to respond; still others as someone who chose to stay behind, in hiding, rather than endure the round-up and long journey. Sharing these pieces allowed participants to debate the choices open (and those unavailable) to people living through the original events—including varying coping strategies used by Cherokee people upon arrival in the West, in what's now Oklahoma.

In retrospect, in the context of this book's framework, and though she didn't use such terms herself directly when she worked with our summer seminar, I see connections between Glancy's specific teaching strategy and the concept of learning legacy, as well as the aspiration of moving from archive-building to social action. Glancy's *Pushing the Bear*, after all, drew on and reassembled a suppressed archive to produce a remapping and a retelling of the Cherokee Removal. To create that narrative, she had retraced the path of the Trail of Tears across the land and had studied the daily lives of people on that painful, enforced journey, as well as the historical documents that could be recovered. Her text blends voices of imagined characters with "real-life" ones. She takes this approach, I believe, to demonstrate the value of integrating the best evidence we can find from suppressed histories with indirect modes of recovery that incorporate what I would term *empathetic visioning and listening*. Thus, Glancy "imagined" the central character Maritole and her family into textual, story-making being. When teaching the book to us, she invited everyone in the institute to generate additional voices so as to expand that imaginative Archive. Adopting such a practice entails certain risks, of course; failing to do careful research first can lead to uninformed perspectives entering a cultural recovery process. But the possible benefits are nonetheless worthwhile, since the potential for promoting self-critical empathy is enhanced when we acknowledge the diversity of perspectives associated with any historical event where power differentials have come into play—as in the Removal or in the assimilationist schools that have been the primary focus of this chapter. In the multiple classrooms where KCAC participant teachers sought to apply Glancy's approach, some admittedly had more success than others. Even when the results were less than ideal, though, our project teachers' ongoing inquiry into their praxis gradually led to refined strategies for teaching about Native cultures in classrooms where students came, mainly, from dominant culture groups.

To enable collaborative evaluation of promising practices over time, we purchased class sets of Glancy's book, rotating use across schools. Teachers supplemented that novel study with field trips to New Echota, both in person and online, and with other resources we exchanged across our team. For instance, some of our teacher participants organized dramatic readings based on scenes in the novel, with one high school group presenting a performance to elementary-age classes studying the topic in their state-mandated history curriculum.[70] Excited as we were about these approaches, when assessing students' responses to our newly developed "Removal units," we discovered that our focus on the horrors of the Trail of

Tears sometimes failed to convey the resilience of the Cherokee people—both those who journeyed to what's now Oklahoma and those who stayed behind, reorganizing as the Eastern Band.

Were we designing KCAC-sponsored Removal curricula today, we would be able to integrate in the additional resource of Glancy's second volume of *Pushing the Bear*, subtitled *After the Trail of Tears*. There, she unflinchingly portrays the challenges characters from her first volume faced upon arrival in Oklahoma's Fort Gibson, "a walled enclosure that reminded them of the stockades in the Southeast from which they had come." But she also determinedly depicts their commitment "to rebuild in the new territory with what they could remember" (3). Addressing the bleak question Glancy identifies in her second novel's "Afterword"—"what was it like to begin again from nothing?"—this sequel is hardly upbeat. But in its author-identified themes of politics, religion, and women's leadership, and in its integration of "historical voices [like the Reverend Bushyhead] mixed with those of fictional characters" (189), this counter-narrative also commingles the "darkness" they faced with "once in a while, a brief spot of light," such as portraits of resettled Cherokee gathering "to make a clearing in the trees for their field" (190). In those moments of hope for the fictional Maritole, her husband Knobowtee, and the children they adopt, readers can find a more forward-looking legacy.

Back during the NEH-funded years of the KCAC project, when Glancy had not yet written her follow-up account, astute teachers seemingly anticipated her eventual move to depict the Western resettlement by wondering how they could convey a resilience theme as part of the Cherokees' living counter-narrative. Patsy Hamby tackled this concern by trying out a different core text, Robert J. Conley's *Mountain Wind Song*, with a class of ninth graders.[71] Conley (Keetoowah Band, Cherokee) addresses the Removal in three interwoven narrative strands, one depicting the nineteenth-century enforced migration and its impact on relationships, another excerpting treaties and other official documents associated with the Removal events, and a third set in the present day, when a Cherokee elder teaches his grandson cultural practices important to the community. Hamby's students worked in three groups, with each team studying closely one of the three interwoven narrative lines in that novel, including digging deeper into related archives for each storyline. Each team then shared their research and interpretations with the whole class. Thus, one group focused on the historical romance of Waguli ("Whippoowill") and Oconeechee, wherein Waguli heads west on the Trail of Tears, thereby becoming separated from his lover. This team's archive-building included landscape mapping, since the two characters embodied different geographic positions assumed by the two branches of the Cherokee tribe, post-Removal. Another group did intensive reading and supplementary research on the official documents in Conley's novel. Initially worried that few students would select this strand, Patsy found this group emerged from their work with an empathetic critique of how the language in such documents was designed to disempower—and an appreciation for why many Native scholars today stress the importance of studying these legalistic archives. The third group worked through the narrative sequence of oral exchanges between the Cherokee elder and his grandchild learner, supplementing their reading with study of Natives' use of material objects and oral texts to transmit culture. That third group, in particular, passed along an essential message of contemporary agency to the class as a whole.

Part of what enabled Patsy's attentive cross-cultural teaching in this case was the shared work of K-university educators who had participated in a precursor to the KCAC initiative. Through a previous NEH grant, several of these same teachers had been involved in Making American Literatures (MAL), a national curriculum development program launched with a summer institute at the University of California, Berkeley, which incorporated inspiring workshops led by Native (Anishinaabe) scholar Gerald Vizenor. Vizenor's teaching about core concepts from his scholarship had already informed the MAL team's exploration of Native culture in that multiyear project; his ideas then carried over into the subsequent KCAC initiative, so that our collaborative curriculum-making in the second case actually linked up with a prior web of shared inquiry. In particular, our study of Native texts for KCAC's "Recovering Displaced Heritages" theme drew from discussions about how best to facilitate study of Native *survivance*—a key concept several overlapping members on both project teams had first studied with Vizenor.[72] By the time Patsy Hamby was teaching *Mountain Wind Song* and the larger story of the "Recovering Displaced Heritages" theme to students some might consider unprepared to grapple with Vizenor's formulations, she had learned transportable ideas from the smaller team who had previously attended the Berkeley institute. So she was ready to invite her class to explore this productive cross-cultural learning legacy. Her supposedly "remedial" students responded with an energy ably described in her essay for *Writing America*, a collection of teacher narratives on the KCAC project.[73] Through teachers-teaching-teachers networking in tune with National Writing Project principles, in other words, a learning legacy had passed from Vizenor's scholarship to an educator across the country—and students who had themselves sometimes been constrained by stereotypes recalling those applied to pupils at assimilationist boarding schools. Crossing multiple cultural boundaries, counter-narrative resources reached new classroom audiences. In a sense, in other words, as we scholars surely hope happens with the work we do, Gerald Vizenor indirectly joined a collaboration with schoolteachers he has never met.[74]

Meanwhile, by sharing responses across their different reading groups, each of the students in Hamby's class came to appreciate how all three strands of Conley's novel are essential to his vision for a Removal counter-narrative—one that takes on the "official" history represented in this case by treaty and court case language, but also another conveying a legend that individualizes that formal history in a love story, as well as a third, showing Cherokee people living and making new history today. By pulling apart the three narrative strands of Conley's novel and then weaving them back together, Hamby and her class became even more aware of how cultural resources gain social power when brought together through research and collaborative reflection. That is, these students came to read the novel as a story about *survivance* in action. Cultural memory, reformed, created a collaborative narrative of hope.

In the respectful, interactive teaching of Conley's grandfather character, students found an affirmative counter-balance to the essential critiques associated with rereading broken treaty documents and confronting the suffering seen in the story of lovers separated by the Removal tragedy. Besides identifying empathetically with the cross-generational relationship depicted in the exchanges between the elder and his grandson, students recognized that narrative thread as emphasizing how Native Americans continue to safeguard their learning legacies, passing down valuable cultural resources to future leaders, and also how learners from other cultural backgrounds might tap into such knowledge from multiple American communities. In line with approaches like Conley's narrative strand celebrating elder-to-child cultural transmission, the next chapter of this book will track another Archive of counter-narratives responding to the painful learning legacy of assimilationist boarding schools by presenting alternative models for cross-cultural teaching grounded in Natives' own educational practices. Like the generous, community-building strategies I encountered in the Standing Peachtree teaching workshop described at the start of this chapter, these learning legacies offer a vibrant, positive foundation of cross-cultural teaching upon which we all can build.

CHAPTER FIVE

Learning from Natives' Cross-Cultural Teaching

"I see myself as *asserting* Native presence where there has been
mostly absence."
   —Lisa King, University of Tennessee, Knoxville

"I love educating. I've done it all my life. My father and my mother
have done it all their lives. And so it's a part of my being."
   —Dennis Zotigh, National Museum of the American Indian

Counter-narrative Voices on the National Mall

The first time I visited the National Museum of the American Indian
(NMAI) on the Mall in Washington, DC, I arrived just in time for a drum-
and-song performance by Dennis Zotigh (Kiowa, San Juan Pueblo and
Santee Dakota) in the sun-drenched Potomac meeting space just beyond
the entryway. Dennis began with soft taps on his hand drum and gradually built to a crescendo. Hearing this inviting call, visitors who had been
scattered around the first floor's large open space, or who were just passing
through the main front doorway, began to congregate, encircling Dennis
in the atrium. After a brief presentation interlaced with humor, and shaped
by his longtime expertise in powwow cultural practices, Dennis answered
questions from the audience. While the queries that afternoon ranged
from insightful to stereotypically ill-informed, Dennis maintained an affirming tone throughout. He clearly welcomed all in attendance, whatever
their background knowledge.[1]

Next, I took one of the overview tours offered several times a day by
members of the interpretive services staff. My guide, Renée Gokey (Eastern Shawnee/Sac-n-Fox), was joined by Susan Sheldon, an NMAI summer
intern and a school-year student at Haskell Indian Nations University in

Lawrence, Kansas. Renée and Susan introduced our haphazardly composed cluster of visitors to several of the museum's exhibits. Afterwards, in the Lelawi Theater, I watched *Who We Are*, a stirring film underscoring the diversity in contemporary Native life. I left that day entranced by the NMAI's vast collections, creative presentations, and stunning architectural spaces. I realized I had barely begun to explore the resources of the place—including, indeed especially, the expert and caring people who teach there, through a range of cultural roles. So I vowed to return and, in the meantime, to read about the museum and its history.

When I began to study journalistic and scholarly reviews of the NMAI, the number of negative assessments surprised me.[2] Had these critics really visited the same place I found to be so intellectually stimulating and welcoming? As I retraced accounts of the museum's initial reception, as well as published defenses of its vision, I was struck to discover the voices of guides like Renée, Susan, and Dennis virtually missing from these analyses. In their survey of mainstream press coverage, in fact, Aldona Jonaitis and Janet Catherine Berlo have pointed to the worrisome significance of this gap in others' reviews—that is, the striking

> blindness to the carvers, weavers, dancers, storytellers, poets, playwrights, singers, and educators who conduct family programs in the Potomac Atrium and the nearby Rasmusson Theater. Innumerable studies have proved that the most important and meaningful part of a museum visit is the visitor's interaction with a knowledgeable person—not an object. No longer can a museum succeed simply by placing beautiful things on its walls; visitors must have some way of personally having a meaningful encounter with those things. And, in a museum dedicated to Native Americans who have themselves urged the exhibit designers to go well beyond the pristinely displayed object, these first-floor performers, artists, and educators are certainly as central to the NMAI—if not more so—than the exhibits on the upper floors.[3]

Such recurring silence across numerous critiques prompted me to reflect on how my own first visit had been affected by the chance to listen to Native teachers' thoughtful interpretations—to hear stories told and small-group conversations guided, on the spot, by people highly invested in the museum's mission. Over several years since then, by combining study of the NMAI's multifaceted exhibits with additional in-person and online conversations with staff members, I've come to see their teaching strategies as another form of Native counter-narrative, reconfiguring the painful heritage of American Indian education by offering a positive alternative vision for cross-cultural learning.

In many ways, the NMAI is perfectly situated to offer such a counter-narrative. The museum is rich in resources, drawing on thousands of archival materials and soaring architecture brought together on the National Mall.[4] On a reclaimed piece of Indian Country now set between the Smithsonian's Air and Space Museum and the US Capital, the NMAI designs exhibitions and programming infused with Native knowledge to proudly announce a "We are still here" message.[5]

Crucial to that theme, I believe, are the staff members who serve as cross-cultural teachers for visitors—the majority of whom are not Natives. Using dialogue and stories to create points of access for intercultural learning, these NMAI educators forge dynamic connections with each audience on multiple levels. For one thing, as Dennis Zotigh would tell me in a fall 2011 interview, they provide corrective counter-narrative content about Native peoples, undoing "stereotypes" and "bad information [visitors] may have come in contact with." This repair work is multifaceted, going beyond the explanatory labels printed alongside various displays from the NMAI's collection. For instance, Dennis has explained, most "students . . . are taught of Indians in the past. And therefore," he notes, "I refuse to dress in traditional clothing. Because I need to be a living, working example that Indians are very much alive in today's society."[6] Besides conveying such vital content knowledge, though, Dennis and his colleagues' overriding approach—their stance toward learner-visitors and their vision for how teaching best happens—is equally important. For instance, for Dennis such teaching represents a commitment to "personal interaction." He believes that "learning should be fun and not threatening." Contextualizing his own view that an "angry" tone "shuts the audience's mind," Dennis observes that "the exact same message can be said another way, where people will say, 'You know, I never thought of that. Let's talk about it. Let's open communication. And let's see what we come up with.'"

When Dennis met with me for our first one-on-one conversation, he highlighted ways in which his past experiences as a student and an educator helped prepare him for leadership at the NMAI. Though his first encounters with white-managed instruction were certainly not as affirming as what he strives to convey through his own teaching, he had parents who, educators themselves, could be "good mentors." Having traveled with them "throughout Indian Country—Alaska to Florida and everywhere in between," he also points to the benefit of having grown up "in a powwow family. A singing family," with a father who "was a pioneer in bringing Plains Culture to other tribes in the Southwest." Among Dennis's previous roles as an educator, he includes having been "a researcher and historian for the Oklahoma Historical Society," a "powwow advisor," a lecturer and storyteller for "kings and queens and children," a curriculum advocate (promoting the infusion of Native culture—including the history of boarding schools—into state-level guidelines), and "doing cultural performances, workshops, and in-service for teachers" at "over 2000 schools, worldwide." All in all, Dennis is a generous teacher whose ethical commitment to intercultural learning brought to mind, the first time I met him, the grandfather character in Robert Conley's *Mountain Wind Song* (chapter 4), but whose platform of NMAI's Smithsonian affiliation brings an even more evident cross-cultural authority to his daily work with diverse audiences.

Dennis and his NMAI colleagues are major role models for my own cross-cultural teaching. If Carlisle and its heritage as the epitome of assimilation education continue to embody a painful learning legacy to be reckoned with, then one important strategy for resisting that history's negative power is to create a positive counter-narrative of intercultural learning. A vital site welcoming all peoples, respecting every perspective they bring, while using story, listening, and dialogue to establish connections, the NMAI enacts, fundamentally, an "un-Carlisle" message. As educators, the museum's interpreters serve as cross-cultural alliance-builders; they carry out a cultural intervention directly tied to the museum's mission, which itself represents an ongoing counter-narrative casting Native peoples in the teaching role previously reserved to white cultural arbiters and their surrogates.[7] Observing visionary teaching practices there, and listening to staff members' reflections on their practice, I've set these stories in conversation with archives (written and oral) of other Native teacher-scholars working at intersections between white and Indian cultures. This chapter synthesizes what I've learned so far.

Native Teachers as Mediators and Guides

As far back as the boarding school movement itself, creative American Indian leaders refuted the flawed premises of assimilation education by asserting, in its place, Native visions of teaching and learning. Counter-narratives carrying out such efforts represent a potent intervention enabling teachers from Indian country to reclaim cross-cultural learning spaces and to assert a brand of educational sovereignty in the process.[8] One aim of this chapter is to highlight examples of these resources from both past and current teachers. These stories of practice-in-action come from a range of sources. One feature they have in common is an effort to forge genuine intercultural learning by turning the Negative Archive of the boarding school legacy on its head.

In place of enforced silencing, these stories of constructive Native teaching demonstrate the efficacy of open, respectful, and affirming communication. In place of a narrow, skills-focused approach, they offer an imaginative avenue to learning and living through the power of story itself and productive sharing of culture-making practices. In place of competitive success-seeking on an individual level, they enact and invite a community-conscious commitment. Taken together, they convey an ironic point from American educational history: the program to assimilate and "civilize" Indians missed a crucial opportunity for the dominant culture itself to become more civilized (in a deep, true sense) by learning from Indian communities' approaches to teaching their children.[9]

Counter-narratives constructed to critique the boarding school legacy are important resources, as outlined in chapter 4. But Native educators from that prior era have also left us a legacy of their own positive teaching stories that can help us reenvision education. Thus, we can surface specific strategies for an alternative brand of cross-cultural teaching by looking to the accounts of teachers who tried, in the midst of the most intense assimilation programs, to enact alternatives to those same oppressive approaches. Certainly, such work was never fully successful, given the power differentials involved in white-managed education of Native students. Yet even in their most tentative forms, these aspirational texts began a process that has reached a fuller level of agency more recently—one I'll describe in more detail later in the chapter.

In whatever period these alternative approaches have been carried out, one productive source for their rhetorical pragmatism and intercultural vision has been what Gerald Vizenor terms *survivance*, as referenced in the previous chapter, and as described, in shorthand, as "survival + resistance."[10] Another has been a willingness to take on the demanding role of *cultural mediator* (often dubbed a *cultural broker*)—a type of border-crossing intercultural engagement that requires the teacher figure to move back and forth into different cultural settings, adapting practices and language from each so as to make sustained connections. Eventually, this work of mediation can create new understandings to be held communally in an aspirational culture space, one my colleague in global learning programs at TCU, John Singleton, has called a "third space."[11] Because competing pressures continue to be exerted from either "side" of this space—that is, from the different cultures these intercultural guides seek to connect—this teaching role brings intense challenges. Yet it also carries great potential. Today, acting as cultural mediators, a growing number of Native educators choosing to teach in cross-cultural situations are drawing on the learning legacy of past responses to the boarding school era to model constructive intercultural praxis. I believe such approaches can be applied on a larger scale, across multiple sites of cultural exchange, and even, at times, toward the creation of new institutional structures, as this chapter aims to illustrate.

In my own learning, the figure of the *cultural mediator* who generates cross-cultural connections has been embodied by several Native educators, some of whose work I've studied (mainly) through their publications and others whom I've been fortunate enough to observe in action and/or learn from conversationally. Notable mentors through their writing have been Zitkala-Ša, Ella Deloria, Ruth Muskrat Bronson, and Esther "Essie" Burnett Horne (herself a student of both Deloria and Bronson). On a more interpersonal level, I've sought guidance from current role models such as Namorah Byrd, Kimberli Lee, Lisa King, Malea Powell, and, at the NMAI, Renée Gokey and Dennis Zotigh. From reading, observing, conversing, and listening, I have tapped into learning legacies grounded in their generous cross-cultural teaching.

Acculturating Children in Indian Country

K. Tsianina Lomawaima and Teresa L. McCarty begin *To Remain an Indian* by quoting Luther Standing Bear. In 1933, they note, he pointed out how, in Lakota society, every "parent was a teacher," and "all elders were instructors of those younger than themselves," so that much learning came through mentoring and positive, self-affirming experiences. Small wonder, then, that Luther Standing Bear also declared: "America can be revived, rejuvenated, by recognizing a native school of thought. The Indian can save America" (xxi). In that vein, I believe that Native approaches to teaching and learning could bring a saving grace—an alternative vision—to much that is troubling American education today. One helpful source for approaches to emulate is in texts about Indians teaching their own children;

and much of this writing was actually generated in response to the oppressive boarding school program.

Zitkala-Ša provides one such example. As outlined in chapter 4, the main focus for "School Days of an Indian Girl" was to counteract the promotional portraits of assimilation instruction appearing in mass media sources like *Frank Leslie's* by exposing abuses in the system. As a calculated set-up to that middle story in the series, Zitkala-Ša's first *Atlantic* installment offered a strikingly positive contrast to the violence in boarding school programs. In vignettes limning Indians' education of children as far more "civilized" than what her first-person narrator would experience at the white-run Eastern school, Zitkala-Ša advocated for a Native approach to teaching the young.

A number of scholars have underscored this dimension of the first story in the *Atlantic* series. In "Zitkala-Ša and Bicultural Subjectivity," Scott Carpenter has extolled the "Yankton education," depicted in the "Impressions" text as an ironic parallel to her boarding school training, with the former emphasizing "tribal custom and knowledge" acquired through nurturing "familial relationships" and exposure to "oral legends" that lead to "civility" (13). Ruth Spack's "Translation Moves" echoes Carpenter's emphasis on learning through extended family interaction and folktales as central to the Native education practices celebrated in "Impressions." For Spack, this approach involves treating each child "with respect as a person who can learn at an early age" and having young people honor their elders as important sources of knowledge, much of which is transmitted through Dakota stories (49, 50–51). Dorothea Susag's "Zitkala-Ša" essay, meanwhile, stresses the "Impressions" narrative's affirmation of maternal teaching as leading the Native child "to value and practice hospitality and generosity to friends and strangers, and to respect the rights of others" (12).

Several scenes in this first *Atlantic* installment portray experience-based and child-focused teaching practices that gradually prepare learners to be productive community members. For instance, the narrator describes how even simple chores such as fetching water or watching over a corn crop become invested with social value because they address communal needs. Like the intricacies of beadwork, hospitality rites are carried out via patterns learned over time through observation and practice. Elders act on the assumption that children are trying their best to become fully vested in these social practices; thus, the young narrator's clumsy efforts to play hostess to an elder's visit during her mother's absence are honored as much as if they had been correctly done. One section of "Impressions," entitled

"The Legends," presents an engaging description of the student-narrator listening to "neighboring old men and women" who told evening stories of Iktomi while the young girl "sat up eagerly listening to every word" (*AIS*, 71, 72). By absorbing not only the legends' details but also the values they represented, she became a member of her community through a gentle, caring brand of acculturation.

On one level, this description of story-based learning invited Zitkala-Ša's original readers to put themselves in the place of the "Impressions" narrator, attending carefully to what her character hears within the story. On another level, this episode alerted those readers to "listen" to the educative voice the print narrative itself was offering.

When reading the "Impressions" essay as offering both an argument for Native teaching of Native children and an alternative model for educating all children, we can see the seeds of a strategy that other Indian writers would embrace in succeeding years. That is, through story, Native authors would attempt to educate white readers about experiential, values-driven avenues to learning—and how story-oriented language, itself, could serve as a powerful teaching vehicle. In published texts like Charles Eastman's various collections of Native folk tales and Zitkala-Ša's own *Old Indian Legends* (1901), both individual stories and the larger narrative framework had more ambitious goals than merely tapping into white fascination with Indian lore as exotic. These publications also offered white readers a chance to be educated by way of the very legends traditionally disseminated by Native teachers to pass culturally significant resources across generations. Unfortunately, many readers of the time failed to embrace such texts as more than curiosities, just as many white educators in assimilationist institutions during Zitkala-Ša's lifetime failed to recognize the assets for cross-cultural learning embodied in the social practices their students were bringing from home to school.

Still, Native writers were persistent in disseminating this potential resource. Author-scholar-educator Ella Deloria labored for years over her *Waterlily* novel, which depicts the lifelong learning of its heroine within the culturally supportive environment of Dakota tribal society. As a textual boundary guide, *Waterlily* synthesized Deloria's own work as a scholar, creative writer, Sioux educator, and, in the words of Susan Gardner's "Introduction," as a keeper of "collaborative cultural remembrance" (viii). As Gardner points out, Deloria faced daunting challenges in preparing all three of her book-length manuscripts, since "the genres and audiences available to her were culturally inappropriate for what she was trying to accomplish" (vii). Acquiring great experiential skill in anthropology through collaborations with Franz Boas, Deloria translated many Sioux texts in support of his research and collaborated with Boas on *Dakota Grammar* (1941). A graduate of Columbia Teachers College, Deloria drew on that preparation in a number of educational positions across a wide-ranging career, including stints as a teacher at the Haskell Indian School in Lawrence, Kansas, and as director of her alma mater, St. Elizabeth's School, on the Standing Rock Reservation. Still, her lack of doctoral-level academic credentials blocked access to the kind of well-paying position in anthropology that Boas and his colleagues at Columbia could claim, even though their many collaborations demonstrate that Boas himself, along with Ruth Benedict and Margaret Mead, benefited greatly from Deloria's talents while also encouraging her own projects. ("Collaboration," in this case, exemplifies the point that not all working partnerships are egalitarian: varying identities brought differing roles, whatever supportive perspectives Boas, Mead, and Benedict may have harbored as individuals). Despite such constraints, Deloria's knowledge of Sioux culture and her great skill at field research eventually coalesced into a well-regarded scholarly text, *Speaking of Indians* (published in 1944), and her *Waterlily* novel, completed in 1947 but published posthumously in 1988.[12]

Waterlily has emerged as an influential text "revered by Sioux (and other Indian scholars)," as Gardner says, but also increasingly appreciated by students from different cultural backgrounds reading it in university courses and by others finding the novel through the Firekeepers paperback series. As an account of how Sioux adults teach their children, *Waterlily* tracks the experiences of the title character from birth through her own transition to adulthood. Pivotal scenes throughout the narrative endorse Dakota ways of acculturating children. For instance, after Waterlily and her mother Blue Bird join the family of Blue Bird's second husband, Rainbow, Waterlily acquires a half-brother, Little Chief, who enthusiastically joins in the family's efforts to tutor the young toddler. Deloria stresses that, despite "the gap in their ages they always played happily together. Little Chief took much credit from the fact that Waterlily learned to walk under his tutelage, and now he was trying to teach her to talk" (*WL* 33–34). He is joined in this endeavor by grandmother Gloku, who cautions patience when Little Chief worries that Waterlily is unusually slow to speak. "'Waterlily has a voice and she will talk soon, when she is ready,'" declares Gloku. "'No doubt she is teaching herself in her mind and trying out new words where nobody can hear her. She does not want to make mistakes and be laughed at'"

(34). Sure enough, "Suddenly, overnight as it were, the child was talking, glibly and well," so that Little Chief, "triumphant," can affirm their grand-mother's assessment. "'She was learning because I was teaching her,'" says Little Chief, as when he pointed out words for various animals and people. Indeed, Gloku avows: "'Yes, you were a good teacher.'" Further, the nar-rator adds: "Gloku was herself an excellent tutor. She had trained her own children well, so that they had good manners and were respected in the tribe. Then she had helped with her grandchildren's training and now she was starting in again with Waterlily" (34).

In such episodes, Deloria provides her readers with an authoritative counter-narrative to the assimilationist educational agenda—a model for acculturating children through patient, respectful, personalized teaching grounded in everyday life. For instance, she has Gloku counsel Little Chief that learners progress at different paces and in different ways. Gloku also reminds Little Chief (and Deloria's audience) that listening can be as pow-erful an avenue to learning as more overt vocal recitation; that learners desire to be respected for their efforts, not aggressively prodded; and that quiet, interior reflection can pave the way to more visible performance. Similarly, this exchange demonstrates how, for the Dakota, teaching of children is a multigenerational communal enterprise. This theme recurs across numerous scenes in the novel, as when Deloria describes elders teaching young children the centrality of gift-giving. "The idea behind it was this: if everyone gives, then everyone gets; it is inevitable" (52). By repeating and self-consciously modeling such maxims for their children, elders ensure that everyone internalizes these concepts. So, as Deloria's narrative establishes, hospitality and generosity become shared values that, in turn, ensure shared social practices. Communal teaching builds on and reinforces community ties.

At one point in the novel, Deloria enacts a deft shift to satire, when members of Waterlily's community travel to a military camp where white soldiers and their families are living. Upon returning home, Waterlily's puzzled uncle describes the whites' behavior toward their children as shocking: "'You should see them—slapping their little ones' faces and lash-ing their poor little buttocks to make them cry! Why, almost any time of day . . . you can hear the soldiers' wives screaming at their children. Yes, they thoroughly scold them. I have never seen children treated so'" (103). Blue Bird (Waterlily's mother) and others listening to this report struggle to make sense of such behavior, asking, "'Why do they do it?'" One Dakota woman speculates that perhaps "'when the children are naughty, that is the quaint way of training them to be good. By talking loudly and fast and by striking them, the people doubtless hope to scare them into good behavior. I know it sounds queer'" (104). Blue Bird—herself such a patient and loving teacher of young children—is appalled by this account. Hugging one of her own offspring close, while "feeling sick with sympathy for the unknown children," she continues to worry over the "horrible lot" of white youngsters, suffering cruel punishment rather than progressing through the loving, gentler, more reliable path to acculturation available within her own Dakota community.

By the time Deloria created this dialogue, these abusive (so-called) teaching approaches, carried out in many boarding school settings, were well known. Setting her narrative in the days before Dakota children would become victims of such punitive environments, Deloria simultaneously shows the superiority of Native teaching and situates the flawed strategies of white education within a cultural system that penalizes (and wounds) whites themselves. Abused as children, adult whites will become the oppressors of Indian children in boarding school settings, even as the more enlightened vision for acculturation that has been validated in the narrative of Waterlily's progress toward adulthood will be undermined by separating indigenous children from their families, where positive learning could unfold in a supportive context.

The connection between Deloria's indirect critique of white-dominated instructional strategies within boarding school settings, on the one hand, and the far more productive model in preassimilation Dakota communities, on the other, was not lost on Diane Wilson. The title of Wilson's book, *Beloved Child: A Dakota Way of Life*, comes from a ceremony celebrated in Deloria's novel—a link that Wilson highlights in a prefatory excerpt from *Waterlily*. On multiple occasions in her narrative, Wilson returns to this textual resource as an inspirational guide toward recovering Dakota approaches for teaching. Repeatedly citing Deloria's text in her own memoir-cum-teaching account, Wilson casts specific elements in Indians' education of their children today as shaped by an awareness of the negative heritage of whites' oppressive policies (including boarding schools as well as removals and other constraints associated with reservation life). But she also celebrates the positive legacy of role model Native educators such as Deloria.

Accordingly, when meeting with Clifford Canku and Yvonne Wynde to discuss contemporary Native teaching approaches as the subject of *Beloved Child*, Wilson begins by referencing "the beloved child ceremony in Ella Deloria's book *Waterlily*."[13] Wilson celebrates Native self-governance and Indian parents' moves to include children in the annual March commemorating past assaults on Dakota rights, especially whites "depriving them of their ability to raise and protect their children" (36). In a series of visits with Native role models who are excelling as educators today, Wilson highlights approaches to acculturating children that are grounded in the vision of all young people as, truly, "Beloved." For example, in conversations with Harley Eagle, his wife, and his children, Wilson directly associates the need to "heal from historical trauma" with a commitment to "raise beloved children" (46). For the Eagle family, homeschooling has represented just such a commitment. However, rather than suggesting that a Native-oriented education program would require home-based teaching, Wilson's conversations with the Eagles stress a broader system, including collaboration within the family, shared activities beyond the small family unit, and "restorative justice"[14] practices using "circle" techniques to "become competent listeners and speakers" who respect and welcome others' diverse ideas (51).

So, too, in chronicling Clifford Canku's "gifts as a teacher and as a spiritual leader," Wilson notes his (and the Dakota) emphasis on learning through "'real-life situations'" rather than "'rote learning'" (85). Hearkening back to preassimilationist acculturation strategies, Wilson honors Clifford's focus on teaching social roles through stages that stress improving character, valuing kinship, and embracing one's role in the family and larger community (87). Taken together, Deloria's *Waterlily* and the allusive *Beloved Child* offer up a positive counter-narrative framework for teaching today, both within and beyond families and local communities.

White Teachers in Assimilationist Zones

When I reflect on the shameful history of Native children being abused by white teachers, I feel overwhelmed by a collective sense of guilt. How can I, as a white teacher myself, ever hope to atone for such horrific practices perpetrated in so many white-run classrooms aimed at "killing" Indians? I can't. But I hope I can draw on studies of that painful history, and on alliances with accomplished Native educators today, to improve my own cross-cultural work. Wondering if white teachers can ever be worthy of trust from Native students and Native educators of today, I take a little comfort from the fact that a few white educators from the assimilationist era did try to cross cultural boundaries and even had a sustained, positive impact on their students. Ella Deloria acknowledged the influence of two such mentors by dedicating *Waterlily* to her anthropologist colleague Ruth Fulton Benedict and, earlier, *Speaking of Indians* to Mary Sharp Francis, a "'beloved teacher and a great missionary'" (quoted by Gardner, vi–vii). So perhaps another relevant site of study for an educator like me is, indeed, the past teaching of whites situated in instructional sites for Indians, where an archive of some partial successes at intercultural exchange can be excavated.

Elsewhere, I've examined the work of white missionary teachers who worked in other cross-cultural settings, including China and Portuguese West Africa.[15] By writing about such figures and trying to historicize the goals of their rhetoric, which was generally intended for white readers and was certainly constrained by their own racial biases and very restricted worldviews, I might have appeared to a hurried reader to be affirming their perspectives. Instead, I have been trying to recover and understand such standpoints, in all their complexity. For example, the aspects of their work that represent resistance (however limited) to then-dominant narratives driving cross-cultural education give us hope for continued progress in intercultural relationships. At the same time, if we ignore the ways in which their pedagogy was bound up with colonizing impulses, we miss equally important responsibilities to critique our own teaching.

In that context, within this chapter highlighting Native teachers as role models for us today, I want to pause here to mark the position of the rare white women educators who resisted (aspects of) the assimilationist program. Perhaps their writings helped pave the way for shifts in other whites' attitudes toward Native people and Indian education. At the least, it appears their teaching had a positive influence on individual students, such as Ella Deloria, who would themselves become teachers. (Sherman Alexie, whose award-winning young adult novel *The Absolutely True Diary of a Part-time Indian* includes affirming portrayals of a few white teachers encountered by his protagonist, seems to envision such a possibility.) Furthermore, educators who find themselves in comparable situations today—perhaps, for example, as white middle-class teachers in urban K-12 schools with "majority minority" student populations,[16] or in post-secondary institutions serving many first-generation college students—may benefit from examining this context so as to reflect critically on their own classroom practices.

What can we who represent "majority" culture to our "minority" students learn from the stories of white educators who made attempts— however limited—to grapple with the practical, intellectual, and ethical challenges of teaching Native students during the boarding school era?

Patricia Carter has pointed out that white women teachers who tried to resist approaches to assimilationist education faced great difficulty. She explains that many of those working in Bureau of Indian Affairs (BIA) schools in the early twentieth century came to their assignments with very inadequate understanding of Native cultures, at best, and that therefore "much of the criticism of the BIA schools has been laid at the feet of the teachers." Carter then suggests that reading autobiographical narratives by teachers themselves yields a more complicated portrait.[17]

Carter's archival research revealed that at least some teachers in BIA schools became self-conscious advocates for students. Carter studied texts by six BIA-affiliated Anglo-American women educators—Minnie Braithwaite Jenkins, Mary Ellicott Arnold, Mabel Reed, Estelle Aubrey Brown, Gertrude Golden, and Flora Gregg Iliff. Carter's research showed that, even though numerous white women were "only in it for the paycheck," others embraced advocacy roles. All six teachers whom Carter studied opposed depictions of Indian students as intellectually deficient. These teachers repeatedly carried out resistance efforts in the boundary space between official policy and actual teaching practice. They defied the taboo against Native language use in the schools, expanded the curriculum to include Native cultural practices, secured enhanced instructional materials, improved school menus with healthier and more appealing foods, acquired better medical staffing and supplies, and addressed oppressive working conditions in places like the institutions' laundries (71–73). As sometimes the victims of sexual harassment and other abuses in the workplace themselves, Carter noted, some Anglo women teachers became vocal promoters of reforming BIA instruction, at the local level of their own work and beyond. Though their efforts were "limited, intuitive, often egocentric, indiscriminative, and [sadly] unproductive," Carter gave them some credit for achieving a resistant stance "consciously political and thus counter-hegemonic," as "they began to struggle for something larger than themselves" (79).

Carter certainly does not claim that her subjects are representative of the cohort of white women in BIA schools at that time.[18] Casting themselves as "disenfranchised workers and powerless change agents who were personally demoralized by the system," the women whose accounts Carter recovered were, she argues, "locked in a never-ending struggle between accommodating and resisting the system" (54). That is, Carter proposes, while individual classroom teachers were used as "tools of the dominant culture to reinforce power relationships," at least some were "questioning, resisting, and trying to change" that very power structure (54–55). Therefore, Carter calls for a nuanced view: we should, she urges, recognize examples of "teacher agency, resistance, and growth through interaction with cultures other than their own" among some individual white educators in assimilationist schools (55).

Meanwhile, if countering the racist structures of assimilationist education was challenging for white women with progressive perspectives, imagine the challenges faced by those Native women who, over time, began to claim positions in Indian boarding schools. As Elaine Goodale Eastman's 1911 fictional depiction of her eponymous *Yellow Star* heroine suggests,[19] even the best educated Indian woman teacher working for white-administered schools could expect to face strong challenges to her authority. At the same time, in evaluating the experiences of real-life Native women who taught during the boarding school era, we must remember that differences in specific institutional settings shaped those situations in widely varying ways.

Indian Teachers among Indians

As research by Amanda J. Cobb and Devon A. Mihuseah has shown, even during the peak years of the assimilationist movement, boarding schools managed by Indian Nations themselves tended to provide a far more supportive learning environment than did the now-infamous white-run enterprises modeled on Carlisle. Cobb's *Listening to Our Grandmothers' Stories*, for instance, demonstrates that the Bloomfield Academy, launched through collaboration between the Chickasaw Nation in Oklahoma in 1852 and missionary partners, is "most significant" for "its very difference from other boarding schools for Native American children" (2). Operating with substantial autonomy as a Nation during the antebellum period, the Chickasaw "founded Bloomfield, not because the federal government demanded it, but because the Chickasaw people knew that literacy training was crucial to their survival as a nation, to their preservation" (6). Accordingly, we might even say that this institution had more in common with Spelman, in terms of its student clientele, its administrative agenda, and its curriculum, than with white-run boarding schools seeking enforced assimilation. Cobb's own grandmother attended Bloomfield from 1924 to 1926 (xvii). Cobb affiliates her study with work by Sally J. McBeth (on schooling among west-central Oklahoma Indians) and K. Tsianina Lomawaima (on Chilocco), who underscore positive aspects of schools where Indians' own agency was honored, including promoting "pan-Indian" conceptions of "a strong, common ethnic identity" (Cobb, *Listening*, 8). Cobb also aligns her findings with those of Devon Mihesuah, who did site-specific archival recovery on the Cherokee Female Seminary.

Overall, while they both take note of class-based bias bound up with full- versus mixed-blood identities, Cobb joins Mihesuah in emphasizing the striking "disparity between the boarding schools founded by southeastern tribes [themselves] and the federally run boarding schools" (9). Though Cobb tracks shifts in emphases in the literacies promoted by successive administrations at Bloomfield (missionary, tribal, and eventually federal), she also demonstrates that the relative wealth of the Chickasaw Nation, its longstanding commitment to providing education for its children (including sending some to Choctaw Academy in Kentucky during the Removal years), and its high degree of control over the institution founded in Oklahoma made for much more positive responses from the alumnae she interviewed than an overgeneralized view of this period's schools would suggest.

Whatever the setting, over time, an increasing number of teachers in the boarding schools were themselves Natives. Gradually, from the close of the nineteenth century and into the early decades of the twentieth, Native educators acquired professional assignments even in white-run boarding school settings. Anne Ruggles Gere has accounted for the notable growth in the number of Natives holding such roles, beginning in the 1890s. One factor leading to this increase, Gere reports, was the development of teacher education programs at the five largest off-reservation schools: Carlisle, Haskell, Genoa, Salem, and Chilocco. Accordingly, by 1899, Gere indicates: "Native Americans comprised 45 percent of the staff of the Indian School Service, the federal agency responsible for administering government-sponsored schools," and "more than 15 percent of the total 1,166 Indian employees" of the organization were teachers; further, "Indians comprised 39 percent of all the industrial teachers, 65 percent of the school disciplinarians, and 4 percent of matrons." Thus, there were "enough Native American teachers," overall, "to ensure that each of the 153 boarding schools (both on- and off-reservation) then in existence could have had at least one" (Gere, "Indian Heart," 39–40).

Garnering more instructor positions did not lead to rapid changes in curriculum, however. Although some institutions allowed Indian teachers to incorporate elements from Native culture into the curriculum, others (like Carlisle and its most committed imitators) were far more constraining. Indeed, Gere explains, "Many schools made it difficult for Native-American teachers to influence the structures or people in the institution, thereby requiring them to use considerable ingenuity to shape the learning environment of their students" (45). Like teachers who today find themselves opposing broad mandates that their knowledge of students' actual needs tells them are misplaced, the educators Gere highlights resisted more on a classroom level than they could systemically.[20]

Given Carter's findings that even the most determinedly empathetic white teachers found any challenges to assimilation practices difficult, and Gere's parallel portrait of the constraints facing Native teachers during the boarding school era, we should not be surprised that Zitkala-Ša's portrayal of herself as a young Indian woman teaching at Carlisle paints a self-portrait of frustration. Thus, in "An Indian Teacher among Indians," the third installment in Zitkala-Ša's 1900 *Atlantic* series, we enter a site of cross-cultural teaching made oppressive by virtue of intense power differentials.

Typically, Zitkala-Ša's original audience would have come to this story last in their reading of the three-part series. Based on its title, we might expect this to be the moment when she would fully articulate an alternative, Native-informed approach to cross-cultural teaching, one overtly countering the white agenda depicted in her middle installment—the Carlisle-based programs by then spread across the continent. Actually, though, we see hardly any of her own classroom teaching here. Instead, this account, briefest of the three *Atlantic* narratives, highlights multiple restraints on her work at Carlisle. One is symbolized in the "small, carpeted room, with ghastly walls and ceiling," where she is to live, in a space that may be assigned as *her own*, but which, in its tomb-like features, is a stark contrast to the "cool, refreshing shade" outside and the wide open plains of her youth (*AIS*, 104–5). Whatever her teaching goals may have been on arrival, she is quickly reminded who is in charge, as the "imposing" Pratt himself pays her a visit, immediately making her feel "frail and languid" in comparison with his "wondrous height" and dictatorial energy (105). Conveying "disappointment" in his survey of her exhausted post-travel appearance, Pratt proffers a "greeting" but also an implied warning (105), reinforced soon afterward when she describes herself as persistently "watched by those around me" once she begins work (106).[21]

Having situated herself at Carlisle in Part I, Zitkala-Ša suddenly shifts not to a teaching scene there but to another journey: she is very quickly sent west to recruit new students.[22] Most of this section describes the sorrowful situation that she finds her mother and brother living in, with her parent's house in disrepair and her sibling having lost his job as a "government clerk" to "a white son" of "the Great Father at Washington" (a pointed reference to rampant nepotism in Indian Affairs appointments). With obvious bitterness, Zitkala-Ša's mother observes that "Dawée [the character standing in for the author's brother David] has not been able to make use of the education the Eastern school has given him," since his advocacy for local Indians against the graft of government officials has led to dismissal from his position (109). In this painful conversation, readers ("listening" with the narrator) encounter the sad results of Indian education programs like the one for which Zitkala-Ša had been sent to recruit. In the narrative's final section, entitled "Retrospection," the author describes her autobiographical persona as reluctantly returning to Carlisle, where, over succeeding months, she recognizes that the "army of white teachers in Indian schools" has internalized a poisoned "missionary creed." Clearly, she finds, this stance entailed "self-preservation" more than unselfish service:

> When I saw an opium-eater holding a position as teacher of Indians, I did not understand what good was expected, until a Christian in power replied that this pumpkin-colored creature had a feeble mother to support. An inebriate paleface sat stupid in a doctor's chair, while Indian patients carried their ailments to untimely graves, because his fair wife was dependent upon him for her daily food. (111)

Furthermore, she observes, when the government finally does attempt to monitor the Carlisle program, what inspectors see is prearranged to paint a falsely rosy picture. Closing her story with a grim overall assessment, Zitkala-Ša condemns the white evaluators of Carlisle and similar institutions for "pass[ing] idly through the Indian schools during the last decade, afterward to boast of their charity to the North American Indian. But few there are who have paused to question whether real life or long-lasting death lies beneath this semblance of civilization" (113).

Why does an essay designated as being by "An Indian Teacher" choose not to depict the writer's own direct instruction of Indian students?[23] I think this absence is related, rhetorically and experientially, to the inescapable limitations facing Native teachers in white-run boarding schools. No Indian teacher working in such a setting would have had access to the level of policy-making, resource-acquiring, or curriculum-designing action required to make system-level changes in the program. Indeed, as "An Indian Teacher Among Indians" demonstrates, Native educators in such environments would have been restricted to calculated maneuvering within a very tight space of agency.[24] By underscoring the exasperating confines she faced as an Indian teacher, rather than depicting any small victories she may have achieved with/for particular students, Zitkala-Ša implicitly calls on her white readers—including the very white women who were, then, the major source for staffing Native classrooms—to take responsibility for changing the status quo. The sophisticated writer who produced this *Atlantic* series was, in effect, using an account of her constrained capacity as a teacher to offer up instruction to her white readers. In her final address to the very cultural and political arbiters whose power was enabling assimilationist teaching, Zitkala-Ša used delineations of its abuses from a trapped teacher's standpoint to craft her plea for reform.

For one sign that this call was heard, in terms of its aesthetic features, but brushed aside as a directive for redesigning Indian education, we can turn to the response of a then well-known literary critic, Elisabeth Luther Cary. Cary's "Recent Writings by American Indians," published in 1902 in *The Book Buyer*, assesses accounts of their schooling by Charles Eastman, Francis La Flesche, and Zitkala-Ša. For Cary, the *Atlantic* pieces offer unmistakable evidence of the author's literary skill: "Zitkala-Ša is not only an educated Indian, but a writer of unusual quality. Her work is nine times heated by the cruelty of her mental and moral experience. If she continues it[,] she can hardly fail to make an impression in a field where differences of race count for nothing and greatness of achievement counts for everything" (25).

Though convinced of Zitkala-Ša's literary skill, Cary nonetheless criticizes the author's tone, contrasting it with La Flesche's account of his schooling as conveying the "radical transformation" undergone with his "many little" schoolmates from a stance "not indifferent to their advantages—certainly not rebellious or bitterly opposed to their surroundings" (22). Directly opposite, Cary finds, is the "different note" struck by Zitkala-Ša's account, which grew out of what Cary dubs an inherent "melancholy," one "that forces sympathy, even where it is not admitted to be rational." Accordingly, for Cary, the "grievances set forth with truly compelling eloquence, are those which only an intensely sensitive nature would nurse and remember, and, after many years, record" (24). As such, they are indeed moving to read about, and they make a worthy "contribution to our literature" by exhibiting genuine "literary value." Yet, although this story is "[s]trange, pathetic, and caustic" enough to "burn . . . into the reader's consciousness," Zitkala-Ša's "emotions, concentrated and violent, strik[ing] us with an electric shock," elicit no call from Cary for programmatic change

(25). The words achieve striking affect, Cary affirms. Yet her review shows no sign of having been enlisted as an ally in a larger political battle against programs aimed at killing Indians' identities through assimilation teaching.[25] For Cary, Zitkala-Ša's call to readers' feelings leads not to self-critical empathy but only to an awareness of literary skill at work.

Alliances as Avenues of Access

A somewhat more positive view than Zitkala-Ša's *Atlantic* story could envision for Native teachers' influence on Indian education had appeared almost a decade earlier in S. Alice Callahan's *Wynema: A Child of the Forest*, published in 1891.[26] Here, intriguingly, access to Native agency hinged on imagining a collaborative approach to cross-racial teaching.

Like Zitkala-Ša's "An Indian Teacher among Indians," this fictional text also positioned its author as writing from a Native perspective. Accordingly, the original "Publisher's Preface" to *Wynema* touted the volume's groundbreaking effort to set forth "the Indians' side of the Indian question told by an Indian born and bred." Concurrently, though, the preface pointed to limits associated with this authentic authorial standpoint, as the validating (and apparently white) "we" publishing voice reasserted the familiar stereotype of a "simple people" full of "inherent weaknesses" that had, this introduction said, left their mark in "the crudeness or incompleteness of the work" at hand (ix). The readers presumably invoked here anticipated those Zitkala-Ša would aim for in 1900: sympathetic, potentially, but nonetheless assuming their own superiority, given widespread views about racial hierarchies at the time. Small wonder, with this audience in mind, that Callahan would have sought the possible rhetorical benefits of creating a *pair* of appealing fictional figures, one white and one (part) Indian. Hence, the narrative tracked a white-Indian alliance rather than assigning textual advocacy to a single character embodying Callahan's own background as an Indian teacher of other Indians, however well-educated and representative of Creek aristocracy.

The novel's title character, Wynema Harjo, is a mixed-blood Muscogee (Creek) Indian who becomes the prized pupil of Genevieve Weir, an idealistic white southerner working at a mission school in the West.[27] The first section of the plot focuses on Genevieve's experiences as a Methodist teacher eager to learn about Muscogee culture. Through the gentle intervention of missionary Gerald Keithly, she gradually recognizes value in Muscogee practices like the Green Corn Dance.[28] In fact, Genevieve develops such a strong affiliation with her students that, during a visit home, she rejects a marriage offer from a family friend because of his anti-Indian prejudice. Meanwhile, Wynema, who has been embracing Genevieve's instruction while continuing to identify with the tribal community, finds the perfect mate in her teacher's brother. A pair of marriages celebrates intercultural possibilities for America's future when Genevieve accepts Keithly's proposal. Along the way, a notable rhetorical strategy for drawing white readers into critique of the United States' misguided Indian policies is Callahan's repeated depiction of these four characters' conversations about issues such as allotment and political corruption undermining the Muscogee community.[29]

In spite of Callahan's efforts to pitch her text to a white readership, the novel seems to have drawn only limited attention when it first appeared in the 1890s ("Editor's Introduction," xvii). But the narrative is significant today—partly for the intricate rhetorical pragmatism it strives to employ. Though written by an author with strong tribal ties, *Wynema* exhibits contradictions somewhat reminiscent of Elaine Goodale Eastman's narratives. With three of the four characters in the marriage plot cast as white, the novel reaffirms the dependent political position of Native peoples. Furthermore, although Genevieve and Wynema both use nurturing rather than punitive educational approaches, and although Reverend Keithly's continued touting of Native culture seems aimed at undermining hierarchies, assimilation remains the most efficacious choice for Indians, as seen in the educational trajectory of Wynema herself. Meanwhile, as in Zitkala-Ša's later account, precious few scenes take readers within the classroom itself, so the narrative lacks alternative models of actual curriculum in action. Instead, Callahan's repeated dialogues around policy issues emphasize how these forces exercise control over cross-cultural pedagogy. In this context, Cari Carpenter has observed how the righteous anger that could have been expressed by Wynema is more fully articulated by Genevieve, replaying a pattern, Carpenter argues, from earlier texts where white women assert moral leadership, pushing Natives into the background in alliances where access to social power, ultimately, is unequal.[30]

These mixed messages may help us better understand the contradictions between Zitkala-Ša's overtly resistant *Atlantic* writing and other elements in her life story, including having traveled and performed with the Carlisle band, having actively opposed peyote use, and having campaigned for US citizenship for Native peoples.[31] Perhaps, reminiscent of Callahan, she came to view sustained (if unequal) collaboration with white leaders as the most productive avenue for achieving reform. In what William Willard has characterized as a politically savvy phase of her career, she engaged in several enterprises after her marriage to Raymond T. Bonnin (a mixed-race Nakota Sioux) that resulted in narratives less "literary" than the *Atlantic* stories so often studied today but, Willard argues, fruitful politically.[32] Along those lines, an October 1918 article in *Forum* locates Zitkala-Ša (identified here by her married name of Gertrude Bonnin) as an inspiring example of Indian women "do[ing] their bit" for the US effort in World War I. Quoting Bonnin, the upbeat report references Indian women's selling "'their most precious bead ornaments in order to give to war funds—especially the Red Cross.'"[33] Here and in her own writings of this period, Bonnin often seems to be promoting Native peoples as eager for, and worthy of, the US citizenship she and others were seeking through organizations such as the Society of American Indians (SAI), a stance at odds with seeing tribal national sovereignty as paramount. Lobbying in Washington, DC, writing and editing for the SAI publication, and building networks within, first, the Republican Party and, later, the Democratic Party, Bonnin and her husband cultivated relationships with allies like John Collier, commissioner of Indian Affairs for the federal government.

One narrative illustrating this alliance-building strategy is the 1924 collaborative report entitled *Oklahoma's Poor Rich Indians*, which Zitkala-Ša cowrote (under her Gertrude Bonnin signature) with Charles H. Fabens (representing the American Indian Defense Association) and Matthew K. Sniffen (for the Indian Rights Association) to document abuses that their subtitle dubs "An Orgy of Graft and Exploitation of the Five Civilized Tribes—Legalized Robbery."[34] With Bonnin serving as a research partner under the auspices of the General Federation of Women's Clubs, the three authors spent "about five weeks in Eastern Oklahoma during the months of November and December, 1923, making a first-hand study" of "the Indian probate situation among the Five Civilized Tribes" (3). Citing the need for radical policy changes to save the tribes there from "pauperization and virtual extermination," the pamphlet calls on readers for immediate aid. Precipitating the investigation were abuses associated with congressional legislation that, in practice, had led to Indian land rights being stolen by unscrupulous "judges, guardians, attorneys, bankers, merchants" in the region (5). Large-scale exploitation of the holders of Dawes Act allotments in Oklahoma arose in the wake of oil discoveries there, as many Natives were declared legally incompetent to manage their affairs and thus rendered easy prey. Besides "excessive and unnecessary administrative costs, unconscionable fees and commissions," the investigative team found far worse manipulations, based in "flagrant disregard of the Indians' welfare" and driven by greed. Among the most heinous charges brought in this report are accounts of "young Indian girls (mere children in size and mentality)" being "robbed of their virtue and their property through kidnapping and a liberal use of liquor" (6). In a separate section of the pamphlet where these crimes are chronicled, the report declares that these "phases of our investigation . . . can be presented best by a feminine mind," so that the horrific details are assigned "to Mrs. Bonnin to describe"—an indication both of the degree to which such cases overstepped moral boundaries and of the trust accorded to her gendered reporting and writing ability, in such a sensitive area.

In this section, the text shifts from a rather detached, though forceful, perspective to a compelling series of narrative case studies rendered in vivid detail, with several episodes including first-person authentication by Bonnin, as in "I personally met Millie Naharkey [one victim], and was struck by her smallness of stature, her child's voice and her timidity" and the associated assessment, "I grew dumb at the horrible things she rehearsed. . . . There was nothing I could say. Mutely I put my arms around her, whose great wealth had made her a victim of an unscrupulous, lawless, party, and whose little body was mutilated by a drunken fiend who assaulted her day and night" (26). Horrified that Millie's "terrified screams brought no help" initially, the author here infuses the kind of intense, affect-oriented description Zitkala-Ša had used years before in her *Atlantic* counter-narratives into a multigenre text that simultaneously invokes gendered sentimental discourse, a witness-oriented authority grounded in Native-to-Native access, and investigative reporting bolstered by an alliance with white male authority.

Similarly, later in this first-person section, Bonnin strategically alludes to the report's title itself while also foregrounding her emotional response to the case of "Martha,—a Shawnee, and widow of an Osage": "I felt an overwhelming indignation at the legal helplessness of a poor, rich Indian woman" (29, 31). Shifting back to a shared "we" voice at its close, this complex account builds to an insistent call for immediate change: "These cases, we think, are sufficient to show the hopelessness of the present situation. . . . There is no hope of any reformation of the present system, and if action is delayed a few years there will be no Indians with property to be protected" (39). Signing the report along with her coauthors, then, Bonnin signals a strategic self-positioning as a border-crossing guide with a voice empowered through collaboration. Capitalizing on the connections desig-

Figure 5.1. Gertrude Simmons Bonnin as a speaker at the Catholic Sioux Congress, Holy Rosary Mission, South Dakota, Pine Ridge Reservation, 1920. Courtesy of the Marquette University Archives, Bureau of Catholic Indian Missions Records, ID (BCIM) 00684.

nated by their various institutional affiliations, she and her coauthors together seek access to cross-cultural intervention. Based on her gender and
her Indian racial identity, she has been able to secure stories otherwise still
suppressed. Based on her alliance with Fabens and Sniffen as coauthors,
she has gained a publication venue aimed at the audience best positioned
to remedy the situation, so that she can channel righteous indignation
through shared agency. While *Oklahoma's Poor Rich Indians* has not (yet)
drawn the same level of attention as the 1900 *Atlantic* memoirs, this text
from later in the author's career illuminates her rhetorical sophistication.
Blending language that echoes official, formal government discourse with
interpolated stories tied to lived experience, this hybrid genre reconfirms
Zitkala-Ša/Bonnin's ability to cross cultural boundaries in public discourse,
varying her composing strategies in line with different contexts. In this
case, as an investigative reporter speaking to her readers in a still-gendered
voice, she offers up a painful story driven by an implied hope for support.

Native Teachers Claiming Authority

Twenty years after the 1924 release of *Oklahoma's Poor Rich Indians*,
Oklahoma-born Cherokee author Ruth Muskrat Bronson published *Indians Are People, Too*.[35] With its six chapters organized like an alternative
textbook aimed at disabusing whites of their familiar misconceptions about
Indian history, Bronson's treatise utilizes such postcolonial rhetorical strategies as a back-of-the-book map of the United States simultaneously mimicking and reconfiguring its usual boundaries by replacing state lines with
icons and notations demarcating Indian tribal nations.[36] To refute racist
stereotypes, she reports that "[p]sychological tests have proved that Indians possess the same capacities as whites," thus undermining one excuse
for the "discrimination and prejudice" still being faced by Indians in the
mid-twentieth century (93). As additional evidence of Indian capability, she
reminds her readers that "Indian youth, in numbers that run to more than
twenty thousand, are fighting in the armed forces all over the world" (125).

Bronson's book creatively binds up a counter-narrative response to
abuses of Native peoples with a positive alternative vision. Initial chapters
excoriate assimilationist teaching's heritage. Chronicling the long-term
negative impact of the boarding school movement, she mocks its rationale and refutes claims for positive results: "The idea back of this policy
was that if Indian children were kept out of the Indian environment long
enough and educated in white ways assiduously enough, they would forget

their Indian background and become 'civilized' by taking on white ways. The implication was that upon graduation the Indian student would be accepted by the white world. He seldom was" (95). Along with such counter-thrusts against dominant narratives, Bronson issues direct polemical calls to an anticipated white readership. For instance, in the opening of chapter 2, entitled "Our Mother, the Land," Bronson rejects the clichéd assessment that "[w]hat happened to the Indian in this country is too bad, but it is over and done with." In its place, she insists that

> deeds of such magnitude cannot be over and done with. They do not stand alone in a period of time. Their tentacles reach out to on-coming generations and touch the lives of people who live centuries after the deeds themselves are only echoes in history. I am an Indian, living in the present now, but I carry the burden and the responsibility of those distant years. So do you, whether you are Indian or white. (33–34)

Bronson's early chapters strike a careful balance between recounting wrongs suffered by America's Indians and acknowledging the support some whites provided.[37] For example, in revisiting the Cherokee Removal, she condemns Andrew Jackson for defying the Supreme Court's decision in favor of the Cherokee and observes: "The Cherokee cause was lost; their confidence in the Federal government destroyed; their faith in the justice and good will of the white man grievously shaken" (40). She poses the righteous query, "Where were the Christian people of the nation? In the records of history their voices are strangely few" (41). But Bronson also praises those same "few" allies for extraordinary courage, thereby offering potential white role models for her readers. In particular, she credits the "compassionate" missionaries who "sharing their hardships, comforting their despair, burying their dead," accompanied the Cherokee "into their exile" (41).

Similarly, she notes, "In 1890, the very same year that the last and most heartless battle was fought with the Dakotas at Wounded Knee, across the continent two Christian women pitched their tent on the edge of the Navajo reservation and began there the labor of sacrificial devotion that developed in the Methodist Navajo mission at Farmington, New Mexico," where these allies endured "criticism and scorn" for "teach[ing] the Indians about the life of Christ" (52). She praises Bishop William Hobart Hare's commitment "to raise up a native ministry" among the Sioux (135).

Figure 5.2. On December 13, 1923, Ruth Muskrat [Bronson] presented President Calvin Coolidge with a copy of *The Red Man in the United States: An Intimate Study of the Social, Economic and Religious Life of the American Indian*, by G. E. E. Lundquist (New York: George H. Doran Company). On June 2 of 1924, Congress would pass—and Coolidge would sign into law—the Indian Citizenship Act. Library of Congress, National Photo Company Collection. (c) Library of Congress, National Photo Company Collection (p. 25, no. 27839).

Much of the book proclaims Indians' inherent right to educate their own children (75), determine their own destiny (80–81), and even model superior approaches to education for whites by restoring Native practices (85–86; 110). Paramount among these values for positive teaching is a commitment "to bring the entire Indian community into the life of the school" (97). In Bronson's resolute demand for "genuine sharing" in the leadership of Indian education, we see a new stage in the process of Natives claiming a right to teach their own children and to have a lasting impact on the larger American community. Quoting Navajo elders who had defended this mandate, Bronson touts their commitment to affiliating the "hearts" of children with their home place and a communal life of "peace and harmony" (160).[38]

That Bronson herself had just such commitments and capabilities as a teacher is evident in the account Esther Burnett Horne includes of Bronson's influence in *Essie's Story*. Describing the mentorship of Bronson and Ella Deloria at Haskell Indian Institute, Horne interweaves narrative examples of their impact with analysis of their teaching goals. So, Horne reports:

> During my senior year, I accompanied Ruth Muskrat Bronson and other students to participate in programs that we presented to schools, to church groups, and to service organizations. Instrumental and vocal music, and talks related to our Indian heritage, were part of the programs. . . . This was my first exposure to public speaking. While on these tours, Ruth arranged for us to stay overnight in people's homes, to eat and to socialize with them. She took us beyond the confinement of the boarding school. Both Ruth and Ella wanted us to learn to survive in a variety of environments. They wanted us to be proud of who we were as Indian people and as boarding school students but also to be comfortable in explaining our identity to the non-Indian world. [39]

Horne's memoir illustrates how some students from her era of the boarding school movement could capitalize on their learning experiences to become revered, productive teachers of other Indians. Pioneer educators like Ruth Muskrat Bronson, teaching at Haskell when Esther was enrolled there from 1924 to 1929, were central to this process as, with each succeeding generation, more Native educators gained authority within the educational system itself. Horne credits both Bronson and Deloria, accordingly, as her role models (41). Reconfirming that affiliation, Horne's memoir tex-tually enacts the stance of rhetorical mediator, with *Essie's Story* straddling the space between personal story of teaching/learning and cultural analysis.

To create what the subtitle designates as *The Life and Legacy of a Shoshone Teacher*, Horne narrated her experiences to her friend and coauthor Sally McBeth, a white anthropologist whose description of their collaboration emphasizes Horne's agency and control over the text. Horne and McBeth explicitly identify their complementary yet distinct roles, as well as their shared feminist values around the cultural power of storytelling grounded in memory. For example, the first voice in the text is Horne's, in a preface, where she describes their "collaborative approach" (vii). In McBeth's lon-ger "Introduction" (xi–xli), she presents an academic perspective on their process: she locates the text in relation to other anthropological life histo-ries but also underlines this narrative's commitment to having Essie's voice claim ultimate authority. Thus, McBeth observes, "Through our intensive work together, Essie and I created a close bond of respect and rapport" that aimed to find meaning in story. She quotes Essie's own affirmation that their "'friendship has enhanced the project'" (xix). At the same time, McBeth acknowledges the differences in their perspectives, outlines traits their project has in common with other "collaborative life histories" (versus "self-authored autobiographies" [xxviii]), and proposes recurring themes she feels are important to Horne's story. The bulk of the text, nonetheless, is Essie's own narrative, and even for the introduction (where McBeth is designated as author), Horne has final say, as she comments on the themes McBeth has highlighted, including Essie's "'relationship to Sacajawea,'" an identity-shaping ancestor; her "'boarding school experiences [being] posi-tive for the most part'" (due to having prominent Native instructors); her own commitment to teaching other Natives; and the pivotal influence of her parents' "'teaching us the many positive things about our Indian culture and the many things that Indian people have contributed to the American way of life'" (xl–xli). All in all, though the learning legacy presented in this text developed through collaboration with partners enacting two different roles, it is ultimately, as designated by the title, *Essie's Story*.

Essie's teaching/learning narrative is grounded in autobiographical memory, but she positions her life in relation to larger historical trends and cultural issues. Thus, she describes her own time at Haskell as "pretty happy," praises the "skills [she] learned" as "beneficial to me through my life," and casts her own account as "soften[ing] the point of view that gov-ernment boarding schools were hellish places with harsh discipline and beatings" (36). She stresses that what made her experience positive was the shift in policy, by the time she was a student and, later, a boarding school teacher, to welcoming both Native instructors and their curricular leadership. Similarly, she uses commentary on such longstanding boarding school practices as a "military regime" to show how Indian students creatively responded to otherwise oppressive approaches by connecting them to Indian values: for herself and her husband (whom she met at school), "military experience . . . taught us self-discipline for our later lives. . . . [W]e both knew that self-control was one of the strongest of the Indian values" (36–37). Horne presents her subsequent goals, when "teaching at the Wahpeton Indian School," in similarly affirmative terms: "to instill in these kids a sense of their dignity and worth as individuals," "to continue to integrate Native American materials into the curriculum," and, overall, "to provide them with the same security and sense of self that my Indian teachers, Ruth [Muskrat Bronson] and Ella [Deloria], had instilled in me" (65).

Further, Essie points to ways in which the BIA, over the years, empowered Native teachers even more than in the early stages of her career, particularly once Dr. Willard Beatty led the organization, beginning in 1936 (69–70). At this point, Horne says, she could move from teaching "Native American culture" "secretly" to an overt leadership of curriculum in line with the goals she had always held, for "our young people to have a pride in themselves as individuals, as American citizens, and as tribal members of sovereign nations" (69). In Horne's view, then, US citizenship and affiliation to a tribe as "sovereign" were at last compatible, and she could teach with both contexts in mind.

Learning from Native Educators Today

Growing numbers of Native teachers are extending the legacy of forebears like Ruth Bronson, Ella Deloria, and Esther (Essie) Horne. Fortunately for American education, they are serving both Native and other students, from diverse backgrounds, in a wide range of settings.[40] Furthermore, if we pay close attention, all of us can learn a lot about effective cross-cultural teaching from these colleagues. I am certainly trying to do so. Besides reading their scholarship and observing them in action, I've benefited from the guidance of gifted Native teachers through in-person and online conversations.[41]

Let me elaborate on this multifaceted learning process itself. This part of my research for writing *Learning Legacies* has entailed building a framework that integrates several vital archives from different types of resources, each of which emerges from the larger Archive of Indigenous knowledge about cross-cultural teaching. All three of these resource types—print and material texts (such as images and culture-carrying objects), observable teaching practices, and personal accounts of teaching—can be viewed, in themselves, as positive counter-narratives offering up alternatives to the negative legacy of assimilationist teaching, with some of these models expressed explicitly and others more indirectly. Before closing this chapter with a focus on the third of these strands—conversations with Native role models about their pedagogy—I want to pause here to comment on how each of these three counter-narrative types actually come together in my own teaching philosophy now. Rhetorically, I've tried to embody that "coming together" in the content and organizational structure for chapters 4 and 5, since this process of moving from inductive exploration of cultural resources to constructing pragmatic value systems also represents an example of how I think the humanities and related fields can effectively develop and convey knowledge for daily life, over time. So, let me highlight, briefly and in turn, each of the three strands assembled for this two-chapter section of *Learning Legacies*, in the hope of making visible connections between inductive story-gathering and conceptual organizing that I have tried to articulate through textual pedagogy in this book, particularly in its Native-focused chapters.

One of these strands, addressed in explications earlier in this chapter, taps into print and other material texts—counter-narratives by Native teachers from the Carlisle era and later, offering up positive alternatives to assimilationist education. Also a part of this important resource from and about cross-cultural teaching is the growing body of Natives' own scholarship incisively interpreting this heritage. Though sometimes my engagement with these scholar-theorists appears in endnotes rather than being addressed in detail in my own narrative proper, I want to emphasize that questions they raise and advice they give have been central to my work. As just one example, I would cite the work of Craig Womack, whose *Red on Red* study of Creek national literatures underscores several points I have tried to honor here: enabling "Indian people to speak for themselves," by "prioritizing Native voices" (4); affirming that such criticism, "written by Native scholars, is part of sovereignty" and the rightful assertion of national identities, such as Womack's focus on Creek culture, as "defined within the tribe rather than by external sources" (14); and, at the same time, recognizing "pan-tribalism" (19).[42] This approach to reading Indian and First Nations educators as in conversation with each other has pushed me to see, in scholarly-creative and creative-scholarly texts like Thomas King's *The Truth About Stories*, a counter-narrative mixture of story-sharing, story-making, and story-theorizing that cuts across national and other boundaries.[43] Close and careful reading of this kind of resource, for me, has included everything from noting recurring images in Ella Deloria's *Waterlily*, to paying respectful attention to objects' and labels' historical context in an NMAI exhibit on treaties, to positioning individual historical narratives by an author like Diane Glancy or Robert Conley within their larger oeuvres, to watching for ways that the beadwork image on her professional website reverberates with rhetorical sovereignty arguments in Malea Powell's academic journal essays. In the classroom, I encourage my students to carry out a parallel brand of patient interpretive work, combining close reading with historical awareness.

A second strand of resources I've been using to explore Natives' own cross-cultural teaching has involved observing and reflecting on cultural practices in action, particularly instances of teaching. I've referenced this type of resource in chapters 4 and 5 via descriptions of Native educators at work. They include my time watching guides like Renée Gokey and Dennis Zotigh at the NMAI, participating in workshops like the Standing Peachtree session in Atlanta, noting the inclusive instructional strategies of Diane Glancy as she taught our KCAC group her own *Pushing the Bear* novel, and taking part in the NEH program led by Professor Gerald Vizenor at the University of California, Berkeley. Through such opportunities, I have certainly been studying important content about Native histories, cultures, and peoples. Equally important, though, I've been assembling and refining a repertoire of teaching practices. (As NEH program officer Janet Edwards once advised me, "A scholar in the act of teaching is a text well worth studying.") By reflecting on these experiences of being taught by Native educators (whether in a classroom or at a powwow), I've carried out readings of practitioner-in-action archives that have complemented and extended my study of material archives such as those captured in print.

Along with these counter-narratives of relatively formal praxis, I've tried to think deeply about experiences that might, on the surface, seem to be disconnected moments of cultural tourism,[44] but that I've sought to position within ever-growing webs of personal learning legacies that I can now share in my classroom and with my readers. So, for instance, I've aimed to be an attentive listener during a Saxman village's self-presentation to visitors in their Tlingit clan house and around their totem collection in Ketchikan, Alaska. There I noted, in particular, the respectful collaborations between elders and adolescent guides, pitched as multivocal oral presentations conveying a resilient sense of community. I've embraced an invitation to join a welcome ceremony at Klahowya Village in Stanley Park, Vancouver, Canada, and appreciated the strategic mix of place-based ceremony and intercultural bridge-building achieved through shared symbolic action. I've admired the elaborate costume-enhanced roundhouse dance by Native Brazilian hosts and then celebrated the good-humored irony of their pointing our admittedly surprised tour group up a hill to their internet-wired home-places. I've listened to Aboriginal Australians tell of their own bitter learning legacy of enforced schooling across multiple generations and heard inspiring stories of how Māori New Zealanders are exercising ecological stewardship. In all these cases, the rich diversity of Indigenous cultures has resonated across far-flung settings, along with a gradually developing portrait of shared values, a pan-tribal vision, if you will, for cross-cultural exchange.

How best to carry these stories of cross-cultural teaching in action to my own students? I can't literally take them along on all my observations of Native teaching, of course. To approximate the impact of my own experiential learning, I can at least craft assignments that push them outside the comfort zone of our "regular" classroom setting, and I can cultivate opportunities for connecting the curricular with the cocurricular, in short-term and longer-term projects that bring them in contact with cultural difference. For instance, whether skyping with a Peace Corps worker who can describe work with an Indigenous population overseas, or collecting and analyzing written responses to a documentary on migrations of Native peoples seeking economic advancement for their families, or sharing transcripts from my interviews with Angolan locals about their experiences in colonial schools—via such modestly intercultural "moments" in my classroom, students in the most self-contained university setting can at least be given opportunities, admittedly at a remove, to observe and interpret cross-cultural experiences in action.

A third strand of my research on Native teaching practices has primarily involved listening. I've tested out and refined my own reflections on learning occasions and my readings of (print and other) narrative reports by inviting educators to "story" their own practice—to theorize it through dialogue. Such a method may seem quite simple, since this brand of research basically entails asking teachers to interpret their own decision-making. But it draws from a strong tradition in teacher research and other fields where self-critique promotes theory-building and theory articulation.

More specifically, I initially came to this third strand for studying Native teachers' learning legacies—*shared conversational analysis*—through prior work as a teacher educator studying reflective practitioners, as Donald Schön has advocated.[45] But when I turned more recently to studying what Shawn Wilson terms "indigenous research methods," I found some strong connections there too. In fact, Wilson's *Research Is Ceremony* could be seen as mapping the inquiry approaches that have directed this two-chapter section of *Learning Legacies*—except that I actually discovered his thoughtful text during the revision stage of this project. (Equally important, of course, as a white teacher-researcher, I should avoid claiming any right to enact a ceremonial Indigenous methodology as if it were my own.)

I certainly do value Wilson's model, though, and plan to draw from it, going forward, as an intercultural researcher committed to sustained collaborative inquiry.[46] In particular, for instance, Wilson argues that "indigenous research emphasizes learning by watching and doing," that it avoids the distancing stance of anthropological participant-observer while using such similar features as seeking face-to-face relationships and shared knowledge-making. Wilson emphasizes that he has "a natural advantage" for researching Native cultures in this way, since such a brand of "participant observation in Indigenous communities has taken place all [his] life" (40). Doing inquiry "within communities that [he is] already a part of," and thus where he already has "rapport," is a stance I can never achieve. But I hope, in adopting an ally-learner stance, I have cultivated as ethical a version of this relationship-building position as possible, since it envisions collaboration that allows for different standpoints and skills to come together respectfully and productively. Specifically, Wilson emphasizes *talking with* and *listening to* individuals as a crucial feature of Indigenous research practice (40–41), including carrying out "deep listening" (59). Says Wilson of his own inquiry into the Ceremony of Indigenous research itself: "As I was listening, I was learning, and as I was learning, I was sharing." Through multiple conversations with colleagues in Canada, Australia, and New Zealand, Wilson explains, "We were helping each other to understand or analyze these lessons and giving each other feedback as we all progressed. The analysis was collaborative and ongoing" (131).

Such an approach is clearly at odds with research interviewing that starts with a hypothesis and tests it out with set queries posed to research "subjects" who become objects of analysis with limited agency. In my case, I understand that I cannot ever approach an insider status. But I can seek a relational brand of knowledge-building that includes going back again

Figure 5.3. National Museum of the American Indian, Smithsonian Institution, Washington, DC, Exterior. Photograph by John Coe Robbins.

and again to reconnect with colleagues who are aiding my inquiry—such as making multiple trips to the NMAI and looping back to interviewees to share the evolution of my thinking and writing—rather than merely carrying out a single instance of "data-gathering" to inform analysis I would then do on my own.

Overall, in other words, consistent with Wilson's framework, I have tried to value relationality, to exercise responsibility, to convey respect, and to uphold reciprocity (70, 72, 77). Below, I share several stories of cross-cultural teaching gleaned from generous Native women colleagues through online and in-person conversations. Taken together, they form an archive of revisionist educational resources, reasserting Native teaching and learning methods, and a collaborative counter-narrative antidote to the legacy of assimilationist education represented by Carlisle and its heirs.

Conversations with Native Teacher-Scholars

In the section above, readers will doubtless have noticed my shift from examining textual archives of Native teaching in the first part of the chapter to giving a first-person narration about the methodological underpinning of my work. As I pointed out in the book's introduction, I recognize the gender-associated need to fold in explanation of how my own storytelling voice in this project is actually theory-driven. In addition, as Shawn Wilson argued in *Research Is Ceremony* and as Thomas King modeled in *The Truth About Stories*, a rhetorical mixing of story and analysis can be helpful to validate the intellectual rigor of narrative inquiry for some audiences. Having provided that scaffolding above, I trust my readers will now take note of the day-to-day integration of theory and practice—of the purposeful exercise of educational sovereignty—evident in the praxis of the Native teachers whose work I survey below: Lisa King, Kimberli Lee, Namorah Byrd, and Malea Powell.[47] The learning legacies from these ongoing conversations now inform my own teaching daily.[48]

Though based in the practice of everyday teaching lives, the stories I pass along from these colleagues do not focus on classroom organizational techniques linked to specific learning outcomes, or construction of particular syllabi, or lesson plans from individual courses. Rather, these reports of dialogues aim more at providing frameworks to help guide readers' own contextualized decision-making and actions. Several factors prompt this emphasis on conceptual frames. One arises from this book's aim to foreground theory at key moments so as to claim an authoritative voice. Another entails a respectful hope that my readers will turn to these scholar-teachers' own accounts of classroom practice details, particularly as seen in the recent anthology *Survivance, Sovereignty, and Story* and its accompanying website. (Several chapters are referenced in this section's endnotes and earlier in my text.) A third rationale assumes that readers who have come this far will welcome a chance to "hear" Native teachers' voices analyzing classroom culture in ways that invite varying localized adaptations instead of seeming to prescribe preset pathways. That said, in my Coda, I will describe a few specific examples of how I am trying to apply their thoughtful guidance in my own teaching.

Lenape (Munsee)/Euro-American teacher-scholar Lisa King has mined her own experience as a learner—including frustrations she encountered and her strategies for addressing them—to guide her work at an institution in the US Midwest, then later at the University of Hawai'i at Mānoa and, more recently, at the University of Tennessee, Knoxville. Hearing from Lisa about teaching in different institutional settings has been especially helpful because, like her, I've had numerous shifts in teaching locations, and I've found that every site brings unique challenges and opportunities for cross-cultural work. Thus, I especially admire King's blending of core principles across multiple settings and her adaptation of curriculum to the needs of students in particular locales.[49]

With energy, vision, openness, and commitment, King locates herself and her teaching within the larger legacy of Native educational history. Thus, she explains, "I see myself as asserting Native presence where there has been mostly absence." King models greater responsiveness to diversity in shaping her curriculum than what she encountered as a Native student herself:

As a student, I remember wanting to see my own experiences and background reflected back to me, or to at least find a way to locate myself in what I was learning. It didn't happen often. I think the breaking point, when I really became determined to take it upon myself to do this work, was when I took a class in life writing/autobiography studies as a graduate student. The professor was well known in her field and a general fount of knowledge on every text we read. That is, until we got to the American Indian author; that was the shortest lecture she gave all semester, and she couldn't really address it in the same depth as the other texts we read. I was so disappointed and frustrated that after that class, I began actively seeking out professors and mentors who would work with me in independent studies and could give me what I needed (since no graduate courses in American Indian literature existed in my department at the time).

But that experience was also double-edged; the classes I was taking across other cultural backgrounds and my own students were revealing my own lapses in knowledge. Given these two factors— wanting my own background respected/reflected as a student, and not feeling as though I knew enough about others as a teacher—I began experimenting with ways to create a classroom experience that would provide some kind of flexibility, where student experience was valuable, but where students also began to recognize other students' experiences and cultures as equally valuable and necessary to consider.

King's classroom is continually informed by her awareness of the complex past history of Indian education and the ongoing impact of that legacy within American culture. In Hawai'i, for instance, this often-painful heritage prompted her to be particularly attentive to the needs of her own Native students. She noted that, when teaching there, she was well aware that many of her students came "from underprivileged backgrounds" and were "struggling with the reality of colonial history, and trying to figure out how best to be themselves in this world and where/how being Native fits into that." So, she said, that while being careful not to "play favorites in my classes, . . . knowing this history I [was] extra careful to provide support for them."

King draws self-consciously on the cultural legacy of Indian education history in responding to student diversity within the classroom. (In this context, in replies to one set of digital interview questions, King offered the example of one introductory-level class's diverse ethnic makeup during her time teaching in Hawai'i: "21 students from a variety of backgrounds: Caucasian/mainland US, Filipino, Japanese, mixed-race students, and Native students in pretty even proportions.") Significantly, she starts with the assumption that all her students will embrace opportunities to broaden their horizons, however limited their exposure to cultural differences may have been before:

> Early on in my teaching career (at a Midwestern university), I became acutely aware of how insulated many students are—especially if they come from the mainstream cultural influences—and also how curious they are to learn about cultures outside of their own experiences when given the opportunity. Much of discrimination, I think, happens because of ignorance, and I became and remain motivated to help students widen their field of vision in the world, and at the very least help them learn how to respect other cultures, even if students don't fully understand them or agree with those perspectives.

Accordingly, for King, foregrounding her own identity and experience is one strategy for cross-cultural teaching:

> I think my experience working from the point of view of contemporary American Indian rhetorics has taught me a lot about how to reach students from a variety of backgrounds. First, I always establish who I am and where I come from, so that they know; I also let them know that they have a lot to teach me. In effect, it's a sort of recognition of cultural sovereignty on a small scale—I'm asking them to respect where I'm coming from, but letting them know that I respect their experience in the world, too. It's also about alliance,

though, and so I also try to build a space where we have common goals in the classroom that everyone contributes to.

Invited to identify some key terms and/or metaphors that direct her work, King named *sovereignty*, *contact*, *dialogue*, and *reciprocity*, with the last of those being crucial since "of course you want to treat others with the same respect you demand."[50] In responding to some possible metaphors for cross-cultural teaching that I asked about, King seemed most drawn to "cultural mediator":

> in many respects, I am the cultural mediator (whether I like it or not), especially for students who don't know much of anything of American Indian studies. At the same time, when I have Native students in class, that role of mediator becomes shared; their experiences will not be the same as mine, and in that respect they also have the ability to teach their classmates (should they wish to share) and I am not the sole source of information (nor should I be).

King also offered a metaphor of her own:

> Alliance Builder. This is work that I see myself doing in every class I teach, and maybe is one of the strongest ways I would identify myself as a teacher. I don't mean this in any sort of saccharine or naïve way. I have had the best of intentions fail. But if I can find a good way to have my students feel affirmed in who they are and in their intellectual abilities, if I can teach them good ways to dialogue with one another, if I can help them be stronger, more compassionate, clear-eyed thinkers together, in mutual respect . . . that's the work I want to be doing.[51]

Alliances are not always easy to create or sustain, of course. King acknowledges, "I have had students lash out at me in journals or in evaluations for asking them to do what they perceive as work unnecessary to their education." Such students, King observes, "generally claim to be content with the world as it is (the 'racism/sexism/discrimination at large doesn't happen, why do we talk about it here?' question), and think my addressing of culturally-related topics is an act of political aggression, no matter how I approach the topic in class."

While acknowledging that challenges can occur in any setting, King also, in a recent update, pointed to the encouraging experiences she's had since her move to a Southern US research institution, where one might expect her to encounter some resistance to the content of her scholarship and the core aims of her teaching. Instead, she explained in email and phone conversation, followed up by an in-person shared meal, although "[t]he University of Tennessee-Knoxville is like night and day to the University of Hawai'i-Manoa in terms of student demographics," so that she is now "teaching mostly white students," she has found encouragement for her work. For instance, she observed, after she had run "a senior-level 'Cultural Rhetorics' course with an Indigenous frame twice as a special topics course, with good success, my department recognized the value of it." In short order, the course was approved as a permanent addition to the curriculum, "as a class in its own right. Student feedback has been heartening," she added: "after the last time I taught the course, the students made their own Facebook page and have continued to carry on the conversations about listening, story, and alliance. I have also recently taught it at the graduate level for the first time, with strong evaluations. This gives me so much hope that no matter where we find ourselves as teachers, we can build these alliances. These learning communities can be developed, woven, cultivated." Overall, King emphasized in another phone talk, "What I want to say is that while the strategies might change depending on the student demographics and the place, this work can be done anywhere."

Often, in fact, "this work" involves helping students reexamine ideas they have internalized because they didn't yet have the tools to critique them. And, as several of the Native women teachers I interviewed suggested, this is a goal that can apply to Native and other minority students as well as those in the United States' current majority demographic.[52]

Along those lines, Kimberli Lee of Northeastern State University in Tahlequah, Oklahoma, points to the fact that, in teaching about American Indian cultural practices, specifically, "it often feels that I have to get students to 'unlearn' so much of what they have passively absorbed about 'authentic Indian-ness,'" since "[s]tereotypes about Native peoples abound and reinscribe themselves constantly through mainstream media."[53] Reflecting back on her own days as a student, Lee echoes King's memories of having little access to mentors with deep knowledge of Native culture. She recalls a former teacher's quick in-class dismissal of "Star Quilt" by Roberta Whiteman, a response Kimberli suggests could be attributable to that instructor's discomfort with her own limited knowledge. Lee draws on such past frustrations in positive ways to fuel her own commitment "to be open to all kinds of genres and authors so I can at least engage my students when they read and have questions."

Lee proposes that this very awareness of the gaps in former instructors' and current students' knowledge actually reaffirms her commitment to teaching across cultures, especially about Native history and social practices. She hopes that coming to see "how Native peoples have shaped and continue to shape American culture at large" will also "allow students to come to know something of themselves."[54] Thus, she envisions, "We can build bridges to one another and find some common space in which to share stories and experiences."

Namorah Byrd, a tenured full professor at Rowan College at Gloucester County, Pennsylvania, describes challenges in line with King's and Lee's reports, while also affiliating with their goals and values. Having begun her career in 1997 as an English composition graduate student instructor and later an adjunct at Temple University, Byrd taught Asian American history and Native American literature there as well. Byrd's pride at having completed multiple degrees (BA, MA, and PhD at Temple) extends to the productive blending of multiple traditions that she achieved in her 2014 dissertation, "The Presence and Use of the Native American and African American Oral Trickster Traditions in Zitkala-Ša's *Old Indian Legends* and *American Indian Stories* and Charles Chesnutt's *The Conjure Woman*." As she points out, "given the difficult history of Native Americans and African Americans [facing challenges] acquiring advanced degrees" from such institutions, she hopes that "other scholars with my heritage [will] think, 'If Namorah could do it, I can do it,'" just as she was "inspired by the educational accomplishments of several Native American and African American authors."

Unlike Lee, Byrd is working today with students who rarely see themselves, primarily, as Natives.[55] She describes herself as having "Native American, African American, Hispanic and European ancestries," and she notes that being a "Professor of Color" often presents challenges since so many white students "have never had an African American or Native American professor, high school, or elementary school teacher prior to landing in [her] classroom." Therefore, she has labored "to invent [her] own teaching methods, particular vocabulary set, and cultural cues for successfully engaging white students," especially since so much of the "cross-cultural teaching literature out there and methods offered, while wonderful and well-meaning, primarily reflect advice directed toward white faculty members. . . ."

Namorah readily concedes that, given her own "cultural experiences," she finds herself more "able to understand the issues of students of color" and finds it "less of a challenge to engage them in the classroom." In her case, Namorah declares: "cross-cultural teaching issues revolve around facing astonished white students who are transparently amazed, and sometimes dismayed, at seeing me enter the classroom and walk up to the desk to unpack my things." Therefore, she explains, she must aid her "white students with the adjustment to having, often for the very first time, a racially and ethnically colored 'expert' providing them with their education." Byrd has observed that "[i]t doesn't take long for us all to enter into a comfortable teaching/learning 'culturally safe' social environment. I use a positive and joyful approach to teaching that recognizes our differences as we move through the difficult task of mastering the subject matter before us." She declares: "I do not shy away from acknowledging that everyone in the room has diverse ideas and experiences that inform how we interrogate literature; instead, through written productions and discussions, we examine how those differences shape and form who we are and how differences inform the America in which we live."

Much of Byrd's cross-cultural teaching goes on outside of academic institutional settings, working as a women's traditional powwow dancer, drummer, and singer. In outreach programs, Byrd capitalizes on resources linked to her own identity. For instance, through "IndiVisible: African-Native American Lives in the Americas," an NMAI project, she facilitated a New Mexico State University workshop blending Native American and African American materials; she modeled oral traditions "through storytelling, drumming, chanting, and dancing" and described how she can "research, teach, and participate in both traditions."[56] She originally learned dancing, drumming, and singing as a member of the United American Indians of the Delaware Valley and *Kanahoochie*: the Native American Women's Singing Circle, a group of Native women that Pura Fé, artist-activist of the singing group Ulali, gathered together in the 1990s for a project enabling Byrd and others to share and learn traditions.[57]

Similarly, she welcomes all cultural traditions into her classroom, inviting students "to 'hear' and understand the thoughts and perspectives of other people." And she self-consciously models that stance: "I explain that we, as scholars, are not obligated to shift our own belief systems just because we respectfully hear each other out; we can 'hear' difference, marvel in its diversity, and be enriched by learning about new things, new ways, and new lives, without shifting from our own base should we care not to do so. This 'permission' seems to create a safe space for us all," a place of "peace" that is still open "to dialogue with each other, without rancor."[58]

Space-shaping and shared action also emerged as themes when I interviewed Malea Powell, a professor of Writing, Rhetoric, and American Culture at Michigan State University. Among many leadership roles she holds, Powell (who is mixed Miami/Shawnee/Euro-American)[59] is one of the vital forces behind both the Standing Peachtree workshop I described in the previous chapter and, more broadly, an ongoing effort by Native scholars to claim a rightful leadership space in academic professional institutions. While some broad-based organizations might be credited with outreach to—or at least a welcoming stance toward—Native scholars,[60] even in such relatively open contexts, they may still encounter problems navigating sustained cross-cultural collaborations. Similar to the challenge of claiming a viable position as a minority teacher in white-dominated classrooms, maneuvering within the complicated social structures of academic organizations can be daunting for scholars coming from any underrepresented group (whether marked by race, gender, geographic region, or social class). But, Powell believes, bringing American Indian and First Nations voices into the vision-guiding and also the operational work of groups like the National Council of Teachers of English (NCTE) and its related Conference on College Composition and Communication (CCCC/"Four Cs"/"Cs") is crucial if Native leadership in the twenty-first century is to hold its rightful place in American educational culture. A specialized educational enterprise like the NMAI or the many regional public and private museums and centers devoted to Native cultures brings with it substantial symbolic capital, practical resources for achieving educational impact, and a special opportunity for Native educators to work together with unquestioned authority. Nonetheless, countering the still-powerful legacy of the assimilationist boarding school movement and its guiding ideology also involves having strong, thoughtful, patient Native teacher-scholars assume leadership roles within organizations that have historically been white-dominated. Having served as "Cs" chair (and thus the primary planner for one of that very large organization's annual conferences), as well as, for several years, having been on the Executive Committee for NCTE, Powell brings to her ongoing work as a teacher and administrative leader at Michigan State University a focused energy and commitment to supporting her Native colleagues while also cultivating fruitful alliances.

I asked Malea to reflect on this aspect of her educational leadership when we sat down together at another national conference—one sponsored by the Society for the Study of American Women Writers. In reference to the Standing Peachtree workshop and its various related enactments in other years at the "Four Cs" conference, Powell said that preparing those sessions regularly together has "created a community of us," that is, a self-conscious affiliation of Native scholar-teachers, in "a space where we can actually share" so as to "work with each other and learn what each other is doing, teaching, and thinking about." Linking those collaborative opportunities for already trained Native scholars with her ongoing efforts to prepare graduate students for future leadership,[61] Powell emphasized in one of our conversations that "to maintain that space" of interconnected growth among university-based Native educators is essential. She stressed that her role models for this work include "the women who have worked with African American lit." Powell also described her own strategy of "watching people" from African American Studies at work *as* educational leaders, seeing how they support "junior scholars" in a never-ending effort at "fighting for more space" for anyone who is marginalized.

Powell also credited artist-colleagues like Robin McBride Scott, who have helped Powell develop meaningful bridges between her study of Native rhetorics and other "practices of making." She emphasized the importance of connecting all the various forms of teaching that transmit Native cultures' learning legacies to the concept of "tradition bearers." Thus, whether as an artist creating beadwork or as an on-site teacher in a "public role" at "one of the traditional dwellings or somebody at the NMAI," Powell explained, "if you are going to put yourself out there, you have to be prepared to teach people." Given the remarkable dearth of accurate information about Native people circulating in the larger culture, she observed, "we can't go out in that kind of public space and not teach people about who you are, who your people are" through a "political, racial orientation" aimed at "communicating . . . the truth versus the mythology." She elaborated: "Your job is to pass culture on and not in some unseen, unchanged, unmediated form," but, "pass it on so it's useful for the future generations."

For Powell, that mandate requires blending teaching that is grounded in, and shares knowledge from, material culture (such as beadwork), but also oral culture and its powerful strategies for supporting communal survival. And besides conveying what we might call the content of Native cultures (including particular sociocultural practices), serving as an effective educational leader, Malea says, also requires cultivating a particular stance toward learners—one that is welcoming, that opens doors. Reaching such a self-positioning isn't easy, she admitted during one of our talks; she reflected back on the experience of attending graduate school at an institution whose "mascot was the Redskins," on being "involved in activism to change that mascot," and on feeling, at that point, intense "anger issues" associated with her own identity as it was positioned by others in what should have been an inclusive learning space. But over time, she indicated, she has learned to seek a kind of "balance" that would promote "putting your anger where it belongs" rather than "acting out." To do so, Powell avers, has moved her from *carrying anger* to *carrying tradition*—to a more "functional rhetorical work" that integrates the arts, rhetoric, teaching, and social action. This purposeful mix, I'd say, represents her personal brand of rhetorical pragmatism, expressed in diverse story forms.

Activist Spaces for New Learning Legacies

By sharing these aspirational accounts of cross-cultural teaching and learning, I do not intend to claim there is one unified or representative "Native approach" to the enterprise. Rather, similar to the work of Jo-Ann Archibald in her chapter on Canadian First Nations women academics in *Restoring the Balance*,[62] I hope both to honor the rich diversity among Native teachers as intercultural leaders and to suggest the benefits majority educators' practice can accrue from studying these examples. I also hope to stimulate the gathering of more such accounts. After all, each educator's story has its own notable value, shaped in part by her own past learning experiences and the institutions where she now works. If all of us who wish to become better cross-cultural teachers seek out such exemplars, we can collaboratively construct "teaching story" archives to support our work. With that goal in mind, I want to return now to a "safe space" for shared learning like that Byrd envisions, one also in line with the "common space in which to share stories and experiences" that Lee promotes. By explicitly inviting cross-cultural alliances like those King aims to build, through the kind of patient organizational leadership Powell has been enacting, the National Museum of the American Indian embodies in its enactment of mission, and through its daily teaching practices, a vision creating new learning legacies accessible to all.

Now in its second decade of public service, the DC branch of the NMAI has been resolutely extending its educational reach to ever-broader audiences. Through enhanced partnerships and new technologies, the museum is ensuring that, compelling though in-person visits to the site itself will continue to be, "visitors" and would-be partners can learn from NMAI archives without setting foot inside its walls. Live webcasts like the symposium on The Great Inka Road, broadcast for free online in late June of 2015, are just one example of this strategic audience expansion. Besides underscoring a *We-are-still-here* message, these teaching practices also proclaim a theme along these lines: *We are "plugged in" to twenty-first century teaching/learning technologies; indeed, we are leading innovators in applying these new archive-building tools; but we are using them in ways that creatively reaffirm our traditional Native vision for community-building pedagogy.*[63] With its development of new counter-narrative networks that integrate creative learning modes into the museum's tradition-keeping cultural work, this commitment to reaching ever-broader audiences aligns with the Smithsonian's overarching goals but also reasserts Native values like hospitality, storytelling, and community curation. This outwardly oriented, proactive work for sustained community engagement is consistent with approaches to museum education also seen at the Jane Addams Hull-House Museum under Lisa Lee and her colleagues (chapter 3). But in the particular NMAI context, these practices simultaneously offer a Native response to both the oppressive heritage of assimilationist education and the dominant culture's standardized model for public education so evident in many classrooms, school districts, and government mandates today. To illustrate how the NMAI is capitalizing on its rich archive of resources to generate new learning legacies using up-to-date teaching tools, I'll return now to Renée Gokey and Dennis Zotigh, two of the museum's talented educators that I introduced earlier.

Let's begin with Renée. To update this project's portrait of her teaching, we set a rendezvous in the Mitsitam first-floor café. ("Mitsitam," in the language of the Delaware and Piscataway, means "Let's eat"—an appropriate signaling of the museum's emphasis on hospitality.)[64] As mentioned above, Renée and I had originally met when she led the afternoon tour I took on an earlier visit, along with my schoolteacher daughter Margaret, several cross-generational family groups, and a half-dozen international guests. Later, Renée and Dennis Zotigh would tell me, that diverse cluster of visitors was typical of the museum's daily visitors. On this follow-up trip, in the autumn of 2011, Dennis and Renée had each agreed to meet with me one-on-one to discuss their work.

I had asked to reconnect because of the skills I'd already seen them both bring to their cross-cultural teaching. I approached our conversations as another occasion for learning about the NMAI but also to hear gifted Native educators reflect on their practice. Like my interviews with Lisa,

Kimberli, Namorah, and Malea, these exchanges represented, from my perspective, not a "study" of "research subjects," by any means, but an opportunity for me to learn from role models—to be a student of their teaching. Given the positive energy I had seen her bring to a randomly formed tour group on my previous trip, I was not surprised that themes emerging from Renée's talk about her NMAI role included her commitment to serving Native youth, her efforts toward building meaningful cross-cultural connections, and, overall, her generosity of spirit.

Renée's descriptions of her strategies for leading visitors through the museum highlighted a vision for intercultural cooperation from which any teacher in today's diverse schoolrooms could learn. While it had been easy for me, during that earlier visit, to identify welcoming techniques she used for engaging learners (such as inviting individual visitors to contribute to the group's dialogue and selecting specific "stops" on the tour in line with their backgrounds/interests), to hear her thoughtful reflections during our follow-up interview reaffirmed my admiration of her strategies. For example, she outlined techniques she used to foreground her own Native identity while also emphasizing the vast array of over five hundred tribal groups in the Americas. Further, she reiterated her commitment to enabling visitors to see Native America all around them and to feel they can connect to those cultures.

Having this conversation in the early stages of my research, I was struck by how differently Renée approached her "captive" audience on a museum tour than so many teachers in the early assimilationist boarding schools did. This thought prompted me to ask her to reflect on how much of the collective mission of the museum is tied to that history. Renée's response centered at first on her grandmother's and other family members' time at Seneca Indian Boarding School. That experience, she indicated, had been full of challenges, but it had also helped her grandmother establish valuable cross-tribal connections.

At the time of this 2011 conversation, one of Renée's duties already involved working with schoolteachers, so she was thinking a lot about how to convey such complicated aspects of Indian history as the legacy of boarding schools and removals—topics which, through her mediation, would later be presented to students in many non-Native communities. She recognized ways that her personal identity and Native knowledge could be marshaled as resources. For instance, she described how, when helping to facilitate a workshop for thirty "Teaching American History" educators from Tennessee, she had integrated oral family histories into her presentation, some of which clearly struck an emotional cord with her audience.

Renée's teaching role expanded further when she was appointed to NMAI's Education Extension Services division. Partly through new technologies, her knowledge now reaches well beyond the museum site in DC on a regular basis, such as in programming for Native youth studying their own cultures. For instance, as she reported in a September 2013 online article, in one project that brought together the Extension Services team with the Miami (Myaamia) Tribe of Oklahoma, NMAI staff enabled young students attending the tribe's Summer Educational Experience in Oklahoma to connect with and analyze resources from the museum's collections through a videoconferencing session led by the associate director for scholarship, Dr. David Penney. As Renée noted in an email reflection she sent to me later, by using new technologies, the teaching team was able to connect the Miami youth to historical photographs and other cultural objects, including some with ties to their own family members. Such a process, for Native learners in particular, can counteract negative connotations often associated with archives as sealed off from daily life and separate from Indigenous peoples themselves.[65]

Noting that "[d]espite a thousand miles of physical separation, the sense of the students' pride in their culture was palpable," Gokey's online description of this partnership in action also exemplified ways that the museum is fostering a new generation's knowledge of Native people's cultural resources. For one thing, Gokey's essay explained, Dr. Penney and other "cultural knowledge bearers," along with the students, discussed how a maple sugaring sap bucket documented the Myaamia practice of making blocks of sugar as part of their tribal traditions. In addition, her essay pointed out, by conversing via the videoconference, students and the program facilitators shared a good-humored yet thoughtful laugh at the irony in a 1910 staged image of two Indiana-based Myaamia that photographer L. M. Huffman had originally labeled "The Last of the Miami." Students raised productive questions about the clear inaccuracies in the photo, including the placement of a tipi in the background (rather than an actual Myaamia home) and the inauthentic costuming (such as a Plains-type headdress).

As Gokey's vivid article chronicled, "Dr. Penney used stories and anecdotes to explain that, in the early 1900s, native people often dressed in ways that supported other people's expectations of what 'real Indians' should look like."[66] Thus, her narrative revisiting of this teaching moment presented yet another layer of learning legacy for the readers of her online story. Accordingly, her blog post moved beyond a straightforward description of that day's conversation to interpretive comments, bringing together the archive of NMAI objects that the students had studied, the process of pedagogy directed by the museum's staff, and the ongoing cultural analysis the participating students would now be better prepared to do, going forward. For instance, her essay noted, "During the adolescent years, young adults invariably explore their identity and stereotypes, trying to reconcile popular ideas of what they 'should' look like as contemporary American Indians and their daily experiences that may not fit into people's expectations."[67] Taken together, the multifaceted narrative elements in this web-based teaching story now provide specific archival resources (such as a photo of the sugar bucket and copies of the white photographer's images); an account of the learning activity itself, as experienced by all the original participants; and a theory-making reflection on the implications of this particular instructional event within the broader context of Native-led education. As such, within Renée's ably executed single text, I can carry out all three layers of reading for learning legacies that I outlined earlier in the chapter: primary and secondary documents as interpreted by Native scholars (in this case, the archival elements analyzed during the videoconference); a scene of practice in action (as in her description of the teaching activities collaboratively carried out); and dialogic reflection on teaching praxis.

Gokey's current role as an educational leader reaching publics beyond the museum's physical space is also evident in her regular contributions to the online quarterly newsletter *Explore NMAI: Educational Resources for Teachers*. Beginning in winter 2014, Renée's welcoming editorial voice on the opening page of each newsletter has been encouraging readers to view the publication as their "source for NMAI educational offerings, including teacher workshops, exhibits and events, classroom resources, and more." By registering online or emailing "questions and teaching ideas," teachers in any location with internet access—that is, basically, anywhere—can now connect to the Native knowledge base assembled there. Addressing a range of topics since its launch, the newsletter has given its readers access to such resources as information about NMAI's groundbreaking exhibit, *Nation to Nation: Treaties between the United States and American Indians* (spring 2015); an analysis of the importance of storytelling for conveying cultural values (winter 2015); and an interactive website entitled American Indian Responses to Environmental Challenges (September 2014).[68] In each issue, Gokey's overview has guided teachers through the resources presented. So, for instance, in spring 2015, she highlighted the on-site exhibition on treaties via a case study that demonstrates the links between treaty violations and Removal politics (focusing, in this example, on the Potawatomi [which translates as People of the Small Prairie] and the Trail of Death). Also, to inform teaching supported by the newsletter, she introduced questions about "removed Indian Nations" and their efforts at "maintain[ing] cultural practices" central to group identity. By providing both access to these stories and interpretive commentary online, Renée and her NMAI colleagues extend the museum's collaborative network to larger teacher-audiences, while building a reservoir of learning legacies that can turn individual archival resources into a shared Archive of pedagogical culture-making.

Like Renée Gokey, Dennis Zotigh employs a version of rhetorical pragmatism to extend the reach of his teaching voice beyond NMAI's physical site through online narratives. One such venue is the "Meet Native America" series, which (as Dennis explains in a headnote for each interview) "invites tribal leaders, cultural figures, and other interesting and accomplished Native individuals to introduce themselves and say a little about their lives and work." To contextualize the interviewees, Zotigh reminds his readers that Native Americans are important people to know, that they are exercising valuable cultural stewardship, and that they are actively leading contemporary lives (that is, they are certainly not vanished). Positioning these texts as part of an ongoing project, Zotigh's recurring headnote also posits that "[t]ogether, their responses illustrate the diversity of the indigenous communities of the Western Hemisphere, as well as their shared concerns, and offer insights beyond what's in the news to the ideas and experiences of Native people today." In this framework, Dennis invites website visitors to envision a productive balance between celebrating "the diversity" among Native communities and seeking to understand their "shared concerns." Further, these written teaching texts help his readers move beyond surface-level looks at "what's in the news" at any given moment to a longer historical view that explores "ideas and experiences of Native people today."[69] The interviews themselves fulfill this vision: ranging from figures like Robert J. Welch (chairman of the Viejas Band of Kumeyaay Indians) to Lora Ann Chaisson (vice principal chief of the United Houma Nation), the series blends its conversational accounts with photos telling visual stories of Indians' daily lives and their social, political, and educational leadership. Overall, by applying this framework for each interview, Zotigh makes vibrant counter-narratives available to the unlimited Web audience and issues a virtual invitation similar to his welcoming performances in the Potomac on-site meeting space. Conversational and contemporary, Zotigh's web texts create a network of learning legacies by blending his personal knowledge of individual Native peoples and cultural practices with his "philosophy that the only bad question is the one that is never asked."[70]

When preparing for one of my follow-up trips back to the NMAI, I took Dennis's advice and asked a question. Could we supplement previous conversations and my readings of his online stories with yet another in-person dialogue, and, if so, what would he most want me to learn? In his reply, Dennis urged me to meet, this time, in October 2012, at an off-site location, the fourth annual American Indian Festival at Patuxent River Park in Upper Marlboro, Maryland. This was an opportunity, I realized, to see his teaching in a context aligned with what he'd told me about coming from a powwow family. Sure enough, by attending the festival, I experienced yet another example of contemporary cross-cultural teaching being carried out by Native educators also eager to honor traditional knowledge and social practices.

Most of those attending the festival—like many who visit the NMAI—were white Euro-Americans. And most, I would guess, were there less for any serious study of Native culture than for an enjoyable family outing. But Dennis knew his audience and ways to reach them. As festival MC, he again encouraged dialogue, welcoming every question. After a traditional hoop dance performance that enthralled everyone, he invited all the children in attendance into the circle to perform a novice version. I had brought along part of my own family—my husband, my daughter Patty, and her husband Ethan. After admiring the young folks' enthusiastic dancing, we wandered through other stations at the festival. Kids were learning to make baskets under the guidance of accomplished crafts-people, recalling Malea Powell's salute to "tradition bearers." Participants also relished foods reminiscent of NMAI's Mitsitam café. My favorite stop, though, was the informal circle hosted by Cherokee storyteller Joseph Stands with Many. With his own updates of traditional tales, this able educator's oral narratives reiterated the efficacy of story-based teaching and listening-to-learn, and of knowledge-making achieved through shared social practices.

Joyful and generative, the learning legacies I left with that day affirmed Dennis's call for me to move beyond the familiar methods of my usual scholarly inquiry to a more communal and aspirational path. In line with the multifaceted practices many Native educators in this chapter have enacted, I vowed to embrace their models for connecting research with community action, integrating the intellectual with the experiential, carrying familial values and interpersonal relations into professional exchanges, and blending the intercultural resources of past Archives with new ones we can all create together today.

Coda

Composing New Learning Legacies

"I made a series of discoveries about myself in relation to my family, my community, and our society. I gained a deeper sense of purpose and meaning as an educator and as a writer."
—Francisco Jiménez, *The Circuit: Stories from the Life of a Migrant Child*, p. 115

"I began to feel again the presence of that unknown history."
—Diane Glancy, *Pushing the Bear, After the Trail of Tears*, p. 187

Envisioning Next Steps

One core premise of this book has been to affirm that cultural resources from the past shape our social actions today. An extension of this basic point has demonstrated how archives (literal repositories of cultural records) and Archives (in a more cumulative sense of culture-in-the-making) can inform current public scholarship. More specifically, I have argued that counter-narratives about cross-cultural teaching from past historical contexts can exercise social power as learning legacies. They provide rich cultural resources to support proactive teaching and civic engagement today.

Undergirding this proposed framework for revitalized liberal arts education has been a belief in the epistemic value of collaboration. When privileged knowledge-makers (including university faculty, museum educators, and social organization leaders) connect with allies who have often been underrepresented in the academy, valuable culture-making occurs. When we work together to apply resources embedded in records of past learning legacies—like the examples explored here from the turn of the twentieth century—we open up dynamic pathways to social justice. In such teaching/ learning partnerships, we can create new counter-narratives, new stories that claim agency through shared activism. Thus, through recovery of past learning legacies and application of their lessons, those of us engaged in liberal-arts-oriented scholarship and teaching show that our work does matter, now and for the future.[1]

What, then, might further applications of this book's argument look like, going forward? In this Coda, I invite readers to envision their own projects, in and beyond the classroom. To help seed such possibilities, I point out some options for teaching and scholarship that elaborate upon this book's framework. As a first step, I describe a few approaches I'm using in my own courses to build on the arguments in *Learning Legacies*. I also forecast several research opportunities derived from the book's concepts. And I outline one just-emerging civic engagement initiative—GlobalEx— that I'm involved in with students, faculty, staff, and community partners. Finally, I reemphasize this book's assertion of writing *about* learning legacies as, itself, a productive way to merge teaching and scholarship. I share all these examples not as blueprints to follow but rather, like the historical cases treated earlier, to encourage readers' own endeavors.

Because I've blended a personal story with more traditional scholarship throughout this book, I should note here that I'm completing this Coda in a specific (auto)ethnographic moment. By the time this book reaches readers in "finished" form, some possibilities I describe here may have come to productive fruition—or at least a budding stage. Others may remain only as hopeful opportunities for future collaborations.[2] Like Jane Addams and her heirs at the Chicago museum bearing her name, I affirm the concept of ever-unfinished business as a reality of shared cultural work. Also, I realize that the particular time when I'm revising this Coda, in the summer of 2016, is shaping specific ideas I have about my future teaching, scholarship, and community engagement: how, for instance, could we live in the United States right now and not be noticing the rhetoric of presidential politics? So consider this a fluid story.

Revising Dominant Narratives

As noted above, one goal of *Learning Legacies* has been to affirm the special benefits we can draw from studying past texts that emerged from inter-cultural teaching situations where counter-narrative rhetoric took center stage. Because I've focused here on the "counter" or oppositional aspects of those cases and their associated texts, readers may be feeling by now that I don't recognize the productive possibilities residing within more dominant narratives. It's true that, in my own classroom, I often make counternarratives a central part of my teaching. But I also emphasize how canonical cultural resources are necessary to explore. In practice, in fact, I often pair the two interactively, as referenced in chapter 2, where I described teaching writings from the *Spelman Messenger* in dialogue with highly traditional poetry by one of TCU's early women educators, Ida Jarvis. In that pairing, I facilitate in-class discussions by asking students to mark linguistic, gender-oriented connections between those two archives of women's texts; these conversations also spotlight how *Messenger* authors made strategic use of lyric poetry conventions even as those same early Spelman authors also exercised resistant rhetorical agency.

One reason I employ curriculum that places traditional cultural resources in dialogue with oppositional ones is because I want students from underrepresented groups to feel they can claim control over canonical material—that they can "own" it and capitalize on its heritage. Here, as in other aspects of my teaching, I draw on the example of Kenyan/US-based author and scholar-teacher Ngũgĩ wa Thiong'o, who blends personal mastery of canonical figures like Shakespeare and William Blake (whom he first studied in colonial schools) with advocacy for indigenous languages and cultural forms. I see my commitment to curricular linkages between canonical and counter-narrative texts as a fundamental refashioning of the Carlisle-type agenda, a revision of the "banking" models like E. D. Hirsch's *Cultural Literacy: What Every American Needs to Know*. New learning legacies that bring dominant narratives and counter-narratives together can capture valuable aspects of established Archives—but also critique and reconfigure them. We can empower all our students to see the potential that traditional cultural narratives still hold for opening access to collaborative agency, provided they are reformulated to serve an inclusive rather than a hierarchical vision. By inviting students to consider these texts as routes to social agency, we help bring the liberal arts' role in public culture to the forefront. Let me briefly cite one example of how I've used a cluster of such texts in courses by placing, at the center of a "learning legacies" venture, a short autobiographical narrative by Francisco Jiménez, *The Circuit: Stories from the Life of a Migrant Child*.

When introducing students to Jiménez's *The Circuit*, in classes ranging from American literature surveys to young adult literature introductions, from my "American Identity" seminar and writing classes to courses in multicultural literature, I zero in on his closing episode's engagement with the Declaration of Independence. As one of American culture's most foundational narratives—a fertile site for considering how writing itself can both embody and invite social action—the Declaration is especially important to study with students who have felt politically marginalized. It's equally useful, though, as a resource for building self-critical empathy among privileged social groups and, as immigrant teacher Hilda Satt Polacheck found in her Hull-House leadership of a naturalization course, for promoting a sense of possibility among those transitioning from marginal identities to more enfranchised ones.

I've found that a historicized reading of the Declaration gains enhanced classroom potential when positioned within intertextual, cross-cultural dialogue. For example, for many years I have had students read the Declaration alongside the 1848 "Declaration of Sentiments" and literally underline ways that the nineteenth-century women's statement of principles both echoed and revised the eighteenth-century one. Additionally, as my students' responses to *The Circuit*'s treatment of the Declaration have shown, comparative interpretation that questions the class-based, racial and ethnic differences associated with the document's place in American Archives is equally essential.

When I teach *The Circuit* now, in the context of learning legacies and cross-cultural exchange, I prompt students to pay careful attention to Jiménez's rhetorical repurposing of the original historical document. Such analysis requires a scaffolded engagement with the earlier chapters that prepare readers for the irony contained in the Declaration's fulsome language, in relation to the central character's (Francisco's) lived experiences in US society. Francisco and his family have survived the dangerous passage from Mexico only to encounter the challenges so many immigrants still face economically, socially, and politically. The young protagonist, clearly based on the author's own life, has struggled, and generally succeeded, at mastering the content of traditional public education, despite his family's constant relocations on "the circuit" that migrant farm workers travel. Then, just at the moment when he's reciting the Declaration, with pride, in a school performance, *la migra* arrives. The reason? To deport family members not born within the United States, including Francisco and his brother Roberto. And yet, rather than reject the idealized vision of this familiar historical document, Jiménez invites readers to revise it: he reconfirms its central values while also seeking ways of resolving its contradictions through social action.[3] What kind of action?

Along the way, leading up to this climactic scene, *The Circuit* has woven in examples of self-critical empathy and associated support for immigrants like Francisco's family—support given by several US-born, fully enfranchised characters, such as the schoolteacher who first nurtured his ability as a writer and an employer who provided a job opportunity, however modest (i.e., school custodian), for his brother. Solidarity that emerges from self-critical empathy, as Jane Addams demonstrated, and as Hull-House museum director Lisa Lee so thoughtfully observed, can be enacted in patient, yet pivotal, ways. That is, what Addams called "disinterested virtue" in her biography of Julia Lathrop, and what Lee termed "radical empathy," is achievable through interactions that need not be overtly revolutionary in order to promote long-term social change.

In fostering others' hopes of achieving such a progression toward social agency, one similar to Jiménez's own transition from illegal child immigrant to university citizen-professor, his "A Note from the Author" resonates with the Archive-to-action framework of *Learning Legacies*. Accordingly, his "Note," a narrative reflection on reconstructing a familial archive, becomes a focal point of my classes' discussion of his text. Jiménez recounts how his hopes to acquire advanced education were eventually enabled through a graduate fellowship at Columbia University. He describes how his mentor there, Andrés Iduarte, led him to craft a thesis that also served as the start-up text for *The Circuit*. That is, like Jane Addams nurturing Hilda Satt (Polacheck), Iduarte spurred Jiménez to begin writing a counter-narrative through artistic expression grounded in personalized historical research. Although intervening years of teaching and administrative service slowed his progress, Jiménez, also like Polacheck and her researcher-editor daughter Epstein, gradually assembled the book-length autobiography of *The Circuit* by persistently building a personal archive situated within a larger historical context:

> In writing these stories, I relied heavily on my childhood recollections, but I also did a lot of background research. I interviewed my mother; my older brother, Roberto; and other relatives. I looked through photographs and family documents, and listened to *corridos*, Mexican ballads, that I had learned as a child. I also went to different places in the San Joaquin Valley where we had lived in migrant labor camps: Bakersfield, Fowler, Selma, Corcoran, Five Points.[4] I visited museums in those towns and read through newspapers from that era. (*Circuit*, 114–15)

Significantly, as Jiménez explains, construction of the archival knowledge he sought wasn't easy: "Unfortunately," he explains, when consulting "newspapers from that era" of his family's migrant experiences, "I found little or no information or documentation in those sources about migrant farm workers." However, even though he was "disappointed," this very gap in the cultural record "convinced [him] even more that [he] should write [his] book." That is, in terms of *this* book's central concepts, I'd say he came to understand the potential counter-narrative value of his own story, even as he recognized that it also reaffirmed some beloved aspects of what's often termed the "American dream." By retrieving what he could, he built a tentative archive, and his effort helped him "recall other experiences [he] had forgotten with the passage of time." This process, in turn, enabled him to position his individual archive within a broader cross-cultural Archive all of us can now access through his writing:

> Looking back at those childhood memories from an adult point of view, I made a series of discoveries about myself in relation to my family, my community, and our society. I gained a deeper sense of purpose and meaning as an educator and as a writer. (115)

By applying the inclusive "our society" to his revisiting of an archive-to-action process, Jiménez also stakes a claim for himself, his "family," and his particular "community" to be recognized as *belonging* to the larger social structures from which some would still exclude him. Indeed, he asserts in a stirring final paragraph, his counter-narrative, partly by virtue of its engagement with the dominant narratives of US culture, can help others fulfill their own aspirations. After all, Jiménez reminds his readers, the "backbreaking labor" of "migrant farm workers and their children" that "puts food on our tables" is indispensable to the larger national society: "Their courage and struggles, hopes and dreams for a better life for their children and their children's children give meaning to the term 'American dream.' Their story is the American story" (116). Like the purposeful pronoun slippage in "our society," in these closing words, *The Circuit* uses rhetorical shifts to "*our* tables," juxtaposed with "*their* children and *their* children's children," to locate Jiménez's authorial voice on both sides of the equation at the same time, and thereby to embody discursively in his own language a very "American dream" of social mobility. This narrative of authorship, especially when read intertextually, stakes a clear claim of belonging based in archival recovery and Archive-making.

As a scholar-educator who seeks to nurture intercultural connections among students, I teach his narrative of familial archive-building alongside his Declaration-framed final episode by asking my classes to unpack specific linguistic linkages across multiple texts. Further, I apply a version of the lesson I learned from visiting Deborah Mitchell's elementary school researchers in downtown Atlanta (chapter 2). I urge students to describe what archives from their own family histories come to mind as they read, and how they might recuperate such records to serve as resources for future learners, as Jiménez has done. Furthermore, while *The Circuit* has long been a staple for my teaching, recent statements from political figures like Donald Trump have opened up additional points of narrative/counter-narrative interaction. These controversial texts can be set in dialogue with witty yet pointed ripostes like former Mexican president Vicente Fox's self-portrait tweet with a Trump tie imported from China, as well as satire on the Trumpian "wall" from *Saturday Night Live*.[5] Such textual juxtapositions—including ones selected to offer a very balanced historical view—help students see and critique the rhetorical dimensions of all such writings, including Jiménez's astutely crafted appeal to affect through a personal story. All in all, the cluster of teaching resources represented by this growing constellation of texts also exemplifies how exchanges between dominant and alternative narratives often lead, over time, to mixed-message Archives—to complex cultural resources containing internal contradictions.[6] Where, we can ask, do students choose to position themselves, from their own stories and toward their own social actions, within this evolving, ever-unresolved Archive?

Creating a Cultural Rhetorics Curriculum

If the angry intensity of Trump's recurring "wall" threats has brought a challenging new dimension to this particular set of narratives, other stories have been offering up a very different call to social action, one envisioning diversity as a resource for promoting critical empathy. At a time when student voices all across the nation have been calling for a strengthened commitment to inclusiveness on campus, I have been looking out for learning legacies that might bring both "traditional" American value systems and the heritage of proactive civil rights leadership together in hopeful conversation.[7] One text I'm now developing for classroom use resides in song.

In "Glory," their stirring anthem for the *Selma* film that chronicled a turning point in the civil rights movement, John Legend and Common simultaneously resist and recuperate elements of dominant American learning legacies. One strand in the song references the nation's tendency to see itself as allied with freedom and justice; its belief that some conflicts are righteous; and its dedication to united, symbolic action for communal good. On that level, Legend's lyrical storyline (re)claims a familiar American narrative for black culture. Yet an ironic interplay between Legend's voice (which references those traditions in a conventional melody) and Common's rap counter-narrative (pushing back in both form and content) forcefully calls out inconsistencies around those very ideals. Thus, "Glory" creates a cross-cultural remix. Celebration and critique combine to sing hope.

For instance, Legend's voice begins with a seemingly straightforward assertion that "One day, when the glory comes / It will be ours." And this strand in the story-song later predicts that, though "Victory isn't won" yet, still "we'll fight on," until we can "cry glory." Meanwhile, Common's tough rap counter-punch invokes "Sins that go against our skin." Since "Justice is juxtaposition in us," Common's counter-narrative avers, "Justice for all just ain't specific enough": the iconic heroine Rosa Parks had to assert her quiet protest as she "sat on the bus" and, today, "we walk through Ferguson with our hands up."[8] With neither lyrical strand sufficient in itself, but both conjoined to claim access to America's mythologizing narrative of glory through rhetorical "Juxtaposition," this song exemplifies the adaptable staying power of counter-narrative as a productive compositional form in our current day.[9]

Encouraged by such telling examples of rhetorical pragmatism in popular culture, and drawing on my own recent research for this book (as humanities scholars often do to enrich our teaching), I'm preparing a new course. I want to introduce undergraduates at my majority-white university, where so many of our students come from relative privilege, to the social significance of counter-narrative texts like "Glory." One strand running through the syllabus will foreground rhetorical representations of minority American learners and teachers—that is, of intersections between racial identity and views on the "right" educational content for members of different race groups in the United States. I envision setting visual imagery like the fists-up photograph of recent black women graduates from West Point in conversation with speeches by Frances Harper, autobiographical essays by Anna Julia Cooper, and journalism critiquing exploitation of black athletes in university settings today—as well as stories from the *Spelman Messenger* and Spelman's Founders' Day performances.[10]

Besides tapping into this book's examination of links between civil/civic rights and education, I want my new course to address cultural rhetorics associated with current citizenship debates, particularly the place of immigrants in American society. I will assign reading sequences to position Jane Addams's descriptions of her evolving settlement teaching next to Hilda Satt Polacheck's written memories of such Hull-House-sponsored learning opportunities for that era's urban immigrants. I will locate both those women's cross-cultural teaching narratives alongside anti-immigration rhetoric like political cartoons stereotyping Chinese arriving in California during the same time period and Gilbert Gonzalez and Vivian Price's award-winning *Harvest of Loneliness* documentary on the 1942–64 bracero "guest worker" program.[11] And I'm developing an assignment whereby students will seek out examples of cultural rhetorics depicting sites of, causes behind, and impacts from various transglobal migrations going on today.

Beyond analyzing others' counter-narratives, however, I also plan to have students in my new course create learning legacies of their own. Texts like *The Circuit*'s "A Note from the Author" can serve as inspiration, through its call for previously disenfranchised people to claim the very cultural resources and Archive-making practices that have so often excluded them. Along those lines, during the spring semester of 2016, I experimented with the final project assignment for a graduate seminar I was teaching on the rhetorical history of "American literature" as a field. Basically, I invited the class to take the reins of their own learning and create personalized projects—curricular learning legacies—aligned with our semester-long questioning of boundaries and processes that have defined (and sometimes constrained) "American literature" as a cultural resource.

Throughout the term, we studied trends that, across the twentieth century and into the twenty-first, have shaped the way "American literature" has been conceived, produced, and packaged within the academy, both in scholarship and in curriculum. We examined the interplay between forces John Guillory has described in *Cultural Capital* and the multifaceted expressive forms of American literature itself that have claimed varying positions within curriculum, and we connected those shifts in curricular content to changes in dominant American value judgments in different historical periods. For example, we asked, what social forces have contributed to feminist recovery of women's writing—a process that certainly has changed the contents of American literature anthologies, courses, and other measures of value, such as doctoral exam lists? Similarly, how and why has memoir recently exerted increasing visibility on bestseller lists and in academic studies of genre in our field? In shorthand, we said, what do "selfies" tell us about life-writing's rise in the academy, and vice versa?

In different stages of the course, we paired up various entries from *Keywords for American Cultural Studies* with relevant primary texts. We noted how various "keywords" (that is, core concepts) that have come to the forefront of scholarship over the past decade or so (such as "diaspora," "ethnicity," and "border") have led to (and reflected) corresponding productivity in new primary texts. In that vein, we read Louise Erdrich's *The Roundhouse* and Sherman Alexie's *The Absolutely True Diary of a Part-time Indian* as well as recent poetry by Native authors alongside Indian/First Nations work in cultural rhetorics by scholars like Lisa King and Malea Powell, as referenced in chapters 4 and 5 here. Thus, we considered how frameworks like "sovereignty" have carried over from scholarship into literature and vice versa. We juxtaposed secondary texts like Aimée Césaire's *Discourse on Colonialism* with his play riffing on Shakespeare's *The Tempest* and with Maryse Condé's *I, Tituba, Black Witch of Salem*; we read Kenneth Warren's *What Was African American Literature?* alongside Percival Everett's *Erasure*.

One goal of the course was to observe ways that the shifting archive of scholarship in American Studies has helped generate new "literary" (and pop culture) texts, and vice versa; that is, we cast research and aesthetic production as interactively connected. One implicit dimension of this examination into how literary fields operate culturally involved asking ourselves how both archives—which are sometimes cast as separate bodies of "primary" and "secondary" texts—could be sites of intervention for us all, and how those very processes of intervention could allow us to reposition American literature field-making as a collaborative public enterprise.

A number of students embraced the chance to reexamine and extend our course's questions by creating final projects consistent with themes in the *Learning Legacies* framework. Thus, for example, Sofia Huggins and Mayra Guardiola collaborated in shared study of Isabel Allende's *Island Beneath the Sea: A Novel*, with each student focusing her analysis in light of scholarly traditions whose growing archives of research resources she had been exploring individually—feminist eco-criticism for Mayra and transatlantic studies' "take" on race history and slave narratives for Sofia. Combining their respective interpretations to address a different section of Allende's novel each week, they produced a month-long series of conversational YouTube videos.[12] That is, these two adventurous young scholars transformed a record of their emergent learning into a public legacy text *about* studying new American literatures dialogically.

That mini-archive now invites others to join the collaboration by adding to the online discussion.

One feature students in the seminar pointed to as cutting across all their end-of-course projects was a willingness to "counter" views of literary Archives (as enacted in curriculum) being determined (solely/mainly) based on ahistorical measures of aesthetic merit. In addition, they contrasted their new view of an ever-evolving Archive of "American Literature" with perceptions about a stable canon. By reenvisioning our work as a broader culture-analyzing and culture-making enterprise, they found, the seminar situated individual texts within a fluid field of social action and thereby encouraged their own sense of individual and collective agency for future shaping of that same dynamic field. Tightly contained archives of "what we should study" shifted to become contingent Archives of ongoing intervention. As an experiment in curriculum, the course itself will bear additional revision. But as a first step, it has surfaced productive approaches for linking literary study with cultural rhetorics—and historical analysis of this academic field with creative generation of new public voices in that landscape.

Researching New Archives' Growth

Beyond empowering individual students as interpreters and creators of new narratives, and beyond specific curricular innovations, this book will further demonstrate its own value as a cultural resource when new scholarship based in its interpretive framework appears. As the case studies here have demonstrated, social movements accrue enhanced power through purposeful use of shared language—a process facilitated when rhetorical pragmatism is deployed to promote cross-cultural learning. Just so, for example, we've seen how Spelman, Hull-House (previously as a settlement, now as a museum), and the NMAI all carry out proactive intercultural stewardship through context-oriented storytelling. So one way to extend the *Learning Legacies* framework would be to examine how such sites' narrative-making strategies are being put to similar use in different social contexts today.

Proactive resources to support social action are available in the Archives of multiple cross-cultural teaching sites from the past. While the previous chapters each began by delving into archives with long histories, a worthwhile extension of this book's argument could immerse, instead, in a nascent archive of current activism. Tapping into just-developing counter-narrative archives could enable us to track their transitions from margin to center, from exploratory storytelling to efficacious blending of narrative and argument, and from loose coalitions to strong collaborations.

Let me cite an example of one just-emerging archive of learning legacies I hope to investigate in the days ahead. As referenced in chapter 3, Lisa Junkin Lopez, formerly associate director at the Jane Addams Hull-House Museum, recently accepted a position as director of the Juliette Gordon Low Birthplace (JGLB) in Savannah, Georgia. When I caught up with Lisa in a May 2016 conversation, I could hear her excitement about new work being developed to usher Girl Scouts who visit the site toward a strengthened sense of personal agency. In line with the biographical heritage of Low herself, with the national organization's vision for the site's potential impact on visitors, and with progressive museum practices she had been applying at Hull-House, Lisa is collaborating with staff there and at the national headquarters to integrate new opportunities for girls' active learning into the birthplace. To illustrate, she passed along a description of the redesigned library. This updated exhibit was curated (by Cindi Malinick, chief executive of cultural resources for Girl Scouts USA, and Estevan Rael-Gálvez, an independent consultant) before Lopez's arrival in Savannah; in fact, its vision was one factor persuading her to make the move from the JAHHM to the JGLB. Literacy as a route to agency is at the heart of visitors' engagement with the library in this reformulated space. "Girls Writing the World: A Library Re-imagined," a one-page overview prepared by the museum staff, explains how the library has shifted its material/spatial and verbal rhetoric away from its previous framing. Before the revision, the exhibit presented "'a southern gentleman's library,'" which "communicat[ed]—tacitly or actively—that reading and writing are the purview [only] of educated men." Now, through its new design, the library's identity has indeed been reimagined:

> Victorian rosewood bookcases that have long graced the room now hold books written by, for and about women on themes of memory, knowledge, poetry, imagination, and wisdom. These books span many cultures and time periods, and visitors are encouraged to examine books rather than simply admire them through the glass. Another bookcase reveals Juliette's love of literature and its role in early Girl Scouting with fiction and nonfiction publications for Girl Scouts and writings by Juliette, her mother and grandmother. . . . An interactive table features audio and video content celebrating women and the spoken word through speeches, poetry, storytelling,

and song. . . . When girls visit with their troops, they are prompted to write a poem that they may choose to share while standing beneath an artistic installation of a "Poe-tree," which represents Juliette's favorite literary genre. . . .[13]

One of my first follow-up research trips after submitting this manuscript will be to the birthplace both of JGL and of US girl scouting—referred to as "the Birthplace." To build upon the model of *Learning Legacies*, I hope to explore representative content from the texts girls have composed in the library and to observe occasions of these writing processes in action. I'm also eager to hear from Birthplace staff about how they perceive this new exhibit as an indicator of where the museum itself can go, in the future, to promote engaged learning. What, we might ask together, is the long-term potential of writing-to-learn activities at the Birthplace? How can those composing options be scaffolded for maximum learning impact? In particular, what types of writing, under what conditions for connecting with the Birthplace's meanings, might be most effective as a bridge to social justice projects?

Given this book's focus on women's cross-cultural teaching, addressing such questions in the context of the JGLB setting seems highly appropriate. One challenge facing such public sites, after all, is the need to bridge between historical eras that are far removed from young visitors' own life experiences and the goals that such institutions aspire to address. If "girls' culture" today is far different from the context of founder Juliette Gordon Low's lifetime, there are, nonetheless, potential connections to be made via both the Archive of the founder's and the Girl Scout organization's history, as a foundation, and newly made archives of girls' authorship created at the site.[14] Hopefully, learning legacies of the past, in this case, can help generate new ones.

Another vital archive for scholarly interpretation of cross-cultural learning today resides in the #BlackLivesMatter (BLM) movement.[15] Using social media to reach across spatial divides, BLM leaders build community. Also, by directing their writing to audiences beyond those already committed to their goals, BLM activists cultivate expanded coalitions. Their storytelling invokes critical empathy toward new alliances, so their compositional archives invite scholarly analysis organized around *Learning Legacies*' main concepts.

To apply this book's mixed methods for researching BLM's stories, we would need to access multiple entry points into its ever-expanding digital

Figure C.1. Girl Scouts writing in response to the Re-Imagined Library Exhibit, Juliette Gordon Low Birthplace (JGLB), Savannah, Georgia. Courtesy of the Juliette Gordon Low Birthplace and Collection of Girl Scouts of the USA. Used by permission.

and performative archive. We would need to interpret historically situated instances of this community's online rhetoric; to engage from a learner stance in shared reflection with its leaders; to locate the movement's activities within larger social networks; and then to tease out relationships among all these interactive elements of engagement. Exploring the cross-cultural public work of #BlackLivesMatter across time and within specific contexts, we could then identify particular learning legacies from its rhetorical efforts to construct shared knowledge and political commitment. That work, in turn, could support expansion of its goals into other contexts. As in earlier chapters of *Learning Legacies*, we might begin with a representative cluster of texts from the movement's record of cultural work—as specific as a string of associated tweets, perhaps. To illustrate, let me reference "The Disruptors," a 2015 CNN online feature story about the coalition's leaders.

A series of narrative profiles, "The Disruptors" posited a connection between writing in social media to support the "rallying cry: Black lives matter" and the ongoing collective enterprise embodied in its slogan, "A movement, not a moment."[16] In this single online essay, we find one intriguing counter-narrative archive of that larger movement—a small story in itself, yet relevant to the *Learning Legacies* framework, as signaled in the "Disruptors" title as well as the rhetorical features of its profiles. Along those lines, CNN's feature report noted: "These activists reside outside traditional institutions and power structures," with some of the most fully engaged being "better known by their Twitter handles than their real names." Yet, as if to amend its own initial characterization of #BlackLivesMatter as only loosely organized, CNN's essay then laid out thirteen story-portraits of movement leaders. These brief but incisive profiles, reminiscent of story portraits presented in the Spelman Founders' Day performance, highlighted their subjects' strategic efforts at network-building through language. Whether in online spaces, through oral exchanges, or via appropriation of more traditional genres, CNN's account indicated, the stories crafted and circulated by these BLM leaders have fostered shared energy and social agency.

In this book's framing terms, I view the CNN essay as demonstrating how these disruptor-authors use counter-narratives to promote social justice, while simultaneously assembling an archive of learning legacies toward discursive institutionalization of BLM itself. Resisting assumptions about political leadership as best articulated through traditional venues such as print text or formal speeches sanctioned by long-established organizations, #BlackLivesMatter asserts a revisionary rhetoric in part by *where* its stories of activism so often appear—in social media and on the street.

Therefore, within this story saluting youthful BLM leaders, CNN's online report both recognized and contributed to an emerging Archive of action residing in alternative public spaces. Thus, as one step toward "organizing the Black Youth Project 100," CNN observed, BLM leader Charlene Carruthers (also a writer for the #SayHerName campaign and an advocate for increasing the minimum wage), helped facilitate a Chicago-based team responding via "digital town halls" to the verdict absolving George Zimmerman in the Trayvon Martin case.[17] Similarly, as "The Disruptors" essay outlined, DeRay Mckesson has acted on his belief that "social media highlights stories that otherwise would go unnoticed." He quit his job as an administrator for the Minneapolis Public Schools to travel the country while contributing op-ed pieces to diverse outlets and acquiring so many online followers that his tweets regularly spawn trending hashtags. Along related lines, CNN's account captioned a photo of Johnetta Elzie with her assertion that social media have enabled "black people to control the narrative by telling their own stories." To illustrate her point, the profile highlighted her mapping of police violence in a sophisticated database. And, in another salute to compact storytelling's ability to marshal organizational strength, "The Disruptors" chronicled how New York's Michelle Taylor used Twitter to assemble twenty-five leaders in twenty-five cities to set up over one hundred vigils after Michael Brown's death in Ferguson, Missouri.[18]

By merging astute use of today's media tools with on-the-scene activism, the movement leaders introduced to readers through CNN's story bring together counter-narrative composing in popular publication spaces (reminiscent of Jane Addams's writing for broad audiences in her day) with the kind of street-level, on-site engagement that Hull-House colleague Ellen Gates Starr chose as her own primary route to civic engagement. In that vein, within this single CNN story on BLM, we can identify recurring language as forming a purposeful connective tissue to support the movement's ongoing institutionalization. That is, both the web-based narrative itself and the rhetoric it identifies with the leaders being profiled are illustrative of, and also contribute to, a growing archive whose still-evolving discourse is becoming a culturally constitutive Archive of shared agency.

Beyond close reading of such texts, another useful methodology for interpreting this burgeoning archive could take its cue from Franco Moretti's distant reading. As advocated by Moretti and others affiliated with the Stanford Literary Lab, distant reading uses quantitative analysis aided by computational modeling to study literature. While other scholars working under the rubric of what's sometimes termed "digital humanities" have developed such projects as making the scattered archives of individual writers and even larger literary movements available in online spaces, Moretti's vision represents a more radical affiliation between "big data" analysis and the study of literature. That is, he advocates assembling huge archive-like databases of language from literary texts and then using quantitative approaches to find meaning within and across that data. By way of such toolkits as corpus linguistics computer programs, distant reading can produce visually oriented, quantitatively conceived analytical records drawn from huge archives of text—for example, diagrams of repeated terms and depictions of cross-text connections shown as building networks of idea exchange. Therefore, using Moretti-style "distant reading" could help us track BLM's narrative networks in multiple directions.

An admitted downside of Moretti's method, though, is its tendency to underemphasize the rhetorical goals and impact of individual texts or even particular writers' oeuvres.[19] So, to incorporate a more mixed-method, rhetorical approach that draws on the *Learning Legacies* framework, we could add a step beyond distant reading's pattern identification to *characterize argumentative aims and methods* repeated across multiple textual exchanges in various public venues. We could then analyze links between these rhetorical features and particular genres and subgenres being employed. Then, too, we could look at comparable rhetorical features and strategies from related cross-cultural contexts, both to better understand the public work of BLM so far and to identify potential techniques the movement could adopt and/or adapt in the future. Along the way, by connecting BLM discourse analysis to other case studies of learning legacies like the ones in this book, we could do comparative work aimed, ultimately, at enhancing the rhetorical efficacy of the movement itself as a call to social action.

Here are some tentative observations along those lines, drawn only from the limited material of the CNN report. In the counter-narratives of the BLM-affiliated authors profiled there, in their ongoing calls for racial progress, I hear echoes of the early *Spelman Messenger*. Like such *Messenger* storytellers as Nora Gordon and Carrie Walls, these #BlackLivesMatter writers insist upon rights to full citizenship for themselves and their communities, and they do so in part by claiming the race-based intellectual authority that resides within their own arguments. For instance, in a tweet of June 10, 2015, as CNN's account notes, DeRay Mckesson positioned himself within a heritage of discourse affirming black identity while also acknowledging the challenges he faces daily because of his blackness: "I continue to talk about race because race continues to impact my life & the lives of those who look like me." Meanwhile, in such rhetorical pragmatism as Johnetta Elzie's data analysis of police brutality patterns, or DeRay Mckesson's addresses to broad audiences online, or Michelle Taylor's decisive coalition-building, I note parallels with strategies like the *Hull-House Maps and Papers*, and Jane Addams's tactical deployment of speaking engagements to convey her theories of action, and the settlement's use of Hull-House theater performances to foster cross-cultural networks. Furthermore, in the use of accessible language sites like Twitter, Instagram, and blogs, as well as in the CNN feature's emphasis on oral exchanges from #BlackLivesMatter gatherings, I see links to the oral storytelling practices and performance texts for communal learning within Native educational traditions. Overall, texts circulating through this current social movement seem to be deploying genre features developed by other counter-narrative practitioners over time—honed for specific exigencies of their own but available, still, to rhetors speaking from similarly marginalized positions today. For instance, the concept and exercise of rhetorical sovereignty as articulated by Native scholars could prove useful to BLM.

In light of such intertextual connections, we might also apply a comparative approach to pursue pedagogical and methodological questions that the CNN narrative itself only implicitly raises. For example, how can a particular teaching text (or a classroom "lesson plan") be fashioned from multiple archival resources that are still acquiring additional layers of meaning, including through the very process of intertextual narration itself? How can effective new learning legacies be composed when their impact depends on complex, even contradictory, discursive materials continually circulating in the culture of this moment? Such questions are essential to examine through broad-based scholarship in an era when the venues for public exchange are increasingly accessible and fluid, yet simultaneously more complicated to navigate. In such a dynamic communications environment, how might an aspiring cultural steward best construct and circulate pragmatic public rhetorics grounded in attentive Archival study?

As noted in prior chapters, studying Native storytelling as a constructive educational practice grounded in counter-narrative rhetoric has helped me begin to address such questions. Here in this Coda, having presented the series of case studies that formed the central sections of this book, I have been taking a more comparative approach. Thus, I would suggest, to fully mine the example of current counter-narrative rhetorics like #BlackLivesMatter, we stand to enrich our analysis by considering parallel texts from Native activists who have, similarly, documented histories of oppression and their continued repercussions while also envisioning alternative models of social justice for our own time. Cherokee author Thomas King provides us with an especially efficacious text to study as a model that bridges between storytelling and theorizing for cross-cultural teaching.

In *The Truth About Stories*, scholar-writer King uses understatement to assert narrative's power to inspire ethical action. Telling and retelling stories from his personal life and from the Archive of indigenous traditions, King repeatedly ends these individual narratives with a comment to readers that seems to belie any confidence in Native/First Nations rhetorical pragmatism. Here, for instance, is the close of his first chapter:

> Do with it [the story] what you will. Tell it to friends. Turn it into a television movie. Forget it. But don't say in the years to come that you would have lived your life differently if only you had heard this story.
> You heard it now. (29)

Despite this apparent reluctance to claim assured ethical impact for his "native narrative," King does celebrate that potential through verbal accretion. Building moral force as his stories mount up across the various sections of his book, partly by braiding candid self-critique together with story-illustrated references to cultural theorists from non-Native contexts, King's message ultimately cannot be missed. *The Truth About Stories* enacts a learning legacy. Consider his closing story, a poignant self-indictment of his "failure" when "Sympathy. Comfort. Understanding" might have helped two friends navigate their adopted daughter's fetal alcohol spectrum disorder (FASD). After John and wife Amy separated due to the husband's escalating frustration, King tells us, John supposedly didn't fault the author for pulling back precisely at the couple's time of greatest need. But King's narrative shows that he blames himself. The end commentary of this chapter, also the final one of the collection, pushes readers to confront the ethical arguments embedded in this story and the others in King's book through a refrain established earlier in the text:

> You can have it if you want. John's story, that is. Do with it what you will. I'd just as soon you forget it, or, at least, not mention my name if you tell it to friends. Just don't say in the years to come that you would have lived *your* life differently if only you had heard this story. You've heard it now. (167, emphasis in original)

King's tone may seem far removed from the frequently assertive postings of #BlackLivesMatter, which issue far more direct calls to self-critical empathy and action. But in both cases, moral energy accumulates gradually, as storytellers purposefully shape their own archive of narrative artifacts. Resonating through intertextuality that reinforces specific verbal tools such as irony and direct address to readers, both counter-narrative voices also remind audiences that the social issues being addressed have arisen from another *lived* archive—a legacy of oppression still evident in too many cross-cultural relationships today. In King's case, for instance, by the time we read of adopted child Samantha's FASD, we have already encountered a layered sequence of stories documenting the suffering of Native peoples at the hands of white imperialism, including how alcoholism's assault on indigenous communities can be traced back to settler-colonialists' introduction of the problem into tribal communities. This counter-narrative rhetoric pushes us to see whites' historically based moral complicity in the disintegration of John and Amy's family. Similarly, once we've recognized the recurring connections between black people's enslavement generations ago and the inescapable heritage of that oppression, then the individual accounts in #BlackLivesMatter's online postings carry cumulative weight. What's up to us as readers, in both cases, is how (and whether or not) we will use this Archive toward the kind of productive responses represented by CNN's aspirational story-portraits in "The Disruptors." Will these counter-narratives move us to purposeful interventions? And what forms might that action take?

Preparing Students for Rhetorical Citizenship

As we imagine potential avenues to agency accessed by *reading* a text like Thomas King's, we should also consider the possible social impact of *writing* such stories. In that context, as educators, presumably charged with preparing our students for active citizenship,[20] we need to ask: Does learning to enact such storytelling generate greater self-critical empathy and associated capacity to become a community leader? And further, assuming these interconnected activities are mutually reinforcing, how can our teaching of reading and writing "skills" support students' growth as participants in intercultural networks, as builders of communal learning legacies, and, more specifically, as makers of counter-narratives?

With these questions in mind, as a teacher seeking to enable students' cross-cultural civic engagement, I want to know more about the prior learning experiences of young leaders such as those profiled in CNN's #BlackLivesMatter story. Intriguingly, imbedded within the profiles of CNN's report, I see an implied link between the educational backgrounds of those young leaders and their current cultural work. Michelle Taylor was trained as a social worker. Brittany Packnett had a career as a third grade teacher and, later, as the director of the St. Louis chapter of Teach for America. Shaun King, raised in rural Kentucky, is a Morehouse graduate. Ashley Yates, CNN reports, "became politicized as a teenager, when her aunt introduced her to the writings of James Baldwin, Sonia Sanchez, and Assata Shakur." Who were Ashley's other teachers, including those at the University of Missouri? Who, at Morehouse, given that institution's heritage as a molder of black male leaders, may have helped inspire Shaun toward activism, and how? Which teachers (including peers) encouraged Umi Selah when he "joined the student government at Florida A&M" and "co-founded a coalition for justice" there? Were there university-based mentors for these young leaders' learning about how to craft their current social media counter-narratives? I hope so.

I am currently seeking to act on that hope by supporting a student-led project called GlobalEX. As I write this Coda, in the summer of 2016, this initiative is still in its infancy. It has grown out of a still-developing cross-cultural collaboration. While I was serving as acting dean for the Honors College, two energetic students—Brian Niebuhr and Ryker Thompson—came to my office one afternoon to pose a cluster of interrelated questions. How, they wondered, could the social boundaries between TCU's increasing numbers of international students and the US-based majority be blurred? What kinds of structured experiences might we create to support bridge-building between those groups? And, assuming we could carry out such a project, how would we assess its impact?

Brian, whose family had hosted several exchange students during his high school years, emphasized that these queries did not represent a wish to "look after" international peers, as if they were somehow less capable academically (quite the contrary, he noted) or uninterested in forming social ties with others from beyond their own homelands. Rather, he stressed, we should be proactively promoting ways that "domestic" students could learn from international ones—so that the two groups might create shared knowledge about each other and about global issues of importance to all.

As a member of the university's Discovering Global Citizenship faculty and staff committee, originally formed in conjunction with our Quality Enhancement Plan (QEP) on global learning, I was eager to address these questions collaboratively.[21] We initiated a conversation with staff leaders of the International Student Services team—John Singleton, Liz Branch, and James English. Soon, our inquiry had moved from tentative conversations to formation of a student leadership team, with four members coming from our campus's current international cohort and four from the "domestic"/ US side. Looking to encourage sustainability beyond a pilot year, students who came on board were all, save one, freshmen. Throughout spring semester 2016, we met regularly. The task we set for ourselves was to envision a pilot program aimed at incoming first-year students in the class of 2020, to launch in fall 2016.

As lead facilitator, Brian began each meeting by revisiting the goals we established in our preliminary discussions and continued to refine over time:

- To provide domestic students with international experience on campus, promoting "Local-Global" learning;
- To promote international students' ability to share knowledge about their home cultures;

- To encourage collaborative learning and reporting on that learning through shared experiences.

By the close of that semester, we had a timeline of activities projected for fall and a to-do list for everyone involved (students [both US-based and international], faculty, and staff) to address, in subgroups or pairs, over the summer. We had tapped several additional project partners from around campus—such as the New Media Writing Studio, whose staff will help us create and maintain an online storytelling space. We had envisioned a structure that would recruit a mix of international and US-based students, then place them in teams of four. Each team, we planned, would move through two stages of shared knowledge-building, first about each other and about global resources on campus and in the metro, second about localized versions of global issues.

In stage one, called EXplore, teams will collaboratively decide on two activities to carry out together as a step toward constructing a "third space" of cross-cultural inquiry, blending their diverse perspectives. These shared learning activities could be as simple, initially, as attending a university-sponsored lecture or film on a global topic together, or visiting a local consulate, or meeting up for dinner with an alumnus who had held a Fulbright Fellowship to hear about the program's structure. In stage two, teams will move to shared social action as each group chooses a particular issue to research in depth in collaboration with community partners (EXchange phase). In a third step (EXtend), every team will develop a strategy for sharing their new knowledge publicly, with campus and community audiences: approaches for this stage might include hosting a forum, giving a performance, or mounting an exhibit. And, for the TCU students, a culminating goal will be to create team-made stories documenting their own learning. Using a web-based reporting space, we aspire to create a start-up archive of learning legacies, a cultural resource for community members within and beyond the university—one that will expand in succeeding years as the project renews itself annually with new participants.

By the time you (my readers) hold this book in your hands, or encounter this text on a screen, we imagine that the GlobalEX project will be well on its way to intercultural storytelling. With the "EX" designating progressive stages of exploration, shared experience, and civic exchange, all of us involved in this pilot project hope you will "google" into our archive via TCU's New Media Writing Studio, then adapt what you find there to start imagining community-building projects of your own. In line with the

Learning Legacies framework I have been presenting here, I suspect you'll see some counter-narrative features in the project's records of work. Situated in a social space outside of a formal academic curriculum, GlobalEX aspires to resist disciplinary constraints, overcome the tight limits of typical school calendars, and undermine the prescriptively performative expectations for students associated with having to earn grades. Organized to operate through a students-leading-students model, some stories will likely be more detailed, vibrant, creative, and thoughtful than others. Some will probably be more clearly grounded than others in the GlobalEX project's stated goals. But if only a few achieve a stance of critical empathy, if only a few compellingly "story" collaborative social action, if only a few are positioned to enable readers' applications in other contexts, then, we think, the pilot will have been successful. In any case, we invite you to examine GlobalEX for yourself.

Writing New Stories of Cross-Cultural Learning

By now, assuming you've read this far, it's doubtless become clear that I hope this book has generated a viable learning legacy of its own. To act on that legacy's aspirations, one venue would certainly be the classroom, so I've tried at various places throughout the text to offer up conceptual models that can operate in diverse instructional settings. In this Coda, I've gone a step further: I've described several specific teaching applications, from individual "lesson-plan" to syllabus-construction level. Another pathway for applying the book's core content, as suggested in the section just above, would extend students' (and educators') shared inquiry and new archival production into the larger community through collaborative projects along the lines of GlobalEX or the Keeping and Creating American Communities program revisited at various points earlier.

A third approach to producing learning legacies entails rethinking scholarship—that is, embracing narratives about collaborative learning and stories about cross-cultural teaching as vehicles for creating academic knowledge.[22] Although I'm hoping the book, as a whole, has successfully demonstrated this pathway, I want to close by honoring two role models whose examples of disseminating learning legacies in their own writing have been especially helpful to me—Sabine Smith and Diane Glancy. I'll reference mentor texts from each below.

First, let me address a question about the organization of this Coda itself. Why end with *writing about writing*? For one thing, writing our own learning legacies helps us accrue experiential authority to enable our students to do the same. That is, consistent with principles I've internalized through the National Writing Project, if I want to nurture students' abilities as writers in particular genres, I need to be a writer too, working in the same forms I am asking students to employ. And as educators, wherever we work—classroom or museum, service organization or informal community group—one of our primary roles is to prepare our students for civic engagement, an ongoing enterprise for which activist literacies are essential. Therefore, based on the case studies I've explored in this book, I am now cultivating my own and my students' capabilities for creating and deploying new counter-narratives, for generating new archives of social action, and for extending the most productive Archives that are already around us, awaiting our efforts to delve into them for everyday use.

If I want to hone my ability to write in such a way, I need to give time to (and carve our professional space for) that priority. Recently, when re-reading notes from my interview with Lisa Lee, former director of the Jane Addams Hull-House Museum, I came across her comments about Addams and Ellen Gates Starr choosing different foci to claim civic leadership themselves. According to Lee, Starr was more committed to "hitting the street," marching with striking women garment workers, for instance, whereas Addams was more inclined to publish a compelling narrative about such demonstrations and their implications. Lee's observation resonated with Addams's own account, in her *Twenty Years at Hull-House* text, of struggling to find a balance between doing settlement work and writing about it.

For scholar-teachers committed to the public humanities today, finding a balance between *doing* activist cultural work and *writing* about it is just as difficult. So I don't have a magic formula for achieving that balance. I've come to understand that collaborative writing, enacted in various configurations, is one way to integrate social action and authorship. Collaboration is time-consuming in itself, of course. But, to see its benefits, we need only look at examples like Jane Addams Hull-House Museum curators' shared reporting on their site-based cultural work, the annual performances at Spelman's Founders Day, or recent publications like *Survivance, Sovereignty, and Story* (emerging over time from collaborative pedagogy workshops by a network of Native scholars). And I can also point to individual role models whose negotiation of this mandate to write via collaborative pathways about their own learning legacies guides my own efforts.

One is Sabine H. Smith, with whom (along with Federica Santini) I co-edited *Bridging Cultures*, a volume of essays by expatriate women academics about finding their place in the US academy. Each essay addresses both personal and institutional frameworks of action for "bridging cultures." Sabine's story achieves especially notable rhetorical power. Consistent with gendered traditions that link the domestic and the political, she courageously positions her own intercultural learning within a complex familial context. Thus, her essay describes a cross-generational conflict connected to her German father's role in, and view of, World War II. In a vivid account of dialogue typical of her uncomfortable visits home, she invites readers both to empathize with Germans seeking to re-vise their personal histories in relation to larger historical narratives and to draw from that complicated learning legacy in ways that will support social justice. These are the very Archival resources she excavates to inform her own cultural stewardship for students in her US classroom today. When Sabine describes her public scholarship projects—such as joining a Holocaust Studies teaching team in Israel or leading students from Atlanta through site visits to former concentration camps—we come to recognize how this scholarly work embodies both a personal and a communal counter-narrative.[23] For me, her writing model is an equally inspiring benchmark, urging me to take on challenging contexts of intercultural learning, as well as to share stories, from a self-critical stance about those experiences.

Along related lines, I've written earlier in this volume about Diane Glancy's impact on the Keeping and Creating American Communities project through her teaching about *Pushing the Bear*. To affirm, here, the longstanding influence of her role model as guiding my writing as well, let me describe my takeaways from two of her more recent narratives. A prolific author of fiction on Native themes, Glancy is also a thoughtful analyst of her own composing processes and of ways that her texts address both literary/aesthetic and educational goals. Her multigenre *Designs of the Night Sky* and the "Afterword" to *Pushing the Bear: After the Trail of Tears*, volume two of her Removal narrative, are prime examples.

In *Designs*, Glancy has created Ada Ronner, a librarian in the Manuscripts and Rare Books Library at an Oklahoma college, and has given this unconventional teacher figure imaginative access to voices from the Native past. Archives, for Ada, become accessible voices shaping what Michel de Certeau calls the practice of everyday life. As Glancy notes in her "Preface," "The novel is a weaving of contemporary voices with several old texts, such as the historical journal of the Cherokee Removal from the South-east to Indian Territory (present Oklahoma)." Ada's story also integrates events from that "turbulent history of a tribe and the survivors of that history still caught in turmoil" (xi–xii). This novel's braiding together of diverse textual forms enables Glancy to raise questions about the relationships between oral and written culture, between books and historical documents, between special collections and public access, between story and lived experience, between author and audience, between the science of formal history and the magic of communally composed words, between culture-making and natural forces like "designs in the night sky," and between artifacts of all kinds and our ways of understanding them. Ada's brand of scholarship—a stand-in for Glancy's with its commitment to communal epistemologies?—embodies a counter-narrative type of knowledge-making, an approach more open-ended and interpersonal than academic, in the traditional sense. Creating a story that is also about the importance of stories and communal storytelling for cultural stewardship, Glancy in this novel conveys a larger agenda for her own work as an author-teacher and, potentially, for others who would write in the service of community-building while, always, encouraging other voices to join in.

Glancy knows such work is difficult. Her account of her process for producing the two *Pushing the Bear* counter-narratives, which reclaimed Removal history through Native storytelling, takes readers along from her early inquiry to her composing stages. Accordingly, her "Afterword" to the second volume of that writing project begins by reflecting back on her girlhood learning about the Trail of Tears when she visited her father's people in Oklahoma. She relocated there after college, she says, and then "began to feel again the presence of that unknown history" (187). To access individual stories that might open up that suppressed cultural heritage, Glancy attended an outdoor drama in Tahlequah, Oklahoma. (That anecdote, for me, conjured up memories of my own family's attendance at "Unto These Hills" in western North Carolina, both as a child with my parents and as a parent with my daughters, a generation later.) She also "visited research libraries and eventually drove the nine hundred miles of the trail, from New Echota, Georgia, to Fort Gibson, Oklahoma, which was called Indian Territory at the time." Glancy's emphasis on how "passing over the land" enabled her "to hear the voices of the people in [her] imagination" (187) reconfirmed, as I was writing this book, that an archive can be far more varied in its make-up than the stereotyped portrait of musty documents encased in a library. Her associated explanation that this imaginative step from travel into "giving voice to history" nurtured my own sense of how multifaceted study of a place-based archive (whether Spelman's Sisters Chapel and quadrangle, Hull-House's dining room, or the NMAI's soaring architecture) can open up deeper layers of a cross-cultural Archive. In Glancy's case, her combination of seeing a performance about the Removal, visiting traditional research libraries, and retraveling the trail herself prepared her to assemble a "communal first-person" viewpoint for her first volume of *Pushing the Bear*, "the one-as-all, as opposed to Western culture's emphasis on the individual" (188). Her inquiry for the second volume was similar. That is, her research for *After the Trail of Tears* affiliated this account with her "other books of historical narrative," such as the *Stone Heart* story of Sacajawea and the recovery of Kateri Tekakwitha's personal history (193) in *The Reason for Crows*. All in all, her reflective memoir of process conveyed a lived-in-place and traveling-across-time commitment to nurturing communities today.

Glancy's culminating image for this "Afterword" on composing "a created voice into historical narrative" comes to her readers as a photograph—a picture of a "rock" that she picked up "at Fort Gibson, the arrival point" that was also the beginning for *After the Trail of Tears*. With this anecdote, Glancy asserts the most humble artifacts' concrete yet imaginative contribution to composing a learning legacy. Through her "picking up" image, she suggests that, with care, any of us can begin connecting to valuable Archives, both in and across time and space.

Like Thomas King's *The Truth About Stories*, Diane Glancy's accounts of narrative-making stop short of claiming a direct social efficacy for such writing. Both of those author-activists leave the doing of cultural work (even if inspired by their storytelling) up to their readers. So here again, a student grateful for others' guidance, I will follow their lead. If you, like those wise mentors, want to move from Archive to action, from counternarrative study to the purposeful shaping of future social history, from recovering learning legacies to composing and circulating your own, then I hope the stories I've shared here will help you find your path.

Notes

Chapter 1

1. See my project description for "Contagion, Quarantine and Social Conscience" online.

2. Thomas King, *The Truth about Stories*. Chapters typically begin with "There is a story I know" and then move to examination of complex ethical issues through the combined lenses of experience and theory. For a case study of story in action in public scholarship, see Patricia Steenland, "Lost Stories."

3. For related discussion of the value of affect in knowledge-making, see Million, "Felt Theory." See also Baker, Dieter, and Dobbins, "Art of Being Persuaded," on Wayne Booth's conception of rhetoric as mutual inquiry requiring humanitarian listening. Also, linked to chapter 3's examination of Hull-House's rhetorical and pedagogical practices, see Ruth Vinz's closing essay in *Jane Addams in the Classroom*. Vinz views the settlement as "part of an ongoing creative attempt [by Addams] to act herself and others into a more democratic space of *being* together," that is, to cultivate a "*transmigration of empathy*" (201, emphases in original). As a note on editing, I should mention that, throughout this book, I use a hyphen in Hull-House, following Addams's own practice, unless I am referencing someone else's title or quoting from a source where the hyphen is not used.

4. Later in this chapter, within the section labeled "Archives as Resources," I discuss my use of the terms "archive" and "Archive."

5. See *Who Can Speak?*, edited by Judith Roof and Robyn Wiegman. For a related discussion of standpoint epistemology, see Santini, Smith, and Robbins, the "Introduction" to *Bridging Cultures*, especially xxiii–xxiv. My primary teaching site as I was completing this book was TCU, which has a substantial endowment and tuition income to support students, faculty, and staff. While a notable percentage of those enrolled receive financial aid, the overall ethos of the institution—including its ongoing building campaign, its substantial library collection and its highly selective admission process, as well as its very visible success in athletics—distinctly marks the institution as privileged. Furthermore, my previous institutions—

Kennesaw State for much of the teaching referenced in this book, and the University of Michigan and the University North Carolina, Chapel Hill, for the bulk of my professorial training—while public, are all relatively well funded and certainly provide extensive access to knowledge-building resources.

6. I discuss this point in a section (16–19) within "Seeking Trust," a *MELUS* essay coauthored with Joycelyn Moody.

7. On reflection as a pathway to rhetorical knowledge, see Liu, "Rhetoric and Reflexivity."

8. In *Autoethnography as Method*, Chang explains that autoethnographic writing should textually represent *method* (the research process), *culture* as one object of study, and *self* as another area of interpretation, including how the identity/self of the researcher interacts with specific cultural groups (48–49, 56). Other useful sources include Denzin, *Interpretive Autoethnography*, and Carolyn Ellis, *The Ethnographic I*.

9. See, for example, Harry Boyte's *Democracy's Education*; David D. Cooper's *Learning in the Plural*; and Julie Ellison, "Guest Column: The New Public Humanists" in *PMLA*.

10. See, in this context, Cheryl Glenn and Jessica Enoch, "Drama in the Archives," where they emphasize the shifting nature of historiographies grounded in archival study and the related impact of scholars' choices about what archival documents to choose and how to study them (336). Applying a Burkean pentad of "Act, Scene, Agent, Agency, Purpose," they posit: "Within the archive (the scene), the researcher (agent) engages (agency) in a variety of recovery and recuperative practices (acts) directed toward a specific end (purpose)" (322). For Glenn and Enoch, a key aspect of agency in archival work resides in the process of doing recovery and in the analysis thereby enabled—interpretive work wherein we must be "accurate," certainly, but also attentive to "what our self-interest is, as well as how that interest might enrich our disciplinary field and how it might affect others," including those "we talk *with* and listen *to*," "whether they are speaking to us in person or via archival materials" (336, emphasis in original). I aim to affiliate with their call for ethical processes recognizing the ways that knowledge drawn from archival sources is ever-changing depending on the agency of the interpreter. I've also tried to answer their invitation for "scholars [to] continue to consider how we might open up even more possibilities for archival recovery"—in this project's case by extending questions of agency to explore how knowledge derived from the archive can support our participation in civic enterprises today.

11. Said McCrory: "If you want to take gender studies that's fine, go to a private school and take it." He added, "But I don't want to subsidize that if that's not going to get someone a job." Bennett (a philosophy major at the University of Texas) asked, on the same radio broadcast: "How many Ph.D.s in philosophy do I need to subsidize?" See Kevin Kiley, "Another Liberal Arts Critic." See too Aamer Madhani, "Obama Apologizes," both available online.

12. See Diane Ravitch, *Reign of Error*, and Emma Brown, "Some parents."

13. Gearan, "Engaging Communities" and Ellison and Eatman, *Scholarship in Public*.

14. In Branson and Robbins, "Going Public," forthcoming, *Cambridge Hand-*

book, and in Branson, Sanchez, Robbins, and Wehlburg, "Collaborative Ecologies of Emergent Assessment: Challenges and Benefits Linked to a Writing-based Institutional Partnership," forthcoming in *College Composition and Communication*, I address these questions along with other colleagues involved in public scholarship.

15. Some scholars purposefully use a plural form—rhetorics—in line with this field's emphasis on how language's rhetorical actions vary according to context. Similarly, for an NEH program I co-led with several National Writing Project (NWP) partners, we titled our initiative Making American Literatures, purposefully choosing the plural form. Here, I generally use singular for consistency's sake, but I appreciate the intent behind preferences for the plural form.

16. Phil Bratta and Malea Powell, "Introduction to the Special Issue" on cultural rhetorics for *Enculturation*. Bratta and Powell's use of the plural form—rhetorics—resonates with their emphasis on situated distinctions in the work of diverse cultural communities. Gilyard's work, quoted in the next section, uses a singular form (cultural rhetoric), perhaps because he seeks to position the term more as a theoretical framework than a cluster of practices.

17. Also relevant is Steven Mailloux's recent consideration of rhetoric's interdisciplinary positioning within the academy and potential benefits of this location and available strategies for doing cultural work through rhetoric. See "Practices, Theories and Traditions," especially Mailloux's citing of Tom Miller's observations on rhetoric's ability to engage in social intervention (134–35). See also Mailloux's *Disciplinary Identities*.

18. See, for example, Schaafsma, ed., *Jane Addams in the Classroom*. On narrative inquiry as a learning method for teachers examining their own practices, see Schaafsma and Vinz, *On Narrative Inquiry*.

19. Richard Enos, personal email communication, August 15, 2015.

20. One writerly tradition useful for understanding counter-narratives comes from postcolonial theory and practices. See, for instance, Homi K. Bhabha, *Location of Culture*, especially chapters entitled "Interrogating Identity" (40–65), "Of Mimicry and man" (85–92) and "Signs taken for wonders" (102–22).

21. Giroux, Lankshear, McLaren, and Peters situate the concept of counter-narratives within a framework of critical pedagogy in *Counternarratives; Cultural Studies and Critical Pedagogies in Postmodern Spaces*. Suggesting that two brands of counter-narratives have acquired broad usage, they view the first as generally mounting "a critique of the modernist predilection for 'grand,' 'master,' and 'meta' narratives" associated with Enlightenment thought (2). The second sense they identify works to counter not only the master/grand narratives but also "the '*official*' and '*hegemonic*' narratives of everyday life: those legitimating stories propagated for specific political purposes to manipulate public consciousness by heralding a national set of common cultural ideals" (2). This approach to making a counter-narrative, they say, aligns the form with the Foucauldian concept of "'counter-memory'" and Lyotard's "'little stories'—the little stories of those individuals and groups whose knowledges and histories have been marginalized, excluded, subjugated or forgotten in the telling of official narratives" (Peters and Lankshear, "Introduction," 2ff. emphases in original).

22. Addams and her colleagues were wise enough not to ignore the authoritative

power of quantitative research and writing tools, however. Spurred on by Henrietta and Samuel Barnett, settlement colleagues from London's Toynbee Hall, Addams encouraged Hull-House residents like Florence Kelley to capitalize on inquiry and dissemination techniques being developed through the then-new social sciences. *Hull-House Maps and Papers* is one example of this blended approach. Similarly, I have tried to adopt and adapt quantitative tools for studying and reporting on my own civic projects, and, despite this book's focus on narrative inquiry, I recognize the potential of techniques such as "big data" analysis in the digital humanities and visualization rhetorics. See, in this context, my discussion of distant reading in the Coda.

23. The Society of American Archivists (SAA) acknowledges the range of meanings for "archives" in discussion of the term on their website. For instance, the entry there notes: "In the vernacular, 'archives' is often used to refer to any collection of documents that are old or of historical interest, regardless of how they are organized; in this sense, the term is synonymous with permanent records." And, as another example of how vernacular meanings differ in different contexts and shift over time, SAA offers this example: "the noun 'archive' is commonly used to describe collections of backup data in information technology literature." I thank my university librarian colleagues Laura Micham (Duke) and Ammie Harrison (TCU) for assistance in identifying and interpreting helpful sources for defining "archive(s)."

24. White movingly contextualizes his "Foreword" discussion of the importance of governmental archives via references to both World War II and the then-current Cold War: "We should expect the continuing crises provided by the discovery of atomic power," he says, to generate concerns about "the threat" that warfare poses to "records themselves," in that "the preservation of archives" is linked to "hope for our civilization" (*Modern Archives*, vii).

25. Already in his 1956 *Modern Archives* book, Schellenberg had pointed to definition challenges associated with using "archive" to apply both to materials and to the places where they reside: "In ordinary conversation, and particularly in professional literature, a distinction must be made between the institution and the materials with which it deals" (11).

26. By way of her study of Annie Ray's diary, Jennifer Sinor's *The Extraordinary Work of Ordinary Writing* implicitly argues for family archives to be valued in feminist recovery efforts. See too Jennifer Bernhardt Steadman and colleagues' "Archive Survival Guide," which points out that progress has been made in rethinking the place of women's materials in archives: "A major shift in archival preservation away from male-dominated histories and collecting foci centered on men's papers and achievements has made space for collecting new texts by and about diverse women and re-cataloging and highlighting documents already in existing collections" (238). In the Coda, I share Jiménez's reflection on the difficulties he encountered trying to use traditional archival collections to contextualize his family's experiences as migrant workers.

27. See, as one example of my previous work in archives and my reflections on process, a coauthored discussion of a collaborative project with Ann Pullen, in "Collaboration in the Archive."

28. Neither Addams nor her colleagues would have used the term "cross-cultural," of course, or a related one that I employ in this book—intercultural. But the anecdotes they marshalled to describe the projects linked to Hull-House nonetheless stressed the vision for social boundary-crossing that was at the heart of the settlement program. Key texts include the "Objective Necessity" chapter of *Twenty Years at Hull-House* and the recurring story of the "Devil Baby," which Addams first addressed in an article for the *American Journal of Sociology* in 1914, then revisited in October 1916 in *The Atlantic*, and returned to in chapter 1 of *The Long Road of Woman's Memory*, 1–24.

29. Examples include Diliberto, *A Useful Woman*; Elshtain, *Jane Addams and the Dream*; Hamington, ed., *Feminist Interpretations*; Jackson, *Lines of Activity*; Knight, *Jane Addams: Spirit in Action*.

30. Atlanta University Center (the AUC Consortium) is comprised of Spelman College, Morehouse College and Morehouse School of Medicine, and Clark Atlanta University. As such, the AUC holds a special place in the heritage and current work of HBCUs, i.e., Historically Black Colleges and Universities.

31. Freire's *Education for Critical Consciousness* and *Pedagogy of the Oppressed* provide important context for such work.

32. For helpful conceptual frameworks and examples, see Alcoff, Hames-Garcia, Mohanty, and Moya, eds., *Identity Politics Reconsidered*.

33. For productive approaches to teaching about the *Cherokee Phoenix*, see Rose Gubele, "Unlearning the Pictures in Our Heads," in King, Gubele, and Anderson, eds., *Survivance, Sovereignty, and Story*, 96–115.

34. Rand, "Why I Can't Visit the National Museum of the American Indian" provides relevant context.

35. Rickard's description was reported by Kristine Ronan in her essay on "Native Empowerment," 137

36. In the pamphlet entitled "Native Artists in the Americas," Keevin Lewis (Navajo), NMAI's Community and Constituent Services Coordinator, located the history of the Native Artists program at the museum within its larger commitment to outreach initiatives that incorporated "listening to the needs of Native people" while contributing to "a growing base of Indigenous cultural knowledge, art, history, and language" that can be "shared with a larger audience" (4, 6–7).

37. One question an anonymous reviewer had asked me to address in revision involved considering whether or not some of the informal interactions I describe in this book represent genuine collaboration. S/he wondered if "the process of engaging others as one pursues one's own work" can actually be viewed as collaboration, and observed that "[m]uch of Professor Robbins' research takes the form of interviews, discussions, observations" toward writing, rather than collaboration in the more traditional sense of "people working together, in some cases to create something. I am skeptical," this reviewer noted, "about how collaborative it is, but eager to be persuaded, and I suspect that many other readers will be the same position. . . ." (Reader's Report #1).

38. Online discussion of Camus's novel in connection with the Ebola outbreak is on the website "Contagion, Quarantine, and Social Conscience: Albert Camus's *The Plague*."

39. On envisioning and enacting next steps beyond initial moves to establish genuine affiliations, see Paul Feigenbaum's *Collaborative Imagination*, where he examines "what it means for contemporary progressives to *earn activism* through literacy education." Feigenbaum suggests: "The imagination—especially when employed communally—offers educators a powerful mechanism for fighting injustice. More specifically, counterhegemonic praxes of literacy education facilitate progressives' *collaborative imagination* of a world in which citizenship is no longer rigged and in which humankind lives in ecological balance with its natural surroundings" (3, emphases in original).

Chapter 2

1. One legacy of the KCAC project is the scholarly work of K-12 teachers of color who began doing research through the program. For two examples, see Sylvia Martinez Spruill's 2013 dissertation, "Assessment in Secondary Environments," and educational texts by Rozlyn Linder, such as *The Common Core Guidebook*.

2. For an overview of the resources initially developed under leadership by Deborah Mitchell, Ed Hullender (Wheeler High School), and others, see "Uplifting a 'New' South" on the KCAC website's "Educating for Citizenship" section.

3. Significantly, the collaboration by teachers in the team studying Spelman was interracial. This pattern would carry forward later in a project developing curriculum for teaching about the 1906 Atlanta race riots.

4. For a calendar of the multiyear KCAC project, visit "Chronology of the KCAC Project's Initial Work" on the program's website. For themes, see "Thematic Content." While the website is dated—such as in lacking interactive conversation—we regularly hear from colleagues using the curriculum. For additional classroom resources, see the companion volume *Writing Our Communities*, eds. Winter and Robbins. For reflective essays by teacher participants, see *Writing America*, eds. Robbins and Dyer.

5. Kennesaw Mountain Writing Project, "Keeping and Creating American Communities: Proposal to the National Endowment for the Humanities" is available online.

6. The *Spelman Messenger*'s first issue appeared in March of 1885 and, on its front page, signaled a goal of promoting the institution via such features as a poem ("Thoughts on Spelman Girls") written in a student voice, a brief history of the institution, and information on tuition (then, with board, seven dollars per month). Subsequent citations, including titles and authors when listed in an issue, will appear within the text, giving the month, year, and page number in parentheses. Material from the *Messenger* is provided courtesy of the Spelman College Archive.

7. Dave Winter, "A Correspondence Between Atlanta Students," in *Writing Our Communities*, 34–44.

8. As Kimberly Wallace-Sanders pointed out to me in conversation, Spelman's placement of its archive in a prominent campus building signals recognition of the key role those materials and the institution's history play in the college's current life.

9. This chapter (indeed, the book as a whole) benefited enormously from guid-

ance provided by Roxanne Donovan, Altheria Gaston, Barbara McCaskill, Stacie McCormick, Joycelyn Moody, and Kimberly Wallace-Sanders. Any errors, though, are my own.

10. Du Bois's poetic characterization of the New England teachers who aimed to help educate the freedmen is sympathetic: "Behind the mists of ruin and rapine waved the calico dresses of women who dared, and after the hoarse mouthings of the field guns rang the rhythm of the alphabet. Rich and poor they were, serious and curious. Bereaved now of a father, now of a brother, now of more than these, they came seeking a life work in planting New England schoolhouses among the white and black of the South. They did their work well. In that first year they taught one hundred thousand souls, and more" ("Of the Dawn," *Souls*, 25).

11. In "Bricks Without Straw," Johnetta Cross Brazzell calls for a more balanced view of the New England teachers who worked in the South—avoiding either over-romanticizing them or lumping all mission organizations and teachers together for critique based on the patronizing, even racist, stances common among some.

12. In *The Souls of Black Folk*, Du Bois points out that a significant amount of the money raised to found institutions like Fisk, Howard, and Hampton came from "the freedmen themselves," who "gave of their poverty" ("Of the Dawn," 29). See also James D. Anderson, *Education of Blacks in the South*, 12.

13. See Dorsey, *To Build Our Lives Together*. On southern whites' and others' contributions to black education in the postbellum era, see Christina Davis's dissertation, "Reconstructing Black Education."

14. On Jacobs's post-Civil War teaching, including with her daughter Louisa, see Jean Fagan Yellin's *Harriet Jacobs: A Life*, 176–86, 199; on the Crafts' efforts to educate blacks in Georgia after the famous international fugitives' return to the United States, see Barbara McCaskill's luminous *Love, Liberation, and Escaping Slavery*, including chapter 4's account of how the libel trial against William undercut their Woodville School, but also the epilogue's treatment of their "legacy of community service, social improvement, and educational and political engagement" (87). Though Charles Chesnutt eventually turned to a legal stenographer career and to authorship, he had teaching and educational administrative experience—and he draws on that background in his fiction. See, for instance, *Mandy Oxendine* and "The March of Progress." For W. E. B. Du Bois's moving account of his experience teaching "in the hills of Tennessee" while a student at Fisk, see "The Meaning of Progress" chapter in *Souls*, 47, 47–54.

15. Jacqueline Jones, *Soldiers of Light and Love*, and Ronald Butchart, "Black Hope, White Power," present thoughtful analysis of the mixed motivations of white teachers serving in the South and the complex connections between their work and Reconstruction politics. See too Eric Foner, *Short History of Reconstruction*.

16. Charlotte Forten's teaching memoir in the *Atlantic* ran in two parts, beginning in May 1864, under the title "Life on the Sea Islands." For a history of the NEFAS's longstanding commitment to black education in the South, as seen through correspondence to and from Boston-based organization leader Ednah Dow Cheney and publication from such texts in the *Freedmen's Record*, see my "Social Action."

17. On Packard's work for the WABHMS, see Read, *Story of Spelman*, 31–34.

18. Packard and Giles began working together in 1854 at New Salem Academy in Massachusetts (Read, *Story of Spelman*, 4). Their skills were so evident that they were hired away to teach in Petersham, then in Fitchburg, and later in Suffield, Connecticut, eventually claiming advanced positions at the prestigious Oread Collegiate Institute in Worcester, Massachusetts (Read, *Story of Spelman*, 19). Their leaving the institute in 1867 seems to have been related to a gender-based conflict with Harris R. Greene, a new principal, and was a blow to the two educational leaders who had grown accustomed to having their talents appreciated.

19. In this sense, my project affiliates with John Ernest's call in *Chaotic Justice* for "an emphasis on the deep structures of the social order that 'race' has both defined and justified historically and on the communal networks that have formed over those deep structures" (5).

20. "A Fifth Generation: The Quarles Family." *Spelman Messenger* (Spring 2012): 12. The feature story included Muriel Ruth Ketchum Yarbrough's comments from Founders Day on April 10 of that year.

21. As I was cross-indexing sources on Spelman's alumnae, I was excited to find a copy of notes Deborah had sent me in early March of 2001 based on her interview with Muriel Ruth Ketchum Yarbrough (who was then 73). The commitment to education "Aunt Ruth" had cited to Deborah was exemplified in an account of an early rural school built by family members just after they had been freed—a school that continued operating until 1941. A recurring theme of this conversation was the family's servant leadership for the race, which Aunt Ruth explained her mother had always "told us, you pass it on!" (Mitchell, Oral History Notes, KCAC project).

22. One noteworthy exception is "The Female Talented Tenth" chapter (19–41) in *Righteous Discontent*, where Higginbotham credits Quarles with "literally giving his life to the cause of Spelman" (23).

23. The opening sentence of a 2005 historical overview by Harry G. Lefever is illustrative: "Spelman College, the nation's oldest and best-known black liberal arts college for women, was founded in 1881 by two New England white women, Sophia B. Packard and Harriet E. Giles" ("Early Origins," 60). While it might be tempting to explain the de-emphasis on Quarles's role solely in racial terms, I suspect that another factor is the tendency of academics to undervalue community activists' contributions to making knowledge and building institutions.

24. In her review of the contributions of Spelman's presidents, from Sophia Packard through Beverly Tatum, Yarbrah T. Peeples credits Read as "developing Spelman into a liberal arts college of high quality" ("Philanthropy," 252).

25. As an example of this peer-style relationship, Taronda sent me a copy of a letter from students in Packard's class one year. Admonishing their teacher that she "must not come into our class in Analogy again until [she felt] stronger," this group from the "Class of '88" confidently assured Packard that they would "get our lessons and go on reciting as usual," while she recovered from an illness. "Don't worry or be anxious about anything, but for the sake of those who love you more than they can express, lay aside every care and we will help the teachers carry on everything just right," they declared ("Dear Miss Packard," n.d., signed by "Class of '[18]88").

26. "Colored Women and Girls" flyer dated April 6, 1881; with archivist notation.

27. Taronda Spencer provided me with a Xerox copy of this undated one-page handwritten description of Mary Ann Brooks from the Sophia Packard Papers, along with a note underscoring how this portrait of Brooks exemplified a tendency, early in the institution's history, for the students to be mature women as well as children. Packard herself references this pattern in the draft for an undated letter to officers of the Woman's American Baptist Home Mission Society. (Based upon the dated April 1882 query to which this draft responds, Packard likely composed her note in spring 1882.) Looking back at the initial days of teaching, Packard observed: "The ages of these pupils varied from the children under 12 most of whom could read to the matrons over fifty that had not ever known their letters." Packard's text includes margin notes and strikeouts indicative of her efforts to provide a balanced report for the upcoming May 1882 board meeting in Boston. Thus, she says: "This school is unique in that we have more mothers than any other school in the South while we have a hundred or more bright promising girls from 15 to 25. . . ." Packard's correspondence is available through the Office of the President: Sophia B. Packard Collection, Archives, Spelman College, Atlanta.

28. I call these texts "semipublic" rather than private because so much of Packard's personal letter writing anticipates a group readership. Thus, similar to the pattern Ann Pullen and I have described in "circular letters" to potential donors by missionaries like Nellie Arnott in a later generation, Packard's "personal" writing often assumes that multiple would-be donors will be evaluating the letters' contents and deciding, on that basis, how much support to provide. See "Introduction," *Nellie Arnott's Writings*, xv–xvi, and chapter 3.

29. Packard's positive personal writings about the African American women being educated at Spelman—along with their self-portraits in the publication launched in 1885—coincide with the determined efforts of postbellum black women professionals to craft positive identities, as outlined in Stephanie Shaw's *What a Woman Ought to Be and to Do*. Shaw argues that this generation of well-educated black women, fully aware that their mothers had endured slavery, were grateful for new opportunities, but also intent on using their new literacies to promote broad social gains. Comparatively speaking, despite the horrors of Jim Crow, "They were the empowered, the advantaged," says Shaw, and "They saw endless possibilities for themselves" individually, while also being "keenly aware of their collective history" (xii). For a counterpoint study addressing working-class contexts, see Xiomara Santamarina, *Belabored Professions*. See also Tera W. Hunter, *To 'Joy My Freedom*.

30. Obvious examples of black women's leadership being affirmed by whites would include Oprah Winfrey, Gayle King, and, on the academic front, such former Spelman presidents as Johnnetta Cole, Audrey Manley, Beverly Tatum, and current leader Mary Schmidt Campbell. However, a speech by Michelle Obama to Tuskegee graduates in spring 2015 (four years after her historic 2011 address at Spelman) offered up a resistant response to assumptions about US society's having reached a postracial stage in terms of accepting black women's social agency. For analysis of the widely varying reactions to the First Lady's speech, see Harvey Mansfield, "Give Michelle Obama a Break" and DeWayne Wickham, "What did you hear Michelle Obama say?" Writing for *USA Today*, Wickham complained about critical press coverage, including a *People* magazine article and a CNN report. For

Wickham, the core message of the address was "the 'double duty' blacks have to our country and our race," as illustrated in her speech's references to the Tuskegee Airmen's serving "with great distinction during World War II," yet "suffer[ing] the indignities of Jim Crow racism" (A7).

31. "Collaboration" can be difficult to sort out in cross-racial situations where whites serve as mediators (even if well-intentioned ones) between black authors and their audiences. See Moody and Robbins, "Seeking Trust." In the case of the *Messenger*, we cannot determine to what extent the published voices of students were encouraged, guided, and/or constrained by white teachers' decision-making. What kinds of student writing might have been excluded from those pages so as to construct the portrait Packard, Giles, and their white supporters sanctioned? As E. Patrick Johnson observes in *Appropriating Blackness*, "The fact of blackness is not always self-constituting," so that, in a white-dominated society, we must wonder not only how "'blackness' is embodied" in a printed space like the *Messenger* but also how "the material reality of the 'black' subject is occluded" (2). Similarly, Rose-ann Mandziuk and Suzanne Fitch identify "layers" of "rhetorical construction" that stand between Sojourner Truth, the original rhetor speaking to audiences, and the verbal portrait of her crafted by white women writers ("Rhetorical Construction," 123).

32. Key texts articulating critical literacy's goals come from Paulo Freire, particularly *Pedagogy of the Oppressed* and *Education for a Critical Consciousness*. Black educational theorist bell hooks, for one, draws effectively on Freire's work in such texts as *Teaching Community: A Pedagogy of Hope* and *Teaching to Transgress*.

33. See Audrey McCluskey, "'Manly Husbands and Womanly Wives'" in *Post-Bellum, Pre-Harlem*, eds. McCaskill and Gebhard, 74–88.

34. Peeples credits Packard and Giles for attracting donors like the Slater Fund and using such resources without giving up their own vision for the school. Thus, the first principals aimed to prepare students to be "teachers, missionaries and church workers," but they also "saw a place for industrial training in the curriculum" ("Philanthropy," 249).

35. As P. Gabrielle Foreman has noted, African Americans had long used their own publications "as the principal public advocate for education and literacy. Essays and editorials that appeared in black papers from their inception in 1827 highlighted the connection between knowledge, economic advancement, self-determination, and personal fulfillment" ("The *Christian Recorder*," 713).

36. Examples include "Spelman's Two Pioneers" (1941), "Spelman College Founders Day Events" (1958), and "Spelman Celebrates 101 Founders Day" (1982).

37. Washington reprinted and discussed his speech in "The Atlanta Exposition Address" chapter of *Up from Slavery*, 217–37. Articles in the *Messenger* that year show how attentively the Spelman community was following news of the Exposition and was capitalizing on the chance to attract new visitors to the campus. One untitled blurb in the December 1895 issue noted: "The Exposition still brings us many friends, both new and old, all of whom we gladly greet. We hope none of our readers who come up to the fair will neglect to report themselves to Spelman" (4).

38. Higginbotham proposes that "At Spelman, as at the other Baptist schools" founded for African American women during this era, "industrial training con-

stituted an important but not preponderant aspect of the curriculum. Industrial training was viewed as enhancing, not diminishing, the school's overall academic direction." Higginbotham—less convinced of Packard and Giles's egalitarian stance than I am—asserts that one factor contributing to this linkage was their belief that the "legacy of slavery" had "left blacks indolent and in need of proper work habits," which could instill a "Protestant work ethic" (*Righteous Discontent*, 33).

39. Before long, Spelman added a more professionally oriented brand of "industrial" education in its "Nurse Training Department," as outlined in an untitled story for the February 1888 issue of the *Messenger*, which also reprints an appreciative report on that program from the influential white-run *Atlanta Constitution* (5).

40. The *Messenger*'s pages drew from the early nineteenth-century periodical- and book-based campaigns for (white middle-class) women's education led by authors such as Sara Hale, Catharine Beecher, Lydia Sigourney, and Catharine Maria Sedgwick. See my *Managing Literacy*, introduction and chapter 1. Women of Packard and Giles's generation had been beneficiaries of these arguments, which they now extended to include southern blacks.

41. Yellin discusses the complicated—and often frustrating—challenges Harriet Jacobs faced in trying to find a white writer to provide an authenticating preface for *Incidents*, something which publishing houses insisted was a prerequisite to their accepting the text. Though twice enduring cruel rejection by Harriet Beecher Stowe, Yellin reports, Jacobs eventually secured support from Lydia Maria Child (*Harriet Jacobs*, 120, 140).

42. As I illustrate in "Social Action," Ednah Cheney published many positive portraits in the *Freedmen's Record*, which she edited for the NEFAS. See, in contrast, chapter 5, "Frances Harper's Literacy Program," in my *Managing Literacy*, which reviews a number of stereotype-filled depictions of the limited abilities of black learners—penned, ironically, by officials of the Freedmen's Bureau in their official reports (157–93).

43. My "Gendering the Debate Over African Americans' Education" focuses on Frances Harper's astute blending of the industrial model with the "talented tenth" framework in *Trial and Triumph*. I juxtapose her stance with Atticus Haygood's 1885 report to the Slater Fund and his 1889 book, *Our Brother in Black* to show how she advocated a curriculum for African Americans that would have appealed to white New South leaders as well as northern supporters of the freedmen by stressing the need for blacks' vocational training (81–84).

44. Praise for the Rockefellers' generosity, understandably, appeared regularly. The first issue, for instance, reported on the family's having enabled the school to develop a campus-type setting with new buildings: "The Spelman Baptist Seminary, formerly called Atlanta Baptist Female Seminary, receives its new name from the large donation made by Hon. J. D. Rockefeller, toward the payment of this property, which insures this Institution ever to be kept as a school for girls and women, in honor of the now sainted father of Mrs. Rockefeller, who was for more than forty years the firm friend of the colored race" (March 1885, 1). On Rockefeller's influential career, including his contributions to Spelman, see Ron Chernow, *Titan*.

45. *Messenger*, April 1891, 3. Sidney Root had been a prosperous antebellum

merchant in Atlanta, amassing a fortune lost during the war. Postwar, Root moved to New York, but he returned to Atlanta in 1878 and became one of the region's "New South" leaders. Though a strong proponent of racial hierarchies, he gave to both Morehouse and Spelman and is credited with bringing Spelman to the attention of the Rockefeller family (Moye, "Sidney Root (1824–1897)," *New Georgia Encyclopedia* [NGE] online). The *Encyclopedia* says of Haygood: "Atticus G. Haygood . . . was a distinguished president of Emory College and a progressive bishop of the Methodist Episcopal Church, South. He gained national prominence as a spokesman for the New South, promoting business and commercial development, and he fearlessly preached reunion, reconciliation, and educational opportunity for African Americans" (Mills, "Atticus G. Haygood (1839–1896)," NGE).

46. See the *Messenger*'s reprint of Warner, "Colored Schools South," May 1887, 1. Barbara McCaskill suggested to me in a personal note that the role enacted by Warner and Haygood in such writings could be termed "cultural amanuensis."

47. Haygood and Hayes, "Spelman Seminary," single-page flyer dated December 1888. Packard and Giles had been using printed flyers to advertise the school since its launch. They also printed advertisements in the *Messenger*.

48. Similarly, from early in the century, see Joycelyn Moody's analysis of how, in Frances Whipple's biographies of Elleanor Eldridge, the white textual manager weaves in "tropes that reify a white masculinist socioeconomic class structure and the racist hierarchizing of whites over Others" ("Frances Whipple, Elleanor Eldridge," 691).

49. See chapter 4, "The National Christian," in Harris, *God's Arbiters*, 104–28.

50. Atticus Haygood's sister, Laura, a celebrity then for her years of mission service in China, visited in November of 1895 and gave a talk based on her teaching overseas (*Messenger*, December 1895, 5).

51. In a context somewhat parallel to the *Messenger*'s, Jessica Enoch argues that the Carlisle School's *Indian Helper* served not to empower students with critical literacy but as "a disciplinary and surveillance device meant to constantly remind teachers and students that they must comply with Carlisle's plan" (*Refiguring Rhetorical Education*, 82). Of course, a key difference between these two institutions' visions is that Pratt famously aimed to "Kill the Indian to save the man," whereas Spelman was cast, from the beginning, as a collaborative uplift endeavor for its students. Nora Gordon's later writing from the Congo (including for her mission organization's periodical) and Walls's postgraduation submissions to the *Messenger* reconfirm their own unmediated writing skills and their affiliation with Spelman's liberal arts learning agenda.

52. This passage seems ironic today in light of the decreasing number of African American males, versus females, completing their high school educations, entering postsecondary settings, and earning advanced degrees. For a thorough analysis of this historical pattern, from prior to the *Brown v. Board* Supreme Court decision through recent data, see Antoine Garibaldi, "Expanding Gender and Racial Gap."

53. Walls's story, like the premise that guided Packard and Giles's vision for Spelman's curriculum, built on arguments for women's education that had been circulating throughout the nineteenth century. Advocates like Sara Josepha Hale and, earlier on, Benjamin Rush and Susanna Rowson, had argued that educated mothers

were essential to the nation. Later, leaders like Catharine Beecher extended the argument to claim that women were the best schoolteachers for young children and therefore needed to be well educated themselves. See my *Managing Literacy*, chapter 3. African American women like Frances Harper and Anna Julia Cooper would adapt that rhetoric—and live its vision—in their own teaching careers.

54. Barbara McCaskill generously pointed out to me that Walls's invocation of the humble log cabin setting affiliated the young teacher's account with others' use of the trope and with its linkage to the mythology around Abraham Lincoln's growing up and studying, early on, in just such a setting. See, for example, Annie L. Burton's descriptions of her post-slavery cabin home, succeeded by her discussion of her first schooling, and leading up to her inclusion of one of her school compositions on Lincoln as becoming a determined reader even while living in his family's humble cabin (Burton, *Memories*, 12, 45, 55–56).

55. Walls was one of many Spelman students already managing schools. An untitled update in the November 1886 issue of the *Messenger* reported: "A large number of the older students who have been teaching during the summer related their experience, testifying of many souls won to Christ. Thus the influence of the work begun in Spelman Seminary is carried, during the summer months, not only through the numerous counties of Georgia, but into other states" (4). Another untitled item in the same issue suggested: "Those of the Spelman girls who spent their vacation teaching were richly repaid in the conversion of over three hundred of their scholars" (2). See too a "Dear Editor" letter from Ida B. Carswell in the December 1887 issue, where she described summer teaching in Gabbettville in "a church, situated in a pretty spot by the road-side, a mile from my boarding place" (December 1887, 2).

56. Benedict Anderson, in *Imagined Communities*, relates the formation of a national consciousness in a range of nineteenth-century settings with the rise of print capitalism and its increasing distribution across otherwise-separated spaces. Reading the same texts, he argues, allowed people who might never meet in person to imagine themselves connected to faraway others. (See, for instance, the opening of chapter 3, 33ff.) Walls's "Exchange" columns clearly tap into this phenomenon.

57. Full texts of some of Walls's writings are available in the Keeping and Creating Communities website's "Educating for Citizenship" section.

58. In *Poets in the Public Sphere*, Bennett demonstrates that nineteenth-century American women poets writing in periodicals used the genre "as a form of *public* speech addressed to concrete, empirically identifiable others" (emphasis in original). Self-consciously claiming access to and participation in a Habermasian public space of "practical discursive" work aimed at "persuasion," women poets of this era were, Bennett shows, attending to aesthetics and affect/emotion, but "in service to swaying the judgments of others on matters of concern to all" (5).

59. See, in this context, Eric Gardner, *Black Print Unbound*; Benjamin Fagan, *The Black Newspaper and the Chosen Nation*; and Frances Foster's *Love and Marriage*, especially the introduction (xiii ff.). Gardner's discussion of the need to explore "church-related *print*" and associated periodicals' role in black culture (10, original emphasis) resonates with this chapter's focus on the *Messenger*. Though the *Messenger* in Spelman's early days certainly had white managers and readers

constraining its contents in some ways, the hybrid blend of genres there anticipates Gardner's call for new literary histories of black writing to cast such scholarship as "an interdisciplinary conversation grounded in the archive, challenging
received 'history,' embracing a wide sense of the 'literary,' and focused on exploring how individuals and groups used the aesthetic, sociopolitical, and philosophical qualities of published words to address, record, and benefit their lives and
those of their fellows" (11).

60. Jennifer Rene Young, in "Marketing," notes that ads for Wheatley's 1773
collection praised her genius, but that "there were critics who sought to dismantle
her career by questioning her intelligence and discrediting her poems." As one example, Young cites a Philadelphia pro-slavery apologist's printed characterization
of Wheatley as "'a Negro girl writing a few silly poems, to prove that blacks are not
deficient to us in understanding'" (214). Another of the published critiques claimed
that Wheatley's writing ability was such an obvious exception to the rule of "this
sable generation" being uneducable that her poems should be ignored (215).

61. In *A Brighter Coming Day*, Frances Smith Foster documented Harper's literary stature and (consistent with Bennett's framework above) the poet's consistent
linkage of lyric craft with political advocacy. Foster declares: "Frances Harper was
the best known and best loved African-American poet prior to Paul Laurence Dunbar" and cites the assessment of one historian of the black press that she was "'the
journalistic mother'" of women writers who succeeded her (4).

62. Setting aside the troubling "thug" discourse recently used to stereotype African American males, a characterization of all black Americans as "ignorant" would
be surprising to encounter today—especially in writing by blacks themselves.

63. For an insistent defense of regular rhythm and rhyme as marks of excellence
in poetry at the turn of the previous century (and sing-song, regular combinations
of both, at that), see George Bourne, "Rhythm and Rhyme" in *Macmillan's*.

64. See Clement and Lidsky, "Danger of History Slipping Away," on the more
recent commitment of HBCU campuses to safeguarding their heritage.

65. Yellin's moving "Introduction" to her biography of Jacobs revisits the multiple stages of her own realization that the "Linda" of *Incidents*—whom Yellin came to
study originally through interest in Lydia Maria Child—might have a recoverable
personal and writerly history, and how, over time, combining patient sleuthing and
collaborations, that history could be reconstructed (Yellin, *Harriet Jacobs*, xv–xxi).

66. Foster characterized her sense of the ongoing reluctance to accept black
writers' authority in "Resisting *Incidents*" (57–75). On the challenge of balancing
appreciation of Jacobs's authorial agency with an awareness of how "racist, classist,
and sexist hierarchies" would still have had an impact on the *Incidents* text, see Holly
Laird, *Women Coauthors*, 59. Moody raises related issues in her nuanced analysis of
the collaboration between Whipple and Eldridge, suggesting that scholars' reluctance to study collaboratively prepared biographical narratives is at least in part the
result of "literary and social historians" viewing the texts as "ventriloquistic and
therefore suspect" and "Anglo-American rather than African American" ("Frances
Whipple," 690).

67. The location of Dunch's own work was China, but he drew on the thoughtful precedent of Lamin Sanneh's work, from an African context, to emphasize that

however clear "the *intent* of missionaries to change a culture" might be in a particular case, their efforts to control the learning of their students should not be "confused with the *actuality* of doing so" ("Beyond Cultural Imperialism," 310, emphases in original; see also 324). For Sanneh, see *Translating the Message* and *Encountering the West* (chapter 2). And, in the case of Spelman's early students, it's crucial to keep in mind that most came from black church environments where they had been "schooled" already to embrace Protestant Christianity and much of its associated cultural heritage, though with a race-based focus.

68. On the tendency of literacy sponsorship to include both constraining and enabling features, see Deborah Brandt, "Sponsors of Literacy."

69. See *A History of African American Theatre* by Errol Hill and James Hatch. Referencing Spelman, Hill and Hatch confirm the strong awareness one former president, Florence Read, had of performance's potential to represent Spelman well—assuming those texts were framed in terms consistent with institutional ethos. Thus, during Read's twenty-seven-year tenure, she was known for "reading and censoring every play produced on campus. Enforcing Rockefeller's strict Baptist morality, Read permitted no sexual innuendoes, profanity, or drinking of alcohol on stage" (256–57). Thanks to Stacie McCormick for this reference. Decorum is still an important feature of Founders Day. The contrast between the lively but self-consciously dignified tone earlier in Sisters Chapel and the free-spirited on-the-lawn celebration and participatory singing and dancing later in the day speaks to this awareness.

70. Personal communication from Stacie McCormick. I thank Stacie for a reminder to consider the differences between a racially mixed audience like those Brooks studied and those on hand for Founders Day at Spelman each year.

71. For an example of Carrie Walls's learning legacy still serving to inspire twenty-first century Spelman students, see Moriah Alyssa's online blog post on "Carrie Walls."

72. In our discussions of this chapter, Kimberly Wallace-Sanders pointed to the important statement Spelman makes through such scenes depicting women working in the sciences together with women in the arts and other fields: in such a vision, she noted, liberal arts learning emerges as valuable in the long term and as interacting with career development, versus being cast as a mere stepping stone or even a potentially dangerous learning avenue to choose, unlikely to lead to productive and practical work.

73. For an overview of mission service in Africa by Howard, Nora Gordon, and other Spelman affiliates of their era, including discussion of African women sent to study at Spelman after contact with these early alumnae, see Sandy D. Martin, "Emma B. Delaney and the African Mission," *This Far by Faith*, 220–38.

74. Atlanta's True Colors Theatre, led by black director, actor, and cofounding artistic director Kenny Leon, is known for performances productively crossing racial lines in content and casting. As Stacie McCormick pointed out in a personal note, having Leon join the Founders Day performance indicates "that Spelman moved forward in embracing more inventive performance strategies as a way to advance the history and mission but also to affirm a relationship with the arts" as a powerful cultural force in the community.

75. For discussion of another year's specific focus in its Founders Day program, see "With 'A Legacy of Change,'" which outlines director Kenneth Green's artistic vision for the then-upcoming Founders Day program of 2010, the year before I attended. This report also notes that his multifaceted performance approach to the occasion began in 2006, when Green "was chosen, along with Jo Moore Stewart, director of publications, to create Spelman's 125th Convocation celebration, 'The River That Flows Through Time,' which set a precedent, changing the format and style of subsequent Founders Day convocations." See Wood, "With 'A Legacy of Change.'" For descriptions of the Founders Day event's content in its previous format, see articles in the *Atlanta Daily World*, referenced above. This still-active venue, now a digital-daily and once-per-week print publication, was founded in 1928 by a Morehouse graduate and was home, especially in its first decades, to many a counter-narrative, given the tendency of Atlanta's white-run newspapers to downplay, misrepresent, and/or erase black perspectives.

76. Tatum's "A Living Legacy" commentary, originally delivered as her convocation speech in the fall of 2014, appeared online via *Inside Spelman* around the time when her transition from the presidency was being honored. It was republished at *HBCUBuzz* in May of 2015. My quotes come from the *Inside Spelman/HBCUBuzz* version.

77. In one sense, the case for forceful self-affirmation in activities like the Founders Day pageant joins arguments asserting the continued need for all women's colleges today to exist, and exist with proud commitment to a gendered heritage, even while moves to "go co-ed" continue among some institutions. As Spelman's affirmation of its unique learning legacies demonstrates, though, the intersectionality of race and gender is crucial to its own unique mission.

78. Warren's premise may refer not as much to literary production by blacks in the United States, per se, but rather to the rise and (he argues) eventual fading of African American literature as a cohesive and necessary *field of study* in academic settings. Thus, he asserts that "African American literature took shape" in response to Jim Crow culture, beginning with the *Plessy* Supreme Court case, and started to lose its central focus and exigency after the gradual victory of the civil rights movement, so that "the coherence of African American literature has been correspondingly, if sometimes imperceptibly, eroded as well" (*What Was*, 2). Forceful refutations of his argument include a review by Marlon B. Ross in *Callaloo* ("Kenneth W. Warren's"). Ross raises several points that bear on this chapter's analysis, such as invoking current performative expressions of black culture (e.g., distinct musical traditions) and the vibrancy of African Americans' participation in social media (Ross, 610). If the first aligns neatly with the annual Founders Day performances, the second could suggest a link between blacks' energetic embrace of social media today and their previous work through venues like the early *Messenger* to build their own intra- and inter-race networks—as well as the echoes of those self-defining, agency-claiming moves in the lively web presence of Spelman today. To study such examples as signaling cultural continuities across time, therefore, offers another form of response to Warren's position. See, in this context, this book's Coda, particularly the discussion of #BlackLivesMatter and its online presence.

79. See, for example, Adams-Bass, Bentley-Edwards, and Stevenson, "That's Not Me I See on TV" and Shirley A. Hill, "Cultural Images and the Health of African American Women." See also Roxanne Donovan's blend of empirical method and theory in "Tough or Tender." Donovan set out "to investigate White college students' stereotypes of Black and White women" by "using an intersectional framework" and to see how those stereotypes resonated with patterns already identified in prior research. Drawing on data from over one hundred white college students, she speculated on both the benefits and the downsides of perceptions of black women as "strong and domineering" and outlined potential interventions to help counter the negative implications of the "Matriarch/Sapphire image." On the lingering presence of related negative stereotypes from as far back as the slavery era, see Jennifer Bailey Woodard and Teresa Mastin, "Black Womanhood"; Micki McElya, *Clinging to Mammy*; Kimberly Wallace-Sanders, *Mammy*; and Wallace-Sanders's edited collection, *Skin Deep, Spirit Strong*.

80. One feminist scholar of color calling for such an approach is Inderpal Grewal, whose 2005 monograph on globalizing gender studies (*Transnational America*) is complemented by her textbook coedited with Caren Kaplan (*Introduction to Women's Studies: Gender in a Transnational World*).

81. See Guy-Sheftall and Wallace-Sanders, "Educating Black Women Students for the Multicultural Future." Spelman's Quality Enhancement Plan (QEP) joined those of many other institutions in focusing on global citizenship. Spelman's effort stands out, though, for thoughtfully positioning that plan in relation to its institutional history.

82. The launch of the Gordon-Zeto Center for Global Education at Spelman and the new programming the center enabled also mark the college's increasing emphasis on global learning. The center, whose name honors Nora Gordon and Flora Zeto (one of the first Congolese graduates of Spelman), was made possible by an anonymous gift of $17 million announced in 2008.

83. Texas Christian University (TCU), founded by Addison and Randolph Clark in 1873 (just a few years before Spelman's opening), was unusual in its early years in welcoming women students to liberal arts learning in a coeducational environment then dubbed AddRan Male and Female College.

84. Examples of other women of color on that semester's syllabus included Maryse Condé, *I, Tituba, Black Witch of Salem*; Louise Erdrich, *The Round House*; Inderpal Grewal, the "Traveling Barbie" essay from *Transnational America*; Anna Julia Cooper, essays and speeches; and Ida B. Wells-Barnett, *Lynch Law in Georgia*. We also studied poetry by Esther Belin and Heid E. Erdrich.

85. Jerri Anne Boggis, Eve Allegra Raimon, and Barbara W, White, eds., *Harriet Wilson's New England*. Describing the Harriet Wilson Project, Eric Gardner suggests that enacting such local projects "asserts that black struggles for identity formation were carried out in specific locations—locations that have often fallen off our maps of early black culture" (*Unexpected Places*, 13).

86. On the crucial contributions of archivists to recovery work, see Robbins and Pullen, "Collaboration in the Archive," Gesa Kirsch, "Being on Location," and Steadman et al., "Archive Survival Guide."

Chapter 3

1. "Death of the Hull House" focuses on the nonprofit organization that attempted to keep a version of the original settlement's programs going, scattered into different neighborhood sites across Chicago, after the bulk of the original settlement's physical resources were demolished in the early 1960s. The association shut down in 2012. This account, like some other writings on the settlement, omits the hyphen Addams and her colleagues used for "Hull-House." I follow each publication's choice in that matter when quoting from a source and use the hyphen otherwise.

2. Subtitled *A Presentation of Nationalities and Wages in a Congested District of Chicago*, 1895's *Hull-House Maps and Papers* signals collaborative authorship on its title page, which labels the book as written "by Residents of Hull-House, A Social Settlement." For thoughtful discussion of challenges associated with coauthorial relationships, see Andrea A. Lunsford and Lisa Ede, *Writing Together*, and Lisa Ede and Andrea A. Lunsford, "Collaboration and Concepts of Authorship."

3. I want to avoid presenting Jane Addams as perfectly egalitarian in her (presentation of) collaborations. If Addams became the "star" of Hull-House mythology, one reason was that she often overgeneralized the identities of her immigrant neighbors when describing their contributions. In her reminiscence about the Labor Museum, for instance, she exalts in how the project overturned the tendency of older immigrants' children to discount their elders' experiential knowledge, and she asserts that craft-sharing at the museum laid "a foundation for reverence of the past which Goethe declares to be the basis of all sound progress" (140). But although she cites John Dewey by name in recalling a conversation with him as helping her conceptualize the museum, the immigrants who were involved early on are unnamed: "a Syrian woman, a Greek, an Italian, a Russian, and an Irishwoman" (*Twenty Years*, 140). On the flip side, the Woman's Club project I referenced earlier had members both from among the settlement's middle-class residents and from the neighborhood. This collaboration—where individuals also go unnamed specifically—cut across social class and ethnic lines. In this context, Hilda Satt (Polacheck) expanded on her comment about the club's being "a real venture in democracy" by adding: "Women from England, Ireland, Germany, Russia, Poland, Sweden, and many other countries were members. Women who had reached the highest educational levels and women who could not read or write sat side by side at the meetings. Women of wealth and women who barely had enough to eat participated in the discussions of the club on an equal basis" (*I Came*, 101).

4. Supporters' efforts to save Hull-House from the wrecking ball ended in 1963, as most of its buildings were razed to make room for UIC. For an example of the *Chicago Daily Tribune*'s extensive coverage of the battle, see "Meeting Set," May 23, 1961. For an illustration of the nationwide reporting on the tear-down and its implications, see "Chicago's Hull House Gives Way" in the *Los Angeles Times*, April 12, 1963.

5. Certainly, important work had been done on Addams and Hull-House by the time of the settlement's centennial, as Margaret Spratt pointed out in her 1991 review of six books for the *Journal of Urban History* ("Hull-House"). But the years

since then have seen an exponential increase in work on Addams and the settlement. One crucial source of support for that process has been the heroic editorial work of Bryan, Bair, and de Angury on the Jane Addams Papers Project, which as of this writing has produced two volumes for *The Selected Papers of Jane Addams*.

6. In contrast to the revitalization of the Hull-House Museum, 2012 marked the closure and bankruptcy filing of the Jane Addams Hull House Association which, for decades after UIC's encroachment on the original site led to their relocation, had sponsored social service programming to continue the settlement's mission, including foster care and domestic violence counseling. See Thayer, "Jane Addams Hull House to close," *Chicago Tribune*, January 19, 2012. Reflecting on her participation in the *Jane Addams in the Classroom* (*JAC*) project, contributor Bridget K. O'Rourke commented on that loss: "my work on Hull-House is part of the landscape of my own memory and sense of place. I'm more conscious of it now for its absence than its presence. The Hull-House Association closed its doors this year, a sad reality for those of us who knew Hull-House (however remotely) as a living reality and not just a historical model" (O'Rourke, "Interview").

7. As one example of current scholars' use of Addams to address "social problems today," from a "feminist pragmatist" stance, see Danielle Lake's "Jane Addams and Wicked Problems" (77). Lake notes "Addams's insights on the need for cooperative action" and praises Hull-House as "a bridge institution" promoting "fellowship, sympathetic understanding, and reciprocity" (78).

8. See the museum homepage, Jane Addams Hull-House Museum. Significantly, even after a shift in personnel described later in this chapter, the vision statement on the website remains unchanged as of this writing, in summer 2016.

9. Recent book-length studies include Joslin, *Jane Addams, A Writer's Life*, and Knight, *Jane Addams: Spirit in Action*.

10. On Addams's work to resolve philosophical conflicts around progressive ideas, see Culbertson, "Jane Addams's Progressive Democracy," and on her leadership of pragmatism as philosophy, see Hamington, *Social Philosophy*. On Addams's interactions with Dewey, see Cunningham et al., "Dewey, Women, and Weirdoes." O'Connell analyzes her work on citizenship ("Jane Addams's Democratic Journey"); Fischer examines Addams's moves to connect a rhetoric of maternalism with her work for peace ("Addams's Internationalist Pacifism"). Other scholars focusing on her contributions to peace movements, feminist thought, and citizenship include Klosterman and Stratton ("Speaking Truth") and Deegan ("Jane Addams on Citizenship"), who touts Addams as an "organic intellectual" (217) and a model of feminist global citizenship, but who asserts the need to critique the limits of her thinking and activism. On Addams as a writer attentive to craft, Duffy ("Remembering is the Remedy") examines her use of reminiscence as a rhetorical tool.

11. Scholars arguing for Addams's relevance today include Danisch, "Jane Addams, Pragmatism and Rhetorical Citizenship," who points to parallels between the waves of immigration in her time and today's context; Harkavy and Puckett, who underscore "Lessons from Hull House" for today's urban universities; and Shields, "Democracy and the Social Feminist Ethics," who argues that Addams's theories provide a "bottom up" vision for "participatory democracy" that "also speaks to the lived experience of public administration" (418). In "Accountability Re-examined,"

Oakes and Young use a case study of Hull-House to argue for a model of assessing organizational effectiveness (such as for nonprofits) in context rather than overrelying on quantitative measures. Téllez and Waxman, in describing effective practices for teaching English Language Learners ("Review of Research"), point to Addams's pedagogy for immigrant children as a model.

12. See, in this context, chapter 2's discussion of the need to recognize that minority-group learners and writers do have opportunities to exercise agency when engaging with a curriculum that is grounded in dominant-culture content and values. I return to this point in chapter 4 in the context of students' written accounts of their responses to assimilation schools aimed at Native American children.

13. During our interview, for example, Lisa Lee referenced Shannon Jackson's *Lines of Activity* as helping to guide work at the museum.

14. My view of Addams's commitment to *story* aligns with Katherine Joslin's *Jane Addams, A Writer's Life*. Joslin argues that Addams's "turn toward the literary and away from the social-scientific is perhaps the distinctive feature of her writing." Joslin, accordingly, sees Addams's writing models—such as Charles Dickens—as coming primarily from literature (15).

15. Frederick Taylor's highly influential *The Principles of Scientific Management* appeared in 1911. On patterns of rhetoric arising over time in scientific writing, see Lawrence Prelli, *Rhetoric of Science*. On interconnections linking urbanization, the growth of bureaucracies in business and in other organizations, and the rise of the male manager during this era, see John Chambers's *Tyranny of Change*. Chambers notes, for instance, that as "[m]ore and more middle-class men worked in the bureaucracies of business," they "began to associate their manhood with specialized knowledge," even as the "middle-class-oriented educational system reinforced this view by largely excluding girls and women from the classical curricula as well as the scientific and mathematical training" required to claim most leadership roles (Chambers, *Tyranny*, 37). Addams and the other college-educated women at Hull-House had to navigate a contradictory space in both their work and their rhetoric, displaying a conservative commitment to approved womanly roles while also carving out space for contributing to new scientific knowledge fields in gender-approved ways. See, on women's relationship to scientific rhetoric, Jordynn Jack, "'Exceptional Women,'" in *Women and Rhetoric*, eds. George, Weiser, and Zepernick.

16. See Valerie Strauss's "'Big data' was supposed to fix education.'" Strauss passes along a call from educational researchers Pasi Sahlberg and Jonathan Hasak. They argue: "big data alone won't be able to fix education systems. Decision-makers need to gain a better understanding of what good teaching is and how it leads to better learning in schools. This is where information about details, relationships and narratives in schools become important. These are what Martin Lindstrom calls 'small data': small clues that uncover huge trends. In education, these small clues are often hidden in the invisible fabric of schools. Understanding this fabric must become a priority for improving education" (para 12).

17. Fortunately, Katherine Joslin's *Jane Addams, A Writer's Life* provides one important exception to the shortage of attention allotted to *My Friend, Julia Lathrop*. Joslin's overview includes revealing details about Addams's research and composing

processes, as well as negotiations with Macmillan representative H. S. Latham and with Paul Kellogg of *Survey Graphic* (250–61). Joslin notes that Latham (based on concerns about the Depression-era publishing marketplace) encouraged Addams to collaborate with Grace Abbott on one volume rather than to try publishing two separate volumes, as originally planned (250, 254). Kellogg, meanwhile, offered to publish parts of Addams's material in his periodical ahead of its appearance within the book. Kellogg's editing of draft material rankled Addams, Joslin reports, but he backed off from aggressive textual interventions after receiving a written complaint from Addams (258–61), even sending an apologetic telegram that reached Addams as she lay on her deathbed and that called the manuscript "luminous" (261).

18. As noted in the introduction, Addams's choice to narrate more than explicate and to write for a broad readership has, sadly, often led to a false dichotomizing of her legacy versus her colleague John Dewey's, with Dewey cast as the theorist and Addams as a practitioner—sometimes even as a practitioner unable to theorize her own work. For instance, even in an essay valuing Addams and "other Hull-House residents" for her "practices" at the settlement (589), Schneiderhan, in "Pragmatism and Empirical Sociology," foregrounds "Dewey's theory of action" (589) as a lens for analyzing women settlement workers, including Addams herself, who "did not always know where they were going with their acts" (613).

19. Joslin (*Jane Addams, A Writer's Life*) argues Addams focused on creating a communal voice depicting shared experience. To explicate this view, Joslin uses Bakhtin's sociolinguistics: "Mikhail Bakhtin's theory of the dialogic urge of the novel, the orchestrating of diverse voices and the depiction of the novelist as ventriloquist, may help us understand how Addams's dramatic use of voices from the street, talking about the issues of the day . . . moved beyond the monologic or static voice of social tracts" (15).

20. In *Peace and Bread in Time of War*, Addams begins with the collaborative actions of "delegates from Holland, England and Austria" and their meeting in the United States: "*we* issued what *we* called a manifesto. . . . *We* were certainly well within the truth when *we* said that '*we* bear evidence of a rising desire and intention . . . to turn a barren disinterestedness into an active goodwill'" (19–20, emphases mine). See also her *The Spirit of Youth*: "*We* cannot afford to be ungenerous to the city in which *we* live without suffering the penalty which lack of fair interpretation always entails. Let *us* know the modern city in its weakness and wickedness. . . . *We* certainly cannot expect the fathers and mothers who have come to the city from farms or who have emigrated from other lands to appreciate or rectify these dangers" (14–15). On Addams's strategic use of "we," and a related choice to make herself a character in her own narratives, see Salazar, *Bodies of Reform*, especially 206, 216, 221–32.

21. Addams coauthored *Women at The Hague* with Emily G. Balch and Alice Hamilton.

22. Examples include Addams's revisiting of the "Devil Baby" story in *The Long Road of Woman's Memory* and her reliance on narrative examples to illustrate concepts, as in chapter II's treatment of the charitable visitor and chapter V's revisiting of Pullman's misguided model community in *Democracy and Social Ethics*. Here too Joslin's assessment, particularly of the late-career publications, is relevant: Joslin

sees Addams's final writings as focusing more and more on "record[ing] a collective consciousness in her reminiscence" (16) while "blending other voices into her own, allowing her to speak through and for the people surrounding her at Hull-House" (*Jane Addams*, 17).

23. Addams, "A Great Public Servant," 280; Addams, *My Friend*, 36.

24. Kathryn Sklar, as early as her 1985 "Hull House in the 1890s" essay for *Signs*, claimed notable social power for the women living and working at the settlement, dubbing them "one of the most politically effective groups of women reformers in U.S. history" (658).

25. For a thoughtful review of the revamped permanent exhibit developed in connection with the settlement's 150th anniversary in 2010—including its enhanced focus "on the residents and immigrants that lived at, worked in, and benefitted from" the settlement (171)—see Dee Harris's "Re-defining Democracy," in *Public Historian*.

26. In an interview focused on the group's reading, writing, and revision processes, similarly, collection editor David Schaafsma shifted from initially referencing "Addams" alongside "Dewey" to using the "Jane" first name (Schaafsma, "Interview").

27. We also shared pivotal classroom experiences in a course with Professor Jay Robinson on the politics of literacy. One recurring assignment for that seminar was writing what Jay called "conversation papers," where we recorded reflective dialogues with our readings. Jay never wrote directly on those papers; instead, he peppered them with sticky notes containing questions to promote more "conversation" during class.

28. As one example of their friendly exchanges, including shared critique, Addams recounts Lathrop's witty assessment of the way they had been introduced at a meeting where the speaker's characterizations reduced them to being old-fashioned "ladies bountiful," a category which Lathrop bemoaned: "Julia Lathrop dryly remarked: 'It is not very complimentary to either of us, J.A., but I am afraid that it is a true word that we are the more highly praised in proportion as we are misunderstood'" (55).

29. Recalling a conversation mixing friendly banter with astute critique, Addams recounts Lathrop's saying: "'Don't generalize on insufficient data, J.A. It is a great temptation but in this case fully one-half of your data is absolutely off. Fifty per cent of inaccuracy is a very large margin'" (132). Similarly, Addams reports on Lathrop's crafty critique of an Addams speech: "'It was a fine story, and at least half the audience enjoyed it immensely, but I was afraid that you told it to relieve your own mind; you certainly did not expect it to convert the Relief and Aid people to our point of view'" (55).

30. This naming of their settlement women's network as "precious" appears in a letter Addams includes in a chapter on Lathrop's friendship with Florence Kelley. This epistle gently (but still wittily, as was Lathrop's wont) takes Kelley to task for failing to report her hospitalization to Lathrop, who describes herself as always "uneasy" when she hears of anyone in their circle "daring to be ill or anything, and not telling me" (89–90). Kelley's own autobiography, originally composed as a series of articles for *Survey Graphic* in 1927, includes one piece ("I Go to Work") fo-

cused on the settlement, where she dubbed Julia Lathrop a "pillar" of Hull-House (Kelley, *Autobiography*, ed. Sklar, 78).

31. Addams, *My Friend*, 4. Hamilton herself was one of Hull-House's most dedicated activists. Having earned a medical degree at the University of Michigan in the 1890s, she became a settlement resident and put her research skills to work to study neighborhood and occupational health issues. As the first woman to earn a faculty appointment at Harvard and the only woman serving on the international health committee for the League of Nations, she—like Lathrop and Addams—became a celebrity figure while also maintaining a strong commitment to the Hull-House women's network.

32. See Alice Hamilton's memoir for treatment of Hull-House's essential role in preparing her for leadership. Notes Hamilton: "I should never have taken up the cause of the working class had I not lived at Hull-House and learned much from Jane Addams, Florence Kelley, Julia Lathrop, and others." (*Exploring/Autobiography*, 16).

33. Victoria Bissell Brown's *The Education of Jane Addams* presents insightful analysis of Addams's youthful learning at home and, later, at Rockford Seminary, but also Addams's work to develop a philosophy that, despite pulling away from established religious practices, maintained a strong commitment to spirituality. Brown declares: "The story told here traces Addams's evolution from an ambitious, arrogant youth caught up in heroic dreams of individual triumph to a young woman humbled by ill health, family duty, and spiritual doubt," and eventually finding "salvation in collective, cooperative action" (6). Brown argues that Addams's education was further honed by settlement practice itself.

34. Though, like Brown (*Education*), I see arrogance in some of Addams's schoolgirl writings, I also recognize continuities between her efforts to bring other young women together in shared learning (such as through the debate club and a student newspaper) and approaches she would develop for teaching at Hull-House.

35. *Hull-House Maps and Papers*, a research project originally taken on with encouragement from Henrietta Barnett, helped establish the settlement's reputation for basing its social interventions in research. Florence Kelley, a major contributor to that publication, also wrote the autobiography referenced earlier and reports about her work in the socialist labor movement, as well as a translation of one of Friedrich Engel's books. The Florence Kelley Collection (MSKell77) is held in the Special Collections at UIC.

36. See Robbins, "Sustaining Gendered Philanthropy," forthcoming, where I track the personal and programmatic support Addams drew from her friendship with Barnett.

37. Jane Addams to Henrietta Barnett, February 3, 1920. Copies of such exchanges from their correspondence are in Dame Henrietta Barnett Papers [hereafter DHBP], Special Collections and University Archives, University of Illinois at Chicago, MSBarn64.

38. Consistent with her own regular use of novel reading as a strategy for considering real-life issues, Addams describes that tendency as evident in others as well: "The popular books are the novels, dealing with life under all possible conditions, and they are widely read not only because they are entertaining, but also

because they in a measure satisfy an unformulated belief that to see farther, to know all sorts of men . . . is a preparation for . . . the remedying of social ills" ("Introduction," *Democracy and Social Ethics*, 8).

39. Interestingly, even within a discussion of how "Teaching in a Settlement requires distinct methods" that focus on "a social atmosphere," with learning occurring "in a medium of fellowship and good will," Addams calls upon her personal *reading* to illustrate her point (427). For instance, she quotes her study of Mazzini to clarify her argument (427), and later in this same "Socialized Education" chapter of *Twenty Years*, she calls on Victor Hugo's Jean Valjean to illustrate how a member of the Hull-House Boys' Club effectively invoked literary allusion when resisting false accusations cast against him (432). She also references courses Ellen Gates Starr taught "in Dante and Browning" and Julia Lathrop's "Plato club" (435). Overall, she says, "residents of Hull-House place increasing emphasis upon the great inspirations and solaces of literature" (434), which (she notes) they were accessing via direct reading, but also by indirect engagements with text through attendance at plays, lectures, and discussions of books.

40. In *Twenty Years*, recalling one of their visits to the United States, Addams describes the "hearty sympathy" she shared with Henrietta Barnett (chapter XVI, 371). But it is in their personal papers where we see the clearest signs of mutual affection, as in Addams's letter praising Barnett's biography of Samuel and in a note back to Addams soon afterwards, which Henrietta signed, "Yours ever in a big strong humble way" (DHBP, MSBarn64).

41. Jean Bethke Elshtain includes this (in)famous speech, under the title "Address of Miss Addams at Carnegie Hall" in *The Jane Addams Reader* (327–40). One of the most controversial passages claimed that soldiers Addams met during her pro-peace tour of Europe reported, in regard to bayonet charges, on "the necessity for the use of stimulants" such as "rum in England, and absinthe in France" to enforce their participation (339).

42. In the 1919 biography of Samuel, Henrietta Barnett served up high praise of Addams several times, a loyal gesture during a period when so many of the American's previously supportive admirers had deserted the Hull-House leader. So, for instance, Barnett characterizes Addams as "a great soul" with "depths of character" enabling her leadership of "that most wonderful of all Settlements" (*Canon Barnett*, 30). Barnett also wrote freestanding articles defending Addams, such as a "Jane Addams" profile for the *Woman's Leader*, June 1, 1923, held in the DHBP collection. For analysis of the shift in popular press depictions of Addams from saintly leader to dangerous traitor, see Shepler and Mattina, "Paying the Price." See too Elshtain's long, revealing quote from Maude Royden, a British peace movement leader, on the contrast between Americans' views of Addams that Royden encountered during a visit to the United States in 1912 versus in 1922–23 (Elshtain, *Jane Addams*, 244).

43. "*My Friend, Julia Lathrop* and *Jane Addams*," 350. Bessie Louise Pierce's evaluation in the same year for *The Mississippi Valley Historical Review* echoed the *SSR*'s criticisms. Pierce wished that Addams's text had offered more of the "valiant, dramatic, real, and intelligent" dimensions of Lathrop's "fight against poverty," i.e., had conveyed a stronger sense of "the struggle" involved in her work (Pierce, "My Friend, Julia Lathrop," 442).

44. See, for example, biographies by Victoria Bissell Brown (*The Education of Jane Addams*) and Louise W Knight (*Citizen: Jane Addams and the Struggle for Democracy*), both of which weave in details of Addams's personal relationships as influencing her activism and her writing. For a look at the bonds of friendship connecting Hull-House women as incorporating both spirituality and vocation, see Eleanor J. Stebner, *The Women of Hull House*. While Addams's influence on highly educated male writer-thinkers like John Dewey has received less attention, exceptions include Charlene Seigfried's "Socializing Democracy: Jane Addams and John Dewey," especially 212ff.

45. Certainly we should not pretend that the generous, respectful stance of Addams and notable Hull-House colleagues toward immigrants was universal. For an opposing view as expressed in fiction set in a related context, see Anzia Yezierska's *Arrogant Beggar* and *Salome of the Tenements*, the latter of which draws on that author's complex relationship with John Dewey.

46. On Polacheck's WPA writing, see Taylor's *Soul of a People*, 55–60. See also the *WPA Federal Writers' Project Collection* in the American Memory Collection, folklore division, at the Library of Congress; examples of Polacheck's work held in that collection are "Little Grandmother" and "The Dybbuk of Bunker Street." The Hilda Satt Polacheck Papers (MSPola75) are held in in the Special Collections at UIC.

47. My original interviews with staff and visits to JAHHM occurred during the tenure of Lisa Lee. In the winter of 2015, Jennifer Scott assumed the director position. Scott's past work with the "International Coalition of Sites of Conscience . . . to create original content for a two-year initiative, the National Dialogues on Immigration," made her a logical choice to assume leadership at Hull-House. See UIC's online announcement by Anne Brooks Ranallo in "NYC Public Historian."

48. Lee and Lopez, "Participating in History" in *JAC*. Striking in the context of Lee and Lopez's "radical empathy" formulation is Jean Elshtain's account of interviewing two Italian American alumnae of Hull-House programs who, as referenced earlier, described their frustration with prior depictions of Addams and the settlement as tainted by class/ethnic bias (*Jane Addams and the Dream*, 9–11).

49. On Nancrede and other aspects of the theater program, see Stuart Hecht, "Edith Nancrede" and "Social and Artistic Integration." For a recent treatment of Starr, cofounder of Hull-House, and Lathrop, see Duran, "Ellen Gates Starr and Julia Lathrop."

50. In the fall of 2015, while I was drafting this chapter, Lisa Junkin Lopez was still serving as associate director under Lee's replacement, but she shortly thereafter became director of the museum linked to the Girl Scout's founding figure. Heather Radke's move to New York also mirrors how some of the settlement's most active residents eventually relocated to take on leadership responsibilities elsewhere, with Addams's encouragement.

51. As Addams so often did, Lee, Lopez, and Radke repeatedly used a first-person-plural "we" when describing their work at Hull-House. Further, each referenced the other two to illustrate key points about the museum's teaching philosophy and practices.

52. In their introduction to *JAC*, Schaafsma and DeStigter explain: "Our interest from the beginning of this project was rooted in Addams's—and her Hull-

House colleagues'—commitment to *listening to* and *learning from* the people living in the neighborhood in which Hull-House was located" (5, emphasis in original).

53. For context on Lee's comments about Addams's rhetoric of pragmatism, see Kaag, "Pragmatism." On rhetorical pragmatism, see also chapter 1.

54. The TAMMS project was collaboratively led by attorneys, artists, and ex-prisoners.

55. See the richly reflective essay collection edited by Adair, Filene, and Koloski, *Letting Go? Sharing Historical Authority*.

56. On links between the Labor Museum and the Arts and Crafts movement, see Stankiewicz, "Art at Hull House." Stankiewicz argues that the Labor Museum "showed process, product, and producer in an effort to illustrate the value of hand-work," even in an increasingly industrial age (37). She also connects ideas behind the Labor Museum and the philosophy guiding T. J. Cobden-Sanderson's promotion of Arts and Crafts activities as transforming society itself into "a potential work of art" embodied by "the union of imagination, spirit, and manual labor" within a liberatory vision (37).

57. Echoes of this position appear in Eisner's advocacy of arts-based and arts-enriched education, as in "What Education Can Learn from the Arts." Among lessons Eisner names are "that form and content cannot be separated" (7), "that surprise is not to be seen as an intruder in the process of inquiry but as a part of the rewards," "that slowing down perception" enhances learning, and that body-based, "somatic" learning is valuable (8).

58. Drawing on work by Dwight Conquergood, Denzin posits that a "feminist, communitarian performance ethic" can be "empowering" for all involved. Thus, Denzin envisions "coparticipatory performances" including dialogue that will promote genuine cross-cultural understanding (*Interpretive Autoethnography*, 80–81).

59. Originally on the museum's website, O'Grady's comments were later retrievable from a WBEZ radio online review of the exhibit by Alison Cuddy, "Home Economics."

60. See "Look At It This Way," an online report. Carried out in 2013, this project was completed during Lopez's interim directorship. Through a partnership enabling UIC students to learn museum curatorial work by doing it, the initiative connected students in the Museum and Exhibition Studies Master of Arts program to JAHHM.

61. Examples include Nina Simon's online "Postcards as a Call to Action" essay and Kass, "Gangs That Came," from the *Chicago Tribune*.

62. The Chicago Freedom School describes its mission in terms consistent with Hull-House's original and current vision: "Founded in 2007, the mission of the Chicago Freedom School (CFS) is to create new generations of critical and independent thinking young people who use their unique experiences and power to create a just world. CFS provides training and education opportunities for youth and adult allies to develop leadership skills through the lens of civic action and through the study of the history of social movements and their leaders" (Chicago Freedom School website homepage).

For one example of the striking e-zines from this partnership, see Rachel Marie-Crane Williams's online "Girls in the System."

63. Some of their contemporaries indicated recognition of the "special relationship" between Smith and Addams, via commentary that might be veiled, yet still supportive. See, for instance, Elshtain, *Jane Addams*, 23. Elshtain does caution against "sexualizing it [their bond] to conform to the political exigencies of our age" (23). On a parallel front, when doing research for *Nellie Arnott's Writings on Angola*, Ann Pullen and I heard about the discreet acceptance sometimes accorded, even by conservative church organizations, to women who worked (and lived) abroad together as missionary couples. In a potentially broader context hinting at questions about sexual practices among the Hull-House residents, Elshtain reports this observation from an interview with Ruby Jane Delicandro: "We've read stupid stories about how the neighbors were suspicious of Hull-House. But we *were* the neighbors. No one we knew was worried about taking her children to Hull-House" (9, emphasis in original).

64. Lee, "Hungry for Peace," 62. In both her opening abstract and her final paragraph, Lee stresses how the museum staff drew on Addams's heritage to guide their work. Thus, she says her "essay explores ways that Addams's legacy and the work at Hull-House around food can inform, educate, and expand the horizon of our imaginations on critical contemporary issues of social justice" (62). Lee also argues: "The efforts of the staff and programs at JAHHM are undertaken . . . with the belief that this extraordinary history of social change and reform can continue to inspire our radical imaginations" (78).

65. Schaafsma and DeStigter affirm the symbolic importance and pragmatic benefits of the restored dining room. Celebrating the reopening in May 2008, they salute programming held there as "a way to renew . . . the Hull-House residents' legacy of carving out 'public spaces where people of all classes and ethnicities can interact' with the aim of creative problem solving" ("Introduction," *JAC*, 1).

66. Vinz's *JAC* "Afterword" notes: "Jane Addams opens *participatory spaces*, both in her writing and through the mortar-and-brick version of Hull-House—to live with and in relation to other people across varied landscapes of difference" (200, original emphasis).

67. Here, as elsewhere in her writing, Addams quotes without attributing her source. While our emphasis today on careful citation would fault Addams, I suspect that such omissions were acceptable to her original readers and may even have been another way for her to signal that collaborative knowledge-building made credit-giving inessential.

68. Junkin Lopez's, Lee's, and Radke's efforts to make the museum's archive-informed practice and philosophy visible are affirmed in Kelland's exhibit review, "Re-Defining Democracy." Citing the museum's ongoing affiliation with "the museological movement away from temple and toward forum," Kelland characterizes the "broad and complex interpretive responsibility" of JAHHM as linking "the mission of civic dialogue to the democratic values of Jane Addams and the residents of Hull House" (783).

69. Schaafsma's dissertation became *Eating on the Street*. DeStigter's *Reflections of a Citizen Teacher* won NCTE's Richard Meade Award for Research in English Education.

70. Examples include Gere and Shaheen, eds., *Making American Literatures*;

Robbins and Dyer, eds., *Writing America*; Winter and Robbins, eds., *Writing Our Communities*.

71. In an interview conducted while he was collaborating with *JAC* contributors on their revisions, Schaafsma observed, in reference to the real-life pressures faced by many students and teachers today: "You're talking about racism. You're talking about classism. You're talking about, to use the postcolonial term, you're talking about the Othering that happens on a daily basis that needs to be addressed." To describe his commitment to participatory research along with public school teachers and students, DeStigter wrote in an online interview: "The most challenging aspect of my work—aside from the time it takes to do ethnographic research, write up field notes, etc.—is to see firsthand how the current educational environment we're living in (one that emphasizes standardized benchmarks/outcomes and high-stakes testing) makes it more and more difficult to listen to the students, to create opportunities for them to bring their experiences and languages into the classroom" (DeStigter, "Interview").

72. In an online interview about her efforts to teach across social divides, Steffen referenced her *JAC* chapter: "What helps our classes be open places for learning is the sharing of stories to bring a vast range of experiences into our context. . . . I use others' and my own stories to build acknowledgement of the differences of our experiences but also, in the sharing of the stories, we force common experiences which help bridge cultures" (Steffen, "Interview").

73. For analysis of what O'Rourke calls the "bayonet speech," see Roskelly's "The Hope for Peace and Bread" in George, Weiser, and Zepernick, eds., *Women and Rhetoric*, 32–47. Addams gave the speech at Carnegie Hall on July 9, 1915. Having recently returned from work in Europe with the Women's International League for Peace, Addams referenced conversations she had with soldiers there. She aimed at presenting a reasoned argument against entering the war. But a brief moment in the talk, where she referenced soldiers' reluctance to use bayonets, became the crux of critics' attacks afterwards, despite the applause garnered at the original event (Roskelly, 34–35).

Chapter 4

1. Powell describes her identity, more specifically, as mixed-blood of Indiana Miami, Eastern Band Shawnee, and Euro-American ancestry, and she emphasizes that distinctions between enrolled and unenrolled should be acknowledged.

2. For an example of Powell's own influential scholarship, see "Rhetorics of Survivance."

3. Workshop leaders represented a range of institutions: Rose Gubele, Central Michigan University; Joyce Rain Anderson, Bridgewater State University; Kimberli Lee, Northeastern State University; Lisa King, University of Hawai'i at Mānoa and more recently University of Tennessee, Knoxville; Gabriela Ríos, Texas A&M University; and Angela Haas, Illinois State University. Resources provided included Angela Haas's syllabus for a course on American Indian literatures and cultures and Lisa King's sample assignment on media analysis to teach about Indigenous

rhetorical sovereignty and alliance. (See material from a later online interview with King in chapter 5.)

4. For a moving account by a current teacher of Dakota language, see Neil McKay, "The Spirit of Language," in *Genocide of the Mind*, 159–65. McKay observes, "I have witnessed many times that Dakotas are very encouraging of others learning Dakota language. . . . I was told that no matter what someone's speaking level is, they are speaking Dakota and that is all that matters" (165).

5. Robert Warrior, *Tribal Secrets*, 123–24. See also Warrior's riveting chapter 3, "The Work of Indian Pupils," in *The People and the Word*, 95–142. Warrior draws on writers ranging from Luther Standing Bear, Gertrude Bonnin, and Charles Eastman to reach imaginative engagement with students who would have worked in the print shop at Santee Normal Training School, which Warrior both compares and contrasts with Carlisle. In his treatment of "an era of Indian policy in which Native youth were targeted to be instruments of transformation" (96), Warrior reminds readers "that Native educational history is best regarded not as a problem to be solved, but as a journey that we are in the middle of" (101).

6. On the complex interpersonal and professional tensions around their collaborative writing, see my "The 'Indian Problem' in Elaine Goodale Eastman's Authorship."

7. See, for example, Baird, "Are Soldiers Murderers?," 43. For a snide description of her cross-race marriage, see "Elaine Goodale Eastman," *Massachusetts Ploughman*, 56.

8. On the history of residential schools in Canada, including similarities and differences between the US and Canadian programs, see the "Separate Schooling Institutionalized" chapter in Charles Leslie Glenn, *American Indian/First Nations Schooling*, 177ff.

9. David Wallace Adams, *Education for Extinction*, 6. Similarly, K. Tsianina Lomawaima and Teresa L. McCarty have underscored the self-serving, contorted reasoning often used to justify assimilation efforts: "The 'civilized' nation assumed that its right to dispossess Native nations went hand in hand with a responsibility to 'uplift' them, and mission and federal 'Indian schools' were established as laboratories for a grand experiment in cultural cleansings, Christian conversion, and assimilation of laborers and domestic workers into the workforce" (*To Remain and Indian*, 4).

10. See Valerie Sherer Mathes, "Helen Hunt Jackson," 141–57. Jackson's writings in support of Native peoples included the nonfiction books *A Century of Dishonor* (1881) and (with Abbot Kinney) *Report on the Conditions and Needs of the Mission Indians* (1883). *Ramona* (1884) represented an effort to use fiction to win support for American Indians, but she was frustrated to find that the love story imbedded in the novel drew more attention from readers than its more political advocacy dimensions.

11. Jon Reyhner and Jeanne Eder stress that "cultural disintegration, not cultural replacement," was typically the result, with the separation from family and the forced immersion into English-only environments being particularly punitive (5). Among other serious problems, "a breakdown in communication between chil-

dren" and their elders cut "Indian people off from their heritage" (*American Indian Education*, 7).

12. See *The Hampton Album: 44 photographs by Frances B. Johnston*. The portfolio's introductory text characterizes Hampton as an "extraordinarily successful experiment in the training of black and American Indian youth, the triumph of an integrated coeducational system of learning-by-doing in the domestic and agricultural arts and crafts, enabling them to teach others to do likewise" (5). Further, several of the photographs conflate the goals and impact of the curriculum for blacks at Hampton with the related aim of Indian assimilation, as in "Class in American History" (11).

13. Robert Francis Engs, *Educating the Disfranchised and Disinherited*, 116–17. Referencing comments from Armstrong's *Lessons from the Hawaiian Islands* as evidence, Engs reports that "Armstrong was much given to comparisons of blacks and Hawaiians, never entirely comprehending how different the two groups truly were, and much to the disservice of both" (74).

14. While Hampton and Carlisle—and their principals Armstrong and Pratt—are rightly associated with the spread of the boarding school model, Charles L. Glenn argues that neither residential schools nor the industrial/vocational curriculum, per se, should be viewed only in terms of having been "imposed on Indians; it was adopted also by the Cherokee Nation after the Civil War as more appropriate for Cherokee-speaking children than the English-medium schools that served the children of the mixed-blood elite" (*American Indian/First Nations Schooling*, 84–85).

15. For an insightful account of this stage in the longstanding battle over Indian education, as well as later developments, see Frederick E. Hoxie, *A Final Promise*.

16. In *The Indian Industrial School*, Pratt himself would attempt to shape the cult of personality associated with his image by crafting a self-serving narrative justifying his work at Carlisle. Published several years after his removal as superintendent, Pratt's account seeks to rescue his legacy by stressing the more affirmative aspects of his program. Besides settling some old personal scores, his narrative emphasizes the long-term potential of Native Americans, presents data to illustrate the successes of many alumni, identifies influential supporters, and touts such milestones as his students' involvement with the Columbian Exposition. Pratt declares: "the whole purpose of the Carlisle school from the beginning was to make its pupils equal as individual parts of our civilization. . . . Indian schools, as I have always contended, should be temporary. . . . Unquestionably the great object to be aimed at should be to have all Indian youth in schools and eventually no purely Indian schools; then and then only is the problem of their proper education really solved" (55).

17. Caskey Russell, "Language, Violence, and Indian Mis-education," 102, 101. Russell also aligned with Ward Churchill's genocide argument by asserting: "The violence, both physical and structural, upon which Indian education in America was founded can be defined, according to the original draft of the Geneva Convention, as a form of genocide under the articles defining cultural genocide" ("Language," 107).

18. Ward Churchill, *Kill the Indian, Save the Man*. His book opens with a "Forward" poem on Charlie Wenjack, "Who died in 1966, aged twelve, running away

from an Indian residential school near Kenora, Ontario" (xi). The poem depicts Charlie walking "on through the snow, / Heading down the railway line, / Trying to make it home" (ll. 2–4).

19. David H. Dejong, "'Unless They Are Kept Alive,'" 261–64, 267, 274. Dejong attributes some of the unhealthy conditions to congressional underfunding but others to the policy of industrial training, which not only prepared students for "obsolete occupations" but also exposed them to unhealthy working conditions. Dejong singles out Carlisle for a particularly high student mortality rate (274–75).

20. Charles Glenn, *American Indian*, 79. Glenn's choice to address both the US and Canadian settings falls in line with the fact that tribal nations' boundaries have certainly never coincided with other dividing lines between North American countries today.

21. Arnold Krupat describes this strand of scholarship as cultivating a cosmopolitan comparativist perspective: "At the most basic level, cosmopolitan perspectives on Native American literatures read them in relation to other minority or subaltern literatures elsewhere in the late-colonial or postcolonial world; cosmopolitan criticism must always in some degree be comparative" (*Red Matters*, 19).

22. In *Decolonising the Mind*, Ngũgĩ highlights themes that reverberate with research on the residential schooling system. To protest the power of colonial education, Ngũgĩ has published some of his writings in the Bantu language of Kenya's Kikuyu people, while demonstrating the strategy of employing the language of colonial education itself to critique, but also show mastery over, such programs in English-language narratives such as *Dreams in a Time of War* and *In the House of the Interpreter*.

23. See Margaret D. Jacobs, *White Mother to a Dark Race* and Katherine Ellinghaus, *Taking Assimilation to Heart: Marriages of White Women and Indigenous Men in the United States and Australia*. Ellinghaus's examination of cross-racial marriages during this period sets these relationships in the larger comparative context of assimilation-oriented goals and policies in both countries. While noting significant differences in the two settings, she stresses how, in both cases, "When such liaisons did take place, especially when they were tolerated or understood as part of an ideology such as assimilation, they exposed the sometimes invisible imaginings by which colonial societies justified their existence" (xii).

24. In "'Survivance' in Sami and First Nations Boarding School Narratives," Rauna Kuokkanen explores survivance strategies counteracting colonizing elements in residential boarding programs in both contexts. She notes how students can work to maintain connections with their home cultures, including by celebrating family and community stories and reenacting familiar social practices (717). She also highlights humor as a survivance strategy (718) and argues that the girls in novels she studied "actively seek to find ways to cope" so as "to negotiate a balance between the lives of home and school." Protagonists manage the "pull between resistance and accommodation" to avoid surrender through creative means (719).

25. Esther G. Belin, "In the Cycle of the Whirl," *From the Belly of My Beauty*, 71. More recently, Laura L. Terrance has drawn effectively on theory from Frantz Fanon and Gayatri Chakravorty Spivak to interpret Zitkala-Ša's "School Days of an Indian Girl." See "Resisting Colonial Education," 623, 622.

26. K. Tsianina Lomawaima, *They Called It Prairie Light*. Lomawaima is one of numerous Native writers drawn to researching boarding schools through family ties.

27. See, in this regard, Amanda J. Cobb, *Listening to Our Grandmothers' Stories*. Cobb's report on the academy her own grandmother attended emphasizes that "Bloomfield was different," in part because "[t]he Chicakasaws had not been relegated to a reservation" and had "a much higher level of autonomy, self-sufficiency, and independence than most other tribal nations." Thus, this was a school founded in 1852, well ahead of the white-dominated assimilation boarding schools, and envisioned to address goals of the Chickasaw Nation itself (6).

28. Brenda J. Child, *Boarding School Seasons*, 11 and 13. As Child notes, the distances between many boarding schools and children's homes often prohibited regular visits in either direction.

29. See also Clyde Ellis, "'A Remedy for Barbarism.'" While critiquing the many problematic features of residential schools, Ellis does point out that some Indian parents sought out such placements for their children as the only readily available access to education (98–99). Ellis also presents testimonials from former students who felt they benefited from their school experiences. Overall, Ellis suggests, "The irony is that, in the process of beginning their new lives, students combined two worlds. Thus there is the seeming contradiction of going to school yet staying Indian" (113). See also Michael C. Coleman's *American Indian Children*, a study of Indian students' narratives, including nineteenth-century accounts such as Francis La Flesche's *The Middle Five*. While "not claim[ing] that this group of one hundred autobiographers is representative of all Indian school pupils during these eight decades" (xii), Coleman notes his initial surprise at how "highly mixed" these published memoirs were in their responses to the assimilation schools (x) and how the texts led him to see important ways in which "the pupil narrators became cultural brokers—mediators—between the white world and their own" (xii).

30. See Nancy Bentley, *Frantic Panoramas*. Bentley argues that, rather than cultivating a disdain for mass cultural forms' expansion during this era, literary writers found ways to tap into these changes, both for subjects to write on and ways to reach audiences. Although she focuses on white writers like Edith Wharton, Kate Chopin, and Henry James, Bentley discusses Gertrude Bonnin (Zitkala-Ša) within a chapter entitled "Celebrity Warriors, Impossible Diplomats, and the Native Public Sphere," which also addresses controversies around Wild West shows like Buffalo Bill Cody's (151–87).

31. Philip J. Deloria, *Playing Indian*. Pointing to British author D. H. Lawrence's analysis of American literature's representations of Native peoples as signaling their crucial role in national identity formation, Deloria notes: "Savage Indians served Americans as oppositional figures against whom one might imagine a civilized national Self" (3).

32. See Armstrong and others from the Hampton Institute, *Twenty-two Years' Work of the Hampton Normal and Agricultural Institute*. The publicity aim of the school's press is acknowledged in the preface: "To keep this progress before the public, on whose intelligent interest it depends, the School has relied on its Annual

Reports, its monthly 'Southern Workman' and occasional pamphlets and outside magazine and newspaper articles . . ." (iii). See also Johnston, *The Hampton Album: 44 Photographs*. These photos, shot in 1899 and 1900, were produced for the Paris Exposition by Johnston "as part of an exhibition demonstrating contemporary life of the American negro" (5).

33. For an insightful discussion of the rhetorical agenda driving texts like the before-and-after photos promoting Carlisle, see Hayes Peter Mauro, *The Art of Americanization at the Carlisle Indian School*. See too Laura Wexler, "Tender Violence." Wexler's essay includes incisive analysis of Zitkala-Ša's *Atlantic Monthly* texts.

34. Amelia V. Katanski, *Learning to Write "Indian,"* 44. Katanski's project resists the binary of casting boarding school students as either assimilated sell-outs or purely resistant, as well as the easy alternative of envisioning them as "caught between." Instead, she insists on examining the complexity of individual experiences and self-representations. She affirms both rhetorical sovereignty and survivance, broadly speaking (14–15). She also observes: "The combination of verbal skills and group identification developed in Indian boarding schools produced a range of texts—from legal briefs to congressional testimony to autobiographical narratives, poetry, fiction, and plays—that explicitly concern themselves with tribal and indigenous sovereignty" (9).

35. Jon Reyhner and Jeanne Eder report that, by 1893, Carlisle had a busy print shop regularly preparing two publications, a monthly (*Red Man*) and a weekly (*Indian Helper*). See *American Indian Education*, 141–42.

36. Enoch, "Resisting the Script," 122. As one telling example of the latter aim, Enoch describes the written response to Zitkala-Ša's *Atlantic* essays, which had, after all, appeared in a venue designed to reach "Pratt's most important and indispensable audience—the white financial supporters and Indian-education sympathizers" ("Resisting," 122). Enoch comments on one especially telling rebuttal appearing in Carlisle's internally produced publication *Red Man* in June 1900 (135–36). For additional analysis in comparative context, see also Enoch's *Refiguring Rhetorical Education*.

37. Leslie Marmon Silko has described how a copy of the novel circulated in her extended family. She likens the book to "an 'extension program' which would reach Carlisle graduates after they returned home." Although researchers tracking the book's history in print archives have amended a few details from Silko's account, the significance of her theme—how Eastern white culture permeated even the Western homes of Natives via such material products—remains unassailable. See Silko's memoir essay online at "Introduction to Our First Catalog of Native American Literature: Leslie Marmon Silko."

38. For example, Carlisle's internally printed *Indian Helper* includes an illustrative (and self-congratulatory) advertisement for the narrative in an 1899 issue: "'Stiya' is the name of a little illustrated book published a few years ago by the Riverside Press, in excellent style, and written by one of our number who has had great experience among the Indians both in the field and at Carlisle. The story is thrilling, and portrays what an educated girl who returns to some of the Indian

Pueblos is liable to have to meet. The character of the girl who overcame every obstacle and came out unscathed is true to life and is built up from actual experiences of returned girls, related to and seen by the author. The book makes a good Christmas present. Price fifty cents, post paid. Address HELPER." See the *Indian Helper* 15, no. 6 (December 1, 1899): 2.

39. Embe [Marianna Burgess]. *Stiya*, 113, 115. Several scholars have identified "Embe" as Burgess. See, for instance, Jane E. Simonsen, *Making Home Work*, 89–90, and Janice Gould, "Telling Stories to the Seventh Generation," 13. Simonsen notes that *Stiya* was first published in Carlisle's *Indian Helper*, which Burgess managed. The frontispiece photograph is labeled "Stiya, Carlisle Indian Girl," but Gould reports that the young woman in that image is actually an Apache student named Lucy Tsisnah, though there was a Pueblo student named Stiya Kowkura attending Carlisle around this time (19 n. 3). Additional photos in the book echo the before-and-after storyline in other portrayals of Carlisle's work by presenting such scenes as "Pueblo children" to contrast the shot of Stiya in Euro-American dress, as well as a "Pueblo Village," with the latter positioned to contrast an image of the manicured Carlisle grounds.

40. Reyhner and Eder set the 1893 circulation of the monthly publication *Red Man* at between two thousand and three thousand, and the weekly *Indian Helper* as high as nine thousand (*American Indian Education*, 141–42).

41. In Scott Laderman, "'It Is Cheaper and Better to Teach a Young Indian,'" see 91–92.

42. Frances E. Willard, "The Carlisle Indian School," 289. Other causes claiming the energetic Willard's authorial attention included suffrage and temperance.

43. Jonathan Baxter Harrison, *The Latest Studies of Indian Reservations*, 184, emphasis in original. Harrison's book was published by the Indian Rights Association (IRA), a white-led group founded in Philadelphia in 1882.

44. For discussion of the relatively flexible approaches to language instruction employed at Hampton up until 1888, when a federal crackdown began forcing English-only methods at all funded schools, see Ruth Spack, "English, Pedagogy, and Ideology." Spack reports that, in the early years of Indian enrollment there, "Hampton allowed students to use their own languages before breakfast and after supper during the week and all day on Sunday." Outside those time frames, the school used a reward system more than punishment to encourage English speaking. In addition, Spack presents examples of individual teachers' using Indian native speakers to translate in the classroom rather than trying to present all instruction in English (7).

45. In *The Voice at Eve*, Goodale Eastman declares: "Although we were not encouraged to acquire the Dakota tongue, I determined to do so, and became rather proud of speaking it correctly enough to be occasionally mistaken for a native when travelling with Indians in the long summer vacation" (25). For additional descriptions of her work in the West and her advocacy around teaching issues, see the book-length memoir published well after her death: *Sister to the Sioux*.

46. Helen W. Ludlow and Elaine Goodale, *Captain Pratt and His Work*, 6–7. Goodale's pro-Carlisle rhetoric in this pamphlet is foreshadowed by a story she published in *The Independent* in 1885, dubbing the school "a center for one of the

great practical and philanthropic movements of our day" and insisting that "[w]e have nothing but praise for the methods employed in the school and for the degree of success attained." Describing "industrial education" via such activities as "cheerful" and "merry" girl laundry workers, Goodale characterizes Pratt himself as "the presiding genius of the place" (Goodale, "Carlisle: The Inlook and Outlook," 3). Goodale's mentor General Armstrong was a guest speaker at Carlisle.

47. On links between Goodale Eastman's writing career and her initial involvement in Indian Reform, see Ruth Ann Alexander, "Finding Oneself through a Cause," 1–37.

48. Examples include Elaine Goodale, "The Indian at Work," and these signed with her married name, Elaine Goodale Eastman: "From Washington," "A New Method of Indian Education," and "A New Day for the Indian."

49. In *The Voice at Eve*, Goodale Eastman references Armstrong's impact on her: "I have always believed that its [Hampton's] founder has been the strongest influence in my life, after my own parents" (22). See also *Sister to the Sioux*, where she contrasts the temperaments of Pratt and Armstrong, critiquing Pratt by way of comparison (22).

50. For an example of scholars' ongoing efforts to criticize Pratt while also giving the man his due, see Reyhner and Eder, *American Indian Education*, where they point to "his ethnocentrism, which prevented him for seeing any good in Indian cultures," but also note, as if echoing Goodale Eastman, "his role in convincing both the federal government and the American public that Indians could and should be educated" (145).

51. "The Indians' Friend: *Pratt, The Red Man's Moses*" presents a short review that opens with this assessment: "It would be difficult to find a more outstanding and complete example of single-mindedness, of unselfish, long-continuous devotion to one conviction and purpose than is afforded by the life story of General Richard Henry Pratt as told in this volume by Elaine Goodale Eastman." The review praises Goodale Eastman's careful research and her deep knowledge of "the Indian problem," as well as "the methods which have been tried for its solution" and the "many individual Indians who have made good under General Pratt's plans, Carlisle, Hampton and other Indian schools" (BR 26).

52. "The Indian Training School at Carlisle, Pa," *Frank Leslie's Illustrated Magazine* (March 15, 1884): 57–59. The lead caption for a full page of illustrations on page 57 offers the following identification: "Educating the Indians—Scenes at the Government Training School At Carlisle, PA—From Photographs and Sketches by James Becker."

53. On the history and cultural work of images in *Frank Leslie's Illustrated*, see Joshua Brown, *Beyond the Lines*. Brown dubs *Leslie's* "the publication that set the pattern for nineteenth-century illustrated journalism" and argues that *Leslie's* "did not simply reflect in its pages the crises of the Gilded Age; rather, its varying representations enacted those crises" (4–5). For Brown, such "images are not the antithesis of print culture but an intrinsic part of its nineteenth-century practice" (5). To locate *Frank Leslie's* place in the booming periodical marketplace of its day, see the classic multivolume study by Frank Luther Mott, *A History of American Magazines*.

54. In the early twentieth century, more Native voices would join Zitkala-Ša's in

describing their own experiences with assimilation education. Key texts include the memoir by Francis La Flesche (Omaha), *The Middle Five*, 1909, with its compelling illustrations by Native artist Angel De Cora, and Charles A. Eastman (Ohiyesa), *From the Deep Woods to Civilization*, 1916. Eastman's narrative continues the life story he began in 1902's [*Memories of an*] *Indian Boyhood*. While such texts can easily be critiqued today as led, by virtue of white sponsorship, into support of assimilation, they nonetheless encourage readers' empathetic response to the challenges of boarding school life. On the ways in which "sponsors" of literacy, even today, can both enable and constrain, see Deborah Brandt, *Literacy in American Lives*. In the case of Charles Eastman's books, questions of course arise about Elaine's role in determining their content. Her biographer, Theodore Sargent, has drawn on Elaine's own correspondence to show she viewed her role as stylistic editor more than content manager, as noted in one letter to her sister Rose, where Elaine insists, "He was and is the *author*—altho[ugh] he wrote very carelessly and would not even try to correct and revise. . . . Naturally, I thought it all over at the time and knew that to appear as *joint author* would be misleading" (*The Life of Elaine Goodale Eastman*, 89, emphases in original).

55. Zitkala-Ša and Doreen Rappaport, *The Flight of Red Bird*, 56–57. Rappaport credits Zitkala-Ša as primary author on the inside title page: "Re-created from the writings of Zitkala-Ša and the research of Doreen Rappaport." The biography's having Puffin as publisher marks its primary audience of young readers, but the respect accorded Rappaport's research is clear from the text's frequently being cited in other studies of Zitkala-Ša. Rappaport uses archival photographs to supplement her creative interweaving of her subject's own writing with contextual narrative. On Zitkala-Ša's *Atlantic* essays as complex autobiographical texts, see Martha Cutter, "Zitkala-Ša's Autobiographical Writings" and Dexter Fisher, "Zitkala-Ša: The Evolution of a Writer."

56. The most recent edition of *The Norton Anthology of American Literature* uses excerpts from all three of Zitkala-Ša's *Atlantic* essays, as well as a portion of "Why I Am a Pagan" and a reprint of "The Soft-Hearted Sioux." The longest excerpt is from "School Days" (see volume C, 1113–20). The Heath anthology, volume C, 5th edition, draws only from the "School Days" narrative (five sections) and "Why I Am a Pagan." *The Bedford Anthology*, volume 2, uses only "School Days." Already in 1994, in "Native American Literatures and the Canon," Patricia Okker was pointing to Zitkala-Ša's increasing presence in American literature anthologies, but also decrying the inadequacy of existing interpretive frameworks for analyzing such Native writers (see especially 88–89).

57. Examples include Dorothea M. Susag, "Zitkala-Ša"; Catherine Kunce, "Fire of Eden"; and Ron Carpenter, "Zitkala-Ša and Bicultural Subjectivity."

58. Young Adult novelist Marlene Carvell drew on the history of her husband's great-aunt Margaret as a Carlisle student to write *Sweetgrass Basket*. Several chapters of this narrative, which alternates between the voices of two sisters (Sarah and Mattie), show Mattie's attempt to escape. Recaptured, Mattie is locked in a cold guardhouse as punishment. By the end of the novel, her body is in the graveyard, and her sister Sarah has little source of comfort beyond the sweetgrass basket that had been Mattie's sole treasure from home. Though aimed at young readers, this

counter-narrative forcefully addresses complex aspects of coercive assimilation, including suppression of Native language and identity. Although one white teacher is cast as sympathetic, the text portrays Carlisle as cultivating narrow-minded, racist authority figures on staff.

59. Louise Erdrich, "Indian Boarding School," 11. Cary Nelson has compiled and posted helpful resources (under the title "About Indian Boarding Schools") to support the teaching of Erdrich's poem.

60. In the biting poem "Euro-American Womanhood Ceremony," Belin contrasts the experience of men at boarding school, where "at least" they were able to learn "a trade," and that of the women, who "were trained to specialize in domestic household work / to mimic the rituals of Euro-American women / to cook roast beef and not mutton / to eat white bread and not frybread / to start a family and not an education / to be happy servants to doctors' families . . ." (*From the Belly*, 20).

61. Laura Tohe, "Introduction: Letter to General Pratt," *No Parole Today*, x. For an insightful discussion of Tohe's use of Diné language and code-switching throughout her oeuvre, see Jessica Safran Hoover, "Rhetorical Sovereignty in Written Poetry," 170–87, in King, Gubele, and Anderson, *Survivance, Sovereignty, and Story*.

62. *Indolent Boys* in Momaday's *Three Plays* collection, 5. In addition to this drama on the Kiowa runaways, N. Scott Momaday's *Three Plays* further critiques boarding school education in *The Moon in Two Windows*.

63. For useful historical context on the school portrayed in this drama, see Ellis, "Remedy." Ellis points out that the Kiowa School near Anadarko had a particularly troubling history of poor administration, with the superintendent at the time of the events in Momaday's play being just one in a series of poor leaders (102).

64. Similarly, note Esther Belin's description of how being "survivors of boarding school 'education,' a process of pure indoctrination and rigid *transformation*," continues to position "natives as chattels to be directed, displayed, and researched" (70, "Cycle/Whirl," *From the Belly*, emphasis added).

65. Cf. whites' criticism of Elaine Goodale, referenced earlier in the chapter, for adopting Lakota language and cultural practices in her own teaching. On sentimental pedagogy being embraced by nineteenth-century women teachers in place of punitive discipline, see chapter 1, "Sparing the Rod," in Richard H. Brodhead, *Cultures of Letters*. See also chapter 3 of my *Managing Literacy, Mothering America*.

66. While revising this book manuscript, I was struck by the cultural capital that memories of Lincoln brought to key figures in each of my core chapters: early Spelman students calling on the log cabin mythology of Lincoln's youthful learning years; Jane Addams, through memories of her father, embracing Lincoln's vision as a guiding force behind the settlement; and/versus Momaday, here speaking through the voice of John Pai, who invokes Lincoln to condemn the boarding schools' ethos and teaching practices as a perversion of that president's legacy.

67. Ellinghaus, *Taking Assimilation to Heart*, 82–83. Acknowledging challenges from the start, Sargent, in *The Life*, points to the Goodale family's negative response to the marriage, a stance he attributes to racism (47). Sargent employs letters from Elaine to family members to track her embittered assessment of the marriage in its final years, which the Eastmans spent apart (106–21). Elaine's intense personality

and her gendered frustrations (including jealousy?) over Charles's more public career should also be taken into account (Sargent, *Life*, 56–57, 60). Though negatively portrayed in late-career writing by his wife, Charles Eastman was, as Sarah Pripas-Kapit points out in a study comparing his public role as physician and author with that of Susan La Flesche (Omaha), "the best- known Indian of the early twentieth century" by virtue of "his numerous writings and speeches on the eastern lecture circuit" ("'We Have Lived,'" 65). Further, as Pripas-Kapit documents, his shift away from a pro-assimilationist perspective deserves more attention. Thus, she notes, "the most significant feature of Eastman's later political philosophy was its rejection of the federal paternalism of which he had once been an agent." He expressed this shift through his leadership in the pan-Indian Society of American Indians (SAI), which asserted Native peoples as "exemplar citizens in a republic corrupted by whites" (71).

68. For a turn-of-the-century celebration of acculturated Indians like Eastman, La Flesche, and others, see Jessie W. Cook, "The Representative Indian."

69. See Vizenor, *Fugitive Poses*, where he explains that "survivance, in the sense of native survivance, is more than survival, more than endurance or mere response; the stories of survivance are an active presence" (15).

70. See "Community Projects: Voices of the Trail," on the Keeping and Creating American Communities website, including a reflection by classroom teacher and KCAC codirector Mimi Dyer.

71. Robert J. Conley, *Mountain Windsong*. Conley, who passed away in 2014, wrote in an array of genres, produced more than forty books, and won numerous literary awards. For a detailed appreciation of this particular novel as worthy of more scholarly attention, see Pamela Fox, *Robert J. Conley's* Mountain Windsong: *Tribally-Specific Historical Fiction*. Fox describes her own efforts to elevate Conley's text as grounded in part in her own Cherokee heritage but also in admiration of his leadership of Cherokee studies at Western Carolina University (see her introduction).

72. Vizenor himself defined *survivance* in his introduction to *Fugitive Poses*, where he also discusses *sovenance*: "Native *sovenance* is that sense of presence in remembrance, that trace of creation and natural reason in native stories; once an obscure [Old French—souvenir] noun, the connotation of sovenance is a native presence in these essays, not the romance of an aesthetic absence or victimry" (15).

73. Patsy Hamby, "Uncovering a Region's Past," in *Writing America*, 64–73. I cite Hamby's essay here not only to direct my readers to its helpful content but also in the hope that more attention will be paid to the cultural authority K-12 teachers bring to studies of classroom practice.

74. On the centrality of Vizenor's *survivance* framework for studying Native cultures, see Lisa King, Rose Gubele, and Joyce Rain Anderson's "Introduction" to *Survivance, Sovereignty, and Story*, 7–8. Similar to our experience with developing curricula through the KCAC project, the editors' introduction to their collection of teaching stories describes a multiyear collaboration, including a series of workshops and collegial conversations supported by the American Indian Caucus (AIC) of the Conference on College Composition and Communication (CCCC). See especially 4–6. I document these cross-community connections here in print text as another

example of how informal and interpersonal exchanges can support sustained collaborations for cross-cultural teaching.

Chapter 5

1. Dennis would later observe: "I know that our visitors . . . come here with different levels and backgrounds of experience and exposure to American Indian culture. And as a museum professional, I have to address them at their level. There is ignorance that is about, but it's most of the time innocent. And there are also scholars, academics, Native people, who are also experts, who come, and I interact with them" (Zotigh, interview).

2. To sample the range of responses the NMAI elicited from academics and museum professionals early on, see the collection of essays introduced by Lisa Jacobson in "Review Roundtable" (47–49). Steven Conn followed up on his critique there with a particularly biting assessment in his later book, *Do Museums Still Need Objects?* (38–39). Taking into account such negative responses to the NMAI, Mara Kurlandsky nonetheless reminded readers in 2011 that the core mission of the museum is being achieved: "The most common critique of NMAI is that it is overwhelming, incoherent and hard to engage with. Even for a museum lover such as myself, there is a certain anxiety upon entering the museum, a sense that one must see everything, read everything and understand everything in order to pay tribute to such a difficult history. But despite this anxiety, and despite the fact that both times I have visited I didn't manage to see or read everything, NMAI communicated its most important message clearly: Native peoples are still here" ("Our Peoples and Our Lives," http://www.exhibitfiles.org/our_peoples_and_our_lives).

3. Aldona Jonaitis and Janet Catherine Berlo, "'Indian Country' on the National Mall," 216–17. In "What Are Our Expectations Telling Us?," Gwyneira Isaac contrasts two of her own visits to the NMAI. She first describes the reactions of a group of "anthropologists and museologists" who, "at home analyzing the architecture and displays," moved toward "critique" of "a number of features [that] confounded us and thwarted our understanding of the goals of the exhibits," producing "critical fodder for future examination and research" (241). She juxtaposes that occasion with a "second visit," when she "found the museum to be a welcoming beacon alight" with "singing" and visitors embracing "the palpable sense of a shared public experience" (242). These differences led her to remember how "meanings are made on the ground in ongoing encounters between displays and the ideational worlds their audiences bring with them into the museum space" (242). For a parallel analysis of the impact of guides in Colonial Williamsburg, see Richard Handler and Eric Gable, *The New History of an Old Museum*, especially the introductory chapter (3–27) and "The Front Lines: Smile Free or Die" (170–207). Handler and Gable sought a more "objective" perspective for their ethnographic enterprise than I have cultivated here, in a project aiming primarily to learn from role models whose expertise I value, if not uncritically, then certainly through a lens of aspiration.

4. Thanks to Bethany Schneider for sharing her essay manuscript, "Reserva-

tion C," which informs my discussion here. See also Douglas E. Evelyn, "A Most Beautiful Sight," in Duane Blue Spruce, ed. *Spirit of a Native Place*, 151–83. Evelyn declares, "Now two centuries of evolving national policy toward American Indians have converged with equally long efforts to shape the National Mall as a place for public inspiration and education. The assignment of the last building site on the Mall to the National Museum of the American Indian restores this long-contested ground to a use that respects its distant past and offers it a new role as a site of reconciliation" (183).

5. For an informative history of NMAI's evolution, including its complex relationship with the George G. Heye collection and the Smithsonian, see Ira Jacknis, "A New Thing," in Lonetree and Cobb, 3–42. Several essays in that collection highlight the collaborative approach to the museum's development; others point to strategies of cultural intervention and reconciliation; still others (such as essays by Sonya Atalay and Amy Lonetree) address shortcomings. See also an essay by George Horse Capture ("The Way of the People") in Duane Blue Spruce, ed., *Spirit of a Native Place*, which examines community consultations with Native tribal groups as a core strategy in the museum's development (30–45).

6. When I asked Dennis what he would most wish young kids who visit the museum to learn there, he suggested that his "biggest point of information" to share with visitors "is that there is no standardized Indian. And taken in historical versus contemporary context, it's important for children to know our cultures evolved, and today we continue to evolve like the rest of human societies. And for some reason, what is taught to them, is stuck in a time warp, and it's unfortunate" (Zotigh, interview).

7. During our first one-on-one interview, Dennis Zotigh recited the museum mission statement to me, identifying its content as a guide for all his NMAI work: "Well, everything I do," he declared, "I consider the mission first. In fact, I always say, [quoting the full mission]: 'The National Museum of the American Indian is committed to advancing knowledge and understanding of the Native cultures of the Western Hemisphere, past, present, and future, through partnership with Native peoples and others. The museum works to support the continuance of culture, traditional values, and transitions in contemporary Native life.'" See "Mission Statement," National Museum of the American Indian, on the museum website.

8. I use the terms "nation" and "sovereignty" self-consciously here, hoping to suggest that these cultural interventions support both tribal identity and a reformed US national one that has been reconfigured to respect and honor Native nations.

9. See the "Coda" for *To Remain an Indian*, where Lomawaima and McCarty argue that American education has much to learn from the historical "footprints of Indigenous struggles for educational, linguistic, and cultural self-determination" (167). They see that heritage as showing how safe spaces for learning "can be constructed as places of difference in which children are free to learn, question, and grow from a position that affirms who they are," a stance "long held within Indigenous communities," one that "has the power to create a more just and equitable educational system for all" (170).

10. See Malea Powell, "Rhetorics of Survivance," 400. See also Anne Ruggles

Gere, "An Art of Survivance," which suggests that Vizenor's term characterizes "American Indian capacity to combine survival with resistance" (649).

11. As outlined later in this chapter, Lisa King suggested the term "cultural mediator" to me in an online interview. I prefer her "mediator" to the "broker" term, partly because "broker" these days carries negative connotations associated with recession-generating abuses in the US economic system. However, several scholars have ably employed the "cultural broker" concept, as in *Between Indian and White Worlds*, edited by Margaret Connell Szasz and referenced in chapter 4.

12. Gardner suggests that Deloria felt quite anxious about publishing in scholarly venues and thus sought reassurance and guidance from mentors such as Ruth Benedict (xxiv–xxv). In contrast, Gardner asserts, "Ella Deloria felt no qualms about releasing *Waterlily*. Conventional ethnology in published form was an impossibility; writing a novel based on that fieldwork was not" (xxv). This view does seem at odds with the positive response to *Speaking of Indians* and with Gardner's own report of Margaret Mead as finding Deloria a strong combination of "'informant, field worker and *collaborator'*" (xxv, emphasis mine). See also Agnes Picotte, "Biographical Sketch of the Author," in *Waterlily*, 229–31.

13. Diane Wilson, *Beloved Child: A Dakota Way of Life*, 74. See also 26, 44, 49, 54, 74, 86–87. Wilson compellingly attributes problems some Native adults have with parenting to the legacy of residential schooling: "A 2003 report, 'American Indian Children in Foster Care,' estimates that one-half of all Native people were either raised in boarding schools or parented by adults raised in boarding schools. As generations of Native children grew up separated from their families, tribes, and cultural traditions, they never learned what it meant to be part of a traditional Native family or any family at all. They were unprepared to teach their own children when they began to have families" (36). Dennis Zotigh made a similar point during our first interview at the NMAI.

14. For more on the concept of restorative justice, see Lisa Lee's discussion of its connections to educational practice in chapter 3, and her "Peering into the Bedroom" essay in *The Routledge Companion to Museum Ethics*, 174–87.

15. See chapter 6 of *Managing Literacy, Mothering America*, wherein I examine the writing of Laura Haygood, a missionary teacher serving in China at the turn into the twentieth century. See also the critical edition I coedited with Ann Pullen: *Nellie Arnott's Writings on Angola, 1905–1913*.

16. See, in this context, an interview with Todd DeStigter in chapter 3.

17. Patricia A. Carter reports that, by 1899, just over half of the BIA teaching corps were Anglo-American women ("'Completely Discouraged,'" 58). Carter is not the only scholar to highlight ways in which (relatively) empathetic white women teachers sometimes resisted the oppressive assimilationist approaches of the boarding schools, even as they faced constraints in such efforts. For example, Lomawaima and McCarty describe the 1890s' Ogalalla Boarding school, where white teacher Thisba Huston Morgan and her colleagues regularly "'chose not to interfere'" when their students set up "camps in the several corners of the playground, complete with tepees" for their "Indian dolls made from sticks" (*To Remain an Indian*, 1).

18. Significantly, Carter contrasts her subjects with other teachers they themselves criticized in their autobiographies as "lifers" incapable of finding other positions—lazy and undedicated, if not incompetent (70).

19. See Goodale Eastman, *Yellow Star: A Story of East and West.* Yellow Star, an orphan of the Wounded Knee massacre who is adopted by a white missionary and educated in New England, gladly takes on the role of on-reservation teacher at Cherry Creek. Though a confident and highly accomplished instructor, Stella faces prejudice from the whites there, who, the author asserts, "should have welcomed her in all sincerity as a fellow-worker" but instead "looked at her critically, even coldly" as an interloper (243), "too self-possessed for an Indian girl" (244).

20. See, in striking comparison, the commentary by schoolteacher Beth Steffen in chapter 3.

21. For today's readers, the Foucauldian undertones of these passages are arresting, given the text's intense focus on surveillance. See Michel Foucault, *Discipline and Punish.*

22. Here, as elsewhere in this account, the narrator is cast as trapped in the role of supporting the same dominating social forces that she had tried so hard to resist in the series' middle story about her own schooling. In line with postcolonial theorists, we could describe her position as "subaltern," both in the general sense of being oppressed by hegemonic power structures and in the more specific sense invoked at times by Homi Bhabha, who has pointed out that subalterns are in a position to subvert colonizing authority even as they appear to support it. That is, while portraying herself as complicit in the work of the assimilationist educational machine—as she recruits new victim-students—Zitkala-Ša simultaneously opposes its power through her narrative's potential impact on her readers, who may come to recognize the colonizing of body and mind being carried out to complement assaults on Indian lands. See Homi K. Bhabha, "Signs Taken for Wonders," *Location of Culture*, 102–22.

23. Virtually the only look into Zitkala-Ša's actual classroom practice is a phrase alluding to "one weary day in the schoolroom" as finally prompting the narrator to leave Carlisle for good, carrying away frustrated memories of the "Christian palefaces" whose visits to her teaching site had seen only what they wanted to find there: "the children of savage warriors [become] so docile and industrious" ("Indian Teacher," 112).

24. N. Scott Momaday affirms this point in his portrayal of Etahdleuh, a male teacher at Carlisle, in *The Moon in Two Windows.* After scenes conveying both Etahdleuh's frustration with school practices and his determined efforts to circumvent the institution's culture to the best of his ability, Momaday has Etahdleuh surprise Pratt, who had offered to adopt this "ideal" student-teacher (156), by leaving Carlisle for the (hopefully) enhanced agency of pastoral work in the West with his wife-to-be, Lame. Momaday's assessment of Etahdleuh is empathetic, as seen in the character Luther Standing Bear's indication that that this former Fort Marion prisoner, now Carlisle teacher, was doing his best "to keep himself an Indian, trying hard, as we all were," within highly constrained circumstances (137).

25. See, in this context, Dian Million's impassioned—and thought-provoking— "Felt Theory," 53–76. Million studies how "Indigenous women . . . created new

language for communities to address the real multilayered facets of their histories and concerns by insisting on the inclusion of our lived experience, rich with emotional knowledges, of what pain and grief and hope meant or mean now in our pasts and futures." She still bemoans ways that "[o]ur felt scholarship continues to be segregated as a 'feminine' experience, as polemic, or at worst as not knowledge at all" (54).

26. For helpful readings of *Wynema*, consult Melissa Ryan, "The Indian Problem as a Woman's Question," 23–45; Siobhan Senier, "Allotment Protest and Tribal Discourse," 420–40; and Lisa Tatonetti. "Behind the Shadows of Wounded Knee," 1–31. Tatonetti, in particular, stresses that Callahan is writing for a white rather than a Native audience (4).

27. Religious schools for Indians (dating back to the pre-Revolutionary era) had a complex history, with notable differences based on individual leadership at particular institutions, denominations' varied emphases in their programs, and shifts in goals over time. Some white teachers working in religious settings, like the Riggs missionary family at Santee in the late nineteenth-century West, strove to establish close ties with the local tribal communities, as seen in Dr. Alfred Riggs's longstanding commitment to teaching in Native vernacular. Elaine Goodale Eastman describes their Santee schools as committed to "leader training" and praises the "able" work there of "the Riggs family for more than sixty years" (*Pratt: The Red Man's Moses*, 119). As Goodale Eastman notes, Carlisle founder Pratt generally viewed missionary educators as competitors. Therefore, she reports, "Notwithstanding his pious Methodist upbringing and earnest Christian faith," Pratt felt church-based teaching could be "damned" for its focus on acquiring converts, first and foremost. Thus, she quotes Pratt as complaining: "'The missionary does not citizenize'" (112). On one side, the fact that a number of influential Indian intellectuals emerged from mission schools and/or embraced Christianity should not be ignored. (See the discussion of Ruth Muskrat Bronson later in this chapter.) On the other, in positioning Ella Deloria within "one of the best-known American Indian intellectual families," Susan Gardner points not only to Ella's being the daughter of Reverend Philip Deloria, longtime Native Episcopal missionary, but also to the eventual decision of her brother, Reverend Vine Deloria, Sr., to resign his own position in the church "in protest against its racist policies" ("Introduction," *Waterlily*, vii). For insightful treatment of one Cherokee woman's early nineteenth-century conversion, see Theresa Gaul's award-winning edition of writings by Catharine Brown, *Cherokee Sister* (15).

28. To exemplify some missionary teachers' affiliating closely with tribal communities, Jon Reyhner and Jeanne Eder cite the case of Reverend Worcester, who was sentenced to four years of hard labor for supporting Cherokee efforts to resist the Removal. See *American Indian Education*, 49. In contrast, Reyhner and Eder note, some missionaries "found nothing to value in Native cultures" (119); further, they document cases of abusive treatment at one Catholic mission boarding school and underscore how a single institution might have both "good and bad teachers" (125)

29. Craig S. Womack (in the "Alice Callahan's *Wynema*" chapter of *Red on Red*) has forcefully faulted the novel's "failure to engage Creek culture, history, and poli-

tics," as seen in its "erasure of Creek voices, the characters' rejection of Creek culture, the many instances of cultural misrepresentation throughout, the lack of any depictions of the nuances of Creek life, the protagonist's repudiation of Muskogean matrilineariry, and the author's choice of a non-Creek and non-Indian viewpoint." For Womack, the novel is most useful "as a document of Christian supremacism and assimilation" (107). For A. Lavonne Brown Ruoff, the scholar whose archival discovery brought *Wynema* to light for today's readers, the novel is significant in spite of its shortcomings, since it "is probably the first novel written by a woman of American Indian descent" ("Editor's Introduction," S. Alice Callahan, *Wynema*, xiii) and because it represents a rhetorically oriented effort to "educate her audience about Muscogee culture, Indians' and women's rights, and the mutual respect between the sexes essential to happy marriages" (xliii).

30. See the "Playing Angry" chapter of Cari M. Carpenter, *Seeing Red*, 29–53. Carpenter acknowledges Craig Womack's critique of the novel but sets its rhetoric in the context of Callahan's mixed-race identity and the "fact that there is little room for American Indian anger" to be openly articulated in "available narratives" of her day, when "anger was figured most readily in the form of a white woman" like Genevieve (52).

31. Ruth Spack has provided insightful analysis of Zitkala-Ša's tour with the Carlisle band, which Pratt arranged soon after publication of the *Atlantic* stories, whose content had left him much aggrieved. Spack uses performance theory and historical context from the Indian author's later career to argue that agreeing to play the violin and recite from Longfellow's *Hiawatha* (in Native costume borrowed from the Smithsonian!) during this tour represented not a capitulation but another strategic engagement with white culture. "Zitkala-Ša, *The Song of Hiawatha*, and the Carlisle Indian School Band," 211–24.

32. William Willard, "Zitkala-Ša: A Woman Who Would Be Heard!," 11–16. On the sophisticated rhetorical strategies at play in Zitkala-Ša's later publications, see Gary Totten, "Zitkala-Ša and the Problem of Regionalism," 84–123. For instance, Totten acknowledges the irony of Zitkala-Ša's 1918 essay urging the government not to turn Carlisle "back into military facilities," since doing so would represent a "'loss of education opportunities only Carlisle can give.'" Totten views her citing of "the government's 'honor-bound obligation to educate the Indian'" as conveying her determination to safeguard such learning as a tool to political power, despite the troubling elements in assimilation teaching that she had experienced herself (107).

33. "Who's She in War Work?," 478–83. The author herself did not abandon pointed critique as a rhetorical strategy during this period, however. See, for instance, "The Red Man's America" poem riffing on "My Country 'Tis of Thee." This biting satire, originally in *American Indian Magazine* in 1917, is reprinted in P. Jane Hafen, ed., *Dreams and Thunder*, 119–20. For a helpful history of *American Indian Magazine* and its precursor *Quarterly Journal of the Society of American Indians*, in the context of SAI's history, see Kathleen Washburn, "New Indians," 380–84.

34. Gertrude Bonnin, Charles H. Fabens, and Matthew K. Sniffen, *Oklahoma's Poor Rich Indians*. Herbert Welsh, president of the Indian Rights Association, wrote a brief preface ("In Explanation," 3). Elizabeth Wilkinson, in "Gertrude Bonnin's

Transrhetorical Fight," gives an apt rhetorical analysis of Bonnin's writing for this collaborative project.

35. Ruth Muskrat Bronson, *Indians Are People, Too*. The biographical sketch provided on the book's copyright page traces Bronson's impressive personal history as a student and teacher, including her attendance at Mount Holyoke and George Washington University, her work as a "teacher of English at Haskell Institute," and her service as "Guidance Officer for the entire Indian Service."

36. On mimicry as a discursive strategy, see "Of Mimicry and Man" in Bhabha, *Location of Culture*, 85–92.

37. Bronson dedicated her book "[t]o Mrs. Fred S. Bennett in deep appreciation of her devoted service to my people" (iii). Mrs. Bennett was long involved in Indian education as a leader of the Woman's Board of Home Missions of the Presbyterian Church.

38. See, along related lines, chapter 2's discussion of the commitment among black community leaders like Father Quarles and his spiritual heirs to servant leadership as a key learning goal for Spelman, in the late nineteenth century and today.

39. Esther Burnet Horne and Sally McBeth, *Essie's Story*, 49. As McBeth states in an introduction responding to Horne's memoir, "What she found in the boarding school setting became an important part of her life. She found Indian friends, Indian teachers, an Indian husband, and a future in the field of Indian education" as a teacher at another off-reservation boarding school in Eufaula, Oklahoma. At the same time, McBeth observes, Horne's life narrative "displays a recognition of the complexity of the boarding school experience," including, in Essie's own words, a critique of its work "'to take the Indianness out of us'"—an effort at which Essie judges that "'they never succeeded.'" In that vein, McBeth's introduction suggests that Haskell can be seen "as adding another level of ethnicity to Essie's already intact identity," combining Shoshone and Pan-Indian selves (xxxiv–xxxv).

40. Certainly progress has been achieved in claiming places of leadership in the academy, in line with prior calls such as that voiced by Roxanne Dunbar Ortiz, "Developing Indian Academic Professionals," 5–10.

41. These colleagues' descriptions of their work sometimes recall formulations offered by Frances Karttunen in *Between Worlds*, which examines cultural mediators going all the way back to Sacajawea and including figures such as Sarah Winnemucca and Charles Eastman's children. See, for instance, Karttunen's description of "individuals, many of them women, who have served as interpreters, translating their languages and also their cultures for outsiders. . . . They functioned as conduits through which information flowed between worlds in collision, translating more than just words and bringing comprehensibility to otherwise meaningless static" (xi).

42. See Jennifer Andrews's "Living History" interview with Native poet-scholar Kimberly Blaeser, who singles out Womack as a leading figure in what Blaeser calls "tribal-centered criticism" (11). In that context, in his introduction to *Red on Red*, Womack declares: "I hope this study encourages young Creek writers to keep writing; to trust their own voices; to tell the stories of family, home and nation; and to know the story of those who told such stories before us" (20). Interestingly, when interviewing Diane Glancy, Andrews asked her opinion on the tribal-centered

criticism that Blaeser (referencing Womack) had seemed to advocate. For Glancy, making such cultural analysis overly specific could bring its own problems. Citing Blaeser's own identity, Glancy noted: "She's Ojibway, she's Chippewa, Anishinaabe. But what about the Cherokee's tribal-centered theory? And then the Creek tribal-centered theory? . . . So what good is it going to do to have all these fractured tribal theories? Can there be an overall theory?" ("Conversation," Glancy and Andrews, 650).

43. King's *The Truth About Stories*, subtitled *A Native Narrative*, uses stories and storytelling to examine how stories can promote change, both within individuals and in the broader social landscape. Crossing boundaries between the printed word and orality, the book is adapted from his 2003 Massey Lectures in Canada, and the stories King shares here also invoke his experiences growing up in California.

44. On the need to cultivate a critical stance toward cultural tourism—one that recognizes issues of power difference linked to globalization, capitalism, and social hierarchies—R. V. Bianchi's "The 'Critical Turn' in Tourism Studies" is especially insightful.

45. See Schön's *The Reflective Practitioner* and *Educating the Reflective Practitioner*.

46. In a modest way, I hope my story-gathering also allies with the "talking circles" Native scholar Andrea M. Riley-Mukavetz has carried out with Native women in the Lansing, Michigan, community and described in "Towards a Cultural Rhetorics Methodology."

47. In a chapter honoring Native agency among learners and teachers, I would stress that I do not view the colleagues who supported this work as "subjects" to be analyzed in the traditional sense of Euro-American research practices but rather as mentors and partners—or, to use Lisa King's term, allies. In this case, a few of the teaching guides discussed in this chapter mainly responded to email queries; others participated in extended in-person conversations that were tape-recorded and transcribed; still others contributed mainly by way of telephone interviews. Most participated in a combination of in-person, telephone, and online conversations, supplemented by email exchanges. All of these partnerships involved multiple exchanges, over an extended period of time. I invited my colleagues to read and help me adjust "their" sections to achieve the most accurate versions of their stories as possible. Because our exchanges became discursively interconnected, and because we revised wordings together, I do not give single specific dates for quotations, as, typically, each such passage now within the text actually took form over several interpersonal exchanges. Accordingly, for interviews, in the bibliography, I provide a listing of the various connecting occasions for each research partner, by month and by year. This pattern holds for interviewees in other chapters.

48. The four Native educators profiled here are not the only ones whose role modeling has had substantial impact on my teaching. For instance, as I hope was clear from earlier references, and as I will highlight more directly in my Coda, Diane Glancy—as both writer and teacher—is a leader whose example I continue to revisit. Further, I would echo Shawn Miller from *Research Is Ceremony*, "In addition to the discussions that were recorded, many more took place that I did not record. These informal talks greatly improved the clarity of my thinking and expanded the relationships I was forming with an Indigenous research [and teaching] paradigm"

(129). For me, one crucial example would be the guidance of Philip J. DeLoria, who met with me over a meal in the early stages of my research on the NMAI and who later addressed follow-up questions during an extended telephone interview.

49. See, for example, King's discussion of how her lessons on representation and stereotypes and associated student assignments have been adapted to expectations for University of Tennessee's English 102 course, in her "Keywords for Teaching," *Survivance, Sovereignty, and Story*, 27–29.

50. When working to enact these terms in day-to-day teaching, I also draw comparatively on the models of Spelman and Hull-House. For instance, *sovereignty* and *contact*, for me, call to mind the generative mix of claiming agency for black learners and their potential as leaders seen in Spelman's Founders Day and their focus on seeking contact with other cultures toward globalized learning. *Dialogue* and *reciprocity*, meanwhile, resonate both with Jane Addams's own writings on her settlement teaching and the practices of the museum educators I interviewed for chapter 3. I've sought to embed these same principles in such teaching documents as the syllabus for a course I teach on "cultural contact zones" and in my daily practices during class meetings, where I strive to honor the diverse experiences and social backgrounds my students bring to learning.

51. As a sign of how she works as an "Alliance Builder" in her classroom teaching, I would reference a thought-provoking handout King provided at the CCCC "Standing Peachtree" workshop referenced in chapter 4. This material situated a media analysis assignment she gives her students within a framework of Native teaching practices.

52. King's incisive *Pedagogy* essay, "Rhetorical Sovereignty and Rhetorical Alliance," outlines shortcomings in such models as critical and contact zones pedagogy: "The assumption that a critical, democratic classroom practice can address the problems confronted by all minorities by giving everyone a voice is . . . highly problematic for any minority group, and particularly for Native communities who are not necessarily seeking equality so much as working to maintain literal and rhetorical sovereignty" (210). In contrast, King convincingly explains, "The voices we consider normative need to be interrogated for the sake of placing them within their own contexts, rather than as prime narrators that might make token space for voices not like theirs" (211). Then, by incorporating the vision for rhetorical sovereignty in the work of leaders like Scott Lyons and Malea Powell, she argues, "respectful alliances in our classrooms" can be developed.

53. Lee teaches a diverse student population that includes a larger proportion of Native students than at many institutions: in Lee's case, "33% of our students identify as Native American." Lee describes Northeastern State as also drawing a notable number of "adult learners" who are "returning to finish their schooling, or just to broaden their horizons."

54. One fruitful approach Lee has used is to bring contemporary Native music into the classroom, as she outlines in detail in "Heartspeak from the Spirit" in the *Survivance, Sovereignty, and Story* collection, 116–37. There, Lee suggests particular songs for teaching about key events in Native history, major concepts such as *Survivance*, and important rhetorical techniques like humor—as well as promoting strong listening skills.

55. Byrd reports that, "Pooling all the students I have taught into one large group, most . . . have been white Americans. The next largest groups . . . have been African American, then Hispanic American . . . , Asian American, and Asian from other countries. It has been rare that students have identified themselves as Native American, although when I ask students, 'Who has Native American ancestry?,' I am always surprised at how many hands go up from people who are ordinarily identifying themselves as being a member of some other American ethnic or racial group."

56. For a report on the project, including the museum exhibit that included display of Namorah Byrd's portrait at NMAI's New York branch and, later, on tour to sites in Texarkana and San Antonio, see Gabrielle Tayac, *IndiVisible*.

57. On Pura Fé and the Ulali Project, see her website.

58. For a powerful reminder that alliances are still far from easy to build in academe—that Native voices, even today, are not always welcome, so that spaces of genuine peace are hard to attain and sustain—see Robert Warrior, "Vandalizing Life Writing," 44–50. Warrior narrates his experience as curator of an on-campus exhibit by Heap of Birds, entitled *Beyond the Chief*; for Warrior, vandalism aimed at the exhibit conveyed "the sense members of the white supermajority on my campus have that they can declare Native perspectives and analysis as wrong, that, with the exhibit, we brought the vandalism on ourselves by being provocative troublemakers. Had we been quiet about our critique and analysis, everything would have been fine. We could have learned, taught, and lived in peace in exchange for our silence" (49).

59. As reported in chapter 4, Powell describes her identity, more specifically, as mixed-blood of Indiana Miami, Eastern Band Shawnee, and Euro-American ancestry, and she notes that distinctions between enrolled and unenrolled should be acknowledged.

60. One example might be the American Studies Association, for which Native scholars Philip J. Deloria and Robert Warrior have served as presidents. A survey of the online program for the fall 2015 ASA conference, held in Toronto, suggests a commitment to including Native and First Nations scholars and topics drawn from their scholarship in selecting session proposals.

61. See Powell's coauthored essay with Andrea Riley-Mukavetz in *Survivance, Sovereignty, and Story*, "Making Native Space for Graduate Students," 138–59. Specific strategies illustrated (and theorized) there include using personal stories to create a web of relations (145), connecting course texts to the landscape of where it is offered (139, 145), and developing a community orientation based in the group (156–57). At TCU, I have had the special benefit of working with, and learning from, doctoral student Natasha Robinson, whose original graduate school training was with Powell at Michigan State.

62. See Jo-ann Archibald, "Creating an Indigenous Intellectual Movement," 125–48, in *Restoring the Balance*, eds. Valaskakis, Stout, and Guimond. Celebrating the leadership of "first-wave First Nations women" producing important scholarship and teaching in Canadian universities, Archibald identifies major contributions by Freda Ahenakew, Marlene Brant Castellano, Olive Dickason, Verna J. Kirkness, and Gail Guthrie Valaskakis. Valaskakis, who was also a coeditor of the volume of

essays in which this piece appeared, is a particularly significant figure for my own study, given her border-crossing identity of having been "born and raised on the Lac du Flambeau reservation in Wisconsin" (140) but working as an academic in Canada; her focus on gender as well as Aboriginal identity (such as in her study of Indian Princess stereotypes); and her emphasis on narrative testimony as an avenue to knowledge-making (141–42). Encouraging my approach here, Archibald advocates for methodology grounded in an "oral tradition" from "First Nations cultures, when life-experience stories are used for educational purposes," with "the listener/reader" being "expected to make meaning with the story given" (127).

63. See, in this context, "Wampum as Hypertext," where Angela Haas forcefully "traces a counterstory to Western claims to the origins of hypertext and multimedia by remembering how American Indian communities have employed wampum belts as hypertextual technologies . . . [using] interconnected, nonlinear designs and associative storage and retrieval methods long before the 'discovery' of Western hypertext" (77).

64. Isaac, "Expectations," in Lonetree and Cobb, 250. In his "Foreword" to *Spirit of a Native Place*, Duane Blue Spruce describes how NMAI planners sought extensive input from Native peoples, whose advice was then summarized in a working document, *The Way of the People* (18). As one telling example, he cites this observation: "*Hospitality is one thing you will always find among Native Americans, and hopefully always will*" (20, emphasis in original). The café seems designed to respond to one recommendation recorded by George Horse Capture in the same collection: "that each visitor should be greeted personally and offered a seat and perhaps a cup of coffee, in the way that Indians welcome guests into our homes" ("The Way of the People," 42).

65. Communication from Renée Gokey discussing NMAI's use of distance learning tools, email received Monday, July 13, 2015.

66. Gretchen M. Bataille notes in her "Introduction" to *Native American Representations*, "Myths about Indians and the West seem impenetrable by facts, and for many people who are not themselves Native American, the stereotypes and misrepresentation remain safer than reality" (7).

67. Renée Gokey, "Not the 'Last of the Miamis,'" *NMAI Blog*. For a similar discussion of the theme of Native people not matching whites' expectations, see Diane Glancy's conversation with Jennifer Andrews (referenced above), where Glancy notes of her own childhood: "my father was Cherokee. I remember him telling me we were Indian, but it wasn't the kind of Indian that the school presented. It took me forever to figure this out as a child. And then you couldn't really present yourself as Indian because it wasn't accepted" (649). Later, when she was first trying to write about her own Indian heritage, she encountered resistance: "all Native heritage was supposed to be Plains Indian. But we would go back to my father's people, the Cherokee, and they were farmers. I never saw a buffalo, I never saw feathers, a war bonnet, no tepees; we had a house, a row of corn, a pig. When you were first able to write about your Indian heritage, editors and publishers wanted Plains Indian material. They didn't want the truth of the kind of Indian you were" (645).

68. NMAI's *Teacher E-Newsletter* assembles all issues of the newsletter for convenient online access.

69. Dennis Zotigh, *Meet Native America*, typically presents two new online profiles per month.

70. In "Introduction & 1st Question," an *NMAI Blog* posting from January 2011, Zotigh not only introduced himself; he also addressed the familiar question, "What do we call you, American Indian or Native American?" by pointing to variations in individuals' and generations' preferences and explaining varying contexts of use for terms. For instance, he points out that "'Indian' usually means an enrolled member of a federally recognized tribe," thus being a "legal term" also reflected in the name of the NMAI and other official titles. Comments added to this blog posting illustrate the wide range of opinions among NMAI stakeholders as to which term(s) would be preferable, and why.

Coda

1. For a forceful call to enact American studies as a critically aware yet aspirational enterprise, see Tomlinson and Lipsitz, "American Studies as Accompaniment." They propose that "American studies can become one of many sites in US society where a collective capacity for democratic deliberation and decision making can be nurtured and sustained. In the process of attempting to build a better society, this work can also lead to better scholarship because its research objects and research questions emerge out of the actual contradictions of social life" (26–27).

2. One factor both constraining and enabling my work going forward was moving back to a faculty role in the early summer of 2016, after two years as an "acting" dean. Though I lost access to some resources open only to administrators (e.g., funds for speakers, access to facilities, and financial support for collaborations), this shift in roles provided the gift of time—including time to complete work on this book, which had been slowed considerably due to my administrative duties. And it freed me up to return to collaborations with some partners with whom I'd worked in the past, outside the TCU community.

3. Eric Sundquist offers a productive context for discussing this text, and particularly Jiménez's closing scene, in "The Humanities and the National Interest." Sundquist observes, "As our principal vehicle for engendering sympathy—the ability to imagine the experience of another, to see ourselves from that perspective, to make another's life our own, if only for a moment—the humanities are not just a means of promoting the 'climate of responsible and watchful stewardship and [the] culture of creative innovation' essential for a strong economy" (here quoting Martha Nussbaum). Also, Sundquist himself argues for the humanities as "a critical means of combating the ignorance and superstition that breed anti-democratic thought, whether abroad or at home, and preparing our young citizens to see themselves" as belonging to a richly diverse nation and world (602).

4. As Shelley Fisher Fishkin astutely notes in *Writing America: Literary Landmarks from Walden Pond to Wounded Knee*, in a view consistent with Jiménez's research of his family story, not all the sites that have played crucial roles in the creation of American literature have achieved such canonical status as being named to the National Historic Register: "What about the literature produced by writers too

poor or too transient to have permanent homes capable of being preserved—such as early-twentieth-century writers who were impoverished workers from China or Russia, for example, or late-twentieth-century migrant farm workers in the Southwest?" (2).

5. Hunter Walker's July 6, 2016, "Donald Trump" essay for *Business Insider* provides multiple examples of what he calls Trump's "doubling down on his controversial comments about Mexican immigrants," including describing them as "'the worst elements in Mexico . . . pushed into the United States by the Mexican government,'" claiming that Mexican cartels are the "'largest suppliers of heroin, cocaine and other illicit drugs,'" and asserting that "'tremendous infectious disease is pouring across the border,'" thereby making the United States "'a dumping ground for Mexico and, in fact, for many other parts of the world'" (para 3).

6. On Trump's plan for a wall to cut off immigration from Mexico, see Bob Woodward and Robert Costa, "Trump Plans Ultimatum." For Trump's broader engagement with immigration-related issues and the potential impact of both his stance and his tone on presidential politics, see Reihan Salam, "Trump's Immigration Disaster" and Linda Chavez, "Donald Trump's America." On the back-and-forth critiques between Trump and Vicente Fox, see Sabrina Siddiqui, "Former Mexican President Vicente Fox Attacks Donald Trump's 'Racist' Ideas."

7. A related impetus for this work is a collaborative effort at TCU to launch a program in Comparative Race and Ethnic Studies, an initiative spearheaded by professors Max Krochmal and Melanie Harris. For one example from an online story-archive of the annual "alternative spring break" civil rights bus tour led by Professor Krochmal, whose leadership has encouraged many other faculty to revisit such movements in both curricular and cocurricular contexts, see the blog post by graduate student James Chase Sanchez: "Civil Rights Bus Tour—Day 5."

8. Common's lyric reference to "Ferguson" clearly invokes the death of Michael Brown in that St. Louis suburb, an event that prompted sustained protests in the local community and beyond, including through social media. Brown's death also generated extensive press coverage that made connections between that event and other cases of young black men being killed under controversial (to say the least) circumstances. For a cluster of texts addressing Brown's death and its larger context within an academic journal, see the Spring 2015 issue of *Cultural Critique*, as described in the editors' unsigned "In the Conjuncture" introduction (115–17). See below in this chapter for a discussion of #BlackLivesMatter, the movement that grew up as one activist response to the Michael Brown case and so many others.

9. In describing the writing process for "Glory," Common told *Daily Beast* reporter Jen Yamato: "We wanted this song to be inspirational. We wanted it to have that pain, but also hope." See Yamato's "John Legend and Common." The "Glory" song was written collaboratively by John Legend, Common, and Che Smith. Like the example of *The Circuit* in this Coda, as well as *Jane Addams in the Classroom* and *The Indolent Boys* earlier, and the role of Frank Quarles in chapter 2, I include this text here in part to signal that my focus on *women's* counter-narratives for *Learning Legacies* is not intended to suggest that only female authors can create such texts.

10. For an insightful analysis of the West Point black women graduates' photo episode, see Dave Philipps, "Raised-Fist Photo." For speeches by Frances Harper,

see Foster's *A Brighter Coming Day* edition; for writings on education by Anna Julia Cooper, including discussion of her graduate study in France, see *A Voice from the South*. On black male youth as "fodder" for university athletics, see Billy Hawkins, *The New Plantation*.

11. James I. Deutsch's review of *Harvest of Loneliness* in *The Journal of American History* offers a thoughtful assessment of rhetorical and historical decision-making shaping the film. On anti-Chinese stereotypes at the turn between the nineteenth and twentieth centuries, including anti-immigration visual rhetoric, see Nicholas Sean Hall's "The Wasp's 'Troublesome Children.'"

12. See, for instance, "Arriba Allende: Discussion Video 3" in the series created by Sofia and Mayra based on study of Allende's *Island Beneath the Sea*.

13. I thank Lisa Junkin Lopez for sharing the one-page write-up that JGLB prepared to characterize the new exhibit and for continuing our conversations about her public scholarship. I have strong personal reasons for being drawn to her new site of archival action. My first full-time teaching position was in Savannah, at Benedictine academy, in the late 1970s. I can call up fond memories of the city's historic tourism, but also of my own preliminary efforts to bring archival recovery into my American literature courses via copies I typed and then mimeographed of local colonial authors' texts. Further, as the daughter of a longtime Girl Scout professional, and a veteran of many Scouting programs, I look forward to reconnecting with that part of my personal heritage.

14. A recent biography, *Juliette Gordon Low*, by historian Stacy Cordery treats the Girl Scout founder's struggles with expectations for Southern genteel femininity; her experiences as a transatlantic wife suffering in an ill-advised marriage match; and her eventual adaptation of the British Robert Baden-Powell's Boy Scout model to launch the Girl Scout movement back in Savannah in 1912.

15. Keeanga-Yamahtta Taylor's *From #BlackLivesMatter to Black Liberation*, especially chapters 6 and 7, provides a scholarly analysis of #BlackLivesMatter that situates the movement in helpful historical context.

16. Appropriately enough, "The Disruptors" had collaborative authorship by Brandon Griggs, Emanuella Grinberg, Katia Hetter, Wyatt Massey, Melonyce McAfee, David Shortell, Tanzina Vega, and Eli Watkins. To note how quickly the #BlackLivesMatter movement began to draw scholarly attention from diverse disciplinary perspectives, see García and Sharif's "Black Lives Matter."

17. Devon Johnson and several colleagues have edited a multivocal scholarly analysis of the Trayvon Martin case and its wider implications, *Deadly Injustice*.

18. See note #9 and references earlier within this chapter to the invocation of Michael Brown's death in the John Legend/Common "Glory" lyrics and in recent scholarship for *Cultural Critique*.

19. Franco Moretti, *Distant Reading*. For critique of Moretti's method, see Katie Trumpener, who suggests scholars seek a middle ground between close reading and Moretti's agenda. "One troubling aspect of Moretti's statistically driven model of literary history is that it seems to necessitate an impersonal invisible hand. . . . His interest, after all, is in trying to identify systemic, overall, large-scale shifts; by this logic, any specific text becomes statistically almost irrelevant," says Trumpener in "Paratext and Genre System," 164.

20. While I would not view this book as a "counter-narrative" response to Stanley Fish's *Save the World On Your Own Time*, I'm aware that some readers might do so. Actually, I think there are important overlaps in our arguments—such as a commitment to empowering students as knowledge-makers by having them thoughtfully and deeply engage with various disciplinary canons. But I also recognize differences in our viewpoints, since I am calling for a pedagogy that promotes social action. Like Fish, I don't expect that "the job of an institution of higher learning [is] to cure every ill the world has ever known," including "poverty, war, racism, gender bias, bad character, discrimination, intolerance, environmental pollution, rampant capitalism, American imperialism, and the hegemony of Wal-Mart . . ." (10). But I do want to prepare students to *participate* in addressing such problems collaboratively—as rhetorically sophisticated citizens.

21. For a full description of the "Discovering Global Citizenship" framework, visit the program website, where the various DGC initiatives are outlined. University reaccreditation through the Southern Association of Colleges and Schools (SACS) requires periodic development and assessment of a Quality Enhancement Plan (QEP); TCU's focus on global learning for its current QEP mirrors a trend at many other institutions.

22. My call for new learning legacies as, themselves, a potential form of scholarship aligns with Ernest Boyer's *Scholarship Reconsidered* and for associated recognition of the "scholarship of teaching" as valuable.

23. Sabine H. Smith, "Perfectly Ambivalent: How German Am I?" in *Bridging Cultures*, 40–60. My collaboration with colleagues contributing to *Bridging Cultures* has deeply enriched all my scholarship and teaching since then.

Bibliography

Archives: Major Collections Consulted and Key Content There

American Antiquarian Society, Worcester, Massachusetts. Numerous publications by and about Hampton Institute, Indian Boarding Schools, and Indian Assimilation.

Congregational Library and Archives, Boston, Massachusetts. Papers related to Sophia Packard and Nora Gordon of Spelman. American Baptist Missionary Union Papers and *Baptist Missionary Magazine*. Papers of the Woman's American Baptist Home Mission Society.

Jane Addams Memorial Collection. Richard J. Daley Special Collections, University Archives, University of Illinois at Chicago University Library. Hull-House Records. Papers and materials on/by various women leaders of the settlement, including the *Hull-House Bulletin* and yearbooks, Addams's scrapbooks, and her extensive personal papers.

New England Freedman's Aid Society, Massachusetts Historical Society. *The Freedmen's Record* E185.2 F85; New England Freedmen's Air Society Records, 1862–78, MS-N101. Documents on/by New England women teaching in the postbellum South.

Spelman College Archives, Spelman College. Sophia B. Packard Papers, 1850–91 and *Spelman Messenger*. Office of the President, Archives, Spelman College, Atlanta, Georgia.

Note: Archival sources such as stories in the *Spelman Messenger* are cited within the text and endnotes.

Interviews, Conversations, and Email Exchanges

Note: The research partners listed below held multiple conversations with me, over several years, in each case. Most also read and responded to drafts of manuscript sections where their input was being incorporated. Accordingly, for a typical quotation or reference within the text, readers should not expect to see a specific date listed but, instead, to find a time frame for the particular reference provided within the text.

Byrd, Namorah. August 2015, September 2012, June 2012, May 2012, January 2012, December 2011, October 2011.

Deloria, Philip. November 2011, October 2011.

DeStigter, Todd. April 2016, November 2015, September 2015, July 2015, June 2015, January 2015, June 2012, January 2012, November 2011, October 2011.

Gokey, Renée. October 2015, September 2015, August 2015, July 2015, January 2013, December 2012, November 2012, October 2012, August 2012, May 2012, December 2011, October 2011, August 2011.

King, Lisa. April 2016, August 2015, July 2015, June 2015, May 2012, January 2012.

Lee, Kimberli. July 2015, June 2015, June 2012, May 2012, February 2012, January 2012, December 2011.

Lee, Lisa. July 2014, March 2014, July 2013, June 2012, May 2012.

Lopez, Lisa Junkin. May 2016, October 2015, January 2014, December 2013, June 2012, May 2012.

Mitchell, Deborah. October 2015, August 2015, summer 2002 (multiple), academic year 2001–2002 (multiple), summer 2001 (multiple), academic year 2000–2001 (multiple), summer 2000 (multiple).

O'Rourke, Bridget. August 2015, March 2015, June 2012, December 2011, October 2011.

Powell, Malea. April 2016, August 2015, July 2015, June 2015, June 2014, October 2012.

Radke, Heather. September 2015, August 2015, May 2015, February 2015, January 2015, November 2014, May 2014, January 2014, May 2012.

Schaafsma, David. November 2015, August 2015, July 2015, June 2015, January 2015, October 2014, September 2014, August 2014, July 2014, March 2014, December 2013, November 2013, August 2013, May 2013, August 2012, July 2012, June 2012, May 2012, January 2012, December 2011, October 2011.

Spencer, Taronda. October 2011, April 2011, March 2011, January 2011, October 2010, August 2010, March 2010, June 2009, summer 2001 (multiple), April 2001, summer 2000 (multiple).

Steffen, Beth. August 2015, July 2015, April 2013, January 2012, November 2011, October 2011.

Zotigh, Dennis. October 2015, September 2012, October 2012, May 2012, December 2011, October 2011, August 2011.

Site Visits

Heard Museum, Phoenix, Arizona.

Exhibits: Remembering Our Indian School Days: The Boarding School Experience; We Are! Arizona's First People; N. Scott Momaday: Art and Poetry.

Huhugam Heritage Center, Gila River Indian Community, Arizona.

Jane Addams Hull-House Museum, 800 South Halsted Street, Chicago, Illinois.

Klahowya Village, Stanley Park, Vancouver, Canada.

Museum of Anthropology, University of British Columbia, Vancouver, British Columbia, Canada.

Museum of the Cherokee Indian, Cherokee, North Carolina.

National Museum of the American Indian, 4th Street and Independence Avenue, SW, Washington, DC.

New Echota Historic Site, Calhoun, Georgia.

Oconaluftee Indian Village, Cherokee, North Carolina.

Saxman Native Village, Ketchikan, Alaska.

Sisters Chapel, Spelman College, 350 Spelman Lane, SW, Atlanta, Georgia.

Sweet Auburn Historic District, Atlanta, Georgia.

"Unto These Hills" Outdoor Drama, Cherokee, North Carolina.

Websites and Web-based Articles

Alyssa, Moriah. *Carrie Walls*. http://moriahalyssa97.blogspot.com/2013/01/carrie-walls.html

Bratta, Phil, and Malea Powell. "Introduction to the Special Issue: Entering the Cultural Rhetorics Conversations." *Enculturation: A Journal of Writing and Culture* 21 (April 2016). http://enculturation.net/entering-the-cultural-rhetorics-conversations

Chicago Freedom School Homepage. http://chicagofreedomschool.org

"Chronology of the KCAC Project's Initial Work." KCAC. http://kcac.kennesaw.edu/welcome/chron.html

Contagion, Quarantine, and Social Conscience: Albert Camus's *The Plague* (Discussion Board). https://jvrfiresides.wordpress.com/discuss

Cuddy, Alison. "Home Economics: The Radical Roots of Domestic Labor." *WBEZ Blogs*. December 12, 2012. https://www.wbez.org/shows/wbez-blogs/home-economics-the-radical-roots-of-domestic-labor/0896e64f-c69e-482f-b10b-31ec3ecbf7a2

"Death of the Hull House." https://nonprofitquarterly.org/2012/08/02/death-of-the-hull-house-a-nonprofit-coroners-inquest

Discovering Global Citizenship. http://qep.tcu.edu/initiatives

Dyer, Mimi. "Community Projects: Voices of the Trail Reflection." Keeping and Creating American Communities, 2001. http://kcac.kennesaw.edu/community_projects/voices_of_the_trail/voicesreflect.html

"Educating for Citizenship." KCAC. http://kcac.kennesaw.edu/thematic_content/educating_for_citizenship/educatpr.html

GlobalEX. TCU, 2015. http://newmedia.tcu.edu/globalex/

Gokey, Renée. "Not the 'Last of the Miamis.'" *NMAI Blog*. September 27, 2013. http://blog.nmai.si.edu/main/2013/09/not-the-last-of-the-miamis.html

Gokey, Renée. *Teacher E-Newsletter*. National Museum of the American Indian, 2015. http://nmai.si.edu/explore/foreducatorsstudents/resources/teacherenewsletters

Griggs, Brandon, Emanuella Grinberg, Katia Hetter, Wyatt Massey, Melonyce McAfee, David Shortell, Tanzina Vega, and Eli Watkins. "The Disruptors." CNN, 2015. http://www.cnn.com/interactive/2015/08/us/disruptors

Guardiola, Mayra, and Sofia Huggins. "Arriba Allende: Discussion Video 3." You-Tube. https://www.youtube.com/watch?v=Z7w8UL6Cn1k&feature=em-subs_digest

Imagining America: Artists and Scholars in Public Life. Syracuse University, 2015. http://imaginingamerica.org

Imagining America: Artists and Scholars in Public Life. *History of PAGE*. Syracuse University, 2015 http://imaginingamerica.org/consortium/student-networks/page/history-of-page

Jane Addams Hull-House Museum. University of Illinois Chicago, Jane Addams Hull-House Museum, 2015. http://www.hullhousemuseum.org

Juliette Gordon Low Birthplace. http://www.juliettegordonlowbirthplace.org

Kass, John. "Gangs That Came to Rule in Seats of Power: Vice Lords Exhibit Reveals Lesser-Known Details About White Gangs Such as Hamburgs." *Chicago Tribune* (June 22, 2012). http://articles.chicagotribune.com/2012-06-22/news/ct-met-kass-0622-20120622_1_gangs-conservative-vice-lords-museum-exhibit

Keeping and Creating American Communities (KCAC). Kennesaw State University, 2001. http://kcac.kennesaw.edu

Kennesaw Mountain Writing Project. "Keeping and Creating American Communities: Proposal to the National Endowment for the Humanities." http://kcac.kennesaw.edu/welcome/pdf_files/original_proposal.pdf

Kiley, Kevin. "Another Liberal Arts Critic." *Inside Higher Ed*. January 20, 2013. https://www.insidehighered.com/news/2013/01/30/north-carolina-governor-joins-chorus-republicans-critical-liberal-arts

Kurlandsky, Mara. "Our Peoples and Our Lives: Review of an Exhibition." *Exhibit Files*. March 15, 2011. http://www.exhibitfiles.org/our_peoples_and_our_lives

"Look at It This Way." http://hullhouse.uic.edu/hull/look/index.html

Madhani, Aamer. "Obama Apologizes for Joking About Art History Majors." *USA Today*. February 19, 2014. http://www.usatoday.com/story/theoval/2014/02/19/obama-apologizes-to-texas-art-history-professor/5609089

Mills, Frederick W. "Atticus G. Haygood (1839–1896)." *New Georgia Encyclopedia*. http://www.georgiaencyclopedia.org/articles/arts-culture/atticus-g-haygood-1839-1896

"Mission Statement." NMAI, 2015. http://nmai.si.edu/about/mission

Moye, Matthew M. "Sidney Root (1824–1897)." *New Georgia Encyclopedia*. http://www.georgiaencyclopedia.org/articles/business-economy/sidney-root-1824-1897

National Museum of the American Indian, 2015. http://www.nmai.si.edu

Nelson, Cary, ed. "About Indian Boarding Schools: Background to Louise Erdrich's Poem." http://www.english.illinois.edu/maps/poets/a_f/erdrich/boarding/index.htm

"PuraFé." *Purafe*, 2015. http://purafe.com

Radke, Heather. "Unfinished Business: 21st-Century Home Economics." *Museum Magazine*. Washington, DC: American Alliance of Museums, 2013. http://www.aam-us.org/about-us/publications/museum-magazine/unfinished-business

Ranallo, Anne Brooks. "NYC Public Historian New Director of UIC's Hull-House

Museum." *UIC News Center.* February 18, 2015. http://news.uic.edu/new-hull-house-museum-director

Rand, Jacki Thompson. "Why I Can't Visit the National Museum of the American Indian: Reflections of an Accidental Privileged Insider, 1989–1994." *Common-Place.* 2007. http://www.common-place-archives.org/vol-07/no-04/rand/

Robbins, Sarah. "Contagion, Quarantine and Social Conscience: Online Fireside and Roundtable." John V. Roach Honors College, 2015. https://jvrfiresides.wordpress.com/about/

Sanchez, James Chase. "Civil Rights Bus Tour—Day 5." https://jameschasesanchez.wordpress.com/2016/03/12/civil-rights-bus-day-tour-day-5

Siddiqui, Sabrina. "Former Mexican President Vicente Fox Attacks Donald Trump's 'Racist' Ideas." *The Guardian.* April 6, 2016. http://www.theguardian.com/us-news/2016/apr/06/vicente-fox-attacks-donald-trumps-racist-ideas

Silko, Leslie Marmon. "Introduction to Our First Catalog of Native American Literature." *Ken Lopez Bookseller.* 1994. http://lopezbooks.com/articles/silko

Simon, Nina. "Postcards as a Call to Action: A Powerful, Political Participatory Experience at the Jane Addams Hull-House Museum." *Museum Magazine.* January 13, 2011. http://museumtwo.blogspot.com/2011/01/postcards-as-call-to-action-powerful.html

Society of American Archivists. "Archives." http://www2.archivists.org/glossary/terms/a/archives

Spelman College. *Inside Spelman.* http://www.insidespelman.com

Steenland, Patricia. "Lost Stories & Cultural Patrimony." *Imagining America.* Spring 2015. http://public.imaginingamerica.org/blog/article/105-2/

Strauss, Valerie. "'Big Data' Was Supposed to Fix Education. It Didn't. It's Time for 'Small Data.'" *The Washington Post.* May 9, 2016. https://www.washingtonpost.com/news/answer-sheet/wp/2016/05/09/big-data-was-supposed-to-fix-education-it-didnt-its-time-for-small-data

Tatum, Beverly Daniel. "Beverly Daniel Tatum Explains Why the Women of Spelman Are the Living Legacy." *HBCUBuzz.* May 21, 2015. http://hbcubuzz.com/2015/05/beverly-daniel-tatum-explains-why-the-women-of-spelman-are-the-living-legacy

Tatum, Beverly Daniel. "A Living Legacy. Convocation Speech Given by Beverly Daniel Tatum. Spelman College, August 21, 2014." http://www.spelman.edu/docs/president_speecheswritings/convocation-2014.pdf?sfvrsn=0

"TCU/About TCU: TCU History." http://www.tcu.edu/90.asp

"Teacher E-Newsletter." NMAI, 2015. http://nmai.si.edu/explore/foreducatorsstudents/resources/teacherenewsletters

Thayer, Kate. "Jane Addams Hull House to Close." *Chicago Tribune.* January 19, 2012. http://www.chicagotribune.com/news/local/breaking/chi-jane-addams-hull-house-to-close-20120119-story.html

"Thematic Content." KCAC. http://kcac.kennesaw.edu/thematic_content/themes.html

Walker, Hunter. "Donald Trump Just Released an Epic Statement Raging against Mexican Immigrants and 'Disease.'" *Business Insider.* July 6, 2016. http://www.businessinsider.com/donald-trumps-epic-statement-on-mexico-2015-7

Williams, Rachel Marie-Crane. *Girls in the System: A Story About Young Women & the Juvenile Justice System.* https://chicagogirltalk.files.wordpress.com/2011/04/girlsforhh4-20final3.pdf

Wood, Angela. "With 'A Legacy of Change,' Green Adds to His Spelman Credits." *Inside Spelman.* http://www.insidespelman.com/with-a-legacy-of-change-green-adds-to-his-spelman-credits

Yamato, Jen. "John Legend and Common on Bringing 'Glory' to the Grammys with a Little Help from Beyoncé." *The Daily Beast.* February 8, 2014. http://www.thedailybeast.com/articles/2015/02/08/john-legend-and-common-on-bringing-glory-to-the-grammys-with-beyonce.html

Zotigh, Dennis. "Introduction & 1st Question: American Indian or Native American?" *NMAI Blog.* http://blog.nmai.si.edu/main/2011/01/introduction-1st-question-american-indian-or-native-american.html

Zotigh, Dennis. *Meet Native America.* NMAI Online. http://blog.nmai.si.edu/main/meet-native-america

Print and Additional Sources

Adair, Bill, Benjamin Filene, and Laura Koloski, eds. *Letting Go? Sharing Historical Authority in a User-Generated World.* Philadelphia: Pew Center for Arts & Heritage, 2011.

Adams, David Wallace. *Education for Extinction: American Indians and the Boarding School Experience.* Lawrence: University Press of Kansas, 1997.

Adams-Bass, Valerie N., Keisha L. Bentley-Edwards, and Howard C. Stevenson. "That's Not Me I See on TV . . . : African American Youth Interpret Media Images of Black Females." *Women Gender, and Families of Color* 2, no. 1 (2014): 79–100.

Addams, Jane. "Address of Miss Addams at Carnegie Hall." *The Jane Addams Reader*, edited by Jean Bethke Elshtain, 327–40. New York: Basic Books, 2002.

Addams, Jane. *Democracy and Social Ethics.* New York: Macmillan, 1915.

Addams, Jane. "Devil Baby at Hull-House." *Atlantic Monthly* (October 1916): 441–51.

Addams, Jane. *Forty Years at Hull-House; Being 'Twenty Years at Hull-House' and 'The Second Twenty Years at Hull-House' in One Volume; with an Afterword by Lillian D. Wald.* New York: Macmillan, 1935.

Addams, Jane. "A Great Public Servant, Julia C. Lathrop." *Social Service Review* 6, no. 2 (1932): 280–85.

Addams, Jane. "Julia Lathrop and Outdoor Relief in Chicago, 1893–94." *Social Service Review* 9, no. 1 (1935): 24–33.

Addams, Jane. "Julia Lathrop's Services to the State of Illinois." *Social Service Review* 9, no. 2 (1935): 191–211.

Addams, Jane. *The Long Road of Woman's Memory.* New York: Macmillan, 1916.

Addams, Jane. "A Modern Devil Baby." *American Journal of Sociology* 20 (1914): 117–18.

Addams, Jane. "A Modern Lear." *Survey* (November 2, 1912): 131–37.

Addams, Jane. *My Friend, Julia Lathrop.* New York: Macmillan, 1935.

Addams, Jane. *My Friend, Julia Lathrop.* With an introduction by Anne Firor Scott.

Urbana: University of Illinois Press, 2004. First published in 1935 by Macmillan.

Addams, Jane. *Peace and Bread in Time of War*. New York: Macmillan, 1922.

Addams, Jane. *The Spirit of Youth and the City Streets*. New York: Macmillan, 1915.

Addams, Jane. *Twenty Years at Hull-House with Autobiographical Notes with Illustrations by Norah Hamilton*. New York: Macmillan, 1910.

Addams, Jane. "Women's Conscience and Social Amelioration." *The Social Application of Religion, The Merrick Lectures for 1907–8*, edited by Charles Stelzle et. al., 41–60. Cincinnati, OH: Jennings and Graham, 1908. Reprinted in *The Jane Addams Reader*, edited by Jean Bethke Elshtain, 252–69. New York: Basic Books, 2002.

Addams, Jane, and Alice Hamilton. "Preface" to *My Friend, Julia Lathrop*, by Jane Addams, 3–4. Urbana: University of Illinois Press, 2004.

Addams, Jane, Emily G. Balch, and Alice Hamilton. *Women at the Hague: The International Congress of Women and Its Results*. New York: Macmillan, 1915.

Alcoff, Linda Martin, Michael Hames-García, Satya P. Mohanty, and Paula M. L. Moya, eds. *Identity Politics Reconsidered*. New York: Palgrave Macmillan, 2006.

Alexander, Michelle. *The New Jim Crow: Mass Incarceration in the Age of Colorblindness*. New York: The New Press, 2010.

Alexander, Ruth Ann. "Finding Oneself through a Cause: Elaine Goodale Eastman and Indian Reform in the 1880s." *South Dakota History* 22, no. 1 (1992): 1–37.

Alexie, Robert Arthur. *Porcupines and China Dolls*. Oroville, WA: Theytus Books, 2009.

Alexie, Sherman. *The Absolutely True Diary of a Part-Time Indian*. New York: Little Brown, 2007.

Allende, Isabel. *Island Beneath the Sea: A Novel*. New York: Harper, 2010.

Anderson, Benedict. *Imagined Communities: Reflections on the Origin and Spread of Nationalism*. New York: Verso, 2006.

Anderson, James D. *The Education of Blacks in the South, 1860–1935*. Chapel Hill: University of North Carolina Press, 1988.

Andrews, Jennifer. "Living History: A Conversation with Kimberly Blaeser." *American Indian Literatures* 19, no. 2 (2007): 1–21.

Andrews, Jennifer, and Diane Glancy. "A Conversation with Diane Glancy." *American Indian Literatures* 26, no. 4 (2002): 645–58.

Andrews, Molly. "Opening to the Original Contributions: Counter-Narratives and the Power to Oppose." In *Considering Counter-Narratives: Narrating, Resisting, Making Sense*, edited by Michael Bamberg and Molly Andrews, 1–6. Philadelphia: John Benjamin Publishing, 2004.

Appiah, Kwame Anthony. *Cosmopolitanism: Ethics in a World of Strangers*. New York: Norton, 2006.

Appiah, Kwame Anthony. *The Ethics of Identity*. Princeton: Princeton University Press, 2005.

Archibald, Jo-ann. "Creating an Indigenous Intellectual Movement at Canadian Universities: The Stories of Five First Nations Female Academics." In *Restoring the Balance: First Nations Women, Community, and Culture*, edited by Madeline Dion Stout, Gail Guthrie Valaskakis, and Eric Guimond, 125–48. Winnipeg: University of Manitoba Press, 2009.

Baird, Major George W. "Are Soldiers Murderers." *The Independent* 43 (June 25, 1891): 3.

Baker, Marsha Lee, Eric Dieter, and Zachary Dobbins. "The Art of Being Persuaded: Wayne Booth's Mutual Inquiry and the Trust to Listen." *Composition Studies* 42, no. 1 (2014): 13–34.

Bamberg, Michael, and Molly Andrews, eds. *Considering Counter-Narratives: Narrating, Resisting, Making Sense*. Philadelphia: John Benjamin Publishing, 2004.

Barnett, Henrietta. *Canon Barnett: His Life, Work, and Friends by His Wife in Two Volumes*. Boston and New York: Houghton Mifflin, 1919.

Bataille, Gretchen M. "Introduction." In *Native American Representations: First Encounters, Distorted Images, and Literary Appropriations*, 1–7. Lincoln: University of Nebraska Press, 2001.

Belin, Esther G. *From the Belly of My Beauty*. Tucson: University of Arizona Press, 1999.

Bennett, Paula Bernat. *Poets in the Public Sphere: The Emancipatory Project of American Women's Poetry, 1800–1900*. Princeton: Princeton University Press, 2003.

Bentley, Nancy. *Frantic Panoramas: American Literature and Mass Culture, 1870–1920*. Philadelphia: University of Pennsylvania Press, 2009.

Bernardin, Susan. "On the Meeting Grounds of Sentiment: S. Alice Callahan's *Wynema: A Child of the Forest*." *American Transcendental Quarterly* 15, no. 3 (2001): 209–24.

Bhabha, Homi K. *The Location of Culture*. New York: Routledge, 1994.

Bianchi, R.V. "The 'Critical Turn' in Tourism Studies: A Radical Critique." *Tourism Geographies* 11, no. 4 (2009): 484–504.

Bilton, Chris. "Knowing Her Place: Jane Addams, Pragmatism, and Cultural Policy." *International Journal of Cultural Policy* 12, no. 2 (2006): 135–50.

Blue Spruce, Duane, ed. *Spirit of a Native Place: Building the National Museum of the American Indian*. Washington, DC: NMAI and National Geographic, 2004.

Boggis, JerriAnne, Eve Allegra Raison, and Barbara W. White, eds. *Harriet Wilson's New England: Race, Writing, and Region*. Durham: University of New Hampshire Press, 2007.

Bonnin, Gertrude, Charles H. Fabens, and Matthew K. Sniffen. *Oklahoma's Poor Rich Indians: An Orgy of Graft and Exploitation of the Five Civilized Tribes*. Philadelphia: Indian Rights Association, 1924.

Bourdieu, Pierre. *Practical Reason: On the Theory of Action*. Translated by Randal Johnson and others. Stanford, CA: Stanford University Press, 1998.

Bourne, George. "Rhythm and Rhyme." *Macmillan's Magazine* (May 1906): 541–49.

Boyer, Ernest L. *Scholarship Reconsidered: Priorities of the Professoriate*. New York: John Wiley & Sons, 1990.

Boyte, Harry C. *Democracy's Education: Public Work, Citizenship, and the Future of Colleges and Universities*. Nashville, TN: Vanderbilt University Press, 2015.

Brandt, Deborah. *Literacy in American Lives*. New York: Cambridge University Press, 2001.

Brandt, Deborah. "Sponsors of Literacy." *College Composition and Communication* 49, no. 2 (1998): 165–85.

Branson, Tyler, James Chase Sanchez, Sarah R. Robbins, and Catherine Wehlburg. "Collaborative Ecologies of Emergent Assessment: Challenges and Benefits

Linked to a Writing-based Institutional Partnership." *CCC: College Composition and Communication*. Forthcoming, 2017.

Branson, Tyler, and Sarah R. Robbins. "Going Public in the Humanities: Undoing Myths, Facing Challenges." In *The Cambridge Handbook of Service Learning and Community Engagement*, edited by Corey Dolgon, Timothy K. Eatman, and Tania D. Mitchell, 244–55. Cambridge: Cambridge University Press, 2017.

Brazzell, Johnetta Cross. "Bricks without Straw: Missionary-Sponsored Black Higher Education in the Post-Emancipation Era." *The Journal of Higher Education* 63, no. 1 (1992): 26–49.

Brodhead, Richard H. "Sparing the Rod: Discipline and Fiction in Antebellum America." In *Cultures of Letters: Scenes of Reading and Writing in Nineteenth-Century America*, 13–47. Chicago: University of Chicago Press, 1995.

Bronson, Ruth Muskrat. *Indians Are People, Too*. New York: Friendship Press, 1944.

Brooks, Daphne A. *Bodies in Dissent: Spectacular Performances of Race and Freedom, 1850–1910*. Durham, NC: Duke University Press, 2006.

Brown, Emma. "Some Parents Revolting against Standardized Testing." *The Washington Post* (March 8, 2015): A4.

Brown, Joshua. *Beyond the Lines: Pictorial Reporting, Everyday Life, and the Crisis of Gilded Age America*. Berkeley: University of California Press, 2002.

Brown, Victoria Bissell. *The Education of Jane Addams*. Philadelphia: University of Pennsylvania Press, 2004.

Bryan, Mary Lynn McCree, Barbara Bair, and Maree de Angury, eds. *The Selected Papers of Jane Addams, Volume 1: Preparing to Lead, 1860–81*. Urbana: University of Illinois Press, 2004.

Bryan, Mary Lynn McCree, Barbara Bair, and Maree de Angury, eds. *The Selected Papers of Jane Addams, Volume 2: Venturing into Usefulness*. Urbana: University of Illinois Press, 2009.

Burgess, Marianna [Embe, pseud.]. *Stiya: A Carlisle Indian Girl at Home, Founded on the Author's Actual Observations*. Cambridge, MA: Riverside Press, 1891.

Burgett, Bruce, and Glenn Hendler, eds. *Keywords for American Cultural Studies*. New York: New York University Press, 2007.

Burton, Annie L. *Memories of Childhood's Slavery Days*. Boston: Ross Publishing, 1909

Butchart, Ronald E. "Black Hope, White Power: Emancipation, Reconstruction and the Legacy of Unequal Schooling in the US South, 1861–1880." *Pedagogical Historica* 46, no. 1–2 (2010): 33–50.

Butchart, Ronald E. *Schooling the Freed People: Teaching, Learning, and the Struggle for Black Freedom*. Chapel Hill: University of North Carolina Press, 2010.

Callahan, S. Alice. *Wynema: A Child of the Forest*. Edited by A. Lavonne Brown Ruoff. Lincoln: University of Nebraska Press, 1997.

Cammisa, Rebecca [director]. *Which Way Home*. DVD. New York: GOOD and White Buffalo Entertainment and HBO Documentary Films, 2009.

Camus, Albert. *The Plague*. Translated by Stuart Gilbert. 1948. Reprint. New York: Vintage Random House, 1991.

Carpenter, Cari M. *Seeing Red: Anger, Sentimentality, and American Indians*. Columbus: Ohio State University Press, 2008.

Carpenter, Ron. "Zitkala-Ša and Bicultural Subjectivity." *Studies in American Indian Literatures* 16, no. 3 (2004): 1–28.

Carter, Patricia A. "'Completely Discouraged': Women Teachers' Resistance in the Bureau of Indian Affairs Schools, 1900–1910." *Frontiers: A Journal of Women Studies* 15, no. 3 (1995): 53–86.

Carvell, Marlene. *Sweetgrass Basket*. New York: Dutton Children's Books, 2005.

Cary, Elisabeth Luther. "Recent Writings by American Indians." *The Book Buyer* 24, no. 1 (1902): 21–25.

Casey, Ethan. *Alive and Well in Pakistan: A Human Journey in a Dangerous Time*. Lahore: Vanguard Pakistan, 2005.

Castellano, Marlene Brant, Lynne Davis, and Louise Lahache, eds. *Aboriginal Education: Fulfilling the Promise*. Vancouver: UBC Press, 2000.

Césaire, Aimé. *Discourse on Colonialism*. Translated by Joan Pinkham. Originally published 1955. New York: Monthly Review Press, 2000.

Césaire, Aimé. *A Tempest: Based on Shakespeare's The Tempest, Adaptation for a Black Theatre*. Translated by Richard Miller. New York: Theatre Communications Group, 1985.

Chambers, John Whiteclay II. *The Tyranny of Change: America in the Progressive Era, 1890–1920*. 3rd ed. New York: St. Martin's Press, 2000.

Chang, Heewon. *Autoethnography as Method*. Walnut Creek, CA: Left Coast Press, 2008.

Chavez, Linda. "Donald Trump's America." *Commentary* (October 2015): 13–19.

Chernow, Ron. *Titan: The Life of John D. Rockefeller, Sr*. New York: Random House, 1998.

Chesnutt, Charles. *Mandy Oxendine*. Edited by Charles Hackenberry. Urbana: University of Illinois Press, 1997.

Chesnutt, Charles. "The March of Progress." In *Charles W. Chesnutt: Stories, Novels, and Essays*, edited by Werner Sollors, 770–81. New York: Library of America, 2002.

"Chicago's Hull House Gives Way for College." *Los Angeles Times* (April 12, 1963): 13.

Child, Brenda J. *Boarding School Seasons: American Indian Families 1900–1940*. Lincoln: University of Nebraska Press, 1998.

Churchill, Ward. *Kill the Indian, Save the Man: The Genocidal Impact of American Indian Residential Schools*. San Francisco: City Lights Books, 2004.

Clark, Carol Lea. "Charles A. Eastman (Ohiyesa) and Elaine Goodale Eastman: A Cross-Cultural Collaboration." *Tulsa Studies in Women's Literature* 13, no. 2 (1994): 271–80.

Clement, Arthur J., and Arthur J. Lidsky. "The Danger of History Slipping Away: The Heritage Campus and HBCUs." *Planning for Higher Education* (2011): 149–58.

Cobb, Amanda J. *Listening to Our Grandmothers' Stories: The Bloomfield Academy for Chickasaw Females, 1852–1940*. Lincoln: University of Nebraska Press, 2000.

Coleman, Michael C. *American Indian Children at School, 1850–1930*. Jackson: University Press of Mississippi, 1993.

Condé, Maryse. *I, Tituba, Black Witch of Salem*. Translated by Richard Philcox. Charlottesville: University of Virginia Press, 1992.

Conley, Robert J. *Mountain Windsong: A Novel of the Trail of Tears*. Norman: University of Oklahoma Press, 1992.

Conn, Steven. *Do Museums Still Need Objects?* Philadelphia: University of Pennsylvania Press, 2010.

Cook, Jessie W. "The Representative Indian." *Outlook* 65, no. 1 (1900): 80–83.

Cooper, Anna Julia. *A Voice from the South. By a Black Woman of the South.* Xenia, OH: Aldine Printing House, 1892.

Cooper, David D. *Learning in the Plural: Essays on the Humanities and Public Life.* East Lansing: Michigan State University Press, 2014.

Cordery, Stacy A. *Juliette Gordon Low: The Remarkable Founder of the Girl Scouts.* New York: Penguin, 2012.

Coward, John M. *The Newspaper Indian: Native American Identity in the Press, 1820–90.* Urbana: University of Illinois Press, 1999.

Culbertson, Graham. "Jane Addams's Progressive Democracy: Hull-House and the Ethics of Reform." *Soundings: An Interdisciplinary Journal* 95, no. 1 (2012): 24–46.

Cunningham, Craig A., et al. "Dewey, Women, and Weirdoes: Or, the Potential Rewards for Scholars Who Dialogue across Difference." *Education and Culture* 23, no. 2 (2007): 27–62.

Cutter, Martha. "Zitkala-Ša's Autobiographical Writings: The Problems of a Canonical Search for Language and Identity in Native American Writing." *MELUS* 19 (1994): 31–44.

Danisch, Robert. "Jane Addams, Pragmatism and Rhetorical Citizenship in Multicultural Democracies." In *Citizens of the World: Pluralism, Migration, and Practices of Citizenship*, edited by Robert Danisch, 37–60. New York: Rodopi, 2011.

Davis, Christina L. "Reconstructing Black Education: Teachers' Impact on Student Learning in the Post-Bellum South." Phd Diss., University of Georgia, 2015.

De Certeau, Michel. *The Practice of Everyday Life.* Translated by Steven F. Rendall. Berkeley: University of California Press, 1988.

Deegan, Mary Jo. "Jane Addams on Citizenship in a Democracy." *Journal of Classical Sociology* 10, no. 3 (2010): 217–38.

Dejong, David H. "'Unless They Are Kept Alive': Federal Indian Schools and Student Health, 1878–1918." *American Indian Quarterly* 31, no. 2 (2007): 256–82.

Deloria, Ella Cara. *Speaking of Indians.* Lincoln: University of Nebraska Press, 1998.

Deloria, Ella Cara. *Waterlily.* Lincoln: University of Nebraska Press, 1988.

Deloria, Philip J. *Indians in Unexpected Places.* Lawrence: University Press of Kansas, 2004.

Deloria, Philip J. *Playing Indian.* New Haven: Yale University Press, 1998.

Denzin, Norman K. *Interpretive Autoethnography.* 2nd ed. Thousand Oaks, CA: SAGE, 2014.

DeStigter, Todd. "In Good Company: Jane Addams's Democratic Experimentalism." In *Jane Addams in the Classroom*, edited by David Schaafsma, 7–31. Urbana: University of Illinois Press, 2014.

DeStigter, Todd. *Reflections of a Citizen Teacher: Literacy, Democracy, and the Forgotten Students of Addison High.* Urbana, IL: NCTE, 2001.

Deutsch, James I. "Harvest of Loneliness—Review." *The Journal of American History* 98, no. 3 (December 2011): 944–45.

Diliberto, Gioia. *A Useful Woman: The Early Life of Jane Addams.* New York: Scribner, 1999.

Donovan, Roxanne. "Tough or Tender: (Dis)Similarities in White College Students' Perceptions of Black and White Women." *Psychology of Women Quarterly* 35, no. 3 (2011): 458–63.

Dorsey, Allison. *To Build Our Lives Together: Community Formation in Black Atlanta, 1875–1906*. Athens, GA: University of Georgia Press, 2004.

Du Bois, W. E. Burghardt. *The Souls of Black Folk: Essays and Sketches*. Chicago: A. C. McClurg, 1903.

Duffy, William. "Remembering Is the Remedy: Jane Addams's Response to Conflicted Discourse." *Rhetoric Review* 30, no. 2 (2011): 135–52.

Dunch, Ryan. "Beyond Cultural Imperialism: Cultural Theory, Christian Missions, and Global Modernity." *History and Theory* 41, no. 3 (2002): 301–25.

Duran, Jane. "Ellen Gates Starr and Julia Lathrop: Hull House and Philosophy." *The Pluralist* 9, no. 1 (Spring 2014): 1–13.

Eastman, Charles A. [*Memories of an*] *Indian Boyhood*. New York: McClure Philips, 1902.

Eastman, Charles A. (Ohiyesa). *From the Deep Woods to Civilization: Chapters in the Autobiography of an Indian*. Boston: Little, Brown, and Company, 1916.

Eastman, Elaine Goodale (Mrs. Charles Alexander Eastman). "Collier Indian Plan Held Backward Step: Instead of Helping the Red Man to Stand on His Own Feet, It Is Seen as Handicapping Him." *The New York Times* (June 3, 1934): E5.

Eastman, Elaine Goodale (Mrs. Charles Alexander Eastman). "From Washington." *Advance* 35, no. 1679 (January 13, 1898): 47.

Eastman, Elaine Goodale (Mrs. Charles Alexander Eastman). "A New Day for the Indian: Commencement at Carlisle School." *New York Evangelist* 71, no. 14 (April 5, 1900): 19.

Eastman, Elaine Goodale (Mrs. Charles Alexander Eastman). "A New Method of Indian Education." *Outlook* 64, no. 4 (January 27, 1900): 222.

Eastman, Elaine Goodale (Mrs. Charles Alexander Eastman). *Pratt: The Red Man's Moses*. Norman: University of Oklahoma Press, 1935.

Eastman, Elaine Goodale (Mrs. Charles Alexander Eastman). "Reviving Indian Customs." *The New York Times* (November 4, 1934): E5.

Eastman, Elaine Goodale. *Sister to the Sioux: The Memoirs of Elaine Goodale Eastman, 1885–1891*. Edited by Kay Graber. With an Introduction by Theodore D. Sargent. Lincoln: University of Nebraska Press, 2004.

Eastman, Elaine Goodale (Mrs. Charles Alexander Eastman). *The Voice at Eve*. Chicago: The Bookfellows, 1930.

Eastman, Elaine Goodale (Mrs. Charles Alexander Eastman). *Yellow Star: A Story of East and West*. 1911. Reprint. Boston: Little, Brown, 1931.

Ede, Lisa, and Andrea A. Lunsford. "Collaboration and Concepts of Authorship." *PMLA* 116, no. 2 (2001): 354–69.

"Educating the Indians—Scenes at the Government Training School at Carlisle, Pa.—From Photographs and Sketches by Joseph Becker" [illustration/figure]. *Frank Leslie's Illustrated Newspaper* (March 15, 1884): 56–57

Eisner, Elliot. "What Education Can Learn from the Arts." *Arts Education* 62, no. 2 (2009): 6–9.

"Elaine Goodale Eastman." *Massachusetts Ploughman and New England Journal of Agriculture* 56, no. 38 (January 19, 1897): 8.

Ellinghaus, Katherine. *Taking Assimilation to Heart: Marriages of White Women and Indigenous Men in the United States and Australia, 1887–1937*. Lincoln: University of Nebraska Press, 2006.

Elliott, Michael A. *Custerology: The Enduring Legacy of the Indian Wars and George Armstrong Custer*. Chicago: University of Chicago Press, 2008.

Ellis, Carolyn. *The Ethnographic I: A Methodological Novel About Autoethnography*. Walnut Creek, CA: AltaMira Press, 2003.

Ellis, Clyde. "'A Remedy for Barbarism': Indian Schools, the Civilizing Program, and the Kiowa-Comanche-Apache Reservation, 1871–1915." *American Indian Culture and Research Journal* 18, no. 3 (1994): 85–120.

Ellison, Julie. "Guest Column: The New Public Humanists." *PMLA* 128, no. 2 (2013): 289–98.

Ellison, Julie, and Timothy K. Eatman. *Scholarship in Public: Knowledge Creation and Tenure Policy in the Engaged University*. Edited by Imagining America. Syracuse, NY: Imagining America, 2008.

Elshtain, Jean Bethke. *Jane Addams and the Dream of American Democracy*. New York: Basic Books, 2002.

Elshtain, Jean Bethke, ed. *The Jane Addams Reader*. New York: Basic Books, 2002.

Engs, Robert Francis. *Educating the Disfranchised and Disinherited: Samuel Chapman Armstrong and Hampton Institute, 1839–1893*. Knoxville: University of Tennessee Press, 1999.

Enoch, Jessica. *Refiguring Rhetorical Education: Women Teaching African American, Native American, and Chicano/a Students, 1865–1911*. Carbondale: Southern Illinois University Press, 2008.

Enoch, Jessica. "Resisting the Script of Indian Education: Zitkala-Ša and the Carlisle Indian School." *College English* 65, no. 2 (2002): 117–41.

Erdrich, Heid E. *National Monuments*. East Lansing: Michigan State University Press, 2008.

Erdrich, Louise. "Indian Boarding School: The Runaways." In *Jacklight: Poems*, 11. New York: Henry Holt, 1984.

Erdrich, Louise. *The Round House: A Novel*. New York: Harper 2012.

Ernest, John. *Chaotic Justice: Rethinking American Literary History*. Chapel Hill: University of North Carolina Press, 2009.

Ette, Ottmar. Translated by Vera M. Kutzinski. "Literature as Knowledge for Living, Literary Studies as Science for Living." *PMLA* 125, no. 4 (2010): 977–93.

Evelyn, Douglas E. "A Most Beautiful Sight Presented Itself to My View." In *Spirit of a Native Place: Building the National Museum of the American Indian*, edited by Duane Blue Spruce, 151–83. Washington, DC: NMAI and National Geographic, 2004.

Everett, Percival. *Erasure*. Hanover, NH: University Press of New England, 2001.

Fagan, Benjamin. *The Black Newspaper and the Chosen Nation*. Athens: University of Georgia Press, 2016.

Feigenbaum, Paul. *Collaborative Imagination: Earning Activism through Literacy Education*. Carbondale: Southern Illinois University Press, 2015.

Feld, Rose C. "Jane Addams Wrote This Biography of Julia Lathrop." *The New York Times Book Review* (December 8, 1935): BR4.

"A Fifth Generation: The Quarles Family." *Spelman Messenger* (Spring 2012): 12.

Fischer, Marilyn. "Addams's Internationalist Pacifism and the Rhetoric of Maternalism." *National Women's Studies Association Journal* 18, no. 3 (2006): 1–19.

Fish, Stanley. *Save the World on Your Own Time*. New York: Oxford, 2008.

Fisher, Dexter. "Zitkala-Ša: The Evolution of a Writer." *American Indian Quarterly* 5, no. 3 (1979): 229–38.

Fisher, Laura L. "Writing Immigrant Aid: The Settlement House and the Problem of Representation." *MELUS: Multi-Ethnic Literature of the U.S.* 37, no. 2 (2012): 83–107.

Fishkin, Shelley Fisher. *Writing America: Literary Landmarks from Walden Pond to Wounded Knee, A Reader's Companion*. New Brunswick, NJ: Rutgers University Press, 2015.

Foner, Eric. *A Short History of Reconstruction, Updated Edition*. New York: Harper Perennial Modern Classics, 2015.

Foreman, P. Gabrielle. "The *Christian Recorder*, Broken Families and Educated Nations: Julia Collins' Civil War Novel *The Curse of Caste*." *African American Review* 40, no. 4 (2006): 705–16.

Forten, Charlotte. "Life on the Sea Islands." *Atlantic Monthly* (May 1864): 587–96.

Fortunate Eagle, Adam. *Pipestone: My Life in an Indian Boarding School*. Norman: University of Oklahoma Press, 2010.

Foster, Frances Smith, ed. *A Brighter Coming Day: A Frances Ellen Watkins Harper Reader*. New York: Feminist Press, 1993.

Foster, Frances Smith, ed. *Love and Marriage in Early African America*. Boston: Northeastern University Press, 2007.

Foster, Frances Smith,. "Resisting *Incidents*." In *Harriet Jacobs and Incidents in the Life of a Slave Girl: New Critical Essays*, edited by Deborah M. Garfield and Rafia Zafar, 57–75. Cambridge: Cambridge University Press, 1996.

Foster, Frances Smith. *Written by Herself: Literary Production by African American Women, 1746–1892*. Bloomington: Indiana University Press, 1993.

Foucault, Michel. *Discipline and Punish: The Birth of the Prison*. Translated by Alan Sheridan. New York: Vintage, 1995.

Fox, Pamela Carmelle. *Robert J. Conley's* Mountain Windsong*: Tribally-Specific Historical Fiction*. Bakersfield, CA: Kemama Publishing, 2013.

Freire, Paulo. *Education for Critical Consciousness*. 1974. Reprint. New York: Bloomsbury Academic, 2013.

Freire, Paulo. *Pedagogy of the Oppressed: 30th Anniversary Edition*. 1970. Translated by Myra Bergman Ramos. Reprint. New York: Bloomsbury, 2014.

García, Jennifer Jee-Lyn, and Mienah Zulfacar Sharif. "Black Lives Matter: A Commentary on Racism and Public Health." *American Journal of Public Health* 105, no. 8 (2015): E27-E30.

Gardner, Eric. *Black Print Unbound: The* Christian Recorder, *African American Literature, and Periodical Culture*. New York: Oxford University Press, 2015.

Gardner, Eric. "Remembered (Black) Readers: Subscribers to the *Christian Recorder*, 1846–1865." *American Literary History* 23, no. 2 (2011): 229–59.

Gardner, Eric. *Unexpected Places: Relocating Nineteenth-Century African American Literature*. Jackson: University Press of Mississippi, 2011.

Gardner, Susan. Introduction to *Waterlily*, by Ella Cara Deloria. Lincoln: University of Nebraska Press, 1988.

Garibaldi, Antoine M. "The Expanding Gender and Racial Gap in American Higher Education." *The Journal of Negro Education* 83, no. 3 (2014): 371–84.

Gaul, Theresa Strouth, ed. *Cherokee Sister: The Collected Writings of Catharine Brown, 1818–1823*. Lincoln: University of Nebraska Press, 2014.

Gearan, Mark D. "Engaging Communities: The Campus Compact Model." *National Civic Review* 94, no. 2 (2005): 32–40.

Gere, Anne Ruggles. "An Art of Survivance: Angel DeCora at Carlisle." *American Indian Quarterly* 28, nos. 3 and 4 (2004): 649–84.

Gere, Anne Ruggles. "Indian Heart/White Man's Head: Native-American Teachers in Indian Schools, 1880–1930." *History of Education Society* 45, no. 1 (2005): 38–65.

Gere, Anne Ruggles, and Peter Shaheen, eds. *Making American Literatures in High School and College*. Urbana, IL: NCTE, 2001.

Gere, Anne Ruggles, and Sarah Robbins. "Gendered Literacy in Black and White: Turn-of-the-Century African-American and European-American Club Women's Printed Texts." *Signs* 21, no. 3 (1996): 643–78.

Gilyard, Keith, and Steven Mailloux. "Conversation with Steven Mailloux." In *Conversations in Cultural Rhetoric and Composition Studies*, edited by Keith Gilyard and Victor E. Taylor, 29–51. Aurora, CO: The Davies Group, 2010.

Gilyard, Keith, and Victor E. Taylor, eds. *Conversations in Cultural Rhetoric and Composition Studies*. Aurora, CO: The Davies Group, 2010.

Giroux, Henry A., Colin Lankshear, Peter McLaren, and Michael Peters. *Counternarratives: Cultural Studies and Critical Pedagogies in Postmodern Spaces*. New York: Routledge, 1996.

Glancy, Diane. *Designs of the Night Sky*. Lincoln: University of Nebraska Press, 2002.

Glancy, Diane. *Pushing the Bear: After the Trail of Tears*. Norman: University of Oklahoma Press, 2009.

Glancy, Diane. *Pushing the Bear: A Novel of the Trail of Tears*. New York: Harcourt Brace and Co., 1996.

Glancy, Diane. *The Reason for Crows: A Story of Kateri Tekakwitha*. Albany: State University of New York Press, 2009.

Glancy, Diane. *Stone Heart: A Novel of Sacajawea*. New York: Overlook Press, 2004.

Glenn, Charles Leslie. *American Indian/First Nations Schooling from the Colonial Period to the Present*. New York: Palgrave Macmillan, 2011.

Glenn, Cheryl, and Jessica Enoch. "Drama in the Archives: Rereading Methods, Rewriting History." *College Composition and Communication* 61, no. 2 (2009): 321–42.

Gonzalez, Gilbert G., and Vivian Price, directors. *Harvest of Loneliness*. Films Media Group, 2010.

Goodale, Elaine. "Carlisle: The Inlook and Outlook Upon Indian Progress." *The Independent* (June 4, 1884): 3.

Goodale, Elaine. "The Indian at Work: Industrial Training in Schools." *New York Evangelist* (September 10, 1885): 1.

Goodale, Elaine, and Helen W. Ludlow. *Captain Pratt and His Work for Indian Education*. Philadelphia: Indian Rights Association, 1886.

Gordon, Nora. "Africa: The Congo Mission." *Baptist Missionary Magazine* (January 1892): 26.

Gould, Janice. "Telling Stories to the Seventh Generation: Resisting the Assimilationist Narrative of *Stiya*." In *Reading Native American Women: Critical/Creative Representations*, edited by Inés Hernández-Avilia, 9–20. Lanham, MD: AltaMira Press, 2005.

Green, Kenneth, producer. *Founders Day 2011; Spelman College: Celebrating the 130th Year*. DVD. April 11, 2011.

Grewal, Inderpal. *Transnational America: Feminisms, Diasporas, Neoliberalisms*. Durham, NC: Duke University Press.

Grewal, Inderpal, and Caren Kaplan. *An Introduction to Women's Studies: Gender in a Transnational World*. 2nd ed. New York: McGraw-Hill, 2005.

Gubele, Rose. "Unlearning the Pictures in Our Heads: Teaching the Cherokee Phoenix, Boudinot, and Cherokee History." In *Survivance, Sovereignty, and Story: Teaching American Indian Rhetorics*, edited by Lisa King, Rose Gubele, and Joyce Rain Anderson, 96–115. Logan: Utah State University Press, 2015.

Guillory, John. *Cultural Capital: The Problem of Literary Canon Formation*. Chicago: University of Chicago Press, 1995.

Guy-Sheftall, Beverly. "Black Women and Higher Education: Spelman and Bennett Colleges Revisited." *Journal of Negro Education* 51, no. 3 (1982): 278–87.

Guy-Sheftall, Beverly. *Daughters of Sorrow: Attitudes toward Black Women, 1880–1920*. New York: Carlson Publishing, 1990.

Guy-Sheftall, Beverly, and Kimberly Wallace-Sanders. "Educating Black Women Students for the Multicultural Future." *Signs* 22, no. 1 (1996): 210–13.

Haas, Angela M. "Wampum as Hypertext: An American Indian Intellectual Tradition of Multimedia Theory and Practice." *Studies in American Indian Literatures* 19, no. 4 (2007): 77–100.

Hall, Nicholas Sean. "The Wasp's 'Troublesome Children.' Culture, Satire, and the Anti-Chinese Movement in the American West." *California History* 90, no. 2 (2013): 42–63.

Hamby, Patsy. "Uncovering a Region's Past to Build a Community Today: Collaborative Learning About Cherokee Heritage." In *Writing America: Classroom Literacy and Public Engagement*, edited by Sarah Robbins and Mimi Dyer, 64–73. New York: Teachers College Press, 2004.

Hamilton, Alice. *Exploring the Dangerous Trades: The Autobiography of Alice Hamilton, M.D., with Illustrations by Norah Hamilton*. Boston: Little, Brown, 1943. Reprint, Beverly, CA: OEM Press, 1995.

Hamington, Maurice. "Community Organizing: Addams and Alinsky." In *Feminist Interpretations of Jane Addams*, edited by Maurice Hamington, 255–74. University Park, PA: Pennsylvania State University Press, 2010.

Hamington, Maurice, ed. *Feminist Interpretations of Jane Addams*. University Park: Pennsylvania State University Press, 2010.

Hamington, Maurice. *The Social Philosophy of Jane Addams*. Urbana: University of Illinois Press, 2009.

Hampton Institute. *Twenty-Two Years' Work of the Hampton Normal and Agricultural Institute at Hampton, Virginia. Records of Negro and Indian Graduates and Ex-Students. Illustrated with Views and Maps*. Hampton, VA: Normal School Press, 1893.

Handler, Richard, and Eric Gable. *The New History in an Old Museum: Creating the Past at Colonial Williamsburg*. Durham, NC: Duke University Press, 1997.

Harkavy, Ira, and John L. Puckett. "Lessons from Hull House for the Contemporary Urban University." *Social Service Review* 68, no. 3 (1994): 299–321.

Harper, Frances. "Learning to Read." In *A Brighter Coming Day: A Frances Ellen Watkins Harper Reader*, edited by Frances Smith Foster, 205. New York: Feminist Press, 1993.

Harper, Frances. *Minnie's Sacrifice, Sowing and Reaping, Trial and Triumph: Three Rediscovered Novels by Frances Harper*. Edited by Frances Smith Foster. Boston: Beacon Press, 2000.

Harris, Dee A. "Re-Defining Democracy: Jane Addams and the Hull-House Settlement." *The Public Historian* 33, no. 2 (2011): 171–74.

Harris, Susan K. *God's Arbiters: Americans and the Philippines, 1898–1902*. Oxford: Oxford University Press, 2011.

Harrison, Jonathan Baxter. *The Latest Studies of Indian Reservations*. Philadelphia: Indian Rights Association, 1887.

Hauptman, Laurence M. Afterword to *Pipestone: My Life in an Indian Boarding School*, by Adam Fortunate Eagle, 171–86. Stillwater: University of Oklahoma Press, 2010.

Hawkins, Billy. *The New Plantation: Black Athletes, College Sports, and Predominantly White NCAA Institutions*. New York: Palgrave Macmillan, 2010.

Haygood, Atticus. *Our Brother in Black: His Freedom and His Future*. New York: Phillips & Hunt, 1881.

Haygood, Atticus, and Rutherford B. Hayes. "Spelman Seminary." Atlanta: Spelman Seminary Press, 1888.

Hecht, Stuart J. "Edith De Nancrede at Hull-House: Theatre Programs for Youth." *Youth Theatre Journal* 6, no. 1 (1991): 3–10.

Hecht, Stuart J. "Social and Artistic Integration." *Theatre Journal* 34, no. 2 (1982): 172–82.

Hegar, Rebecca L. "Transatlantic Transfers in Social Work: Contributions of Three Pioneers." *British Journal of Social Work* 38, no. 1 (2008): 716–33.

Higginbotham, Evelyn Brooks. *Righteous Discontent: The Women's Movement in the Black Baptist Church, 1880–1920*. Cambridge, MA: Harvard University Press, 1993.

Hill, Errol G., and James V. Hatch. *A History of African American Theatre*. Cambridge: Cambridge University Press, 2003.

Hill, Shirley A. "Cultural Images and the Health of African American Women." *Gender & Society* 23, no. 6 (2009): 733–46.

Hirsch, E. D. *Cultural Literacy: What Every American Needs to Know*. New York: Vintage Books/Random House, 1988.

hooks, bell. *Teaching Community: A Pedagogy of Hope*. New York: Routledge, 2003.

hooks, bell. *Teaching to Transgress: Education as the Practice of Freedom*. New York: Routledge, 1994.

Hoover, Jessica Safran. "Rhetorical Sovereignty in Written Poetry: Survivance through Code-Switching and Translation in Laura Tohe's *Tséyí/Deep in the Rock: Reflections on Canyon de Chelly*." In *Survivance, Sovereignty, and Story: Teaching American Indian Rhetorics*, edited by Lisa King, Rose Gubele, and Joyce Rain Anderson, 170–87. Logan: Utah State University Press, 2015.

Horne, Esther Burnett, and Sally McBeth. *Essie's Story: The Life and Legacy of a Shoshone Teacher*. Lincoln: University of Nebraska Press, 1998.

Horse Capture, George. "The Way of the People." In *Spirit of a Native Place: Building the National Museum of the American Indian*, edited by Duane Blue Spruce, 30–45. Washington, DC: NMAI and National Geographic, 2004.

Hoxie, Frederick E. *A Final Promise: The Campaign to Assimilate the Indians, 1880–1920*. Lincoln: University of Nebraska Press, 2001.

Hucks, Darrell Cleveland, Kenneth Fasching-Varner, and Marcelle M. Haddix. "Teaching Trayvon Martin and Black Lives Matter: Resources for Education." *Journal of Adolescent & Adult Literacy* 58, no. 7 (2015): 608–10.

Hunter, Tera W. *To 'Joy My Freedom: Southern Black Women's Lives and Labors after the Civil War*. Cambridge, MA: Harvard University Press, 1998.

"In the Conjuncture: For Michael Brown." *Cultural Critique* 90 (2015): 115–17.

"The Indian Training School at Carlisle, PA." *Frank Leslie's Illustrated Magazine* (March 15, 1884): 59.

"The Indians' Friend: PRATT, THE RED MAN'S MOSES. By Elaine Goodale Eastman." *The New York Times Book Review* (December 1, 1935): BR 26.

Isaac, Gweneira. "What Are Our Expectations Telling Us?: Encounters with the National Museum of the American Indian." In *The National Museum of the American Indian: Critical Conversations*, edited by Amy Lonetree and Amanda J. Cobb, 241–66. Lincoln: University of Nebraska Press, 2008.

J. H. M. "The Hampton Institute." *The Unitarian Review and Religious Magazine* (April 1877): 4, 7.

Jack, Jordynn. "'Exceptional Women': Epideictic Rhetoric and Women Scientists." In *Women and Rhetoric between the Wars*, edited by M. Elizabeth Weiser, Anne George, and Janet Zepernick, 223–39. Carbondale: Southern Illinois University Press, 2013.

Jacknis, Ira. "A New Thing?: The National Museum of the American Indian in Historical and Institutional Context." In *The National Museum of the American Indian: Critical Conversations*, edited by Amy Lonetree and Amanda J. Cobb, 3–42. Lincoln: University of Nebraska Press, 2008.

Jackson, Shannon. *Lines of Activity: Performance, Historiography, Hull-House Domesticity*. Ann Arbor: University of Michigan Press, 2003.

Jacobs, Margaret D. *White Mother to a Dark Race: Settler Colonialism, Maternalism,*

*and the Removal of Indigenous Children in the American West and Australia, 1880–
1940*. Lincoln: University of Nebraska Press, 2009.

Jacobson, Lisa. "Review Roundtable: The National Museum of the American Indian." *The Public Historian* 28, no. 2 (2006): 47–49.

Jarvis, Ida V. *Texas Poems*. Nashville, TN: Gospel Advocate Publishing, 1893.

Jiménez, Francisco. *The Circuit: Stories from the Life of a Migrant Child*. New York: Houghton Mifflin, 1999.

Johnson, Devon, Patricia Y. Warren, and Amy Farrell, eds. *Deadly Injustice: Trayvon Martin, Race, and the Criminal Justice System*. New York: NYU Press, 2015.

Johnson, E. Patrick. *Appropriating Blackness: Performance and the Politics of Authenticity*. Durham, NC: Duke University Press, 2003.

Johnston, Frances B. *The Hampton Album: 44 Photographs by Frances B. Johnston from an Album of Hampton Institute with an Introduction and a Note of the Photographer by Lincoln Kirstein*. New York: Museum of Modern Art, 1966.

Jonaitis, Aldona, and Janet Catherin Berlo. "'Indian Country' on the National Mall: The Mainstream Press Versus the National Museum of the American Indian." In *The National Museum of the American Indian: Critical Conversations*, edited by Amy Lonetree and Amanda J. Cobb, 208–40. Lincoln: University of Nebraska Press, 2008.

Jones, Jacqueline. *Soldiers of Light and Love: Northern Teachers and Georgia Blacks, 1865–1873*. Chapel Hill: University of North Carolina Press, 1980.

Jonsberg, Sara Dalmas. "Yankee Schoolmarms in the South: Models or Monsters?" *The English Journal* 91, no. 4 (2002): 75–81.

Joslin, Katherine. *Jane Addams, A Writer's Life*. Urbana: University of Illinois Press, 2004.

Juliette Gordon Low Birthplace. "Girls Writing the World: A Library Re-Imagined. Excellence in Exhibition—Brief Explanation of the Exhibit." Unpublished two-page exhibit overview, Savannah, GA: JGLB, 2016.

Junkin, Lisa. "Sex in the Museum: Building Relationships and Pushing Boundaries at Jane Addams' Hull-House Museum." In *The Radical Museum: Democracy, Dialogue & Debate*, edited by Gregory Chamberlain, 135–49. London, United Kingdom: Museum Identity, 2011.

Kaag, John Jacob. "Pragmatism and the Lessons of Experience." *Dedalus* 138, no. 2 (2009): 63–72.

Karttunen, Frances. *Between Worlds: Interpreters, Guides, and Survivors*. New Brunswick, NJ: Rutgers University Press, 1994.

Katanski, Amelia V. *Learning to Write "Indian": The Boarding-School Experience and American Indian Literature*. Norman: University of Oklahoma Press, 2005.

Kelland, Laura. "Exhibition Review: 'Re-Defining Democracy and the Hull-House Settlement.'" *Journal of American History* 98, no. 3 (2011): 782–86.

Kelley, Florence. *The Autobiography of Florence Kelley: Notes of Sixty Years. Edited and Introduced by Kathryn Kish Sklar*. Chicago: Charles H. Kerr, 1986.

King, Lisa. "Rhetorical Sovereignty and Rhetorical Alliance in the Writing Classroom: Using American Indian Texts." *Pedagogy* 12, no. 2 (2012): 209–33.

King, Lisa. "Sovereignty, Rhetorical Sovereignty, and Representation: Keywords for Teaching Indigenous Texts." In *Survivance, Sovereignty, and Story: Teaching American Indian Rhetorics*, edited by Lisa King, Rose Gubele, and Joyce Rain Anderson, 17–34. Logan: Utah State University Press, 2015.

King, Lisa, Rose Gubele, and Joyce Rain Anderson. "Introduction—Careful with the Stories We Tell: Naming Survivance, Sovereignty, and Story." In *Survivance, Sovereignty, and Story: Teaching American Indian Rhetorics*, edited by Lisa King, Rose Gubele, and Joyce Rain Anderson, 3–16. Logan: Utah State University Press, 2015.

King, Lisa, Rose Gubele, and Joyce Rain Anderson, eds. *Survivance, Sovereignty, and Story: Teaching American Indian Rhetorics*. Logan: Utah State University Press, 2015.

King, Thomas. *The Truth About Stories: A Native Narrative*. Minneapolis: University of Minnesota Press, 2005.

Kirsch, Gesa E. "Being on Location: Serendipity, Place, and Archival Research." In *Beyond the Archives: Research as a Lived Process*, edited by Gesa E. Kirsch and Liz Rohan, 20–27. Carbondale: Southern Illinois University Press, 2008.

Klosterman, Eleanor M., and Dorothy C. Stratton. "Speaking Truth to Power: Jane Addams's Values Base for Peacemaking." *Affilia: Journal of Women and Social Work* 21, no. 2 (2006): 158–68.

Knight, Louise W. *Citizen: Jane Addams and the Struggle for Democracy*. Chicago: University of Chicago Press, 2008.

Knight, Louise W. *Jane Addams: Spirit in Action*. New York: W. W. Norton, 2010.

Krupat, Arnold. *Red Matters: Native American Studies*. Philadelphia: University of Pennsylvania Press, 2002.

Kunce, Catherine. "Fire of Eden: Zitkala-Ša's Bitter Apple." *Studies in American Indian Literatures* 18, no. 1 (2006): 73–82.

Kuokkanen, Rauna. "'Survivance' in Sami and First Nations Boarding School Narratives: Reading Novels by Kerttu Vuolab and Shirley Sterling." *American Indian Quarterly* 27, nos. 3 and 4 (2003): 697–726.

Laderman, Scott. "'It Is Cheaper and Better to Teach a Young Indian Than to Fight an Old One': Thaddeus Pound and the Logic of Assimilation." *American Indian Culture and Research Journal* 26, no. 3 (2002): 85–111.

La Flesche, Francis (Omaha). *The Middle Five: Indian Boys at School*. Boston: Small, Maynard, and Company, 1909.

Laird, Holly A. *Women Coauthors*. Urbana: University of Illinois Press, 2000.

Lajimodiere, Denise. "A Healing Journey." *Wicazo Sa Review* 27, no. 2 (Fall 2012): 5–19.

Lake, Danielle. "Jane Addams and Wicked Problems: Putting the Pragmatic Method to Use." *The Pluralist* 9, no. 3 (2014): 77–94.

Lee, Kimberli. "Heartspeak from the Spirit: Songs of John Trudell, Keith Secola, and Robbie Robertson." In *Survivance, Sovereignty, and Story: Teaching American Indian Rhetorics*, edited by Lisa King, Rose Gubele, and Joyce Rain Anderson, 116–37. Logan: Utah State University Press, 2015.

Lee, Lisa Yun. "Hungry for Peace: Jane Addams and the Hull-House Museum's Contemporary Struggle for Food Justice." *Peace & Change* 36, no. 1 (2011): 62–79.

Lee, Lisa Yun. "Peering into the Bedroom: Restorative Justice at the Jane Addams Hull House Museum." In *The Routledge Companion to Museum Ethics: Redefining Ethics for the Twenty-First Century Museum*, edited by Janet Marstine, 174–87. New York: Routledge, 2011.

Lee, Lisa Yun, and Lisa Junkin Lopez. "Participating in History: The Museum as a Site for Radical Empathy, Hull-House." In *Jane Addams in the Classroom*, edited by David Schaafsma, 162–78. Urbana: University of Illinois Press, 2014.

Lefever, Harry G. "The Early Origins of Spelman College." *The Journal of Blacks in Higher Education*, no. 47 (2005): 60–63.

Legend, John, and Common, performers. "Glory, from the album *Selma*," Columbia Records, 2014. Produced by John Legend. Written by John Stephens, Lonnie Lynn, and Che Smith.

Lewis, Keevin. "Introduction." *Native Artists in the Americas: National Museum of the American Indian Native Arts Program: The First Ten Years*. Washington, DC: National Museum of the American Indian, Smithsonian Institution, 2007. 4–7. Museum Brochure.

Linder, Rozlyn. *The Common Core Guidebook: Informational Text Lessons 3–5*. Atlanta: The Literacy Initiative, 2013.

Liu, Yameng. "Rhetoric and Reflexivity." *Philosophy and Rhetoric* 28, no. 4 (1995): 333–49.

Lomawaima, K. Tsianina. *They Called It Prairie Light: The Story of Chilocco Indian School*. Lincoln: University of Nebraska Press, 1995.

Lomawaima, K. Tsianina, and Teresa L. McCarty. *To Remain an Indian: Lessons in Democracy from a Century of Native Education*. New York: Teachers College Press, 2006.

Lonetree, Amy. "Missed Opportunities: Reflections on the NMAI." *American Indian Quarterly* 30, no. 3–4 (2006): 632–45.

Ludlow, Helen W., and Elaine Goodale. "Captain Pratt and His Work for Indian Education." Philadelphia: Indian Rights Association, 1886.

Lunsford, Andrea A., and Lisa Ede. *Singular Texts/Plural Authors: Perspectives on Collaborative Writing*. Carbondale: Southern Illinois University Press, 1990.

Lunsford, Andrea A., and Lisa Ede. *Writing Together: Collaboration in Theory and Practice*. New York: Bedford/St. Martin's, 2011.

Lyons, Scott Richard. "Rhetorical Sovereignty: What Do American Indians Want from Writing?" *CCC: College Composition and Communication* 51, no. 3 (2000): 447–68.

Mailloux, Steven. *Disciplinary Identities: Rhetorical Paths of English, Speech, and Composition*. New York: MLA, 2006.

Mailloux, Steven. "Practices, Theories, and Traditions: Further Thoughts on the Disciplinary Identities of English and Communication Studies." *Rhetoric Society Quarterly* 33, no. 1 (2003): 129–38.

Mandziuk, Roseann M., and Suzanne Pullon Fitch. "The Rhetorical Construction of Sojourner Truth." *Southern Communication Journal* 66, no. 2 (2009): 120–38.

Mansfield, Harvey. "Give Michelle Obama a Break." *Wall Street Journal* (May 20, 2015): A13.

Martin, Sandy D. "Spelman's Emma B. Delaney and the African Mission." In *This

Far by Faith: Readings in African-American Women's Religious Biography, edited by Judith and Richard Newman Weisenfeld, 220–35. New York: Routledge, 1996.

Mathes, Valerie Sherer. "Helen Hunt Jackson as Power Broker." In *Between Indian and White Worlds: The Cultural Broker*, edited by Margaret Connell Szasz, 141–57. Norman: University of Oklahoma Press, 1994.

Mauro, Hayes Peter. *The Art of Americanization at the Carlisle Indian School*. Albuquerque: University of New Mexico Press, 2011.

McCaskill, Barbara. *Love, Liberation, and Escaping Slavery: William and Ellen Craft in Cultural Memory*. Athens: University of Georgia Press, 2015.

McCluskey, Audrey Thomas. "'Manly Husbands and Womanly Wives': The Leadership of Educator Lucy Craft Laney." In *Post-Bellum, Pre-Harlem: African American Literature and Culture, 1877–1919*, edited by Barbara McCaskill and Carolyn Gebhard, 74–88. New York: New York University Press, 2006.

McElya, Micki. *Clinging to Mammy: The Faithful Slave in Twentieth-Century America*. Cambridge, MA: Harvard University Press, 2007.

McKay, Neil. "The Spirit Language." In *Genocide of the Mind: New Native American Writing*, edited by MariJo Moore, 159–65. New York: Thunder Mouth Press, 2003.

"Meeting Set by 'Save Hull House' Group." *Chicago Daily Tribune* (May 23, 1961): A7.

Mihesuah, Devon A. *Cultivating the Rosebuds: The Education of Women at the Cherokee Female Seminary, 1851–1909*. Urbana: University of Illinois Press, 1997.

Miller, Shawn. *Research Is Ceremony: Indigenous Research Methods*. Winnipeg, MB: Fernwood Publishing, 2009.

Million, Dian. "Felt Theory: An Indigenous Feminist Approach to Affect and History." *Wicazo Sa Review* 24, no. 2 (2009): 53–76.

Minor, DoVeanna S. Fulton, and Reginald H. Pitts, eds. *Speaking Lives, Authoring Texts: Three African American Women's Oral Slave Narratives*. Albany: State University of New York, 2009.

Mitchell, Deborah. "Oral History Notes, KCAC Project." Unpublished research notes, 2001.

Momaday, N. Scott. *Three Plays:* The Indolent Boys, Children of the Sun, *and* The Moon in Two Windows. Norman: University of Oklahoma Press, 2007.

Moody, Joycelyn. "Frances Whipple, Elleanor Eldridge, and the Politics of Interracial Collaboration." *American Literature* 83, no. 4 (2011): 689–717.

Moody, Joycelyn, and Sarah R. Robbins. "Seeking Trust and Commitment in Women's Interracial Collaboration in the Nineteenth Century and Today." *MELUS* 38, no. 1 (2013): 50–75.

Moretti, Franco. *Distant Reading*. London: Verso, 2013.

Mott, Frank Luther. *A History of American Magazines, 1885–1905*. Cambridge, MA: Harvard University Press, 1957.

"*My Friend, Julia Lathrop* and *Jane Addams*." *Social Service Review* 10, no. 2 (1936): 350–51.

"Negro and Indian: The Hampton Institute Experiment." *The Advance* (July 2, 1891): 24.

New-England Freedmen's Aid Society. *Extracts from Letters of Teachers and Super-*

intendents of the New-England Freedmen's Aid Society. Fifth Series. Boston: John Wilson and Sons, 1864.

Ngũgĩ Wa Thiong'o. *Decolonising the Mind: The Politics of Language in African Literature.* Portsmouth, NH: Heinemann, 1986.

Ngũgĩ Wa Thiong'o. *Dreams in a Time of War: A Childhood Memoir.* New York: Anchor, 2011.

Ngũgĩ Wa Thiong'o. *Globalectics: Theory and the Politics of Knowing.* New York: Columbia University Press, 2012.

Ngũgĩ Wa Thiong'o. *In the House of the Interpreter: A Memoir.* New York: Random House, 2012.

Oakes, Leslie S., and Joni J. Young. "Accountability Re-Examined: Evidence from Hull House." *Accounting, Auditing & Accountability Journal* 29, no. 6 (2006): 765–90.

O'Brien, C. C. "'The White Women All Go for Sex': Frances Harper on Suffrage, Citizenship, and the Reconstruction South." *African American Review* 43, no. 4 (2009): 605–20.

O'Connell, Tom. "Jane Addams's Democratic Journey." *Contexts* 9, no. 4 (2010): 22–27.

Okker, Patricia. "Native American Literature and the Canon: The Case of Zitkala-Ša." In *American Realism and the Canon*, edited by Tom Quirk and Gary Scharnhorst, 87–101. Newark: University of Delaware Press, 1994.

Oread Institute. "Oread Institute for Young Ladies. Worcester, Mass." Worcester, MA: Tyler & Seagrave, 1866.

O'Rourke, Bridget K. "'To Learn from Life Itself': Jane Addams's Democratic Experimentalism." In *Jane Addams in the Classroom*, edited by David Schaafsma, 32–42. Urbana: University of Illinois Press, 2014.

Ortiz, Roxanne Dunbar. "Developing Indian Academic Professionals." *Wicazo Sa Review* 1, no. 1 (1985): 5–10.

Ostman, Heather. "Maternal Rhetoric in Jane Addams's *Twenty Years at Hull-House*." *Philological Quarterly* 85, no. 3–4 (2006): 343–70.

Pastorello, Karen. "'The Transfigured Few': Jane Addams, Bessie Abramowitz Hillman, and Immigrant Women Workers in Chicago, 1905-15." In *Jane Addams and the Practice of Democracy*, edited by Marilyn Fischer, Carol Nackenoff, and Wendy Chmielewski, 98–118. Urbana: University of Illinois Press, 2009.

Peeples, Yarbrah T. "Philanthropy and the Curriculum: The Role of Philanthropy in the Development of Curriculum at Spelman College." *International Journal of Educational Advancement* 10, no. 3 (2010): 245–60.

Penney, David W. "Scholarship for Leadership." *American Indian* (Spring 2015): 12.

Peters, Michael, and Colin Lankshear. "Introduction: Postmodern Counternarratives." In *Counternarratives: Cultural Studies and Critical Pedagogies in Postmodern Spaces*, edited by Henry A. Giroux, Colin Lankshear, Peter McLaren, and Michael Peters, 1–39. New York: Routledge, 1996.

Philipps, Dave. "Raised-Fist Photo by Black Women at West Point Spurs Inquiry." *The New York Times* (May 7, 2016): A1.

Picotte, Agnes. "Biographical Sketch of the Author." In *Waterlily*, by Ella Cara Deloria, 229–31. Lincoln: University of Nebraska Press, 1988.

Pierce, Bessie Louise. "Book Reviews: *My Friend, Julia Lathrop* by Jane Addams." *The Mississippi Valley Historical Review* 23, no. 3 (1936): 441–42.

Polacheck, Hilda Satt. *I Came a Stranger: The Story of a Hull-House Girl*. Edited by Dena J. Polacheck Epstein. Urbana: University of Illinois Press, 1991.

Powell, Malea. "Rhetorics of Survivance: How American Indians Use Writing." *CCC: College Composition and Communication* 53, no. 3 (2002): 396–434.

Pratt, Mary Louise. *Imperial Eyes: Travel Writing and Transculturation*. 2nd ed. New York: Routledge, 2008.

Pratt, Brigadeer General R[ichard] H[enry]. *The Indian Industrial School: Carlisle, Pennsylvania. Reprint of the 1908 Text with an Introduction by Robert M. Utley, Recognizing the Centennial of the Carlisle Indian School*. Carlisle, PA: Cumberland County Historical Society, 1979.

Prelli, Lawrence J. *A Rhetoric of Science: Inventing Scientific Discourse*. Columbia: University of South Carolina Press, 1989.

Pripas-Kapit, Sarah. "'We Have Lived on Broken Promises': Charles A. Eastman, Susan La Flesche Picotte, and the Politics of American Indian Assimilation During the Progressive Era." *Great Plains Quarterly* 35, no. 1 (2015): 51–78.

Rappaport, Doreen, and Zitkala-Ša. *The Flight of the Red Bird: The Life of Zitkala-Ša; Re-Created from the Writings of Zitkala-Ša and the Research of Doreen Rappaport*. New York: Puffin Books, 1999.

Ravitch, Diana. *Reign of Error: The Hoax of the Privatization Movement and the Danger to America's Public Schools*. New York: Alfred A. Knopf, 2013.

Read, Florence Matilda. *The Story of Spelman College*. Princeton: Princeton University Press, 1961.

Residents of Hull-House, A Social Settlement. *Hull-House Maps and Papers: A Presentation of Nationalities and Wages in a Congested District of Chicago*. New York: Thomas Y. Crowell, 1895.

Reyhner, Jon, and Jeanne Eder. *American Indian Education: A History*. Norman: University of Oklahoma Press, 2004.

Riley-Mukavetz, Andrea. "Towards a Cultural Rhetorics Methodology: Making Research Matter with Multi-generational Women from the Little Traverse Bay Band." *Rhetoric, Professional Communication and Globalization* 5, no. 1 (2014): 108–25.

Riley-Mukavetz, Andrea, and Malea D. Powell. "Making Native Space for Graduate Students: A Story of Indigenous Rhetorical Practice." In *Survivance, Sovereignty, and Story: Teaching American Indian Rhetorics*, edited by Lisa King, Rose Gubele, and Joyce Rain Anderson, 138–59. Logan: Utah State University Press, 2015.

Robbins, Sarah. "Gendering the Debate over African Americans' Education in the 1880s: Frances Harper's Reconfiguration of Atticus Haygood's Philanthropic Model." *Legacy: A Journal of American Women Writers* 19, no. 1 (2002): 81–89.

Robbins, Sarah. *Managing Literacy, Mothering America: Women's Narratives of Reading and Writing in the Nineteenth Century*. Pittsburgh: University of Pittsburgh Press, 2006.

Robbins, Sarah. "Rereading the History of Nineteenth-Century Women's Higher Education: A Reexamination of Jane Addams' Rockford College Learning as

Preparation for Her *Twenty Years at Hull-House* Teaching." *Journal of the Midwest History of Education* 21 (1994): 27–45.

Robbins, Sarah, and Ann Ellis Pullen, eds. *Nellie Arnott's Writings on Angola, 1905–1913: Missionary Narratives Linking Africa and America*. Anderson, SC: Parlor Press, 2011.

Robbins, Sarah, and Mimi Dyer, eds. *Writing America: Classroom Literacy and Public Engagement*. New York and Berkeley, CA: Teachers College Press and NWP, 2005.

Robbins, Sarah R. "Domestic Didactics: Nineteenth-Century American Literary Pedagogy by Barbauld, Stowe, and Addams." PhD diss., University of Michigan, 1993.

Robbins, Sarah R. "Social Action in Cross-Regional Letter Writing: Ednah Cheney's Correspondence with Postbellum Teachers in the U.S. South." In *The Edinburgh Companion to Nineteenth-Century American Letters and Letter-Writing*, edited by Celeste-Marie Bernier, Judie Newman, and Matthew Petheis, 287–301. Edinburgh, UK: Edinburgh University Press, 2016.

Robbins, Sarah R. "Sustaining Gendered Philanthropy through Transatlantic Friendship: Jane Addams, Henrietta Barnett and Writing for Reciprocal Mentoring." In *Poverty, Giving, and the Culture of Altruism: Transatlantic Philanthropy 1850–1920*, edited by Frank Christianson and Leslee Thorne-Murphy, forthcoming.

Robbins, Sarah R., Sabine H. Smith, and Federica Santini, eds. *Bridging Cultures: International Women Faculty Transforming the US Academy*. Lanham, MD: University Press of America, 2011.

Robbins, Sarah Ruffing. "The 'Indian Problem' in Elaine Goodale Eastman's Authorship: Gender and Racial Identity Tensions Unsettling a Romantic Pedagogy." In *Romantic Education in Nineteenth-Century Literature: National and Transatlantic Contexts*, edited by Monika M. Elbert and Lesley Ginsberg, 192–208. New York: Routledge, 2015.

Robbins, Sarah Ruffing, and Ann Ellis Pullen. "Collaboration in the Archive: Finding, Shaping, and Disseminating Stories from a Missionary Writer's Network." *Legacy: A Journal of American Women Writers* 30, no. 2 (2013): 287–305.

Rohan, Liz. "A Material Pedagogy: Lessons from Early-Twentieth-Century Domestic Arts Curricula." *Pedagogy* 6, no. 1 (2006): 79–101.

Ronan, Kristine. "Native Empowerment, the New Museology, and the National Museum of the American Indian." *Museum & Society* 12, no. 1 (2014): 132–47.

Roof, Judith, and Robyn Wiegman, eds. *Who Can Speak? Authority and Critical Identity*. Urbana: University of Illinois Press, 1995.

Roskelly, Hephzibah. "The Hope for Peace and Bread." In *Women and Rhetoric between the Wars*, edited by Ann George, M. Elizabeth Weiser, and Janet Zepernick, 32–47. Carbondale: Southern Illinois University Press, 2013.

Ross, Marlon B. "Kenneth W. Warren's *What Was African American Literature?*: A Review Essay." *Callaloo* 35, no. 3 (2012): 604–12.

Russell, Caskey. "Language, Violence, and Indian Mis-Education." *American Indian Culture and Research Journal* 26, no. 4 (2002): 97–112.

Ryan, Melissa. "The Indian Problem as a Woman's Question: S. Alice Callahan's *Wynema: A Child of the Forest.*" *American Transcendental Quarterly* 21 (2007): 23–45.

Salam, Reihan. "Trump's Immigration Disaster. His Campaign Has Set Back the Cause of Border Enforcement." *National Review* (May 9, 2016): 24–25.

Salazar, James B. *Bodies of Reform: The Rhetoric of Character in Gilded Age America.* New York: New York University Press, 2010.

Sanneh, Lamin. *Encountering the West: Christianity and the Global Cultural Process: The African Dimension.* Maryknoll, NY: Orbis Books, 1993.

Sanneh, Lamin. *Translating the Message: The Missionary Impact on Culture.* Maryknoll, NY: Orbis Books, 1989.

Santamarina, Xiomara. *Belabored Professions: Narratives of African American Working Womanhood.* Chapel Hill: University of North Carolina Press, 2005.

Santini, Federica, Sabine H. Smith, and Sarah R. Robbins. "Introduction." In *Bridging Cultures,* edited by Sarah R. Robbins, Sabine H. Smith, and Federica Santini, xxi–xlii. Lanham, MD: University Press of America, 2011.

Sargent, Theodore. *The Life of Elaine Goodale Eastman.* Lincoln: University of Nebraska Press, 2005.

Schaafsma, David. *Eating On the Street: Teaching Literacy in a Multicultural Society.* Pittsburgh: University of Pittsburgh Press, 1993.

Schaafsma, David, ed. *Jane Addams in the Classroom.* Urbana: University of Illinois Press, 2015.

Schaafsma, David, and Ruth Vinz. *On Narrative Inquiry: Approaches to Language and Literacy.* New York: Teachers College Press, 2011.

Schaafsma, David, and Todd DeStigter. "Introduction: In Search for a Form: Jane Addams, Hull-House, and Connecting Learning and Life." In *Jane Addams in the Classroom,* edited by David Schaafsma, 1–6. Urbana: University of Illinois Press, 2014.

Schellenberg, T. R. *The Management of Archives.* With a Foreword by Jane F. Smith. Washington, DC: National Archives and Records Administration. First published in 1965 by Columbia University Press.

Schellenberg, T. R. *Modern Archives: Principles and Techniques.* With a New Introduction by H. G. Jones. Chicago: Society of American Archivists, 1996. First published in 1956 by University of Chicago Press.

Schneider, Bethany. "Reservation C." Manuscript in progress. Bryn Mawr, 2004, 1–18.

Schneiderhan, Erik. "Pragmatism and Empirical Sociology: The Case of Jane Addams and Hull-House, 1889–1895." *Theory and Society* 40 (2011): 589–617.

Schön, Donald A. *Educating the Reflective Practitioner: Toward a New Design for Teaching and Learning in the Professions.* San Francisco: Jossey-Bass, 1990.

Schön, Donald A. *The Reflective Practitioner: How Professionals Think in Action.* New York: Basic Books, 1984.

Seigfried, Charlene Haddock. "Learning from Experience: Jane Addams's Education in Democracy as a Way of Life." In *Ethical Visions of Education: Philosophies in Practice,* edited by David T. Hansen, 83–94. New York: Teachers College Press, 2007.

Seigfried, Charlene Haddock. "Socializing Democracy: Jane Addams and John Dewey." *Philosophy of the Social Sciences.* 29, no. 2 (1999): 207–30.

Senier, Siobhan. "Allotment Protest and Tribal Discourse: Reading *Wynema*'s Successes and Shortcomings." *The American Indian Quarterly* 24, no. 3 (2000): 420–40.

Shaw, Stephanie J. *What a Woman Ought to Be and to Do: Black Professional Women Workers During the Jim Crow Era.* Chicago: University of Chicago Press, 1996.

Shepler, Sherry, and Anne F. Mattina. "Paying the Price for Pacifism: The Press's Rhetorical Shift from 'Saint Jane' to 'The Most Dangerous Woman in America.'" *Feminist Formations* 24, no. 1 (2012): 154–71.

Shields, Patricia M. "Democracy and the Social Feminist Ethics of Jane Addams: A Vision for Public Administration." *Administrative Theory and Praxis* 28, no. 3 (2006): 418–43.

Sicherman, Barbara. *Well-Read Lives: How Books Inspired a Generation of American Women.* Chapel Hill: University of North Carolina Press, 2012.

Simonsen, Jane. *Making Home Work: Domesticity and Native American Assimilation in the American West, 1860–1919.* Chapel Hill: University of North Carolina, 2006.

Sinor, Jennifer. *The Extraordinary Work of Ordinary Writing: Annie Ray's Diary.* Ames: University of Iowa Press, 2002.

Sklar, Kathryn Kish. "Hull House in the 1890s: A Community of Women Reformers." *Signs* 10, no. 4 (1985): 658–77.

Small, Sandra E. "The Yankee Schoolmarm in Freedman's Schools: An Analysis of Attitudes." *The Journal of Southern History* 45, no. 3 (1979): 381–402.

Smith, Sabine H. "Perfectly Ambivalent: How German Am I?" In *Bridging Cultures*, edited by Sarah R. Robbins, Sabine H. Smith, and Federica Santini, 40–60. Lanham, MD: University Press of America, 2011.

Spack, Ruth J. "English, Pedagogy, and Ideology: A Case Study of the Hampton Institute, 1878–1900." *American Indian Culture and Research Journal* 24, no. 1 (2000): 1–24.

Spack, Ruth J. "Translation Moves: Zitkala-Ša's Bilingual Indian Legends." *Studies in American Indian Literatures* 18, no. 4 (2006): 43–62.

Spack, Ruth J. "Zitkala-Ša, *The Song of Hiawatha*, and the Carlisle Indian School Band: A Captivity Tale." *Legacy: A Journal of American Women Writers* 25, no. 2 (2008): 211–24.

"Spelman Celebrates 101 Founders Day." *Atlanta Daily World* (March 28, 1982): 1.

Spelman College. "The Sustaining Vision: 130 Years and Leading: Commemorating the One-Hundred Thirty Anniversary of the Founding of Spelman." Performance and Printed Program. Atlanta: Spelman College, 2011.

"Spelman College Founders Day Events Friday." *Atlanta Daily World* (April 6, 1958): 1.

"Spelman's Two Pioneers to Be Honored During Anniversary." *Atlanta Daily World* (March 30, 1941): 5.

Spratt, Margaret. "Hull-House and the Settlement House Movement: A Centennial Reassessment." *Journal of Urban History* 17, no. 4 (1991): 410–20.

Spruill, Sylvia. "Assessment in Secondary Environments: How Co-Teachers Navigate the Competing Demands of Theory, Policy, and Practice." EdD Diss., Kennesaw State University, 2013.

Stankiewicz, Mary Ann. "Art at Hull House, 1889–1901: Jane Addams and Ellen Gates Starr." *Woman's Art Journal* 10, no. 1 (1989): 35–39.

Steadman, Jennifer Bernhardt, Elizabeth Sanders, Elizabeth Engelhardt, Frances Smith Foster, and Laura Micham. "Archive Survival Guide: Practical and Theoretical Approaches for the Next Century of Women's Studies Research." *Legacy: A Journal of American Women Writers* 19, no. 2 (2002): 230–40.

Stebner, Eleanor J. *The Women of Hull House: A Study in Spirituality, Vocation, and Friendship*. Albany: State University of New York Press, 1997.

Steedman, Carolyn. *Dust: The Archive and Cultural History*. New Brunswick, NJ: Rutgers University Press, 2002.

"Stiya" [Advertisement]. *Indian Helper* (December 1, 1899): 2.

Sundquist, Eric J. "The Humanities and the National Interest." *American Literary History* 24, no. 3 (2012): 590–607.

Susag, Dorothea M. "Zitkala-Ša (Gertrude Simmons Bonnin): A Power(Ful) Literary Voice." *Studies in American Indian Literatures* 5, no. 5 (1993): 3–24.

Szasz, Margaret Connell, ed. *Between Indian and White Worlds: The Cultural Broker*. Norman: University of Oklahoma Press, 1994.

Tatonetti, Lisa. "Behind the Shadows of Wounded Knee: The Slippage of Imagination in *Wynema: A Child of the Forest*." *Studies in American Indian Literatures* 18, no. 1 (2004): 1–31.

Tayac, Gabrielle. *Indivisible: African-Native American Lives in the Americas*. Washington, DC: Smithsonian, 2009.

Taylor, David. *Soul of a People: The WPA Writers' Project Uncovers Depression America*. Hoboken, NJ: John Wiley & Sons, 2009.

Taylor, Diana. *The Archive and the Repertoire: Performing Cultural Memory in the Americas*. Durham, NC: Duke University Press, 2003.

Taylor, Frederick Winslow. *The Principles of Scientific Management*. New York: Harper & Brothers, 1913.

Taylor, Kay Ann. "Mary S. Peake and Charlotte L. Forten: Black Teachers During the Civil War and Reconstruction." *The Journal of Negro Education* 74, no. 2 (2005): 124–37.

Taylor, Keeanga-Yamahtta. *From #BlackLivesMatter to Black Liberation*. Chicago: Haymarket, 2016.

Téllez, Kip, and Hersh C. Waxman. "A Review of Research on Effective Community Programs for English Language Learners." *The School Community Journal* 20, no. 1 (2010): 103–20.

Terrance, Laura L. "Resisting Colonial Education: Zitkala-Ša and Native Feminist Archival Refusal." *International Journal of Qualitative Studies in Education* 24, no. 5 (2011): 621–26.

Thomas, Veronica G., and Janine A. Jackson. "The Education of African American Girls and Women: Past to Present." *The Journal of Negro Education* 76, no. 3 (2007): 357–72.

Thompson, Carol C. "The Lessons of Non-Formal Learning for Urban Youth." *The Educational Forum* 76 (2012): 56–68.

Tinker, George E. "Preface: Tracing a Contour of Colonialism: American Indians and the Trajectory of Educational Imperialism." In *Kill the Indian, Save the Man: The Genocidal Impact of American Indian Residential Schools*, by Ward Churchill, xiii–xxxi. San Francisco: City Lights, 2004.

Tohe, Laura. *No Parole Today*. Albuquerque, NM: West End Press, 1999.

Tomlinson, Barbara, and George Lipsitz. "American Studies as Accompaniment." *American Quarterly* 65, no. 1 (2013): 1–30.

Totten, Gary. "Zitkala-Ša and the Problem of Regionalism: Nations, Narratives, and Critical Traditions." *American Indian Quarterly* 29, nos. 1 and 2 (2005): 84–123.

Treuer, Anton. *Everything You Wanted to Know About Indians but Were Afraid to Ask*. Saint Paul: Minnesota Historical Society, 2012.

Trumpener, Katie. "Paratext and Genre System: A Response to Franco Moretti." *Critical Inquiry* 36, no. 1 (2009): 159–71.

Tuggle, Darren. "Scaling Fences with Jane, William, and August: Meeting the Objective and Subjective Needs of Future University Students and Future Teachers." In *Jane Addams in the Classroom*, edited by David Schaafsma, 99–111. Urbana: University of Illinois Press, 2014.

Vail, Erin. "Surveying the Territory: The Family and Social Claims." In *Jane Addams in the Classroom*, edited by David Schaafsma, 127–45. Urbana: University of Illinois Press, 2014.

Valaskakis, Gail Guthrie. *Indian Country: Essays on Contemporary Native Culture*. Waterloo, ON: Wilfrid Laurier University Press, 2005.

Valaskakis, Gail Guthrie, Madeline Dion Stout, and Eric Guimond, eds. *Restoring the Balance: First Nations Women, Community, and Culture*. Winnipeg, MB: University of Manitoba Press, 2009.

Vinz, Ruth. "Afterword. The Fire Within: Evocations." In *Jane Addams in the Classroom*, edited by David Schaafsma, 193–212. Urbana: University of Illinois Press, 2014.

Vizenor, Gerald. *Fugitive Poses: Native American Indian Scenes of Absence and Presence*. Lincoln: University of Nebraska Press, 1998.

Wakefield, Laura Wallis. "'Set a Light in a Dark Place': Teachers of Freedmen in Florida, 1864–1874." *The Florida Historical Quarterly* 81, no. 4 (2003): 401–17.

Wallace-Sanders, Kimberly. *Mammy: A Century of Race, Gender, and Southern Memory*. Ann Arbor: University of Michigan Press, 2008.

Wallace-Sanders, Kimberly, ed. *Skin Deep, Spirit Strong: The Black Female Body in American Culture*. Ann Arbor: University of Michigan Press, 2002.

Walls, Carrie. "Children's Exchange Column." *Spelman Messenger* (1886–88): various.

Warren, Kenneth W. *What Was African American Literature?* Cambridge, MA: Harvard University Press, 2011.

Warrior, Robert. *The People and the Word: Reading Native Nonfiction*. Minneapolis: University of Minnesota Press, 2005.

Warrior, Robert Allen. *Tribal Secrets: Recovering American Indian Intellectual Traditions*. Minneapolis: University of Minnesota Press, 1995.

Warrior, Robert Allen. "Vandalizing Life Writing at the University of Illinois: Heap of Birds's Signs of Indigenous Life." *Profession* (2011): 44–50.

Warrior, Robert Allen. "The Work of Indian Pupils: Narratives of Learning in Native American Literature." In *The People and the Word: Reading Native Nonfiction*, edited by Robert Allen Warrior, 95–142. Minneapolis: University of Minnesota Press, 2005.

Washburn, Kathleen. "New Indians and Indigenous Archives." *PMLA* 127, no. 2 (2012): 380–84.

Washington, Booker T. "The Atlanta Exposition Address (Chapter XIV)." In *Up from Slavery: An Autobiography*, 217–37. New York: Doubleday, 1907.

Watson, Yolanda L., and Sheila T. Gregory. *Daring to Educate: The Legacy of the Early Spelman College Presidents*. Sterling, VA: Stylus, 2005.

Wells-Barnett, Ida B. *Lynch Law in Georgia*. Chicago: Chicago Colored Citizens, 1899.

Wexler, Laura. "Tender Violence: Literary Eavesdropping, Domestic Fiction, and Educational Reform." In *The Culture of Sentiment: Race, Gender, and Sentimentality in Nineteenth-Century America*, edited by Shirley Samuels, 9–38. New York: Oxford, 1992.

"Who's She in War Work?: The Ears of the Army." *Forum* (1918): 478–83.

Wickham, DeWayne. "What Did You Hear Michelle Obama Say?" *USA Today* (May 12, 2015): A7.

Wilkinson, Elizabeth. "Gertrude Bonnin's Transrhetorical Fight for Land Rights." In *Women and Rhetoric between the Wars*, edited by M. Elizabeth Weiser, Ann George, and Janet Zepernick, 48–62. Carbondale: Southern Illinois University Press, 2013.

Willard, Frances E. "The Carlisle Indian School." *The Chautauquan: A Weekly Newsmagazine* 9 (1889): 289–90.

Willard, William. "Zitkala-Ša: A Woman Who Would Be Heard!" *Wicazo-Sa Review* 1, no. 1 (1985): 11–16.

Williams, Heather Andrea. "'Clothing Themselves in Intelligence': The Freedpeople, Schooling, and Northern Teachers, 1861–1871." *The Journal of African American History* 87 (2002): 372–89.

Wilson, Diane. *Beloved Child: A Dakota Way of Life*. Minneapolis: Borealis Books and Minnesota Historical Society Press, 2011.

Winter, Dave. "A Correspondence between Atlanta Students." In *Writing Our Communities: Local Learning and Public Culture*, edited by Dave Winter and Sarah Robbins, 34–42. Urbana, IL, and Berkeley, CA: National Council of Teachers of English and NWP, 2005.

Winter, Dave, and Sarah Robbins, eds. *Writing Our Communities: Local Learning and Public Culture*. Urbana, IL, and Berkeley, CA: National Council of Teachers of English and NWP, 2005.

Womack, Craig S. *Red on Red: Native American Literary Separatism*. Minneapolis: University of Minnesota Press, 1999.

Woodard, Jennifer Bailey, and Teresa Mastin. "Black Womanhood: *Essence* and Its Treatment of Stereotypical Images of Black Women." *Journal of Black Studies* 36, no. 2 (2005): 264–81.

Woodward, Bob, and Robert Costa. "Trump Plans Ultimatum to Make Mexico Pay for Wall." *Washington Post* (April 6, 2016): A5.

Yellin, Jean Fagan. *Harriet Jacobs: A Life*. New York: Basic Books, 2004.

Yezierska, Anzia. *Arrogant Beggar*. New York: Doubleday, Page & Co., 1927.

Yezierska, Anzia. *Salome of the Tenements*. New York: Boni, 1923.

Young, Jennifer Rene. "Marketing a Sable Muse: Phillis Wheatley and the Antebellum Press." In *New Essays on Phillis Wheatley*, edited by John C. Shields and Eric D. Lamore, 209–46. Knoxville: University of Tennessee Press, 2011.

Zangwill, I. *Children of the Ghetto: A Study of Peculiar People*. New York: Macmillan, 1896.

Zitkala-Ša. *American Indian Stories, Legends, and Other Writings*. Edited by Cathy N. Davidson and Ada Norris. New York: Penguin, 2003.

Zitkala-Ša. *Dreams and Thunder: Stories, Poems, and the Sun Dance Opera*. Edited by P. Jane Hafen. Lincoln: University of Nebraska Press, 2001.

Zitkala-Ša. "Impressions of an Indian Childhood." *Atlantic Monthly* 85, no. 507 (1900): 37–47.

Zitkala-Ša. "An Indian Teacher Among Indians." *Atlantic Monthly* 85, no. 509 (1900): 381–87.

Zitkala-Ša. *Old Indian Legends*. With illustrations by Angel De Cora. Boston: Ginn and Company. 1901.

Zitkala-Ša. "School Days of an Indian Girl." *Atlantic Monthly* 85, no. 508 (1900): 185–94.

Index

Page numbers in italics refer to figures.

345